Research Matters

A Guide to Research Writing

Rebecca Moore Howard
Syracuse University

Amy Rupiper Taggart
North Dakota State University

McGraw Hill
Connect Learn Succeed™

The McGraw·Hill Companies

This book is printed on acid-free paper.

1 2 3 4 5 6 7 8 9 0 WCT/WCT 0

ISBN: 978-0-07-338374-3
MHID: 0-07-338374-0

Vice President, Editorial: *Michael Ryan*
Editorial Director: *Beth Mejia*
Publisher: *David S. Patterson*
Director of Development: *Dawn Groundwater*
Senior Sponsoring Editor: *Christopher Bennem*
Developmental Editor: *Janice Wiggins-Clarke*
Editorial Coordinator: *Zachary Norton*
Supplements Editor: *Sarah Colwell*
Executive Marketing Manager: *Allison Jones*
Media Project Manager: *Thomas Brierly*
Production Editor: *Anne Fuzellier*
Designer: *Andrei Pasternak*
Cover Design: *Gearbox*
Interior Design: *Elise Lansdon*
Photo Research Coordinator: *Nora Agbayani*
Photo Research: *Deborah Bull*
Illustrator: *Ayelet Arbel*
Production Supervisor: *Louis Swaim*
Composition: *9.5/11 ITC Garamond Light by Thompson Type*
Printing: *45# New Era Matte Plus, Quebecor World*

Cover image: Howard Sokol/Index Stock Imagery/Photolibrary
The credits section for this book begins on page 396 and is considered an extension of the copyright page.

Library of Congress Cataloging-in-Publication Data

Howard, Rebecca Moore.
Research matters / Rebecca Moore Howard and Amy Rupiper Taggart. — 1st ed.
p. cm.
Includes bibliographical references and index.
ISBN-13: 978-0-07-338374-3 (alk. paper)
ISBN-10: 0-07-338374-0 (alk. paper)
1. English language—Rhetoric. 2. Academic writing. I. Taggart, Amy Rupiper. II. Title.
PE1408.H68522 2010
808'.042—dc22 2009030576

www.mhhe.com

The love, support, and patience of our families and loved ones—Tom Howard, Mike Moore, Jack Richardson, Melisa Richardson; Mark, Ella, and William Taggart—have made it possible for us to write this book. *Research Matters* is dedicated to the memory of Rebecca's sister, Sandy, and Amy's father, Glenn.

Dear Colleague:

Thank you for taking the time to consider *Research Matters*! You might find yourself asking, "What makes this text distinctive as a research guide?" We'll answer that question here.

Drawing on our own teaching and research, we emphasize what we believe to be central to research writing: the responsibility that comes with entering conversations. We think of students not just as consumers of information but as potential producers of knowledge, as well. As such, they have responsibilities to other writers who have been conversing and building knowledge on their topics—other writers who have poured the foundation on which they will build. They have responsibilities to the audiences of their texts to provide enough good information and to give their readers a sense of where that information comes from. They have responsibilities to the topic, to treat it fairly and to represent it fully. And they have responsibilities to themselves as learners, to give themselves the time, space, and energy necessary to complete the research well and to learn from it.

To support students, we offer concise explanations of research concepts, overviews of research processes, materials that can serve as models for their work, teaching and learning activities to support their development as researchers, and resources for further information. Together, the parts of the book signal to readers that responsible writers take research seriously and have a wide range of skills and knowledge to help them do it well. Throughout, we remind readers that writing and research are lifelong endeavors, not simply assignments to be completed and forgotten.

Sincerely,

Rebecca Moore Howard and Amy Rupiper Taggart

Rebecca Moore Howard has researched and published extensively on literacy education and plagiarism. She has been driven by a concern that plagiarism circumvents the education that she regards as instrumental in individual development and essential for a democratic society. She is Associate Professor of Writing and Rhetoric at Syracuse University.

Amy Rupiper Taggart has researched and published on teaching writing and rhetoric in school and community settings. Her interest in language as social action energizes and informs her teaching and research, allowing her to explore the intersections among writing, rhetoric, and social and individual change. She is Associate Professor of English and Director of First-Year Writing at North Dakota State University.

Responsibility to Other Writers

Research Matters helps students recognize and respect their role in their own writing and research by focusing on four key areas of responsibility:

1. **Responsibility to other writers**
2. **Responsibility to audience**
3. **Responsibility to topic**
4. **Responsibility to self**

Found Bibliographic Entry

Visual hallucinations in schizophrenia: Confusion between imagination and perception. Brébion, Gildas; Ohlsen, Ruth I.; Pilowsky, Lyn S.; Neuropsychology, Vol 22(3), May 2008. pp. 383-389. [Journal Article]

Revised Bibliographic Entry

References [APA style—see chapter 20]

Brébion, G., Ohlsen, R. I., & Pilowsky, L. S. (2008). Visual hallucinations in schizophrenia: Confusion between imagination and perception. *Neuropsychology, 22*, 383–389.

9f Drafting to Avoid Plagiarizing and Patchwriting

ore about ▸▸▸
aking notes, 93–105
Drafting, 161–72

From notes to first drafts, many of the techniques for avoiding plagiarizing and patchwriting are similar. If you have taken effective notes with attention to how each source might be useful to your study and with care to preserve quotations where appropriate and alter them fully where useful, you should have little trouble avoiding plagiarism. However, all writers make mistakes sometimes. As a result, it is a good idea to do some double-checking when you get to the drafting stage. When you expose your document to readers, your responsibilities to others become particularly critical.

To continue best practices for using sources at the drafting stage, take the same care as you move your notes into the document that you took when you made them initially:

- If you have a quotation in your note, include the quotation

for c
your
y int
One
separ

Writing Responsibly **Avoid Patchwriting**

As you summarize, check to make sure that you are not *patchwriting*—duplicating the language of the source with minor changes. Check your language against that in your source, and revise if you have done any of the following:

- used more than a few *key terms* from the text
- presented the ideas in the *same order* as the source
- used the *same sentence structure* as the source

If you find that you are patchwriting, revise your summary using your own words.

Research Matters teaches students to recognize and respect other authors, not only by citing their work accurately but also by treating their ideas fairly.

Research Matters demonstrates that writers must be responsible to their audience by citing and integrating research clearly, allowing readers to see where their information came from and the nature of that information.

Responsibility to Audience

Make It **Your Own**

For a research paper that you have drafted, show how you have integrated supporting evidence from sources by listing:

1. Three different sentences in your paper that demonstrate how you varied your choice of signal words
2. Three other sentences in your paper that demonstrate how you provided context and identified source authors
3. Three other sentences in your paper that demonstrate how you incorporated quotations fairly into your own prose by adding, deleting, or changing words

Did you find all nine sentences in your paper? If not, consider revising to integrate supporting evidence from sources into your prose more effectively.

More about ▸▸▸
In-text citation:
MLA style, 231–45
APA style, 291–301
Chicago style, 334–51
CSE style, 361–63
Quotation, 97, 97–99, 99–105, 108–109, 109–11, 181–86
Documentation:
MLA style, 246–71
APA style, 302–16
Chicago style, 334–51
CSE style, 363–75

15e Creating Transparent, Elegant Citations

A citation names the source that you are talking with, and the other cues you provide reveal the nature of that conversation. To cite well—to go beyond simply naming the source—is to make your conversation "transparent." Your goal should be not only to name your sources, but also to make obvious how you are using them.

By breaking up your citation, putting a signal phrase at the beginning and a page citation at the end, you can show *how much* and *which parts* of your text are derived from the source. In the following example, it is clear that the first sentence is the writer's statement of her own ideas, the second is a paraphrase from the Rosenfeld source, and the third is a quotation from Rosenfeld:

> The effects of music go beyond mere entertainment. Rosenfeld asserts that music not only brings pleasure to the soul but can also heal the body. "There may be, as yet, no empirical evidence that the cosmos sings, but the belief that music heals is old and ubiquitous" (89).

The last name of the author of the source (or, in the absence of an author, the first words of the title) is identified.

Quotation marks enclose exact copying from the source.

The page from which the quotation comes is identified.

Especially if your use of a source is paraphrase without quotation, you need to show where your use of the source *ends*. The page

Make It Your Own!

Responsibility to Topic

Writing Responsibly Made-up "Evidence"

In May 2005, a stem cell expert resigned his position at Seoul National University following revelations by the journal *Nature* that his laboratory had falsified data. Hwang Woo Suk's case is not an isolated one: In 2002, for example, Bell Laboratories fired star researcher Jan Hendrik Schon for falsifying data. Commentators have noted that competition was a factor in these cases: The desire for acclaim and advancement had become more important than the desire for truth.

The highly competitive academic environment may tempt you, too, to make up "facts" to support a thesis in a paper. It is easy to alter data, invent statistics or quotations, or manipulate an image so that it "shows" what you want it to. Resist the temptation: the short-term benefits are not worth it. Not only are you likely to get caught—fabricated evidence often *sounds* fake—but you would also be sacrificing the opportunity to learn something about your topic and about the writing process.

Incorporating the counterevidence to your claims

More about ▸▸▸ Counterevidence, 150–52

Advertising almost always suppresses counterevidence. Shampoo ads, for example, tell you the benefits of the product, but not its shortcomings. The shampoo may eliminate dandruff, but it may also make your hair dry and brittle—you are likely to find only the positive information in the ad. In recent years, government regulations and public pressure have brought counterevidence into ads for potentially dangerous products such as tobacco and alcohol.

Academic writing, on the other hand, usually benefits from the inclusion of counterevidence. The purpose of most academic writing is not to sell products but to explore and explain ideas. Demonstrating that you have considered all sides of a thorny problem and have come to a reasonable resolution of it requires that you include

...esearched argument, ask ...Have you included these ...ng counterevidence in an ...complexity of the issue ...nce to form its own well- ...t offers this paragraph of ...tcomings of her research:

...mple size (n = 54) with ...le college students. The

Writing Responsibly Keeping an Open Mind

As a writer, you also have a responsibility to avoid bias: Read sources with an open mind, use reliable sources, consider evidence that undermines your position, avoid exaggerated claims, and criticize unreasonable or poorly supported conclusions but not the people who hold them. Sound research considers all sides of an argument. Be especially careful as you evaluate sources that you immediately agree or disagree with: Just because you agree with them does not mean they are reliable sources, nor does your disagreement invalidate them.

Research Matters helps students recognize their responsibility to provide reliable information about their topic at a depth that does the topic justice.

Responsibility to Self

Research Matters emphasizes the responsibility of writers to themselves, to take their writing seriously and to approach writing tasks as an opportunity to learn about a topic and to expand their scope as writers.

All the same, if a cure were found, woul[...] cripple, but I'm only occasionally a loon[...] brand of theology God doesn't give bonus points for a limp. I'd take a cure; I just don't need one. A friend who also has MS startled me once by asking, "Do you ever say to yourself, 'Why me, Lord?'" "No, Michael, I don't," I told him, "because whenever I try, the only response I can think of is 'Why not?'" If I could make a cosmic deal, who would I put in my place? What in my life would I give up in exchange for sound limbs and a thrilling rush of energy? No one. Nothing. I might as well do the job myself. Now that I'm getting the hang of it.

—Nancy Mairs, "On Being a Cripple"
(*Plain Text: Essays,* Tucson: U Arizona P, 1986)

bedded in a quotation)

Achieves closure by answering questions

14g Drafting Responsibly

[...]e more aspect of writing to keep in mind while you are drafting is [...]*iting responsibly.* Because writing is so challenging and because so [...]ch is often riding on the success of writing projects, it is easy for [...]er objectives (getting an A, impressing the boss, looking clever to [...]nds, finishing the task quickly) to get in the way of fulfilling your [...]ponsibilities as a writer. At the drafting stage, ask yourself the fol-[...]ing questions to make sure you have worked responsibly so far:

- Have I done enough research to answer my research question without making too many assumptions?
- Have I acknowledged any counterevidence in my draft?
- Have I documented any sources I have referred to in my draft, whether quoted, paraphrased, summarized, or reproduced (images and other media)?
- Have I avoided misrepresenting my sources?

More about ▸▸▸
Introducing counter-evidence, 150–52, 173–76
Citing your sources and avoiding plagiarism, 106–19

[...]le Student Essay: First Draft

[...]irst draft of Erin Buksbaum's essay on social networking sites [...]

▸▸▸Additional samples from Erin

Writing Responsibly — The Big Picture

Another way to think about revising is to focus on your responsibilities to your *audience,* your *topic, other writers,* and *yourself*:

- Have you provided your *audience* with a worthwhile reading experience?
- Have you covered your *topic* fully and ethically?
- Have you represented borrowed ideas accurately and acknowledged all your *sources,* whether you have quoted, summarized, or paraphrased?
- Have you developed a voice that readers will find credible, represented your ideas clearly and powerfully, and written in a voice that reflects *your best self?*

Research Matters Makes Responsible Writing Easier!

Research Matters empowers students to own their ideas and to view their writing as consequential, and it equips them with a powerful set of tools that can help put responsible writing into practice. Developed by studying the workflow of students and their instructors through hours of ethnographic, qualitative, and quantitative research, *Research Matters* offers:

- **a flexible, powerful toolkit**
- **a familiar, web-based interface including an authority-based keyword search**
- **proven course architecture**
- **market-tested content**
- **additional learning, writing, editing, and research resources**

The Tools for Writing Responsibly

Research Matters includes a web-based assignment and assessment platform that connects students with their coursework, their classmates, and their instructors.

- **Customized Learning Plans.** *Research Matters* promotes original thinking and writing by giving instructors a system for individualizing content, assignments, and learning plans. *Research Matters* recognizes that different students need different plans to become responsible writers.
- **Documentation Tools.** Students can practice being responsible to other writers and to their sources and learn to meet the documentation requirements of an assignment through numerous interactive, step-by-step citation activities for a wide range of print and electronic sources.

Students: Visit **ShopMcGraw-Hill.com** to purchase registration codes for this exciting new product. Instructors: Contact **English@mcgraw-hill.com.**

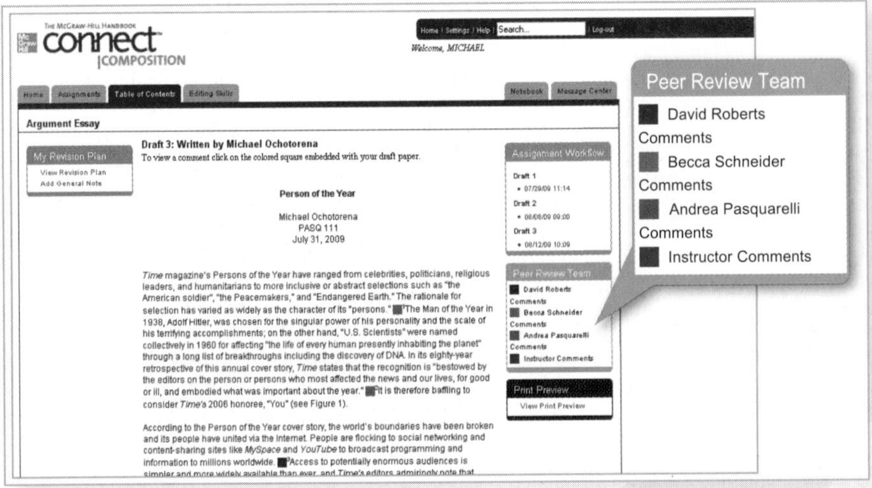

Superior Peer Reviewing Capability

Research Matters provides superior peer review capability, allowing students not only to see and consider the comments of others but also to create a roadmap for revision based on the feedback they receive. The *Research Matters* peer review system embraces the idea of a writer's responsibility to audience and self, providing a better way for writers to understand their readers, to recognize the impact of their writing on others, and to revise their work in a way that honors the contributions of their peers. Instructors can use the technology to organize peer groups that reflect classroom dynamics, improving the peer review experience for their students.

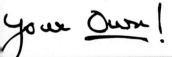

Acknowledgments

Writing *Research Matters* has been a thrilling and reciprocal learning experience. We hope readers will learn from *Research Matters* as much as we learned from the process of creating it. *Research Matters* is the product of many, many individuals' efforts beyond those of the coauthors whose names appear on the cover. We are grateful to all who have helped make *Research Matters* possible: students, editors, copyeditors, designers, and citation and documentation experts.

Students—including Erin Buksbaum, Dan Long, and Lydia Nichols from Syracuse University; Abrams Conrad from American University; Amy Ehret from Illinois State University; Heather DeGroot from James Madison University; Alicia Keene from University of Maryland; and Alea Wratten from SUNY–Geneseo—have generously provided relevant writing samples that will help other students envision good research writing. Thanks to them and to the students who also provided writing for Rebecca Moore Howard's companion handbook, *Writing Matters*. All those who contributed to the handbook also affected *Research Matters* in large and small ways.

We also want to thank the many reviewers who offered candid evaluations and suggestions for improvement. Their understanding of what works at their institutions and in their classrooms provided us with invaluable help in choosing what to include, what to leave out, and how to shape each part.

Manuscript Reviewers

Angelina College: Howard Cox, Patty Rogers
Bakersfield College: Jennifer Jett
Bluefield State College: Dana Cochran
Boston University: Matthew Parfitt

> **. . . a really practical resource that is addressing the needs of contemporary college students.**
>
> —Moumin Quazi, *Tarleton State University*

Bowie State University: Stephanie Johnson
Capital University: Kevin Griffith
Cecil College: Craig Frischkorn
Central Oregon Community College: Cora Agatucci
Clark State Community College: Laurie Buchanan, Cecilia Kennedy
Edinboro University of Pennsylvania: Wendy Warren Austin
Edmonds Community College: Greg Van Belle
Florida State University: Deborah Coxwell-Teague
Georgia Gwinnett College: Thomas Clancy
Georgia Perimeter College: Kari Miller
Greenville Technical College: April Childress
Indian River State College: April Van Camp
Indian University-Purdue University Indianapolis: Anne C. Williams

> **. . . thoroughly presents the benefits to and responsibilities of students as they pursue researched essay projects.**
>
> —Carol Watt, *Lane Community College*

Jones County Junior College: Cheryl Windham
Jones County Junior College: Susan Blackledge, Phillip Wedgeworth
Lane Community College: Carol Watt
Loyola University Chicago: Margaret Loweth
McHenry County Community College: Cynthia Van Sickle
Metropolitan State College of Denver: Rebecca Gorman, Jessica Parker
Metropolitan State University: Jenni Runte
Mount Hood Community College: Jonathan Morrow
North Idaho College: Amy Flint
Northern Virginia Community College—Alexandria: Brian Delaney
Northern Virginia Community College—Loudoun Campus: Arnold Bradford
Northwest Florida State College: James Suderman, Patrice Williams
Northwest Missouri State University: Robin Gallaher
Palm Beach Community College: Patricia McDonald, Vicki Scheurer
Palo Alto College: Ruth Ann Gambino, Caroline Mains, Diana Nystedt
Pioneer Pacific College: Jane Hess
Rogue Community College: Laura Hamilton
Salem State College: Rick Branscomb

San Antonio College: Alexander Bernal
Seton Hall University: Nancy Enright
South Texas Community College: Joseph Haske
Southern Illinois University–Edwardsville: Matthew S. S. Johnson
Southwestern Illinois College: Steve Moiles
St. Clair County Community College: John Lusk
St. Johns River Community College: Melody Hargraves, Elise McClain, Jeannine Morgan, Rebecca Sullivan

"Innovative ideas, effective examples, and good organization . . ."
—Barbara Chambers, *Jones County Junior College*

Tarleton State University: Moumin Quazi
Tennessee State University: Samantha Morgan-Curtis
Texas A + M University—Kingsville: Laura Wavell
University of Illinois at Urbana-Champaign: Grace Giorgio
University of Maryland—University College: Andrew Cavanaugh
University of Northern Iowa: Gina Burkart
University of Texas—San Antonio: Marguerite Newcomb
University of Wisconsin at Marathon County: Christina McCaslin
Valdosta State University: Richard Carpenter, Jane Kinney, Chere Peguesse
Wesley College: Linda De Roche
Westminster College: Susan Gunter
Westmoreland County Community College: Michael Hricik
Wharton County Junior College: Mary Lang, Sharon Prince
Wharton County Junior College: Mary Lang (design designation missing)
Wichita State University: Darren DeFrain
William Woods University: Greg Smith

Design Reviewers

Bakersfield College: Jennifer Jett
Bluefield State College: Dana Cochran
Edmonds Community College: Greg Van Belle
Georgia Perimeter College: Kari Miller
Indian University–Purdue University Indianapolis: Anne C. Williams
McHenry County Community College: Cynthia Van Sickle
Metropolitan State College of Denver: Rebecca Gorman, Jessica Parker
North Idaho College: Amy Flint
Northern Virginia Community College—Loudoun Campus: Arnold Bradford
Northwest Missouri State University: Robin Gallaher
Rogue Community College: Laura Hamilton
South Texas Community College: Joseph Haske
Southern Illinois University–Edwardsville: Matthew S. S. Johnson
University of Northern Iowa: Gina Burkart
University of Wisconsin at Marathon County: Christina McCaslin
Westmoreland County Community College: Michael Hricik
Wharton County Junior College: Mary Lang

Components of *Research Matters*

For Instructors

All of the instructor ancillaries described below, created by Andy Preslar, Lamar State College, can be found on the password-protected instructor's side of the text's Online Learning Center. Contact your local McGraw-Hill sales representative for log-in information.

Instructor's Manual

The *Instructor's Manual* provides a wide variety of tools and resources for enhancing your course instruction, including an overview of the chapter, considerations for assigning, applications for freshman comp and other courses, learning outcomes, strategies and tips for teaching, and exercises and activities.

Test Bank

The *Test Bank* offers multiple choice, true/false, and fill-in-the-blank questions covering key concepts in the text. These test items are available on the instructor's Online Learning Center as Microsoft

Word files and in EZ Test, a simple-to-use electronic test bank that allows instructors to edit questions and to add their own questions.

PowerPoint Slides

The PowerPoint presentations cover the key points of each chapter. The presentations serve as an organizational and a navigational tool integrated with examples and activities. Instructors can use the slides as is or modify them to meet their individual needs.

Personal Acknowledgments

Research Matters represents the efforts of a team of teachers, writers, researchers, editors, and designers, but it also reflects the family who supported us: Tom Howard, senior lecturer in University Studies at Colgate University, has worked with Rebecca Moore Howard from the beginning to the end; Mark Taggart, multimedia specialist with Left Brain Media, provided ongoing support and child care at key moments in the development of the book; Ella and William Taggart distracted Amy Rupiper Taggart from the book so that she was able to view it with fresh eyes; Shirley Rupiper offered extra help, particularly in the final phase.

The entire McGraw-Hill team has provided excellent support and guidance to make *Research Matters* possible and keep it moving apace. Our thanks go to Jane Carter, Senior Development Editor; David Chodoff, Senior Development Editor; Steve Debow, President for Humanities, Social Sciences, and World Languages; Beverley DeWitt, whose clear-eyed copyediting helped us avoid many mistakes; Anne Fuzellier, Senior Production Editor; Dawn Groundwater, Director of Development, Psychology, Education, English, and Political Science; Alison Meier, Production Editor; David Patterson, Publisher for English; Marty Moga, Permissions Editor. Special thanks go to Janice Wiggins-Clarke, Development Editor, who gracefully kept track of tasks and schedules; and Christopher Bennem, Senior Sponsoring Editor for Rhetoric and Composition, who helped us see the big picture as the book progressed.

Contents

Part One Preparation Matters

Part Two Information Matters

1 Owning Your Research

IN THIS CHAPTER

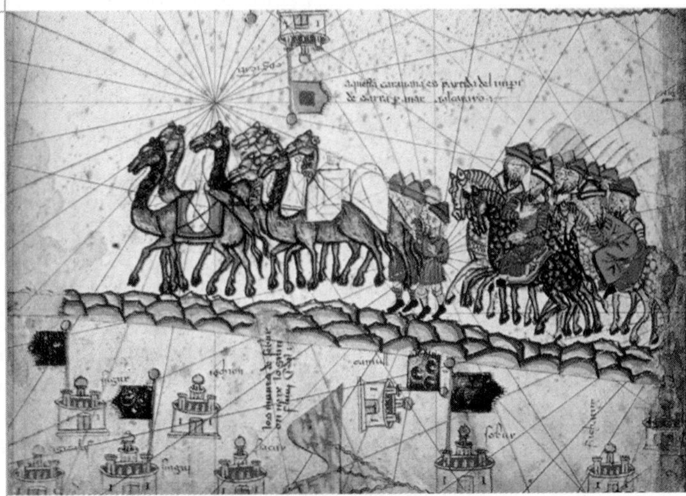

Ancient travelers making the trip to Europe across Asia faced a perilous journey. Writers, especially those new to the process, may worry that writing a college-level research project resembles this trek: Both seem to entail long, arduous expeditions through unfamiliar, sometimes harsh terrain, and both present the unwary with many opportunities to lose their way. Writers might also be unclear why they are making the trek—what lies at the other end that is worth the time and energy? Good preparation, though, can fill the journey with rewards rather than anguish. As a dependable map helped travelers stay on track, so too will this chapter and the ones that follow provide guideposts for writing your research project. Being clear about the goal and the rewards of the journey can make research a process of exploration and discovery rather than one of tired retracing of steps.

1a Understanding the Benefits

Why are you making this trek? Research is taught and required throughout high school and college for a host of reasons:

- **To build knowledge.** Your research project should help you understand your topic better. Ideally, it will also help your readers come to a more nuanced understanding of the issues, ideas, and information.

More about ▸▸▸ Analysis, 20

- **To develop analytical skills.** Researchers break down information into parts that can be examined and managed; they focus on smaller pieces of large problems so that people can see them more clearly.

More about ▸▸▸ Evaluation, 22

- **To develop evaluative skills.** Each time you encounter a source, you must determine whether it is good or even the best one. This evaluative decision comes from comparison with other sources and with standards dictating what a good source is.

More about ▸▸▸ Claims and evidence, 174–77 Thesis statements, 142–47

- **To understand and practice supporting claims with evidence.** To affect other people's beliefs and actions, you must be persuasive. Few people change their minds, however, without compelling evidence. Research projects involve developing a clear claim, often in the form of a thesis statement, and making sure the information you offer supports that claim, so that your readers will agree with you or at least consider you to be reasonable.

More about ▸▸▸ Conducting research in the disciplines, 222–29

- **To develop an understanding of academic discourse.** Members of particular disciplines and professions share some common ways of talking, thinking, writing, and acting. If you are an outsider to the group, these can seem like obstacles or unclear communication. While one research project will not teach you all of the writing techniques you need for college (these will differ from class to class and discipline to discipline), paying attention to how research is done in one context will help you determine which questions to ask when you have a research task in another context.

More about ▸▸▸ Setting a schedule, 43–44 Keeping records, 93–98 Organizing your project, 148–59

- **To learn about and practice project management.** Virtually all jobs, especially the professional jobs for which most college graduates prepare, involve complex projects that require pacing, prioritizing, organizing, and breaking down into tasks that can be easily completed. Research projects are similar: There are steps you must take, information to organize and track, and an end goal.

1b Tapping Personal and Professional Interests

A Chinese proverb says, "Instructors open the door. You enter by yourself." In a college class, research can seem like something an instructor makes you do, something that is disconnected from your life and interests. Yet most instructors hope you will be able to connect what you learn and do in school with your interests and goals. Finding ways to make connections between your research project and your interests is up to you, both in and out of school.

Recognize that you conduct research all the time Think about the times you have had a question, ranging from one that could be answered by a single source to one for which you constantly seek more information. If you are a video gamer, you have probably done research to learn how to deal with new challenges in the game. Maybe you have just saved up enough money to buy a car and want to find a fuel-efficient, affordable, but sporty vehicle. You are motivated to find the right car and are willing to spend some time asking the right people and reading the right resources. While the experience of doing this daily research may feel less structured than your academic research, the best academic research will also come from personal motivation and may draw on a similar range of resources.

Use personal experiences as stimuli If your family has a history of genetic diabetes, you might be more motivated than others to understand some aspect of diabetes research. A student athlete might be invested in understanding Title IX, which bans discrimination based on sex or gender in schools, including athletic activities. Think about who you are, where you come from, how you spend your time, and what forces affect you every day. In these parts of your own identity lie sources of curiosity.

Another way to define your interests is to explore what annoys, worries, or upsets you. Have you felt annoyed when talking about a particular topic with friends or family? Is there something you have read recently that excited you? Starting with an emotionally charged topic will require some care: You will need to explore the topic as a learner, rather than just looking for evidence to support what you already believe. Still, your emotions may motivate you to exert extra intellectual energy.

Start to see yourself as a professional Professionals of all stripes conduct research, even when their titles are not "researcher." An architect planning a building researches its location, its purpose, the qualities of the materials that will be used, and traffic patterns. Corporate managers conduct research on motivating people. Doctors keep current on the latest medical research. What are your long-term goals as a professional in training? Thinking about your professional goals may suggest additional topics that will not only fulfill the assignment requirements but also help you develop professional knowledge. If you are not sure what roles research and writing play in your chosen field, conduct an informational interview with a professional working in it.

1c Developing an Interest Inventory

How can you make a personal connection with your topic when it is not "How do I play Resident Evil better?" Start by taking a few minutes to develop an interest inventory for yourself. An *interest inventory* is a list of all the things you find worth thinking, reading, and talking about daily. Begin with a simple list: all of the things you can think of that interest you, like this:

Amy's Interest List

• music	• local history
• travel	• health and wellness
• kayaking	• race relations
• yoga	• politics
• the environment	• women's issues
• food	• art

Next, put those topics into table format with other general topic areas such as politics, technology, religion, current affairs, education, history, and culture. Raise questions about the intersections of these topics. Here is what one column of the table ("Food") might look like:

General Topic Area	Food
Politics	How does the US Food and Drug Administration (FDA) define "organic" foods?
Technology	How does seed modification constitute intellectual property that can be patented like technology?
Religion	Did Native Americans use food in spiritual ceremonies? If so, how?
Current Affairs	Genetically modified organisms (GMOs) are illegal in Europe. How does this differ from what's permissible in the United States? Why?
Education	What do nutritionists think of school food programs?
	Should schools allow beverage companies to advertise on their premises?
History	How did Europeans learn to cultivate crops in the New World?
Culture	What does America's consumption of fast food say about us as a culture?

When you list things you are interested in, you have already generated some topic areas and key terms for searches. Now when you conduct a preliminary search to see what other people are talking about, you might find academic conversations about the very things you like most.

More about ▶▶▶
Key-term searching, 54–65

EXERCISE **1.1** Developing an Interest Inventory

Without worrying for now about the research assignment you might have in hand, develop an interest inventory that has at least five general categories.

Then, choose your two favorite categories and create tables for those two categories with potential topics under politics, technology, religion, current affairs, education, history, and culture.

1d Finding Space in the Assignment

Sometimes your research assignment will constrain your choices. In a way, the constraint is helpful because it provides a focus. However, developing personal investment with the topic can be challenging. Think about your interest inventory and try to connect your topics to the assigned one. For instance, if you are interested in music while the assigned topic is environmentalism, you could merge those interests to study musicians who take a stand regarding the environment or music industry advances with an environmental impact. Most instructors welcome initiative and creativity, as long as you find a way to connect your interest to the goals and focus of the assignment.

More about ▶▶▶
Analyzing the assignment, 38–40

1e Making Room in Your Schedule

To explore and complete your assignment well, start planning now. Find some time in your schedule that is usually available, and make that your "research project time." Put it on your calendar and use it. This will help prevent procrastination and the faulty idea that the project can be completed the night before it is due. Later, when you develop your project proposal, you can break down your schedule further and get more specific about your plan. For now, at least schedule the following tasks:

More about ▸▸▸
Project proposals, 48
Brainstorming, 26–27
Taking notes, 93–105

- Reread the assignment.
- Brainstorm ideas (using your interest inventories and other brainstorming techniques such as freewriting and talking to peers).
- Read for discovery, to find more ideas.
- Begin a research notebook, blog, or other notes file.

Then, use the corresponding chapters in this book to complete each task.

1f Reading for Discovery

More about ▸▸▸
Reading sources, 11–23

Still having trouble finding something both interesting and appropriate? Reading what other people are talking about can help spark new ideas. If you have no topic at all in mind, you will need to browse.

- Visit a news website or pick up a newspaper.
- Look through a reference work, such as an encyclopedia.
- Return to things you have read for class or pleasure.
- Think about extending projects you began in other classes (but remember that you will need to create something new for this project, and you will also need your instructor's prior approval).
- Wander through a library and find a section that draws your attention. Browse the books there with an open mind. You may discover fascinating topics you had never heard of before.

As you browse, write down the topic areas of articles or books you find you would be willing to read. Do not rule anything out yet as "not good for school." Your instructor, consultants at your campus writing center, or even your classmates may be able to help you adapt the topic to an academic setting.

Tech

Using Tags to Develop Interest Inventories

Web 2.0 tools have made it even easier to track your interests. You may still want to keep a document on your computer with an interest inventory, but consider using a free online bookmarking program such as *digg, del.icio.us*, or *ThoughtMesh* to keep track of websites you find useful and interesting. Over time, your *del.icio.us* account will build a tag cloud that is much like an interest inventory. Eventually, when you have tagged many sites, your primary interests will show up in boldface, as in Figure 1.1.

FIGURE 1.1 Sample Tag Cloud

1g Raising Questions

More about ▸▸▸
Developing your research question, 34–35
Drafting research questions, 40–41

Perhaps the best way to own a research project is to start with authentic questions. Good research answers questions—for the writer as well as the reader. Avoid choosing a topic about which you intend to "prove" the correctness of your beliefs. Research projects are an opportunity to expand your knowledge.

Consider your areas of interest and questions you have about them. Perhaps you read an article somewhere or heard someone on talk radio saying that elections are unfair because the voting systems differ from state to state. You might want to ask the question "What has happened in response to complaints about ballot methods and their inconsistencies across the nation?" Or, having a dim memory of your high school civics class, you might want to freshen your knowledge and put it in the context of the upcoming election by asking, "What is the history of the electoral college system, and what kinds of challenges have been leveled against it?"

A second way to work from questions is to think of a problem, and use the research to find a solution. This approach is especially appropriate when your assignment is to write a formal proposal, whose hallmark is a problem-solution structure. These might be campus problems: How can the campus expand its recycling program? Or they might be community problems: How can the city increase home ownership and reduce renting?

Make It **Your Own**

To get a sense of the problems that affect you directly and that might make fruitful research topics, focus in on groups with which you are involved.

- List all of the groups to which you belong, including church groups, student organizations, nonprofits at which you volunteer, and even informal groups that share common goals.
- Now choose a group and brainstorm a list of all the problems you perceive it to have, and/or consult with the group to determine what problems exist.
- Consider attending the next group meeting and asking members what kinds of information would help them solve these problems.

Think about pursuing a research project in response to one of these problems and bringing your findings to the group when you are finished. Along the way, continue to consult with group members.

1h Developing Confidence: What Do You Already Know?

More about ▸▸▸
Freewriting, 25–26
Brainstorming, 26–27

Individuals sometimes procrastinate when they feel overwhelmed and believe they have nothing to say on a topic. One way to reduce the feeling of being overwhelmed is to write freely for about ten minutes on a topic, not worrying about writing coherently or cleanly, just to explore what you already know. You are not a blank slate; allow yourself to really think about what you know on the assigned topic or one you might consider as your research topic. Another benefit of this task is that you can make sure you do not rewrite things you already know as the bulk of your research project.

1i Presenting Your Research in an Alternate Form

More about ▸▸▸
Designing and presenting your project, 204–21

Some assignments require that you present your research in traditional research essay form. However, some instructors and some assignments may be more open in terms of format and audience. Take advantage of this opportunity, particularly if you have multimedia or design skills that might make it more interesting to you to move away from the traditional academic essay form. You might feel you "own" the piece more in another medium or genre. Would your information reach a broader audience on the Web? Would the topic lend itself well to audio and visual enhancement? Think about the ways in which research is presented through documentary films; multimedia-enhanced websites; even print genres such as proposals, commentaries, and fact sheets. If you are already comfortable with the essay, moving into a new genre will also expand your flexibility in presenting research. Just be sure an alternate genre or approach is appropriate in your class.

1j Discussing Potential Topics

Sometimes just batting ideas around with others can help you generate ideas that will help you connect to the research project. This can be as casual as a late-night chat with your roommate ("What do you think about . . . ?") or as formal as a scheduled brainstorming session with a collaborative group.

Work **Together**

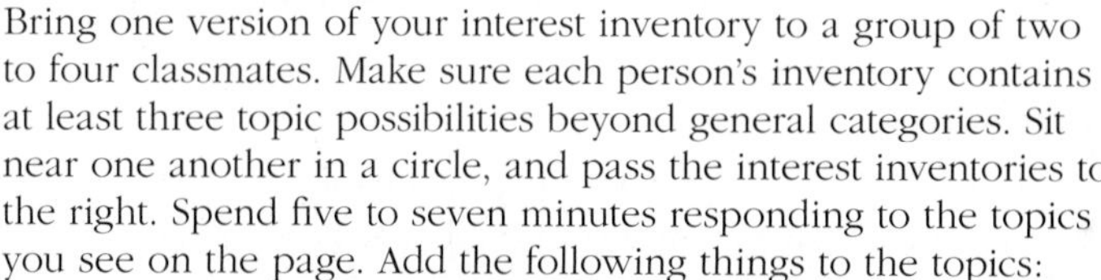

Bring one version of your interest inventory to a group of two to four classmates. Make sure each person's inventory contains at least three topic possibilities beyond general categories. Sit near one another in a circle, and pass the interest inventories to the right. Spend five to seven minutes responding to the topics you see on the page. Add the following things to the topics:

- More subtopic possibilities
- Your initials next to the topic that seems most interesting and focused
- Questions for your peer about the topics represented there
- At least one research question that could be answered on the focused topic (for example, if your peer has written "student apathy" and "elections," you might develop this question: "What factors contribute to political apathy among Generation Y students?"

After the allotted time is up, pass the sheets again to the right until everyone in the group has commented on all the inventories. Return the sheets to their authors and, as a group, talk about topics you found interesting, ways to focus, and avenues to pursue next.

Quick Reference: Owning Your Research

If you have just been handed a research project assignment sheet and do not yet feel invested in the project, try some of these techniques:

- Set aside an hour or two in your schedule each week for this project. Do not let other things encroach on that time.
- Think about your personal and professional goals. What information do you need to achieve those goals?
- Develop or refer to an existing interest inventory or a tag cloud you have developed using Web 2.0 tools like *del.icio.us*. Which topics stand out?
- Find a little corner of the assignment topic (if it is not an open topic) that corresponds to your existing interests and goals. What kind of fusion happens when you put the topic area together with one of your interests?
- Return to sources you have read, or expand the kinds of things you read. Is there an existing conversation you might be interested in joining?
- Take a potential topic, and write a couple of pages with your internal editor turned off. What do you already know? What seems to be missing in your knowledge?
- Consider fresh ways of presenting research. Would you like experience presenting research in documentary, hypertext, proposal, or another form?
- Sit down with a friend and talk about possible topics. Does anything your friend says spark an idea you can get excited about?

A Final Thought

If you are interested and invested in your research, it will show. You will learn from the project, and your readers will be much more likely to read what you have written with pleasure.

2 Reading Your Sources

IN THIS CHAPTER

Reading sources is always an interaction, much more like chemistry than it might first appear. In chemistry, one chemical reacts with another, each having an effect. Readers' experiences similarly intermingle with what is in a text, and this intermingling is an exciting part of the research process. Even when we read purely for pleasure, the experience allows for—and often demands—more than mere *comprehension,* or getting something out of a text. Active reading also means *reflection* and *interpretation,* or putting something in, as well. In college courses and beyond, reading often entails *response,* an opportunity for readers to write about the text and put themselves in conversation with it. This chapter focuses on three stages of the critical reading process: *reading to comprehend, reading to reflect,* and *reading to write.*

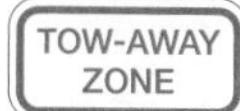

2a Reading to Comprehend

We constantly read texts. Some, like signs or labels, are just one- or two-word messages.

Advertising slogans are a bit longer, and directions for assembling a shelving unit are longer still. Even longer are newspaper articles or stories in a magazine. These different types of texts all share a common goal: to communicate information quickly, simply, and clearly.

Most texts you read in college have a different objective: to engage you in the complexities—not the simplicities—of an issue. This urge to examine complexity encourages both writers and readers to make well-informed, carefully considered judgments. *Critical reading* is more than an attitude; it is a set of skills—or a process that includes the following steps:

- previewing the text
- reading to get the gist
- rereading

Previewing the text

The more you know about a text before you begin reading, the more efficiently you will be able to read. Far from adding to your reading load, *previewing* texts saves you time in the long run, allows you to read more in the time allotted, and enables you to read with greater comprehension. Before you settle down to read a text, try some of the following *prereading strategies:*

- **Read the abstract.** Many scholarly journals provide abstracts—or summaries—of their articles, either in the table of contents or at the beginning of each article. Reading the abstract can introduce you to the main ideas you will encounter in the text.
- **Read the table of contents.** When reading books, look first to the table of contents to see which chapters are likely to address most directly issues of importance to your work.
- **Read the headings.** If the text is organized with headings and subheadings, skimming these will often give you a helpful outline.

- **Scan figures and illustrations.** Graphics might represent important ideas and can convey a complex process to you immediately.
- **Read the introduction and conclusion.** The introduction and conclusion usually contain a text's central ideas and arguments, important questions, and major discoveries or conclusions.
- **Read only the first sentence of each paragraph.** Not all first sentences are topic sentences, but most introduce or summarize what a paragraph will cover.
- **Use the index.** When reading a book, consult the index to find sections where your key terms appear. (You will want to read those sections closely.)

Reading to get the gist

After using several prereading strategies, you are ready to read the entire text from beginning to end. As you do, circle words or phrases you have questions about, but press on without looking them up. If you do not understand a passage, keep moving; for now, resist rereading or taking substantial notes. When you have finished one read-through, put the text aside and write down what you remember, no matter how fragmentary.

Rereading

Engaging with—or even just comprehending—a difficult text requires more than one reading. After you have read the entire selection from beginning to end, reread it. Retrace your steps carefully, and take time to puzzle over complexities. Look up unfamiliar words, and highlight or underline the most important, interesting, and difficult concepts. In the margins, write your questions, reactions, insights, and arguments. Connect what you read to what you know, have read, or have experienced.

More about ▸▸▸
Annotating, 15–17

Viewing visual texts to comprehend

In our information-based society, much information is communicated visually, and we strive to be savvy readers of that information. When you are reading for research projects, information graphics can be useful but sometimes perplexing sources of information. It is very easy to misread a visual display of information.

Here are some ways to approach a visual text for comprehension:

- **Determine the visual's audience, purpose, context, and author.** These contextual aspects will often help you quickly to understand the text better. If you find an information graphic during a web search that is out of its original context, this process of going back to ask who produced it and why is especially important. Data on infant mortality rates produced by US insurance companies as opposed to information on infant mortality gathered by the United Nations would likely have a very different focus and intent, for instance.

More about ▶▶▶ Using visuals as support, 177–79

- **Look for keys or codes.** Labels are important to interpreting information accurately. On a chart or graph, for instance, the axes will be labeled. On a pie chart, color-coding is often used to distinguish different categories of information.
- **Pay close attention to how numbers are displayed.** To make large numbers easier to represent, information graphics sometimes use the numbers 1–100 but indicate that those numbers stand for millions or even billions.
- **Avoid relying only on the visual.** If a description or analysis accompanies the graphic, read that, too. Compare your understanding to the description.

2b Reading to Reflect

When you think about what you are reading and connect it to your prior experiences, to other readings, and to the larger world, you are practicing *reflective reading.* The text initiates a conversation in which a critical, reflective reader participates.

Keeping a reading journal

Writing while reading helps us discover both what we know and what we want to learn more about. The latter, our curiosities, may become research topics. A great way to write reflectively is to record your intellectual and personal responses to texts in a *reading journal.* Articulating your responses to what you read helps build a deeper understanding and a sense of taking part in—not just taking in—your education.

More about ▶▶▶ Taking notes, 93–105

Your reading journal is a good place to do any or all of the following:

- List and define specialized vocabulary in the reading.
- Summarize the main idea and supporting points in the reading.
- Respond to ideas you encounter through freewriting, clustering, or brainstorming.
- Record your own ideas in response to the reading: what you agree with, disagree with, need to learn more about, or just find interesting or important.
- Compare and connect what you have read previously to this piece.

More about ▶▶▶
Summary, 18–19
Idea-generation techniques, 24–31

When you are reading specifically for a research project, your reading journal will evolve into a more formal research log. It is a good idea to get into the practice of keeping bibliographic information with your journal entries so that, when you decide on a topic, you can easily go back to items you have already noted in your journal and use them as resources for the research project.

More about ▶▶▶
Research logs, 25, 97
Citation, 122
Documentation, 221–28

Annotating

Like reading or keeping a journal, *annotating* (marking notes directly on a text and in its margins) is a highly individual activity. Even if you have developed an efficient and useful system, revisit it from time to time, considering alternatives that may improve the process. As you hone your own effective system, keep the following suggestions in mind:

- Use a highlighter or colored pen to mark important ideas. Rather than marking whole sentences, try to highlight as few words as possible, allowing the truly important points to stand out.
- Read with a pencil in hand. When you have ideas or questions, if the book is yours, write them in the margin.
- Circle or underline passages or words you have questions about or might want to respond to.

In addition or instead, you might want to take notes in a separate location: in a computer file, notebook, blog, or wiki.

More about ▶▶▶
Choosing an organizer to fit your work style, 93–96

Sample Annotated Text

Here is how one student approached the task of annotating the text "How Hip-Hop Lost Its Way and Betrayed Its Fans" by Brent Staples. The annotations define unfamiliar vocabulary, note reflections, and make connections.

How Hip-Hop Music Lost Its Way and Betrayed Its Fans

I loved "Just Walk on By" (same author)

Too strong? Rap sometimes glamorizes, but it can raise awareness, too.

By BRENT STAPLES

(12 May 2005)

African-American teenagers are beset on all sides by dangerous myths about race. The most poisonous one defines middle-class normalcy and achievement as "white," while embracing violence, illiteracy and drug dealing as "authentically" black. This fiction rears its head from time to time in films and literature. But it finds its most virulent expression in rap music, which started out with a broad palette of themes but has increasingly evolved into a medium for worshiping misogyny, materialism and murder.

There are certainly negative images out there, but there are many positive African American role models, too (including Staples).

virulent—extremely infectious or damaging. Why is rap the most "virulent" music?

Central argument—raises an important issue but overgeneralizes.

"palette" compares music to painting

misogyny—hatred of women

This dangerous narrowing of hip-hop music would be reason for concern in any case. But it is especially troubling against the backdrop of the 1990's, when rappers provoked a real-world gang war by using recordings and music videos to insult and threaten rivals. Two of the music's biggest stars—Tupac Shakur and the Notorious B.I.G.—were eventually shot to death.

Have things changed since then?

People who pay only minimal attention to the rap world may have thought the killings would sober up the rap community. Not quite. The May cover of the hip-hop magazine *Vibe* was on the mark when it depicted fallen rappers standing among tombstones under the headline: "Hip-Hop Murders: Why Haven't We Learned Anything?"

Is this logic backwards? Sometimes gangsta rappers are violent, but does their music describe the violence or cause it?

The "rap community" isn't entirely gangsta rap; there are other kinds of rap/hip-hop out there.

Many people "learned" or were not involved in the violence: Kanye West, Chuck D., Public Enemy, etc.

The cover may have been prompted in part by a rivalry between two rappers that culminated in a shootout at a New York radio station, Hot 97, earlier this spring. The events that led up to the shooting show how recording labels now exploit violence to make and sell recordings.

True—recording labels are marketing an image.

At the center of that Hot 97 shootout was none other than 50 Cent, whose given name is Curtis Jackson III. Mr. Jackson is a confessed former drug dealer who seems to revel in the fact that he was shot several times while dealing in Queens. He has also made a career of "beef" recordings, in which he whips up controversy and

Example: 50 Cent and the release/marketing of "The Massacre"

heightens tension by insulting rival artists.

He was following this pattern in a radio interview in March when a rival showed up at the station. The story's murky, but it appears that the rival's entourage met Mr. Jackson's on the street, resulting in gunfire.

No concrete proof that 50 Cent planned a gunfight to promote his album. Is the inference fair? I think so.

Mr. Jackson's on-air agitation was clearly timed to coincide with the release of "The Massacre," his grotesquely violent and misogynist compact disc. The CD cover depicts the artist standing before a wall adorned with weapons, pointing what appears to be a shotgun at the camera. The photographs in the liner notes depict every ghetto stereotype—the artist selling drugs, the artist in a gunfight—and includes a mock autopsy report that has been seen as a covert threat aimed at some of his critics.

Is it the marketing or the art itself that is "misogynistic" and "supremely violent"? Note: Listen to this song.

The "Massacre" promotion raises the ante in a most destructive way. New artists, desperate for stardom, will say or do anything to win notice—and buzz—for their next projects. As the trend escalates, inner-city listeners who are already at risk of dying prematurely are being fed a toxic diet of rap cuts that glorify murder and make it seem perfectly normal to spend your life in prison.

In many neighborhoods, kids grow up seeing people going to prison all the time, so for them it is normal.

Critics who have been angered by this trend have pointed at Jimmy Iovine, the music impresario whose Interscope Records reaped millions on gangster rap in the 90's. Mr. Iovine makes a convenient target as a white man who is lording over an essentially black art form. But also listed on "The Massacre" as an executive producer is the legendary rapper Dr. Dre, a black man who happens to be one of the most powerful people in the business. Dr. Dre has a unique vantage point on rap-related violence. He was co-founder of Death Row Records, an infamous California company that marketed West Coast rap in the 1990's and had a front-row seat for the feud that led to so much bloodshed back then.

I wonder who these other critics are?

impresario—entertainment manager or promoter

Good example of author's point—even in the name of the record company.

The music business hopes to make a financial killing on a recently announced summer concert tour that is set to feature 50 Cent and the mega-selling rap star Eminem. But promoters will need to make heavy use of metal detectors to suppress the kind of gun-related violence that gangster artists celebrate. That this lethal genre of art has grown speaks volumes about the industry's greed and lack of self-control.

A pun?

Can art be "lethal"?

But trends like this reach a tipping point, when business as usual becomes unacceptable to the public as a whole. Judging from the rising hue and cry, hip-hop is just about there.

tipping point—the moment when something rare becomes much more common

Hip-hop is still popular. Does he just mean against gangsta rap?

Summarizing

When we take notes, we often *paraphrase* a text, rephrasing the writer's ideas in our own words; paraphrasing pushes us to understand the specifics of what we are reading. When we *summarize,* we go a step further, presenting the main ideas in a piece in *condensed* form, a great way to reinforce and process a text. When writing a summary, you may need to use key terms from the text—calling a German Shepherd a "Central European canine bred for shepherding" is just silly—but be careful to avoid repeating the author's language and phrasing unnecessarily. Selecting a phrase here and a phrase there—a "greatest hits" approach—is a surefire way to fall into "patchwriting," a form of plagiarism.

More about ▶▶▶
Paraphrase, 98–99
Summary, 98–99
Patchwriting, 99–105
Plagiarism, 106–19

Instead, read the text through at least twice to identify its main idea and key supporting evidence. Then write your summary, omitting less important supporting details and using language and organization that is meaningful to you (not borrowed from the source). Finally, check your summary against the text. Is it accurate? Is it brief?

If the text you are summarizing is long, consider summarizing it in sections rather than tackling the whole thing at once. It is still a good idea to complete a reading of the full text before you start, but you can write each section's summary separately.

Alea Wratten's summary of "How Hip-Hop Music Lost Its Way and Betrayed Its Fans" (p. 19) condenses the text, representing its main claims in her own words.

Quick Reference → **Steps for Writing a Summary**

1. After annotating a text, put the text aside so that you are no longer looking at it.
2. On a clean sheet of paper or in a new document on your computer, try to recapitulate the main ideas from what you have just read.
3. Check the text to make sure you have conveyed the main ideas and the major supporting points without distortion or undue influence (are too many words in your summary like the language in the text?).

Writing Responsibly — Avoid Patchwriting

As you summarize, check to make sure that you are not *patchwriting*—duplicating the language of the source with minor changes. Check your language against that in your source, and revise if you have done any of the following:

- used more than a few *key terms* from the text
- presented the ideas in the *same order* as the source
- used the *same sentence structure* as the source

If you find that you are patchwriting, revise your summary using your own words.

Student Summary of "How Hip-Hop Music Lost Its Way and Betrayed Its Fans"

In this essay, *New York Times* writer Brent Staples claims that both rap music and the way it is marketed perpetuate racial stereotypes and glorify violence, materialism, and sexism. Citing the example of an actual gang war in the 1990s, Staples argues that rival rappers use their music to insult each other and initiate violence. Staples worries that many inner-city kids, who already face poverty and violence on a daily basis, will buy the myth of a glamorous "gangsta rap" lifestyle and maybe even wind up in prison. He feels that white and black record producers are both to blame for the direction hip-hop has taken, and he hopes concert organizers will use security precautions to make sure that the violence they sell doesn't go beyond the lyrics or marketing materials. Staples closes the essay by saying he feels that the public will not stand for much more of this; if hip-hop continues in this vein, it will not last.

2c Reading to Write

As a critical reader, you are always readying yourself for the next step: writing. Once you have identified a text's claims, you are ready to interact with them through *analysis, interpretation, synthesis,* and *critique.*

More about ▶▶▶
Analysis, 38–39
Synthesis, 180–81
Evaluation, 80–82

Analyzing

Critical comprehension of a text involves more than being able to repeat or even summarize it. You must be able to take the text apart, to understand how it works. Critical reading requires analysis.

To *analyze* is to divide something (in this case, a text) into its component parts, to figure out what each part means and how the parts fit together. Those "parts" may be in the text itself—its various claims and evidence, for example. Or "parts" may refer to the text and its author, publisher, reader, and intended audience. Finally, in the case of multimedia texts such as a documentary film, "parts" might mean the spoken language, the images, and the music. How do the separate parts of the text work together—or conflict with each other? As you analyze, ask the following questions:

More about ▶▶▶
Claims, 85–86
Evidence/counter-evidence, 174–77

- What major *claims*—or arguments—does the text make?
- What types of *evidence*—examples or data—does the text offer for its claims? Is the evidence based on facts; on the writer's opinion, interpretation, or logic; or on authoritative sources?
- What options does the text allow its readers? Must readers either agree or be wrong? To what extent does the text consider alternative or conflicting viewpoints?
- How is the material in the text organized? What can you observe about its style and word choice?
- Who is the text's author? What other work has he or she done? How does this text build upon or diverge from the author's previous work?

Interpreting

After you use summary and analysis to understand the general meanings and mechanisms of a text, you can enter the text through *interpretation.* As you read, try to draw inferences about what may be below the surface of the text. Use the following questions to help guide your interpretation:

- What does the text assume to be true without actually claiming it?
- What inferences can you draw from the text? Beyond its explicit claims, what do you derive from factors such as the author's tone and choice of words?
- Where does the text leave gaps or present contradictions? Can you explain them?
- When and where was the text written? What else was going on at that place and during that time? How does the text draw on or diverge from its historical context?
- Who published this text? Who sponsored the research? What influence might those facts have on the way the text presents information, arguments, and evidence?
- For whom was the text written and who might be left out?

Synthesizing

College research assignments demand that you *synthesize*—connect what you have read to ideas in other texts or to the world around you. The skills and techniques used in summary, analysis, and interpretation all play key roles in synthesis. When you synthesize, you work with multiple texts, identifying and explaining the relationships you perceive among them. Throughout and after college, the techniques of synthesis will be important whenever you read—for integrating what you learn into what you already know. As you synthesize, ask the following questions:

- What else have you read or experienced that this text explains, illustrates, clarifies, complicates, or contradicts? How does this text respond to other texts?
- What claims or points in each text do you find especially compelling? How do compelling points in one text connect to ideas in others?
- What claims could these texts, taken together, provide evidence for? What purposes could they serve?
- How does considering these texts together enhance your understanding of a topic or change your thinking?
- What might others gain by seeing these texts together?

Critiquing or Evaluating

More about ▸▸▸
Evaluating information, 80–92

A *critique* is a well-informed evaluation or review, an argument based in evidence and established criteria. Writing a highly effective research project requires that you critique sources to figure out where you stand in the midst of the arguments and which of the existing arguments are most worthy of attention.

To critique well, a reader must carefully consider a text's content, intent, and meaning, as well as how it compares with or informs other texts. The ideal critical reader approaches a text skeptically yet with an open mind. Remember that writing a critical response does not necessarily involve *criticizing*. In fact, your critique may be entirely positive.

Critical reading and writing draw on the component activities of reading for comprehension, reading reflectively, and reading analytically. To these, critiquing adds the activity of evaluating sources and making judgments about them based on the criteria for effective, authoritative, and trustworthy texts. For a successful critique, ask yourself questions like these:

- What qualifications do you have (or lack) for judging this text? What beliefs and/or prejudices do you bring to the text?
- What beliefs and/or prejudices do you detect in the text?
- What authority or expertise does the author have regarding the topic?
- What is the intended purpose of this text? Does the work achieve it? Can you offer a critique of this purpose?
- What kind of relationship and power dynamic does the text establish between writer and reader? How well is the relationship established, and how well does it serve the text's purpose?
- Who is the text's intended audience? What differences are there between that audience's experiences, knowledge, and culture and your own?
- Based on your analysis (or breakdown) of the text's argument, does anything seem to be missing? Is any of the evidence questionable?
- Does the text use emotion to manipulate its audience?

More about ▸▸▸
Author credibility, 82–84

As you prepare to respond to a text, consider *your* audience. If you want your critique to resonate with people who have not read the original source, use just enough summary to help readers understand

Quick Reference **Ways of Reading Critically**

- **Analyzing:** breaking a text down into parts to study its meanings and mechanisms
- **Interpreting:** going below the surface of a text; drawing inferences about it based on contextual clues, omissions, suggestions, and assumptions
- **Synthesizing:** connecting a text to relevant ideas in other texts and personal experiences; drawing comparisons and relationships among ideas
- **Critiquing:** crafting a well-informed evaluation or review of a text through analysis, interpretation, and synthesis

Tech

Critical Response to Digital Texts

Online texts pose significant and unique challenges for the critical reader.

- **Filter for authority.** All web pages a Google search displays may seem equally authoritative, but they are not. Some sites are set up by scholars or experts, but many others are created by children or hobbyists exploring their interests, by retailers selling a product, or by advocacy groups seeking support.
- **Filter for accuracy and appropriateness.** A website might look official and well composed but offer information that is inaccurate or inappropriate for your research purpose.
- **Filter for manipulation.** A website's design—its language, images, spoken text, and music—may exert a profound influence, discouraging readers from exercising critical judgment.

the context of your critique. If your audience is familiar with the text, do not devote space to paraphrasing an idea; instead, refer and then respond to it.

A Final Thought

As you read sources for your research project, engage actively in the conversation you "hear." What do you bring to the conversation? Who do you believe and why? What is missing in the conversation? If you comprehend the texts you encounter, you will be able to reflect on your responses to them and write in response to them.

3 Exploring and Sharpening Your Topic

IN THIS CHAPTER

Working with blunt tools is slow, tedious work. The chef with a dull knife struggles to create a beautiful product, while a sharp blade cuts easily and quickly. The work is easier and the product better. As with physical sharpening, writers need to work to sharpen their own vision of a project before they get too far into it. A blurry or dull idea makes searching for information, developing a thesis, and recognizing gaps difficult, among other challenges. Taking the time to look around, explore, and then focus your topic as tightly as possible increases the odds that you and your readers will like and learn from the finished product.

3a Exploring Research Topics

A typical first response to an academic research assignment is to choose a topic that you are already interested in or one that will be easy to research. These are legitimate considerations, but before committing yourself, be sure that enough appropriate sources are available on that "interesting" topic or that the "easy" topic will really interest your readers—and you.

Invention techniques allow you to generate several possible topics before settling on one. No single strategy works for everyone, and most writers use several methods. The following sections explain some of the more common strategies for selecting a research topic. If you have tried some of these before, experiment with the others; drawing on new visual and verbal techniques may increase your creativity. And remember that you can return to these invention techniques over and over throughout your project, whenever you get stuck, need a jump start, or simply want to rev your intellectual engine.

Maintain an interest inventory, idea journal, or commonplace book.

In the nineteenth century, the philosopher Ralph Waldo Emerson wrote his essays from ideas he had jotted down in a notebook. In the twenty-first century, writers often use PDAs or weblogs (commonly known as *blogs*) to store ideas. Whatever medium you use, you may find that keeping an interest inventory, an idea journal, or a commonplace book is an effective part of the creative process.

More about ▸▸▸
Interest inventories, 4–5
Keeping a reading journal, 14–15
Keeping a research journal or log, 97

An *interest inventory* is typically a list of topics and subtopics that are of ongoing interest to you. An *idea journal* is a place to record your thoughts about projects you are working on. Like a diary, an idea journal is something to write in every day. Unlike a diary, though, it is not a record of the events of your life, but a record of the events of your *mind*.

Whereas an idea journal records your own ideas, a *commonplace book* records the ideas (quotations, summaries, paraphrases) of *others* that you might find useful in the future. You can also use your commonplace book to record your reactions to those ideas. As you jot notes in your commonplace book, record your sources and use quotation marks carefully to separate others' words from your own.

More about ▸▸▸
Avoiding plagiarism, 106–19
Taking notes, 93–105

Freewrite.

Have you ever found yourself sitting in front of a blank screen, knowing you had to begin writing but just not being able to get started? When the writing must begin and you are blocked, try *freewriting:* writing the first thing that enters your mind and then continuing to write nonstop for ten to fifteen minutes (or for a set number of pages). What you write about does not matter; if you draw a blank, just write (or type) the same word over and over again until something comes to you. To be useful, freewriting must be fast and spontaneous.

Here is a sample of freewriting for Erin Buksbaum's essay on social networking sites:

▶▶▶Sample student essay "Is Social Networking a Serious Danger?" by Erin Buksbaum, 170–71

Not sure what I want to write not sure what I want to say would rather be at the gym or just catching up on sleep. Stayed up too late last night doing my MySpace page. Finally managed to get that video to play when it opens. Prob. should take down that pic of Hannah from Friday night, but it's really, really funny. Maybe she shld just put it on her page, but she hardly ever updates. I hope my mother—or Hannah's mother—doesn't look at it! OMG!

Once the time has elapsed, read through what you wrote. You might find a usable idea: Buksbaum's essay topic—social networking sites like MySpace—appears in this freewriting snippet, for example. But the exercise is also beneficial for freeing the mind and getting over writer's block.

Some writers like to use a variation on freewriting to help them develop ideas. Instead of starting from the first idea to pop into their heads, they start from something specific: their general topic (if they have one), a quotation, a memory, or an image. If they stray from the topic, they just keep writing, trying to circle back to it. This is *focused freewriting.*

Brainstorm.

A prewriting strategy to help writers develop their ideas is *brainstorming* (or *listing*): writing down everything the writer can think of on a topic. Brainstorming—either alone or with friends, classmates, or colleagues—is something every writer should do all the time. It helps get ideas percolating and provides a record of that percolation, which can come in handy at the drafting stage. Here is a snippet of brainstorming for Erin Buksbaum's topic, social networking sites:

Anyone with an email address can use a social networking site
Lots of networking sites: Facebook, Friendster, Bebo . . .
People post tons of pictures, not only of themselves, of friends, too
Other things they post: name, school, job, fave bands, books, movies, etc.
Easy for friends to stay in touch and meet friends of friends
Easy for people to track down other people—old classmates, people with shared interests, etc.
Do criminals take advantage of networking sites? Are people aware of this?

Brainstorming can be done for a specific length of time or in bits and pieces over the course of several days. Avoid waiting for inspiration, though. A good, focused idea usually takes a little effort and time and will reward you by being interesting and manageable.

Cluster.

Clustering (also called *mapping* and *webbing*) is a visual method for identifying and developing ideas. Because it shifts your focus from print to visual composition, clustering may spur your imagination.

Here are the three simple steps for creating a cluster:

1. Write your topic in the middle of the page, and draw a circle around it.
2. Write other ideas related to your topic around the central idea bubble, and draw a circle around each of those ideas.
3. Draw connecting lines from the word bubbles to the central topic or to the other word bubbles to show relationships among the ideas.

When creating a cluster, keep two things in mind:

1. Keep your topic and idea notes brief—writing more than a word or two in each bubble will make the diagram difficult to read.
2. Create your cluster diagram in pencil—you will make many changes as you work. Or, put each item on a sticky note so you can move them freely.

The cluster diagram in Figure 3.1 (p. 28) was used to generate ideas for a paper on the topic "social networking sites."

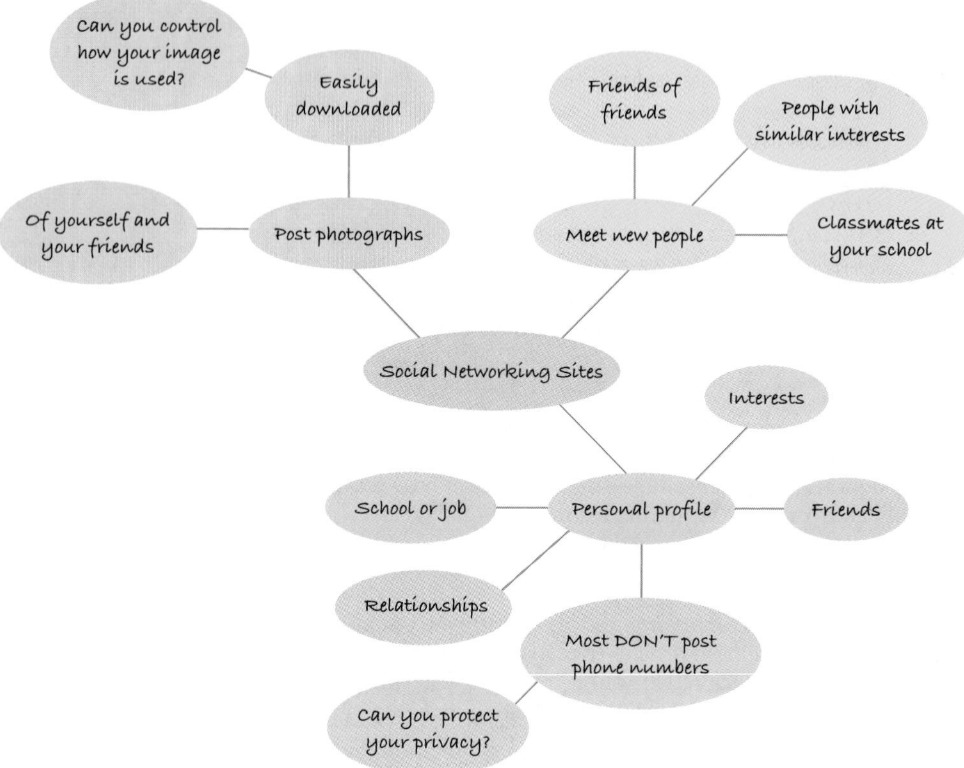

FIGURE 3.1 A Cluster Diagram

Answer an expanded list of journalists' questions.

Journalists' questions—who, what, when, where, why, and *how*—can not only help you generate ideas about your topic, they can also help you figure out what you need to learn. When considering a topic, ask yourself:

- **Who** are the key figures? (people)
- **What** happened, what did they accomplish, or what are the issues? (events/accomplishments/issues)
- **When** and **where** did the main events occur? (context)
- **Why** did the key figures do what they did, or why did these events transpire as they did? (reasons)
- **How** did it happen? (process)

As a college student, you will also benefit from adding two questions to the journalists' list:

- What is the **significance**?
- What are the **consequences**?

Asking the expanded list of journalists' questions for a paper on the risks of using social networking sites could generate the following questions:

Who uses social networking sites?
What do social networking sites allow users to do? What forms of communication do they allow?
When did social networking sites become popular?
Where can one find information on users of social networking sites (statistics)?
Why do people use social networking sites? Why do they post information about themselves?
How might social networking sites be abused?
What social significance does the popularity of social networking sites have?
What consequences might result from posting too much personal information?

Discuss your topics with friends and classmates.

At every stage of the process, it can be useful to share ideas and writing. As you work to focus a topic, consider showing one or two peers some of your exploratory work, such as a cluster, your journalists' questions, or a brainstormed list. Ask them to pay attention to things that seem particularly interesting, ideas that still seem fuzzy, ways to sharpen those fuzzy ideas, items they might add to a cluster, and so on. Do the same for them. This mirrors productive relationships professional writers often have with other writers.

Use the internet, the library, and classroom tools.

A quick internet search can help stimulate ideas when you are faced with a new topic. Start by searching a *subject directory,* a collection of websites organized into groups by topic and arranged hierarchically

More about ▶▶▶
Searching a subject directory, 73–74

from most general to most specific. (Two useful subject directories are listed in the Find Out More box on p. 31.) By clicking through a list of topics from most to least general, you can get a sense of the range of subject areas related to your topic.

More about ▸▸▸
Searching news sites, 76
Searching for blogs, 75

For very current topics, you might search a news site or find a relevant blog. Blogs are journals chronicling an individual's thoughts and ideas or responses to events. Specialized blogs can provide insight into what those studying your topic are thinking right now. You may need to use a specialized search engine to turn up blogs. (The Find Out More box below lists some reliable news sites and some search engines that specialize in blogs.) Figure 3.2 shows a blog entry on Erin Buksbaum's topic, social networking sites.

Another resource for generating ideas about your topic is the reference sources provided by your college library. Browse through general encyclopedias and dictionaries to get a sense of how your topic is

FIGURE 3.2 A Blog Entry on Social Networking

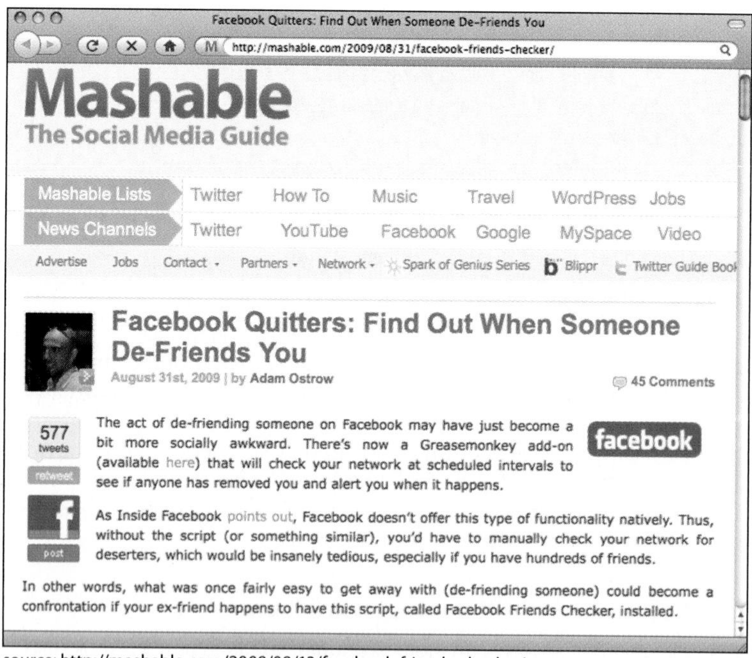

source: http://mashable.com/2009/08/13/facebook-friends-checker/

Find Out **More . . . Internet Sources for Exploring a Topic**

Subject directories

Internet Public Library <www.ipl.org>—an academic subject directory

Yahoo! <www.yahoo.com>—a good general subject directory

Online news sources

BBC News <news.bbc.co.uk>

CNN <cnn.com>

Google News <news.google.com>

New York Times online <www.nytimes.com>

Yahoo! News <news.yahoo.com>

Weblog search engines

Blogsnow <www.blogsnow.com>

Google Blogs <blogsearch.google.com>

Technorati <www.technorati.com>

usually discussed, or turn to specialized dictionaries or encyclopedias to get a more detailed introduction.

Finally, if you are writing about topics that were introduced in class, you can begin by reading (or rereading) course materials, such as your textbook, class notes, and any handouts your teacher has distributed. All can provide context or help you identify a topic that interests you.

More about ▸▸▸
Finding reference sources, 59–60, 77

Tech

Keeping Track of Preliminary Web Searches

As you browse the internet for ideas, keep a list of "favorites" or "bookmarks," and refer to this list when you draft.

To *bookmark* a website, while looking at the site you want to record for later, go to the Bookmarks drop-down menu. Then choose "Add Bookmark" or "Bookmark This Page." Your browser may ask you whether you want to save the bookmark to a particular folder.

If you realize that you forgot to bookmark an important page, use your *browser's "history"* (a drop-down menu) to find the page again. Each browser keeps track of where you were for the past five or ten clicks.

Not working on your own computer? Instead of bookmarks, you might want to start a *blog* or a *wiki* (for a group project) where you can copy the URLs and paste them with the date you visited them and even a note about what you valued there.

You can also set up an account on a *social bookmarking service* such as *del.icio.us* or *digg,* so that your bookmarks will be accessible from any internet-connected computer.

3b Focusing Your Topic

After you have generated some ideas, the next step is to ensure that your topic is not overly broad, too narrow, too common, or inappropriate for the occasion. Some topics (the drinking age and the death penalty, for example) have become hackneyed: It is very difficult to write something engaging on these topics. Others, such as hot topics in *Sports Illustrated* and *Spin,* may be new and compelling to you but may not lend themselves to the critical insight that is the objective of most academic writing.

Narrowing your topic

It is typical to begin with too broad a topic. Thus, once you have chosen a general topic, narrow it enough that you can conduct research and write about it in insightful ways, given the time you have and the length of the assignment. Narrowing means finding a viable subtopic.

Just as they can help you to explore a topic, idea-generating techniques—such as freewriting, brainstorming, and clustering—can help you narrow your topic. Figure 3.3 shows how a cluster can be used to determine a narrow and productive focus. Also, consider the examples in this chapter for a reminder of how each strategy leads from general seed ideas to sprouts of more manageable and focused topics.

More about ▸▸▸ Subject directories, 73–74

Besides traditional invention techniques, databases and subject directories are also incredibly useful resources for narrowing a topic because they organize information into topics and subtopics. For instance, if you are a business major and are trying to focus a topic related to your major but are new to the field, you might go to the Librarians' Internet Index,<www.lii.org>, starting at the home page and clicking first on Business. The page that opens lists a host of subtopics (Figure 3.4).

From this list, you might choose "Corruption & Fraud" because it sounds intriguing to you. After each subtopic, as in Figure 3.4, you will notice a number. This indicates the number of resources organized under that category. Clicking on "Corruption & Fraud" will lead you to new subtopics that will increasingly refine your focus. Figure 3.5 shows the subtopics under Corruption & Fraud in the Business category.

When your own brain is not producing sufficiently narrowed topics, using databases and subject directories can alleviate stress and lead you to subtopics you did not know existed.

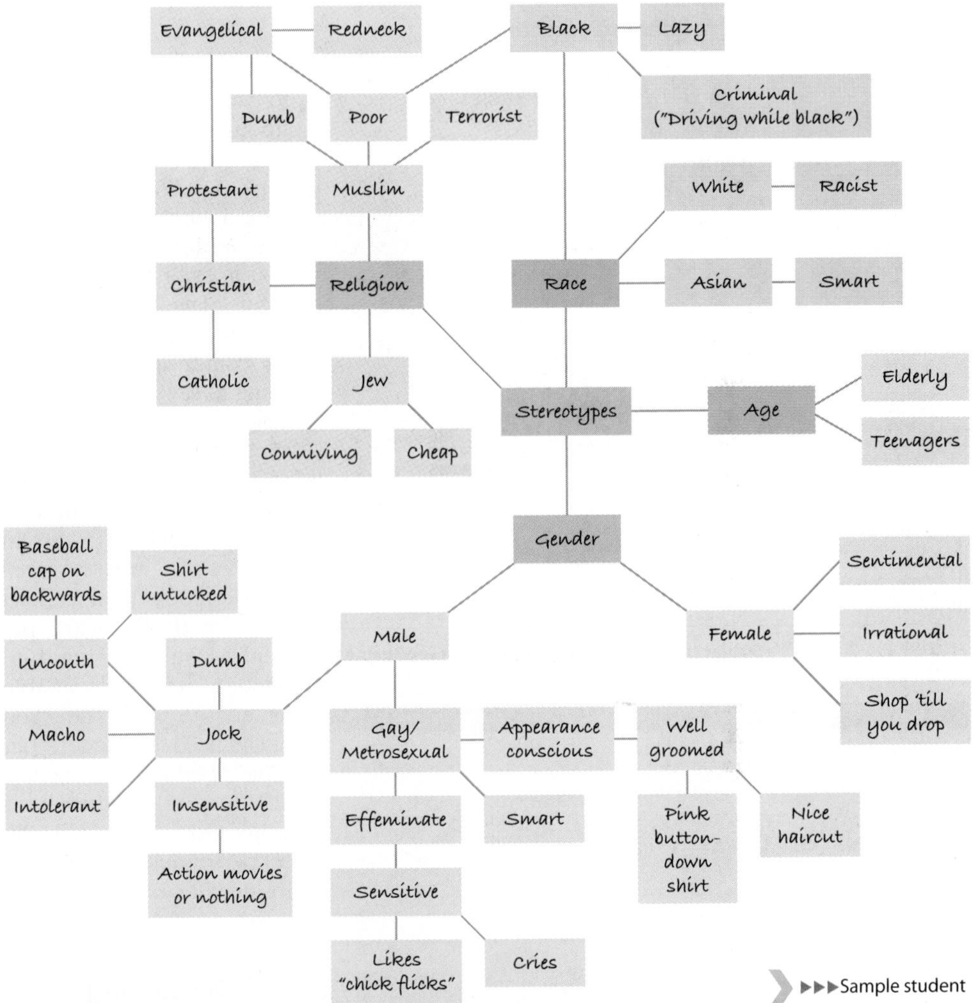

▶▶▶Sample student paper "The Power of Wardrobe" by Heather DeGroot, 321–32

FIGURE 3.3 A Cluster Diagram for Narrowing a Topic The development of Heather DeGroot's paper begins with the general topic "stereotypes" and then narrows, first to gender-based stereotypes, then to male stereotypes. With several gender stereotypes about men's dress, DeGroot ultimately focused on the influence that stereotypical male dress exerts on the behavior of other men.

More about ▸▸▸
Effective searching, 51–52

Broadening your topic

It is rare that a topic becomes too focused and needs to be broadened. Before broadening your topic, work to make sure you have used good search strategies to find information on your topic. It can sometimes appear as though nothing exists on the subject because you are not looking in the right places. However, if you find yourself struggling to come up with something to say about the topic you have selected, your topic may be too narrow. If, for example, you were thinking about exploring whether social workers in your county are pressured to overreport their contact hours with Medicare patients, you may not find enough readily available material to work with. You would need to broaden your topic, perhaps to include all US social workers or a larger group, such as medical personnel (which would include doctors, nurses, and technicians).

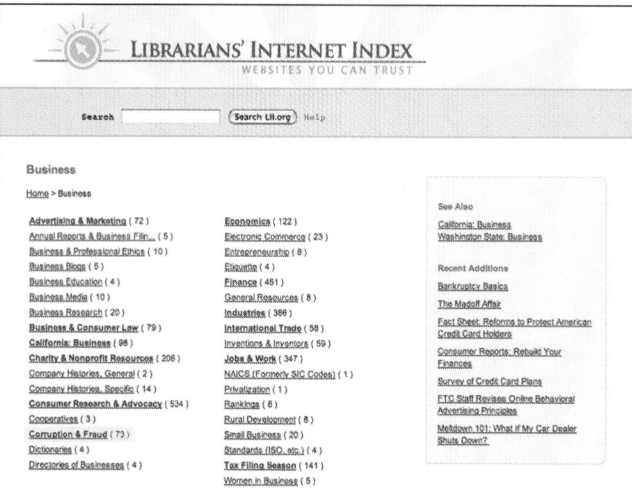

FIGURE 3.4 An Online Subject Directory, Subcategories under Business

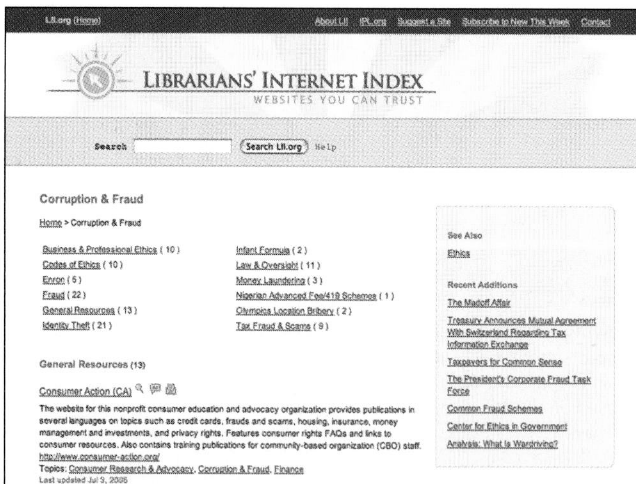

FIGURE 3.5 Corruption & Fraud Subcategories under Business at Librarians' Internet Index

3c Developing Your Research Question

All of this exploration should lead to at least one question that can drive your research. As you have seen through Erin Buksbaum's

Quick Reference **Developing a Research Question**

- **Figure out what you do not know.** Where are the gaps in your invention materials?
- **Determine what has not been said.** Is there any gap in the research conversation that you have started to notice?
- **Return to your interests.** Write down a question related to the most stimulating categories in your interest inventory, reading journal, commonplace book, or other invention materials.
- **Work from a hypothesis to a question.** If you have the sense that something might be true but are not certain, write down the hypothesis—for example: "I think too much time spent texting might contribute to students' doing poorly in school." Then, rephrase it as a question: "Is too much texting leading to kids' doing poorly in school?" However, if you already are certain you have the answer to the question you are asking, you will need to develop a different question.
- **Think about scope.** Which question do you feel you could answer in the time and space of the project? If entire books (rather than chapters in books or articles) have been written in answer to the question you have now, you should probably tighten your focus further.
- **Use the keywords of your study in your question.** Make your question specific. For example, note the difference between "How can the internet be abused?" and "What are the risks of using social networking sites, and how can users avoid those risks?"
- **Determine whether the question is answerable.** Use your exploratory source searches to determine whether anyone seems to know how to answer the question.
- **Consider your readers.** If your audience is anyone other than your teacher, what do you know about them? Will your research meet their interests and needs?

examples, developing multiple questions on a single topic can lead you to find the one that will be the best fit for you and the project at hand. After trying several of the idea-generating or invention strategies in this chapter, take some time to develop a question that will provide the primary focus to your research. Use the suggestions in the Quick Reference box above to make the shift from topic to question.

More about ▶▶▶
Drafting research questions and hypotheses, 40–41

A Final Thought

With a question in hand and with invention materials in which you have generated keywords, you are prepared to dive more deeply into your project, whether that means writing a clear project proposal or beginning your search for answers. Keep all the materials you have generated so that you can return to them as you work. They should help you to continually refine your focus as the project progresses and evolves.

4 Writing a Research Proposal

IN THIS CHAPTER

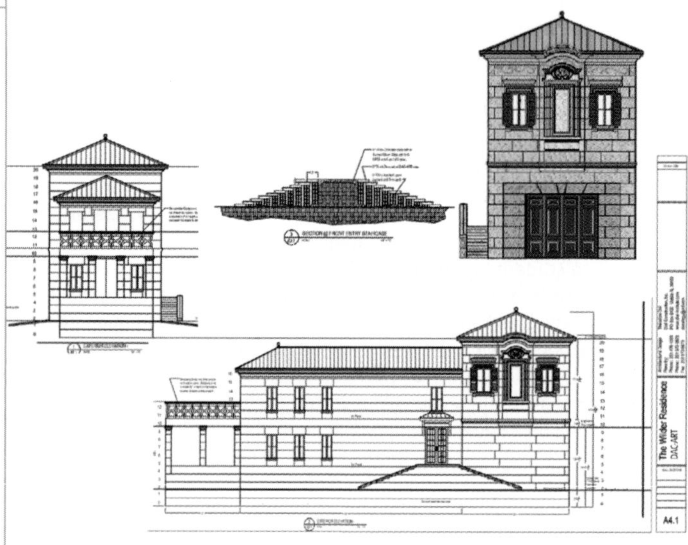

A *research proposal* is a plan, one created to be read by someone other than you. It is the first formal pitch of a project. Similarly, architects' pitches come, in part, in the form of drawn plans. These plans are done with great care and attention to detail, and they take into account location and client constraints. You are the architect of your project. Careful planning at the project proposal stage can save time and energy later and offers you the opportunity to get focused feedback from your instructor and others.

4a Understanding Typical Components of a Research Proposal

Your instructor will probably define the information required for your research proposal, as it will depend in part on the assignment requirements. However, research proposals share some common features:

- Identification of the *topic* you have chosen.
- A specific *question* within the topic area that your research will answer.
- A *hypothesis,* or working thesis statement. Your research project should not begin with your thinking you already know the answer to your question. Still, you probably have some ideas about what you might find. Write up your ideas as a hypothesis you will test with your research.
- A *statement of significance.* Answer these questions: Why should anyone care about this question and topic? What is its importance?
- What you *already know.* Your existing knowledge provides a baseline for you and your instructor. It might even include experiential knowledge that has compelled you to pursue this particular topic. It will also include information you have started to gather and read for the project.
- What you *need to know.* Completing this section allows you to identify areas in which you will need to do more reading and research.
- The *methods* you will use to acquire information. Your methods for gathering and processing information should match the question you ask. That is, think about what resources will best answer the question. Will you need to look at archival materials? Survey a population? Read expert sources? Apply a theory?
- A *schedule* or *timeline* for managing the parts of the project. Break the project into bite-sized chunks, tasks that can be completed in two hours or less.
- A *working bibliography* of sources or a *literature review.* Identify the sources you may need to use (a working bibliography), or suggest how your study fits into a body of existing research (a literature review).

More about ▸▸▸
Exploring research topics, 24–31
Developing a research question, 34–35

Other possible components of the proposal or prospectus may include:

- A specific *audience* to which you will direct the researched writing. If your instructor has not specified an audience and wants you to determine one, consider who might be most invested in the outcomes of your research.

- A *genre* choice. In what form will you deliver the research? The answer will depend in large part on your audience and purpose.

4b Analyzing the Rhetorical Situation

Before you can complete a research proposal, you will need to understand the assignment and its *rhetorical situation:*

- **Purpose:** what you hope to accomplish with the text
- **Audience:** who will be reading the text you produce
- **Tone:** your attitude toward your subject and audience, expressed through the words you choose
- **Context:** the setting (academic, business, personal, public) in which your text will be "consumed"
- **Genre:** the type of work you will produce—a scholarly essay for a psychology class, a formal proposal (not a project proposal but a final researched project) for a campus organization, a research report for a business

Attention to all of these issues as well as to a variety of practical factors, such as knowing the due date and length of the assignment, is essential to effective assignment analysis. Before you can write an effective project proposal, you will need to understand these factors.

Establishing a purpose

The classical *purposes* for researched writing are

- to inform
- to interpret
- to persuade
- to solve a problem

Analyzing the assignment for purpose

The details of the assignment as well as its purpose will be expressed—explicitly or implicitly—in the assignment and in the instructor's discussion of it. Analyze the language of the assignment to determine its purpose:

- Does the assignment ask you to *describe, compare, discuss, explain,* or *review* (in the sense of provide an overview)? If so, the purpose of the assignment is *informative* (or *expository*): You must use reasons and evidence (facts, statistics, examples) to explain something to your reader.

- Does the assignment ask you to *analyze, interpret,* or *comment*? If so, the purpose of the assignment is *interpretive.* You must offer insight into trends or patterns you see through the gathering of evidence, data, and expert opinion. Your goal is to persuade readers that yours is the most logical and reasonable interpretation of the situation.

More about ▶▶▶
Analysis, 20
Interpretation, 20–21
Evaluation, 22–23

- Does the assignment ask you to *assess, evaluate, argue, critique,* or *propose*? If so, the purpose of the assignment is *persuasive* or *argumentative:* You must make a claim with which readers may agree or disagree, and you must present reasons and evidence in support of your position, in an effort to persuade your readers to adopt your point of view or at least to consider it reasonable.

Identifying and addressing the assignment's audience

For a piece of writing to be effective, the writer must make a careful analysis of the intended reader (or readers). Consider the audience's expectations: Are you addressing a *specialist audience*? That is, do your readers already possess a good deal of information about the topic, and are they reading your document to learn more? Or are you addressing a *general audience,* readers who may have a good deal of experience reading (say, they read sections of the *Los Angeles Times,* the *Philadelphia Examiner,* and the *Manchester Guardian* online every day) but who have only a passing interest in your topic and are expecting to learn the basics?

Consider, too, the *beliefs* of your audience. Do they already hold strong opinions about your topic, or are they likely to be open-minded? All of these considerations will have a powerful effect on the choices you make as a writer.

Having figured out what kinds of people will make up your audience, you should next consider what will make your writing most successful for this group:

- What information will your audience need to understand and appreciate what you are saying?
- What kinds of language, examples, evidence, or reasons will be most effective with your audience?

Considering context

Four of the broad contexts for which you are likely to write, now and in the future, are *academic, business, personal,* and *public*. Research plays a role in all of these contexts, yet each presents its own demands. Personal contexts often privilege relationship over efficiency, while business contexts privilege the opposite. Because your primary present context for writing is school, it is most likely that an academic context—one in which learning, knowledge development, and rationality are valued—will shape your research project.

Determining genre

In literature classes, you may have learned that poetry, drama, fiction, and nonfiction are the four major literary *genres*. You may also have learned that fiction has many subgenres, such as the mystery, romance, or spy novel. But genre extends beyond literature to types of writing as varied as informed commentaries published in magazines to public policy proposals, investigative reports, and instructional manuals. Whatever type of writing you embark on, consider the expectations readers of that genre will have. If you are unfamiliar with the type of writing you will be doing, read several examples of the genre, and try to determine what all the examples have in common. Do most of them value particular types of evidence? Is there a typical tone? Are there common sections or structures?

More about ▸▸▸
Developing a research question, 34–35

4c Drafting Research Questions and Hypotheses

To research effectively, you need to know what you are looking for. Since many college assignments ask you to go beyond the facts to an opinion based on knowledge and supported by information, start with a question that is difficult or impossible for you to answer definitively but that is nevertheless worth pursuing:

CONCEPTUAL QUESTION Would writers still be motivated to write if their work were not protected by copyright laws?

Then break down the broad conceptual question into specific, focused subquestions that you can answer through research:

SPECIFIC QUESTIONS Why did the United States adopt international copyright regulations?

Did the adoption of copyright regulations in the United States lead to an increase in the rate of publication?

To devise research *hypotheses*, turn your specific research questions into statements that express the answer you expect to find. As you conduct research, you will learn whether your hypotheses are true or false, and your thesis will grow naturally from your research hypotheses.

Your specific research questions will be most effective when you:

- Include concrete keywords that you can use in web, database, and catalog searches.
- Formulate a tentative hypothesis in response to your question, but be open to revising your response.
- Devise new questions if your research provides few appropriate sources that address your topic.

The research questions below, for Lydia Nichols's paper on underground comics, demonstrate the technique.

▸▸▸Sample student papers
"Holy Underground Comix, Batman!" by Lydia Nichols, 278–89
"The Power of Wardrobe" by Heather DeGroot, 321–32

Keywords: "comics"; "graphic novels"; "underground comics." Combine with "audience"; "internet"; "market"; "artists"; "genre"; "experimentation"

Hypothesis: Characteristics of underground comics may make them unsuitable for mainstream distribution.

Research questions: What are the characteristics of mainstream comics? What are the characteristics of underground comics? What is the history of each? What is the value of each? What are audiences' responses to the characteristics of underground comics?

EXERCISE 4.1 Devising Research Questions and Hypotheses

Devise five research questions for the topics you have already begun exploring. Turn one of these research questions into a research hypothesis using the guidelines in section 4c.

4d Providing a Rationale

The project rationale is the "so what?" part of the project proposal. At each stage of your project, you should have a sense of why you are pursuing your research question and why someone other than you might be interested in reading the results of the research.

In the rationale section of your proposal, consider answering the following questions:

- What are your personal motivations for looking into this topic?
- What other groups might find the information helpful, and why?
- In what way is the question too complex to answer easily? (Is this a new phenomenon worth exploration? Does the question require the insight of multiple perspectives?) How will your study help to shed light on the issues?

4e Establishing Methods

More about ▶▶▶
Gathering information, 50–56
Developing new information, 129–40
Archival research, 128–31
Field research, 131–40

Every research project employs methods for finding and interpreting information. Methods should not be arbitrary but should fit the question being asked. Some of the primary methods you might use for your project include:

- **Textual research.** Many questions have been answered fairly well by experts in their respective fields. It is often entirely appropriate for student researchers to rely on others' work (secondary research) as the primary evidence and answer to a research question. Your *interpretation* of that existing research is part of your contribution to answering the question.
- **Archival research.** Primary research involves searching through original documents and objects for answers. For this kind of research, you might go to an archive or a museum to study the holdings there. An example of a question well suited to archival research is "What was the nature of Marion Mahony Griffin's working relationship with Frank Lloyd Wright?" Because these two architects worked together, many documents, such as letters and memoranda, are likely to exist from their collaborations.
- **Field research.** Through observations, interviews, questionnaires, and surveys, you can develop your own data to answer

your research questions. Going into the field means drawing new information from people and places. A field researcher might ask the question "What percentage of parents in the Southside school district is satisfied with the educational system, and what are the perceived problems?"

- **Application of theory.** To understand a case, situation, artifact, or text, a researcher might use theoretical tools for interpretation. A question that might be answered through the application of feminist theory to texts, for example, would be "What do alcohol advertisements reveal about power relations between men and women?"

In the methods section of your proposal, first identify which of these methods you will use. Then be as specific as possible about the process you will use to get and interpret information. Specifying the process is especially important for field research. What questions will you include on your survey? Where do you plan to distribute it? Often it is appropriate to combine existing expert studies with your own archival research, field research, or application of a theory.

4f Setting a Schedule

Writing an effective and successful research project takes much more than reading a few things and sitting down to write. Complex projects like these—and many you will do in your jobs and life—require project management. To set a reasonable and complete schedule, begin by considering the practicalities:

- **When is the project due?** Knowing your project deadline is critical to good time management. Once you have determined the due date, work *backward* with a calendar to set a realistic schedule, one that takes into account your other responsibilities and leaves time in case you need to devise a new research question, do additional research, or revise a second (or third) time.
- **How long is the assignment?** Knowing the length requirements will give you a better idea of the scope of your project.
- **What types of research are required?** Will you be expected to do *secondary research*—gathering information from books and articles—or *primary research*—developing your own evidence through questionnaires, interviews, observation, or

primary materials such as letters, memoranda, case law, or works of literature?

- **Must you turn in a portfolio with the final version of the project?** If the instructor requires you to provide a portfolio, you may be asked to include any or all of the following: your notes from the idea-generating process, your working hypothesis, your outline, your working bibliography, your research notes, your first draft, and a reflection letter. Keep copies of these if a portfolio is part of the assignment.

4g Choosing Research Sources Strategically

More about ▸▸▸ Gathering information, 50–66

Even at the proposal stage, you should have a sense of what has already been said about your chosen topic. Your chief concern as you begin researching will be to find enough relevant and reliable sources to answer your research questions. It is also important to ask yourself the following questions:

- How many sources do you need to consult?
- Can you rely only on websites, blogs, and other online sources, or do you need to consult books, print periodicals, and government documents? Will images, movies, or sound recordings be relevant to your research?
- Will classic authorities be useful, or should you concentrate on more recent sources?
- Are popular sources acceptable, or should you use only scholarly sources?

4h Building a Working Bibliography

More about ▸▸▸ Search strategies, 50–66

After you have determined the types of sources you might need, you are ready to begin your search. Researchers generally find it more efficient to prepare a *working bibliography,* a list of sources they may want to consult, than to identify and retrieve sources one by one. First conduct keyword searches in databases and library holdings, developing a list of *all* the promising sources on your topic. Then see how many of the sources you can find (interlibrary loan will help with sources not held by your library). Finally, preview each of the sources, to see which will best help you answer your research question(s). Starting with a working bibliography ensures that you will be using the best sources available, rather than just the first ones you could find.

Tech

Citation Help

There are now free citation builders online that will significantly reduce the time you have to spend getting your citations right. The two most used are

Bibme <http://www.bibme.org/>

Easybib <http://www.easybib.com/>

But be cautious: You need to understand citation well enough to recognize which style sheet you need to use, what you need to put into the builder, and what each category of information is. Otherwise, your bibliography will be a mess. Remember that the builder is not smarter than you are. Check its work.

More about ▸▸▸
MLA style:
In-text citations, 231–45
List of works cited, 246–71
APA style:
In-text citations, 291–301
Reference list, 302–15
Chicago style:
In-text citations, 334–51
List of works cited, 334–51
CSE style:
In-text citations, 361–63
Reference list, 363–75

Your working bibliography should include all the information you will need to locate the source and cite it in your paper. The "working" part of "working bibliography" means that you may add and subtract sources from this initial list, but it should be as comprehensive as you can make it at the proposal stage.

Noting information you will need later

Most of the information you will need to include in your working bibliography is the same for all source types and includes the following:

- Full name of author or artist
- Title and subtitle of book or article
- Publication data (such as title of journal, volume/issue number, publisher or vendor name, date of publication)
- Access information (such as catalog number or URL and date of access)

More about ▸▸▸
Taking notes, 93–105

For a detailed list of the information you will need in your working bibliography, see the Quick Reference box on pp. 46–47.

4i Annotating Your Working Bibliography

More about ▸▸▸
Annotating sources, 122–23

Even if your instructor does not require an annotated bibliography, annotating potential sources can save you time later (when you return to sources that looked promising or if you decide to do more research on the topic at another time). An *annotation* is typically a single paragraph that summarizes and perhaps evaluates the source.

Quick Reference: Information to Include in a Working Bibliography

Publication	Author	Title and Subtitle	Publication Data	Access Information
Books (printed)	–Full name of author (including editor, translator, artist, performer, director, conductor, sender of posting, etc.)	– Title and subtitle of book; edition number – If part of series, title of series, volume number and total number of volumes (if relevant)	– City (and state for less common cities) of publication – Name of publisher – Year of publication	– Call number and library where found (if you visited more than one)
Books (online)		– Same as for printed books	– Same as for printed books	– Date first accessed – Database or project name – Sponsoring organization – Date of e-publication – URL – Call number and library where found (if you visited more than one)
Articles or chapters (in printed periodical, book, or reference source)	– Same as for books	– Title and subtitle of article	– Title and subtitle of periodical – Volume and number or volume and season of publication – Page number (first–last)	
Articles (database)	– Same as for books	– Same as for printed article	– Same as for printed articles; use paragraph or section numbers if page is not provided – If published online only, day/month/year of publication	– Date first accessed – Name of online subscription service, URL of home page, and name of subscribing library – URL or link path for

Publication	Author	Title and Subtitle	Publication Data	Access Information
Newspaper (printed)	– Same as for books	– Title and subtitle of article – Title of newspaper in which it appeared	– Date and edition (national edition, late edition) – Page number(s) – Section designation (if given) – City of publication (if not mentioned in newspaper title)	– Library where found (if you visited more than one)
Newspaper (online)	– Same as for books	– Same as for printed newspaper	– City of publication – Date of publication	– Date first accessed – URL of article
Web source (electronic)	– Same as for books	– Title of website; title of web page – Subject line (email message, posting) – Word or two describing source (email, online posting, blog posting) – Sponsoring organization		– Date first accessed – Date posted or last updated – URL or link path for web page; email address of moderator, if no URL
Audiovisual sources	For creators other than author, composer, visual artist, indicate role: director, performer, producer, etc.	– Title and subtitle of work – Medium or distinguishing characteristic (DVD, videocassette, LP, map, interview, etc.)	– Studio or manufacturer – Date of release or year of creation – Location where held or performance space and city – Television or radio network that produced or broadcast it	If online: – Date first accessed – Date posted – URL or link path

If you decide to annotate your working bibliography, place each annotation immediately following the bibliographic information for the source. Dan Long's annotated bibliography, which appears at the end of Chapter 10, illustrates how useful it will be to have such information at hand when you begin drafting your research project.

Make It **Your Own**

For a research project that you are working on, create a working bibliography of at least ten sources. Choose a mix of source types, including books, scholarly articles, newspaper and magazine articles, reference works, websites, pamphlets, government publications, visuals, multimedia, and audio sources. Then locate and annotate the five most promising sources, recording complete publication information and taking preliminary notes on what the source covers and how useful it might be for your research project.

4j Developing a Literature Review

More about ▶▶▶
Synthesis, 21
Situating your research in a conversation, 173–90

Extended literature reviews often become part of a research project, relating the new research to what others have said about a topic. In a project proposal, a brief literature review offers readers something similar. Primarily, though, creating an overview of what you have already read about your topic indicates that you have a good enough sense of the conversation to develop an informed question. Work from your notes or annotated bibliography, and write two to three paragraphs that identify the primary strands of the discussion. Avoid just moving from author to author if you can; instead, try to group articles and arguments based on similar stances or topics. Why are these sources relevant to answering your question, and what part of the question do they not address?

4k Formatting the Project Proposal

Typically, a project proposal has a header containing standard information such as your name, the date, the instructor's name, and "Research Project Proposal." In the body of the proposal, use subheadings so that your instructor can quickly see that you have addressed all of the required areas. Finally, format the working bibliography using the appropriate style sheet (MLA, APA, *Chicago*, CSE).

Work Together

Before submitting your proposal, exchange it with one or more classmates. Peer review will reduce the chance that your instructor will need you to rewrite the proposal before you move on with the project. Ask your reviewers to check for the following things:

- Have you included all of the information that your instructor requested?
- Is there anything that needs clarification?
- Is your research question narrow enough to be answered in the space and time of this project?
- Can your classmates recommend any search strategies or sources to help you answer the question?

Quick Reference: Checklist for Planning a Research Project

- **Analyze purpose, audience, and other requirements.** What type of research are you expected to do? Who will be reading your results? What goals do you and the audience have for the research? When is the project due, and how long should it be?
- **Choose and focus a topic.** Explore possible topics by assessing the number and types of sources available, your knowledge of the topic, your own interests, and the knowledge and interests of your audience.
- **Form research questions and develop a hypothesis.** Use the question(s) to structure your investigation and the hypothesis to focus and organize your research project.
- **Choose research methods.** Which are more appropriate to your task: primary or secondary materials? scholarly or popular sources?
- **Identify strategies for managing time, resources, and panic.** Set up a calendar, a research log and note-taking system, and a working bibliography.

A Final Thought

The planning process helps you to envision the project and the work you will need to do to answer your research questions. A good plan will reduce negative surprises and make the work much more manageable.

Writing Responsibly: A Checklist

Audience

- ❑ Have you chosen a topic that is appropriate and interesting to your reader?
- ❑ Does your title prepare your reader for what follows?
- ❑ Does your thesis focus your reader's attention on your main point?
- ❑ Will your reader find the reasons you supply logical and compelling?
- ❑ Have you supplied enough relevant evidence to persuade your reader to accept (or at least to consider) your position?
- ❑ Will your reader find your project logically organized?
- ❑ Will your reader find your paragraphs clearly organized and tightly focused?
- ❑ Have you provided transitions to guide your reader?
- ❑ Is your project written at an appropriate level for your reader?
- ❑ Is your tone appropriate to your reader?
- ❑ Have you revised, edited, and proofread your project so that your reader will find the writing clear, correct, and powerful?

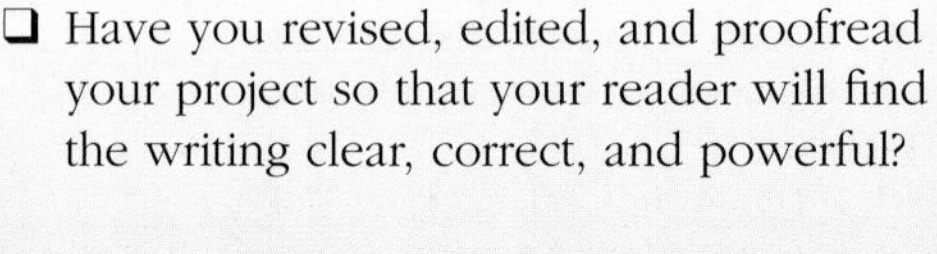

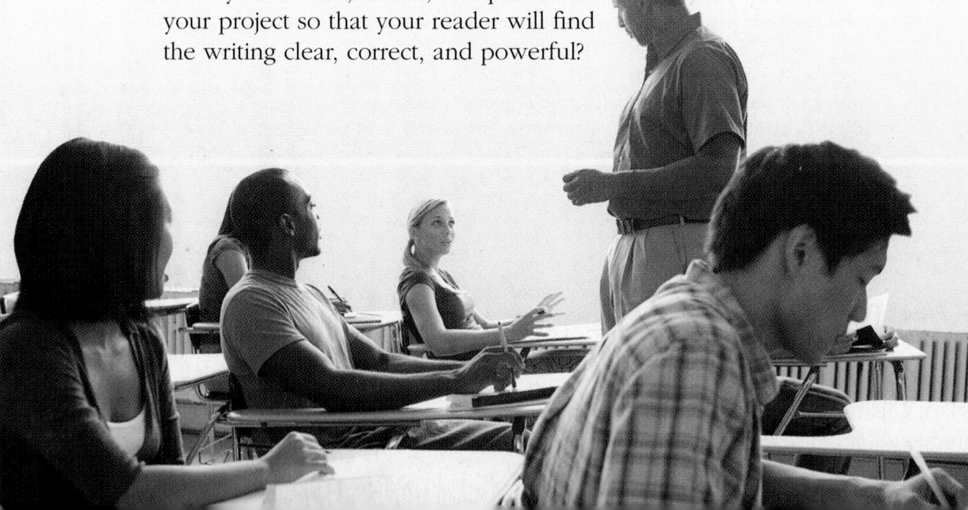

Writing Responsibly: A Checklist

Other Writers

- ❑ Have you given credit to those from whom you have borrowed words or ideas, whether you have summarized, paraphrased, or quoted material or whether your source is printed or online?
- ❑ Have you avoided patchwriting by paraphrasing borrowed material fully, putting the text into your own words and sentence structures?
- ❑ Have you represented the ideas of other writers accurately and fairly?
- ❑ Have you treated other writers respectfully, even when you disagree with them?
- ❑ Have you considered alternative viewpoints?
- ❑ Have you addressed alternative perspectives that conflict with your own position?

Topic

- ❑ Have you explored your topic thoroughly and creatively?
- ❑ Have you conducted research (when needed), using the most in-depth and reliable sources available to you?
- ❑ Have you provided logical reasons that support your thesis?
- ❑ Have you provided sufficient evidence to support your claims?
- ❑ Have you used visuals when they are the most effective way of presenting supporting evidence or when they provide a visual example (and only when they are appropriate to your context and genre)?
- ❑ Have you assessed your sources carefully and presented evidence from reliable sources?
- ❑ Have you represented ideas borrowed from sources accurately and fully?

Lydia Nichols

Ms. Concannon

Writing 205

6 April 2009

Holy Underground Comics, Batman! Moving Away from the Mainstream

Audience/Topic: Nichols chooses a title that reflects her topic and draws the reader in.

When most people think of comic books, predictable images usually come to mind: caped heroes, maniacal villains, deeds of incredible strength, and other typical elements of super-powered adventures. Undeniably, characters like Batman, Superman, and Spider-Man are the most prominent features of the comic book landscape, in terms of both popularity and of revenue (Wright xiv). However, there is more to comic books than superpowers and secret identities. Underground comics (also known as *comix*), printed by small publishers or by individual artists, are very different from what is usually expcected in the genre. While far less well-known than their superhero counterparts, underground comics often offer an innovative and more sophisticated alternative to mainstream titles.

Topic: Nichols uses reliable sources, including scholarly books (see list of works cited, pp. 356–57).

Audience: Nichols chooses a topic that engages both the writer and her reader.

Audience: Nichols writes at a level appropriate for college-level readers, and writes clearly and correctly.

Almost from the beginning, comic books were associated with superheroes. The first comic books appeared in the early 1930s, nearly four decades after comic strips such as *Yellow Boy* began appearing in the major newspapers. Yet comic books did not gain widespread popularity until June of 1938, when writer Jerry Siegel and artist Joe Shuster debuted their character Superman in *Action Comics* #1 (Daniels 9). Superman was an immediate success, and he quickly inspired the creation of copycat superheroes in other comic books. The protagonists

Audience: Nichols starts the paragraph with a topic sentence to focus the reader's attention.

Audience: Nichols uses a transition ("Yet") to prepare readers for a contrasting idea.

Topic: Nichols provides an accurate summary of information borrowed from Daniels.

This paper appears in full on pp. 278–89.

of these comics each had their own strengths and vulnerabilities, but the stories all shared a basic formula: individuals with extraordinary abilities battling against evil and struggling to maintain a secret identity. These superhero comics, though similar to each other, set the comic book industry on its feet, paving the way to profits and sustained success (Daniels 9). Over the decades and even today, the best-selling comics have typically been in the superhero genre.

Other writers: Nichols paraphrases fully to avoid "patchwriting."

While artists and writers over the years have certainly done inventive work in superhero comics, some similarity in mainstream titles was for many years unavoidable. This was due to the creation in 1954 of the Comics Code Authority (CCA), an organization formed by a number of the leading comic publishers to regulate the content of comics (Heller 101). It set very explicit standards, dictating what content was allowed in comic books and what content was expected. Some parts of the code are incredibly specific and controlling:

Self: Nichols writes in a voice that is true to herself and appropriate to her audience, context, and genre.

Other writers: Nichols represents the ideas of others accurately and fairly.

Self: Nichols has revised, edited, and proofread to make the essay the best reflection of herself that it can be.

> The letters of the word "crime" on a comics magazine shall never be appreciably greater in dimension than the other words contained in the title. The word "crime" shall never appear alone on a cover. . . . Restraint in the use of the word "crime" in titles or subtitles shall be exercised. (qtd. in "Good Shall Triumph over Evil")

Other writers: Nichols uses quotations as support and cites sources.

Other rules were more general—vague enough to allow the CCA a free hand in shaping content. One read, "Respect for parents, the moral code, and for honorable behavior shall be fostered" (qtd. in "Good Shall Triumph over Evil"). The CCA also regulated the presentation of criminals and criminal acts, themes of religion and race, and dialogue, especially profanity. While the CCA had no legal authority,

Self: Nichols synthesizes information from a variety of sources to provide the reader with something original.

This paper appears in full on pp. 278–89.

Yourself

- ❑ Have you used the writing assignment to learn something new and to expand your scope as a writer?
- ❑ Have you represented your ideas clearly, powerfully, and accurately?
- ❑ Have you integrated your own ideas or your own synthesis of sources to provide a text that is original and interesting?
- ❑ Have you used language inclusively, avoiding bias and representing yourself as a respectful person?
- ❑ Have you written in a voice that is true to yourself and in keeping with your context (academic, business, public, personal) and genre (college essay, PowerPoint presentation, newsletter)?
- ❑ Have you revised, edited, and proofread your project to make sure your presentation reflects the effort you have put into the writing?
- ❑ Is your project the best representation of yourself that you can make it?

5 Gathering Information

IN THIS CHAPTER

Novice researchers today are cursed with a wonderful gift—the internet. A simple search on *Google* or *Yahoo!* can provide ready access to a mountain of information—some excellent, much unreliable—but this mountain can collapse in an avalanche, becoming a roadblock to effective research. The inexperienced researcher, relying exclusively on open sources (digital resources that do not require registration or payment for access), may miss out on important information available in books, articles, and documents that are accessible through the library, and even sources buried deeper in the Web. Experienced researchers avoid the open-source avalanche with advanced techniques that reduce the onslaught to a manageable number of relevant web pages. They also move beyond the open Web to the library—virtual or physical. This chapter will help you become experienced with non-internet resources.

5a Choosing Research Sources Strategically

Your chief concern as you begin researching will be to find enough relevant and reliable sources to answer your research questions. It is also important to consider the following questions:

- What types of sources will best answer your question? Can you use websites, weblogs (blogs), and other sources you can find online? Do you need to consult books, print periodicals, and government documents? Will images, movies, or sound recordings be relevant to your research?
- Will classic authorities be useful, or should you concentrate on more recent sources?
- Are popular sources acceptable, or should you use only scholarly sources?

***More about* ▸▸▸**
Finding reference works, 59–60
Using an online catalog to find books, 60–63
Using databases to find articles, 52–58
Differentiating between scholarly and popular sources, 52
Finding websites and blogs, 67–78
Finding pamphlets and government documents, 63–65
Finding multimedia sources, 78–79
Using visuals and other media, 130–31
Archives in primary documents, 128–31
Interviews, 131–35
Surveys, 137–40
Observations, 135–37

Consulting a variety of sources

Consulting online sources alone is an alluring prospect. With the myriad of resources now available online, you might think you will never have to enter a library again. Think again. It is a rare project that does not benefit from a variety of sources:

- **Reference works** such as dictionaries, encyclopedias, biographical resources, maps, atlases, almanacs, and statistical reports offer a sound overview of your topic.
- **Books** provide in-depth analysis.
- **Scholarly articles** report the research of experts in the field.
- **Newspaper and magazine articles** offer information about recent events.
- **Pamphlets and government publications** offer information and data that may be available nowhere else.
- **Visual, multimedia, and audio sources** can enliven your research and offer new data.
- **Websites** are useful for quick answers but also often offer sound information from reliable sources.
- **Archival materials** provide insight into history and lived experiences.
- **Field research** provides data about specifically selected populations.

The ease of finding and accessing sources should take a back seat to source quality and relevance.

Consulting authoritative sources: Scholarly versus popular sources

Popular books and *magazines* are published for a broad audience and address a topic of general interest. Because popular books and magazine articles assume little or no prior knowledge and define any specialized vocabulary they may use, they are usually accessible to a general audience. But because they are often written by journalists and other nonspecialists who may lack advanced scholarly training on the topic, they are not always the best information sources.

Scholarly books and *journals* are published by university presses, commercial publishers, or academic organizations for distribution primarily to academic libraries and to scholars in that field. Significantly, scholarly books and articles are *peer reviewed:* Before they are chosen for publication, they are reviewed by other specialists, who may require revisions before acceptance. These steps assure readers that the work represents the most current, most reliable information and opinion on the topic. For most college research assignments, instructors will expect you to rely on scholarly publications for your research.

More about ▸▸▸ Differentiating between scholarly and popular sources, 82–84

5b Finding Periodicals Using Databases and Indexes

Indexes are collections of bibliographic information for articles in periodicals (magazines, journals, and newspapers). They are organized so that you can look up the articles by author, title, and date. In library research, a *database* is now understood as any electronic index of sources that includes an abstract (a summary) or a full-text link to those sources.

Increasingly, subscription indexes and databases are available online through your library's website. The library at the University of Denver (Figure 5.1) is typical in that the link to its database offerings is on the library's home page. To use your library's indexes and databases, you will need to sign in, usually with your student identification number or a username and password.

Finding an appropriate database or index

When searching for articles in magazines, newspapers, or journals, you will need to consult an index or database. College libraries generally

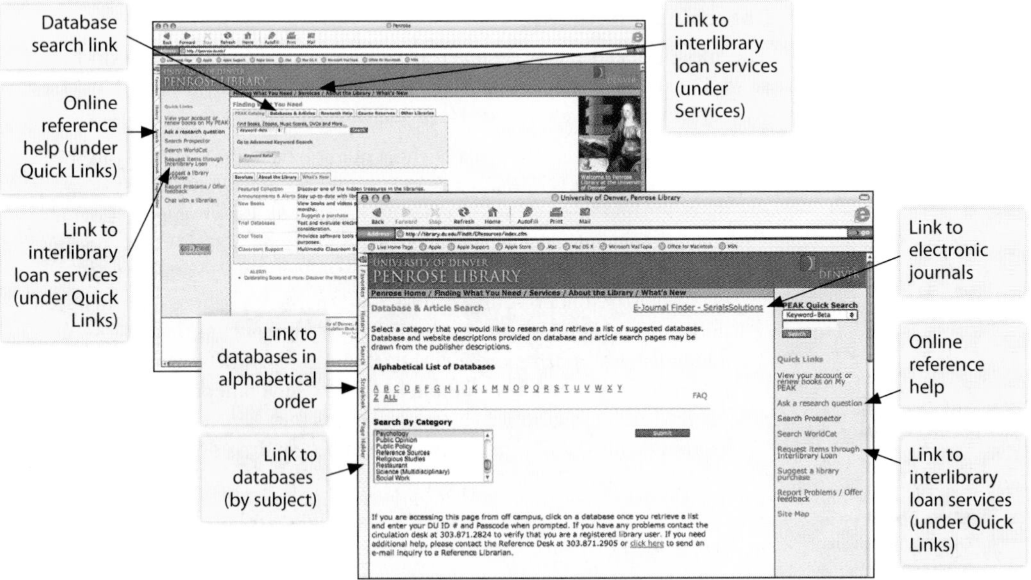

FIGURE 5.1 Home Page and Database Access Page for the University of Denver Library

offer an all-purpose database like *ProQuest Research Library, Academic Search Premier,* or *Expanded Academic ASAP,* which indexes both general-interest newspapers and magazines and scholarly journals.

College libraries also offer a wide variety of discipline-specific databases and indexes. The University of Denver, for example, offers more than 300 online databases—from *ABELL: Annual Bibliography of English Literature and Languages* to *Worldwide Political Science Abstracts*. Thus, the first step in finding appropriate articles for your college research project is to identify the databases and indexes that will be most appropriate for your search. Go to your library's database access page or consult with a reference librarian to find the right ones.

When searching for articles on your topic, be sure to consider the following:

- The types of periodicals the database indexes—popular periodicals, scholarly sources, or both
- The types of sources that are most appropriate for your purpose, audience, context, and genre
- The types of sources that are most appropriate to your topic

More about ▸▸▸
Purpose, 38–39, 144–46, 192, 205
Audience, 39, 193–94, 205
Context, 40
Genre, 40

Searching a database

More about ▶▶▶ Conducting a keyword search, 68–70

The most effective way to learn how a database works is to conduct a search yourself with advice from a reference librarian; the second-best way is to learn by example. Here is an example:

> To begin her research, Lydia Nichols might have typed "comics" in the *ProQuest* search box. Such a search would have generated a list of almost 130,000 items—far too many to be helpful. But *ProQuest* provides a variety of tools for narrowing the search (Figure 5.2). Clicking on the Topics tab reveals a list of terms used to index subjects related to Nichols's, such as "underground comics" and "genre." A search for articles on underground comics reduces the search results (or "hits") to 287—still a long list, but much more focused. Using the Advanced tab allows researchers to search on multiple keywords simultaneously, narrowing the list further. Figure 5.2 shows the results for a search on both "underground comics" and "genre"; this search brought the number of sources down to a manageable 22.

More about ▶▶▶ Using a metasearch engine, 71–72

Just as metasearch engines such as *Dogpile* and *Surf Wax* allow you to send your keyword search out to several search engines simultaneously, most databases allow you to search simultaneously through all the databases provided by the same vendor. If you find several databases that index periodicals on subjects that are appropriate for your research, searching them simultaneously can save you time and effort.

Finding copies of articles

Once you have generated a list of articles from your searches of indexes and databases, you will be ready to retrieve copies of the articles. Some you can link to directly from the database where you found the citation (see Figure 5.2, "Full text" links); those you can print, download to your hard drive, or email to yourself.

Some databases, however, provide only abstracts (or summaries) of sources, and a few provide the bibliographic citation only. While it may be tempting to skip sources to which you cannot get immediate, full-text access, you will miss out on many useful sources if you rely solely on those that can be delivered instantly to your desktop.

When the database does not provide a direct link to the full text of the article, take the following steps:

1. Check your library's list of electronic journals; look for a link to the list on the library's home page (Figure 5.3) or on its database access page.

Find Out **More . . . Conducting a Boolean Search**

Most databases (and some search engines, like *Yahoo!*) use Boolean logic to narrow a search. Boolean logic relies on the "operators" AND, NOT, and OR (in all-capital letters) to expand or narrow a search. It also uses signs (usually parentheses) to group words into phrases and wildcard characters (* or ?) to stand in place of letters so that you can search for different forms of a word at the same time.

AND	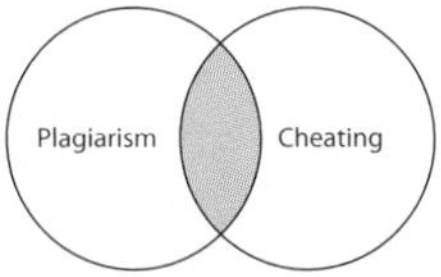 Plagiarism / Cheating Plagiarism AND cheating	Narrows the scope of a search by retrieving items that include both terms.
OR	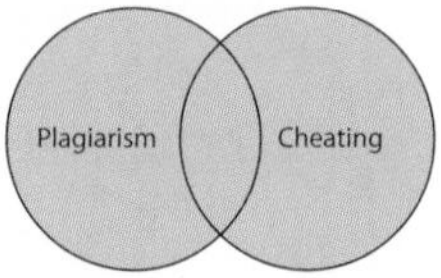 Plagiarism / Cheating Plagiarism OR cheating	Expands a search by retrieving items that include either term.
NOT	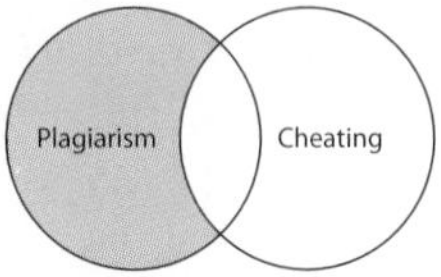 Plagiarism / Cheating Plagiarism NOT cheating	Narrows a search by retrieving items that include one term but not the other.
NEAR	Plagiarism NEAR college	Narrows search by retrieving items with terms within a certain proximity of each other.
(/)	(plagiarism in college) plagiarism AND (college OR education)	Groups terms into phrases, so only items that include the phrase are retrieved. Also used to group Boolean operators.
*** / ?**	*plagiar** to search for *plagiarism, plagiarist, plagiarize,* and *plagiary* simultaneously	Wildcard characters allow you to search for more than one version of a word at the same time by replacing the letters that are different in each word with an asterisk (*) or a question mark (?).

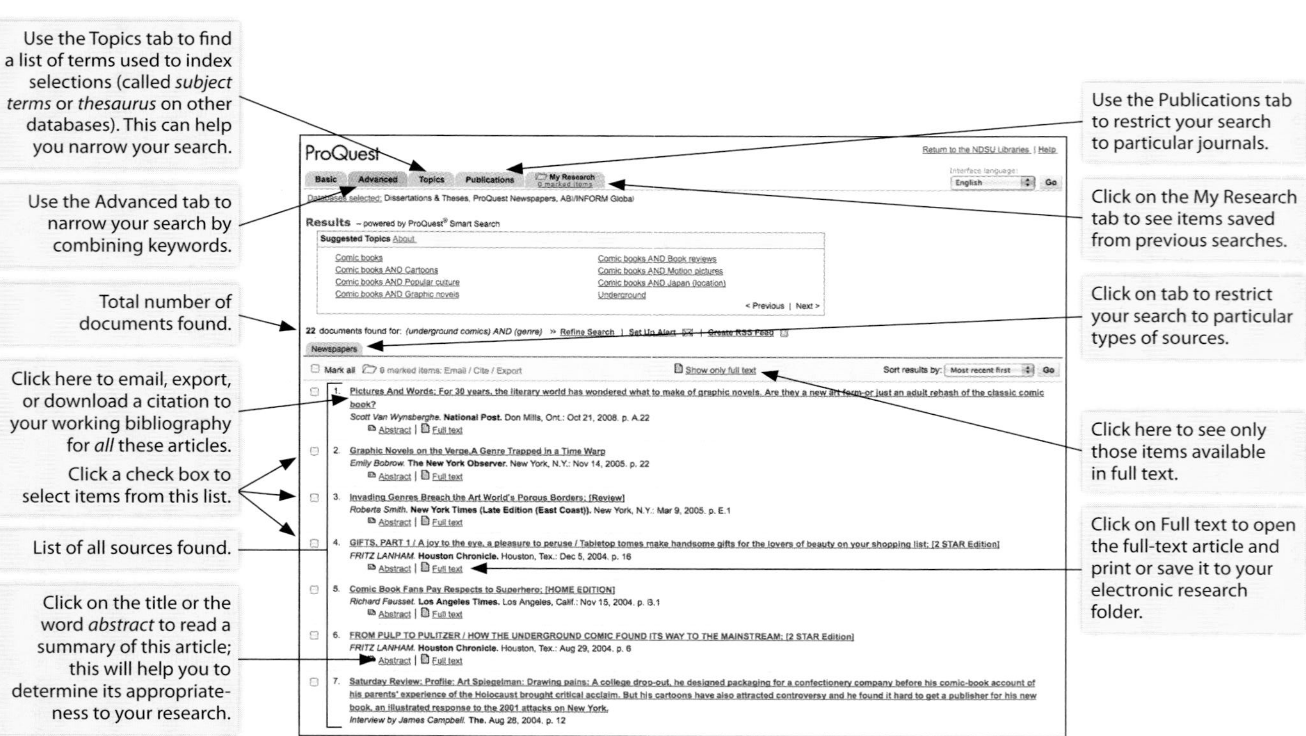

FIGURE 5.2 Search Results for "Underground Comics AND Genre"

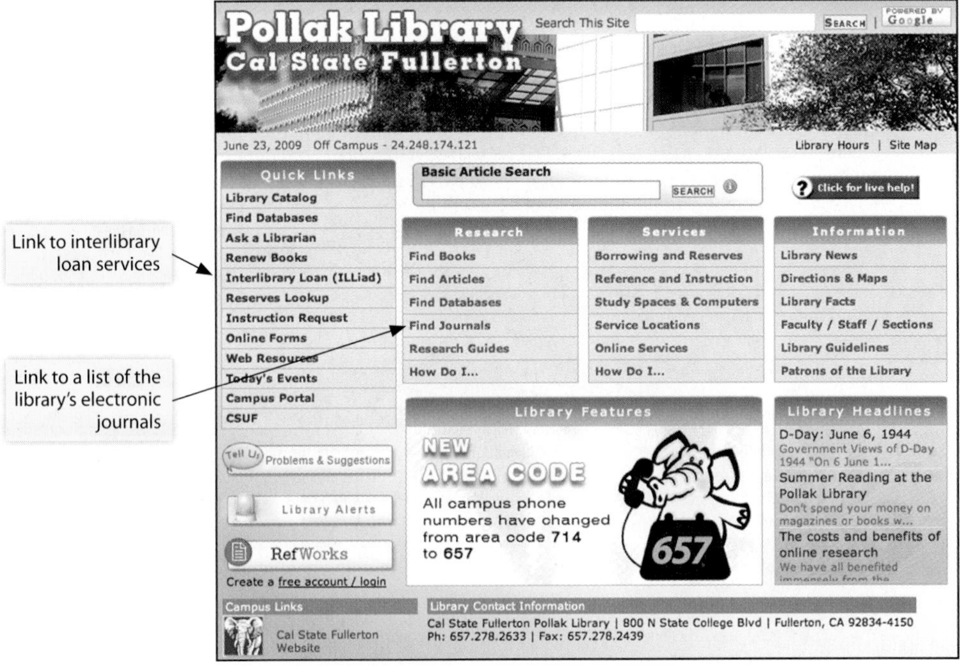

FIGURE 5.3 Link to Interlibrary Loan and Electronic Journal List on Home Page
California State University–Fullerton's library provides these links on its home page.

2. If the journal or issue you want is not available online, check the library's catalog to see if your library subscribes to the print version of the journal. It will likely be housed in one of three places: the Periodicals room, the shelves of bound periodicals, or on microform or microfiche.
3. If your library does not subscribe to the journal you need, you can request a copy through *interlibrary loan (ILL)*. Most libraries now allow you to place interlibrary loan requests directly from the library's website. Many library sites organize ILL under "Services" links. Because it can take two weeks or more for ILL materials to arrive, be sure to start your research well in advance of the due date for your project.

More about ▸▸▸
Using a library's electronic catalog, 61–63

Figure 5.4 (p. 58) summarizes the process of searching for periodical articles.

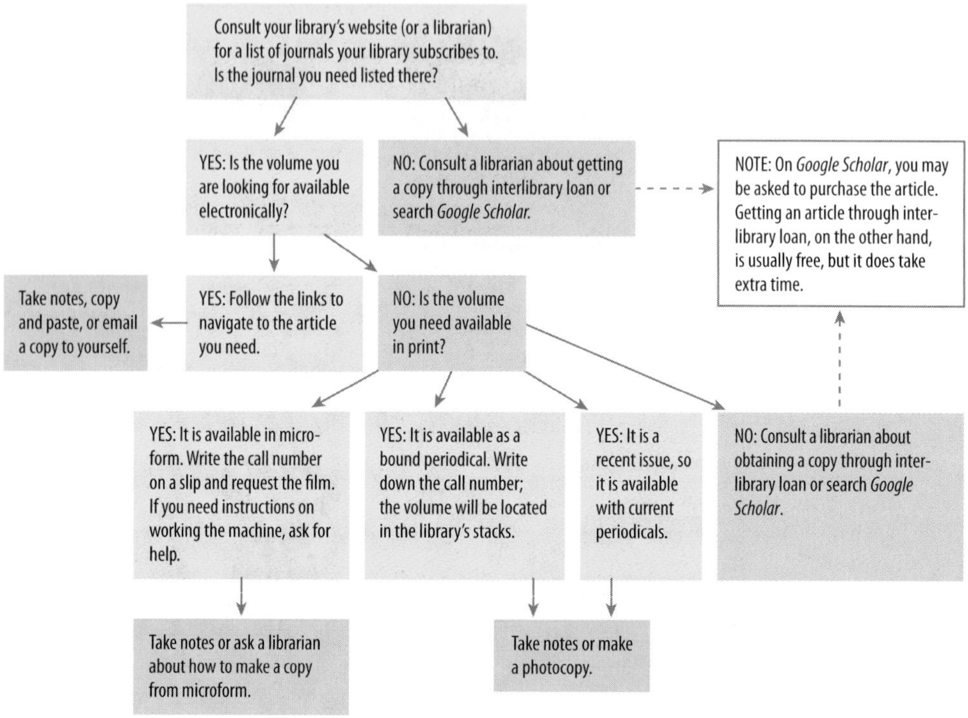

Consult your library's website (or a librarian) for a list of journals your library subscribes to. Is the journal you need listed there?

YES: Is the volume you are looking for available electronically?

NO: Consult a librarian about getting a copy through interlibrary loan or search *Google Scholar.*

NOTE: On *Google Scholar*, you may be asked to purchase the article. Getting an article through interlibrary loan, on the other hand, is usually free, but it does take extra time.

Take notes, copy and paste, or email a copy to yourself.

YES: Follow the links to navigate to the article you need.

NO: Is the volume you need available in print?

YES: It is available in microform. Write the call number on a slip and request the film. If you need instructions on working the machine, ask for help.

YES: It is available as a bound periodical. Write down the call number; the volume will be located in the library's stacks.

YES: It is a recent issue, so it is available with current periodicals.

NO: Consult a librarian about obtaining a copy through interlibrary loan or search *Google Scholar*.

Take notes or ask a librarian about how to make a copy from microform.

Take notes or make a photocopy.

FIGURE 5.4 The Process of Finding an Article

More about ▶▶▶
Creating a working bibliography, 44–45

EXERCISE 5.1 Searching Databases

Using your research topic, search a general database (such as *ProQuest Research Library* or *Academic Search Premier*) to find citations of three or more promising articles, and add them to your working bibliography. Then perform the same search on a subject-specific database (such as ERIC, an education database). Compare the results: How many hits did each search provide? How do the types of sources compare? How many articles were available in your library, as full-text documents linked to the database entry, or as items available in electronic journals, or in print journal articles in your library's periodicals department?

5c Finding Reference Works

In its online and hard-copy reference works, your college library offers a good starting place for research, regardless of whether you are new to a topic or expert in it.

Many reference sources are now available online, and you will be able to link to them from your library's home page. But some (especially more specialized sources) are still available only in hard copy or on CD-ROM in your college library. To find them, type the name of your subject area (for example, "American government" or "psychology"), the Boolean operator AND, and the type of source you are searching for ("dictionary" or "encyclopedia" or "bibliography") in the search box on your library's electronic catalog; then hit Return. You can also talk with a reference librarian.

More about ▶▶▶
Specialized reference works:
Literature, 222–25
Humanities, 222–25
Social sciences, 226–29
Sciences, 226–29
Boolean operators, 55, 70

Finding dictionaries and encyclopedias

In addition to whatever online tools they may use, most writers keep a hardbound desktop dictionary at hand, to verify spellings, look up definitions, and gather additional brief information about words. For this sort of information on usage and spelling, any number of collegiate dictionaries can do the trick.

An unabridged dictionary provides more—more words, more examples of usage, a more complete etymology showing the word's roots in other languages. The most extensive unabridged dictionary is the *Oxford English Dictionary,* a multivolume work providing the entire history of English words and showing the ways in which their meanings have changed over time.

Specialized dictionaries are written for students and scholars in specific academic fields. They often provide a comprehensive introduction to the topic as well as a list of further resources. If, for example, you want a deeper understanding of what *absolutism* means to a political scientist, you will need to turn to a source like the *Blackwell Dictionary of Political Science,* which offers a long paragraph explaining the term, followed by three recommended sources on the topic.

General encyclopedias can offer an overview of your topic and a list of further resources. Some, such as the *Encyclopedia Britannica,* are available in print but may also be accessible through your library's database listings. Others are likely to be available in your college library's reference collection.

Specialized encyclopedias will provide more specific, detailed information than will a general encyclopedia. From reading a specialized encyclopedia on your topic, you can expect not only general information but also a sense of how scholars in the field approach the topic. You are likely, too, to find a brief bibliography of what are considered the most authoritative sources on the topic.

Finding almanacs and yearbooks

Almanacs and yearbooks are annual publications offering facts and statistics. Traditionally, almanacs and yearbooks have offered a wide variety of information, such as when each phase of the moon will occur or the time at which the sun will rise or set on a given date, the population and annual per-capita income of nations, and chronologies of events for the past year. The best-known general-purpose almanac is the *World Almanac and Book of Facts,* which has been published annually since 1923. Others, such as the *Almanac of American Politics* or the *Yearbook of Immigration Statistics,* focus on a specific topic but provide a wide body of statistical and tabular data on that topic.

Finding biographical reference works

Biographical resources can provide you with the facts and events of people's lives (both the famous and the fairly obscure), such as their education, their accomplishments, and their current position. These references can also help you understand the historical context in which the person lived or in which his or her works were produced. Biographical resources available to researchers are indexed in *Biography Index* and in the annual versions of *Current Biography.*

Finding bibliographies

***More about* ▸▸▸**
Annotation, 120–27

Bibliographies list sources on a particular topic, providing the information you need to locate the source in your library's stacks or through interlibrary loan. They are often annotated—that is, they provide an abstract or brief summary of the source—so that you can tell without locating the book or article whether it is likely to be relevant to your research.

5d Finding Books

While reference works can give you an overview or direct you to other sources, it is in books that you are most likely to find extensive, in-depth treatments of your topic.

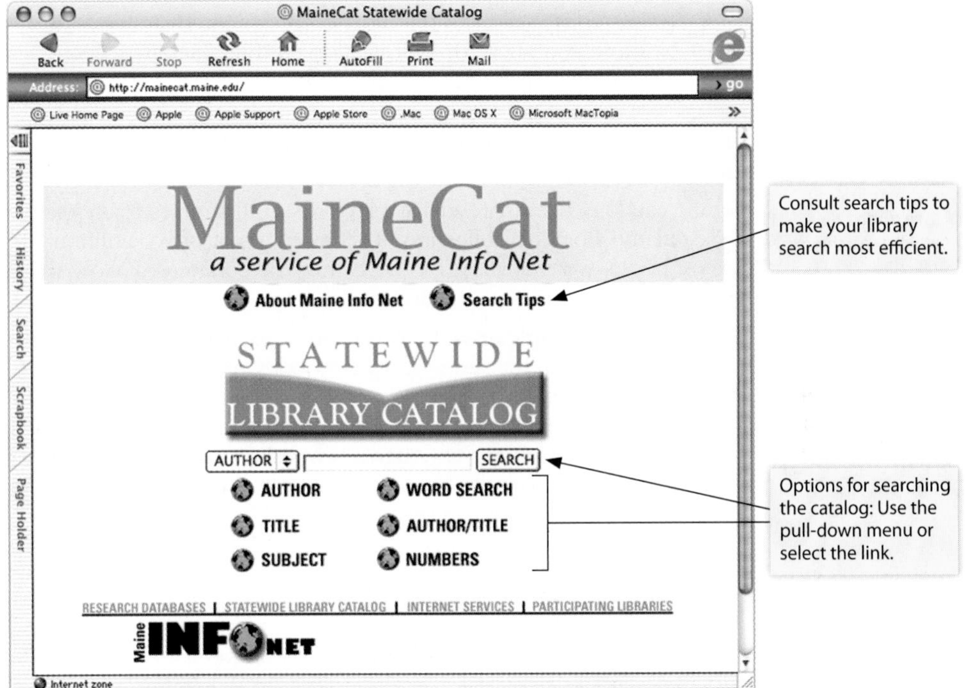

FIGURE 5.5 Search Screen for Maine Info Net The Maine Info Net consortium allows researchers at several colleges (including the University of Maine, Colby College, Bates College, and Bowdoin College) to search each library's holdings through one catalog and order books from any of those libraries through interlibrary loan.

Searching the library's catalog

Library catalogs index the library's holdings by author, title, and subject heading. In addition, you can now search catalogs by keyword and call number, as shown in the search screen for Maine Info Net (Figure 5.5).

- To search by *author,* most library databases ask that you enter the author's last name first, but you should check the catalog's "Help" or "Search Tips" screen to determine which order your own library's catalog specifies.
- To search by *title,* omit the subtitle and any articles (*the, a,* or *an*) at the beginning of the title.

- To search by *subject*—the most popular search strategy—is a bit more complicated, so it is addressed in a separate section below (pp. 61–63).

Searching by subject using the Library of Congress subject headings

More about ▸▸▸ Keyword searching, 68–70

Library catalogs use a preset list of words and phrases to index the books in the library's collection. The terms used by your library to catalog books were devised by the Library of Congress. Follow these steps to find the terms you need:

1. **Find your topic area.** Look for your topic area in the classification outline in the series of big red books aptly titled *Library of Congress Subject Headings* (or *LCSH* for short) shelved in the reference section of the library. You can also find this list of topics online at the Library of Congress's website <www.loc.gov/catdir/cpso/lcco/lcco.html>. The classification outline demonstrates how the Library of Congress organizes published materials:

   A – General works
   B – Philosophy. Psychology. Religion
   C – Auxiliary sciences of history
   D – History (general) and history of Europe
   E – History: America
   F – History: America
   G – Geography. Anthropology. Recreation
   H – Social sciences
   J – Political science
   K – Law
   L – Education
   M – Music and books on music
   N – Fine arts
   P – Language and literature
   Q – Science
   R – Medicine
   S – Agriculture
   T – Technology
   U – Military science
   V – Naval science
   Z – Bibliography. Library science. Information resources (general)

The letter at the left (from A to Z) is the first letter in the call number your library assigns to every item in its collection. Because libraries organize books according to call numbers, you can consult a map of your library to find out where the books beginning with each letter are shelved.

2. **Find your subclass heading.** Turning to the correct letter section of the *LCSH* for your topic will bring you to a list of subheadings (or subclass headings) for that general category. You will now have a two-letter code, such as PR.
3. **Find your subject heading(s).** Once you identify the appropriate subclass heading for your topic, look for an even more specific topic. The call number will now include the two-letter category heading plus a series of numbers indicating the more specific topic, like this: PR908.

   At this point, you need to turn to the printed *LCSH* volumes to find the specific subject headings the Library of Congress uses to categorize books within this sub-subclass. Those subject headings would look like this:

   English literature—Diaries—Bibliography

   English literature—Diaries—History and criticism

   English literature—Diaries—Women authors—History and criticism

   Use the relevant subject headings to search your library's catalog. You can also use the first part of the call number—PR908—to search your library's catalog for all the books it holds on this subject.

Selecting the full record for a book will also bring up the Library of Congress subject headings under which that title has been classified. You can then use those subject headings to search your library's catalog for related subjects. A subject search of the combined Carleton College and St. Olaf College catalog using the subject terms "English diaries—history and criticism" turns up nine items (Figure 5.6, p. 64).

5e Finding Government Publications and Other Documents

Government agencies, businesses, nonprofit groups, and libraries provide rich resources, including statistical data, annual reports, archives of records, and documents from the past.

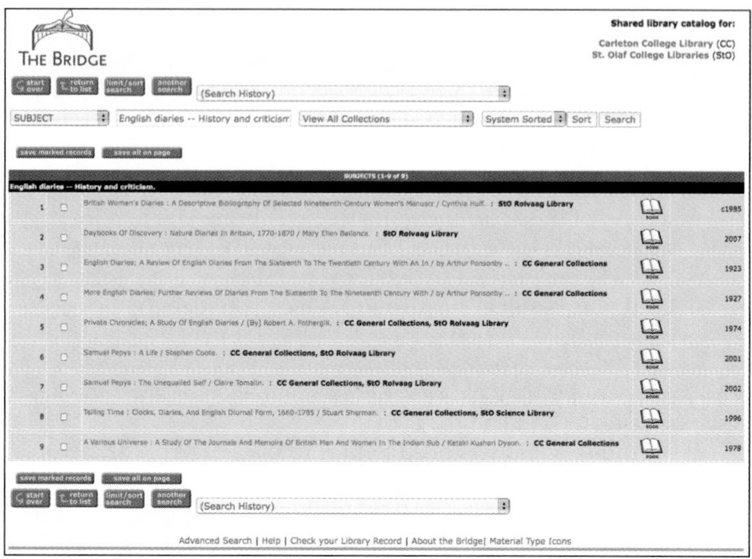

FIGURE 5.6 A Library Search by Subject

Finding government publications

If you are researching a social, legal, or political issue or need up-to-date statistics about almost any group, you may find valuable information in government publications. US government publications include information from all three branches of the government—the executive, legislative, and judicial. More than 300,000 government documents are available in electronic format, free of charge. You can order printed government documents from the Government Printing Office (for a fee), or you can visit one of the 1,250 libraries that act as depositories for government documents. (To find a depository library in your area, visit <www.gpoaccess.gov/libraries.html>.) Many state and local government documents are also now online, as are the documents of many foreign governments. A list of useful websites for federal, state, local, and foreign government documents appears in the Quick Reference box on p. 65.

Many other resources may be included in your library's list of databases, such as the *CQ* (for *Congressional Quarterly*) *Electronic Library* and *Lexis-Nexis Congressional.*

Finding pamphlets, brochures, and annual reports

Until recently, most libraries collected pamphlets, brochures, newspaper clippings, and annual reports in filing cabinets called the Vertical

Quick Reference **Accessing Government Documents Online**

European Union <europa.eu.int/index_en.htm>
FedStats <www.fedstats.gov>
FedWorld Information Network <www.fedworld.gov>
Library of Congress: Thomas <thomas.loc.gov>
National Institutes of Health <www.nih.gov>
Northwestern University Library <www.library.northwestern.edu/govpub/resource/internat/foreign.html>
Organization for Economic Cooperation and Development <www.oecd.org>
State and Local Government on the Net <www.statelocalgov.net>
USA.Gov <www.usa.gov>
US Census Bureau <www.census.gov>
US Government Printing Office <www.gpoaccess.gov/cgp>
United Nations <www.un.org/documents>

File. Today, many libraries have eliminated their Vertical File because items you could only find in print ten years ago are now readily available online. Now if you are doing research on a charitable organization or looking for an annual report, you can usually find the same information at the organization's website that you would have found in the Vertical File.

5f Finding Sources in Special Collections: Rare Books, Manuscripts, and Archives

Many libraries house collections of rare books, manuscripts, and archives. Rare-book collections can include a variety of texts, such as Bibles printed during the early days of the printing press, original documents from the Revolutionary or Civil War period, and first editions of books by writers such as T. S. Eliot and Jack Kerouac. Manuscript collections may include letters by politicians or works by writers in their own hand. Archives include documents, records, and memorabilia that preserve the historical record of an institution or an event. Harvard College and the *New York Times,* for example, both have archives that preserve their history.

More about ▸▸▸
Doing primary research on original documents, 128–131

To find such sources, search your library's catalog and the internet using your keywords plus the words "rare book," "manuscript," or "digital archive." Pertinent items from special collections can enliven your understanding of your topic and enhance your appreciation of its social or historical significance.

5g Finding Multimedia Sources

Photographs, graphs, charts, and drawings have long been a staple of research papers in disciplines such as art history, film studies, history, geography, geology, political science, psychology, and sociology. With research in all disciplines now being shared through multimedia presentations and websites, the demand for multimedia resources has also grown. Many library catalogs list not only books but also audiocassettes, films, manuscripts, maps, musical scores, slides, and sound and video recordings. Look for a drop-down menu from which you can select the type of resource you need. (This menu may be labeled "Record type," "Material," or "Format.") Additional multimedia resources can be located through search engines that index non-HTML files such as Google, AllTheWeb, and AltaVista Advanced searches.

More about ▶▶▶
Creating graphics, 206–14
Using visuals as support, 177–79
Formatting papers, 272–89, 317–32, 352–60, 375–85

In addition to finding multimedia materials in a library's collection or online, you can also create your own graphics (tables, charts, and graphs) by putting data from a government website, an almanac, a yearbook, or your own research into a spreadsheet program to create a table, chart, or graph.

Make It **Your Own**

For a research topic for this or another class, create a working bibliography with sources from at least five of the following categories: scholarly journals, popular periodicals, scholarly books, popular-press books, letters, email messages, newsletters, electronic bulletin boards, discussion lists, websites, government documents, films, still images, maps, statistical reports, pamphlets, and audio recordings. See p. 44 for what to include in your working bibliography.

A Final Thought

It is easy to get trapped in an avalanche of internet-accessible information, but there are many rewards in searching the library. Both the library's web portal (its home page and web site) and its physical location offer trustworthy resources. And do not forget the librarians, who are often the best guides through an effective research process.

6 Meeting the Challenges of Online Research

IN THIS CHAPTER

Jorge Luis Borges, an Argentinean writer, describes in "The Library of Babel" a library so vast it contains all possible information imaginable, even every variation of wrong and mistyped information. All the answers in the universe might be found there, if only one knew how to search it. Readers today often think Borges anticipated the internet's vast reaches and the challenges of finding the right or best information it contains. The more the Web proliferates, the more skills and knowledge it demands of those who come looking. Understanding the ways search engines work and the organization of the Web can help make the difference between an online search that turns up lots of junk and one that quickly leads to real answers.

6a Web and Database Searches: Developing Search Strategies

To find information on the Web, researchers typically begin with a search engine, like *Google* or *Yahoo!* Search engines scan billions of Web pages for whatever words the user enters and return the links they uncover in order of relevance, as determined by criteria the search engines set. (*Google*, for example, ranks its results based on the number of other pages that link to that site, while a *Yahoo!* search ranks results in part on the number of times a search term turns up.) The results retrieved from each site can differ because of varied relevancy criteria, as well as because the search engines index different web pages. For that reason, it is always a good idea to run a search on multiple engines. A list of popular search engines appears in the Quick Reference box below.

Before using a search engine or web directory for the first time, read about how it works. Look for links (often at the bottom of the page) called "About" or "Help" to find answers to frequently asked questions (FAQs) or advice about how best to conduct a search on that site.

Using keywords

The most common way to begin a web search is to type a word into the search box of a search engine and then click on the Search button or hit your Return key. A search on *Google* for the word "robotics," for example, yields the results shown in Figure 6.1.

***More about* ▶▶▶**
Library electronic catalogs, 61–63
Library periodicals databases, 52–58

This kind of searching is very easy, and it yields plenty of results—in this case, more than 85.5 million of them. How helpful are these search results? Not very. Too much data has been delivered.

Popular Search Engines and Web Directories

Alta Vista <www.altavista.com>
Ask <www.ask.com>
Dmoz <dmoz.org>
Excite <www.excite.com>
Gigablast <www.gigablast.com>
Google <www.google.com>
HotBot <www.hotbot.com>
Infoseek <www.infoseek.com
Live Search <www.live.com>
Yahoo! <www.yahoo.com>

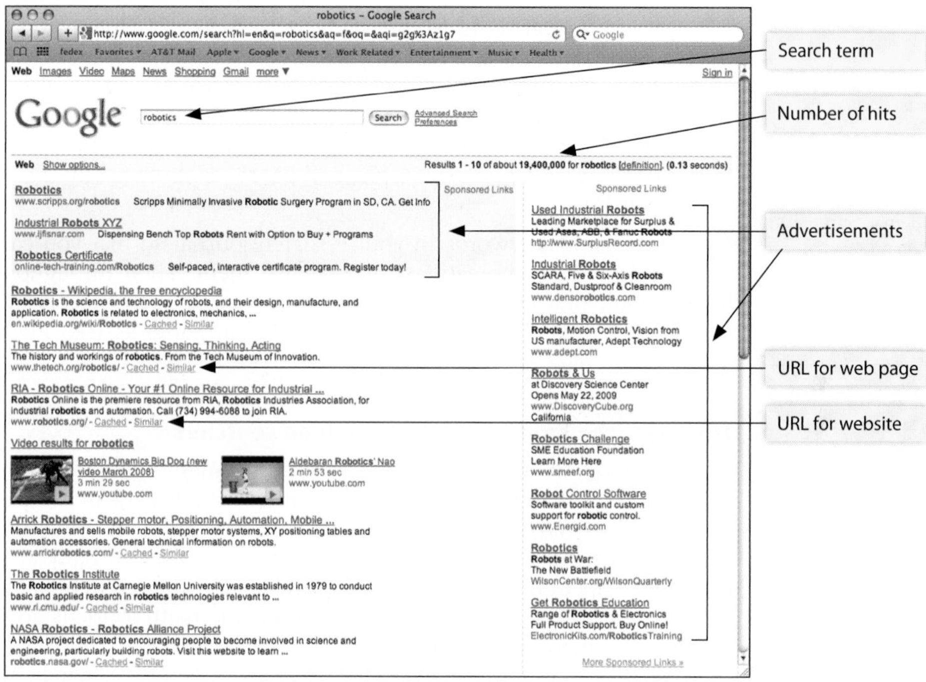

FIGURE 6.1 A Simple Keyword Search on *Google*

A better way to begin is to create a list of search terms for your topic and then to use them to search the Web systematically. Since search engines—unlike your library's electronic catalog or the periodicals databases your library subscribes to—do not use a systematic list of terms, you must rely on your ingenuity to come up with a list of effective keywords. Here are some suggestions for making an effective list:

> ***More about*** ▸▸▸
> Generating ideas, 24–31

1. Begin by reviewing whatever prewriting you have already done, underlining the distinctive nouns you find there (including names, titles, acronyms) and compiling these nouns into a list.
2. Next, add variant spellings ("Beijing" for "Peking," for example) and synonyms (such as "generalization" for "stereotype"). A thesaurus can help you find alternatives. Also add related concepts for your terms; in a search for "robotics," for

example, you could search the larger category of "automated technologies" or the related category of "artificial intelligence."

3. Browse the results of your early searches to find additional keywords. A "robotics" search turns up information on military uses, jet propulsion, and robotics research labs, for instance.
4. As you read about your topic, add possible keywords to your list.

More about ▸▸▸
Keeping a research journal, 14–15
Planning, 49
Drafting, 161–72
Revising, 191–203

Keep your list of keywords in your research journal so that you can track terms (and combinations) as you use them. Then throughout the research, drafting, and revising stages of your project, conduct new keyword searches to flesh out areas of your paper as your ideas develop.

Using search engine math and Boolean searches

More about ▸▸▸
Boolean searching, 55

Beyond having finely tuned keywords, using combining and limiting strategies is also critical to search effectiveness. Boolean searches use the primary search terms AND, OR, and NOT for combining and limiting. Search engines sometimes recognize these terms, but many also use symbol operators (+, -, " ", *). So, for instance, when searching for a topic on robotics, you might use search engine math to focus your results better than just putting "robotics" in the search box.

A long series of terms can be effectively combined for a search. To find out who originated thought on robotics, you might conduct the following search: +robotics +inventor +origin* (the asterisk allows the engine to find all variations of the word: *origin, original, originals, originate, originated*). To search for how the military is involved in developing and using robotics, you might use the following string:

Quick Reference **Search Engine Math**

Operator	Function	Example
+	Always include	+robotics
-	Do not include	-lab
" "	Look for the phrase exactly as typed	"robotics lab"
*	Search for words with this root and various endings	Robot*

+robotics +military -training. From this search you could limit the results once you found the area of military robotics you were interested in: +robotics +military +vehicles. Be sure to check which search strategies the search engine you are using recognizes before you enter either Boolean terms or search engine math.

Using Advanced Search options

Another method for refining searches is using Advanced Search screens built into the search engines and directories. The *Google* Advanced Search page, for example, allows you to search for sites that contain the word "anorexia" and the phrase "social class." Whereas a simple Google search using the terms "anorexia," "social," and "class" returns links to 508,000 web pages, an advanced search for the word "anorexia" and the phrase "social class" (rather than the separate words "social" and "class") reduces the number of "hits" to 29,000.

The Advanced Search page also allows you to search for results only in languages that you can read, for pages that have been updated recently, and for sites that are published in noncommercial domains (sites with URLs, or addresses, that end in *.org, .gov,* or *.edu,* rather than *.com*). The Advanced Search options are illustrated in Figure 6.2 (p. 72).

Notice that the Advanced Search page allows you to add ("with **all** of the words") and subtract ("**without** the words") terms much as you can with search engine math. Going directly to the Advanced Search page when you conduct online research can save you some time reviewing how the engine works.

Using metasearch engines

You may have a favorite search engine, one that you go to automatically when you have a question. But because search engines index different web pages and use different methods to rank sites, for serious research you will need to consult more than one. One way to search multiple sites simultaneously is through a *metasearch engine* that sends your keyword search out to several search engines at once and then returns the top results from each, usually compiled and with the duplicate entries deleted. If you enter "obesity" and "culture" in the search box at the metasearch engine *Dogpile,* for example, you will get a manageable 66 "hits," many of them quite promising.

Search for an exact phrase.

Eliminate irrelevent items.

Narrow results to sites in English or other languages.

Limit results to specific file types such as .pdf.

Limit results to specific domains such as *.edu* and *.org*.

Narrow results to recently updated pages.

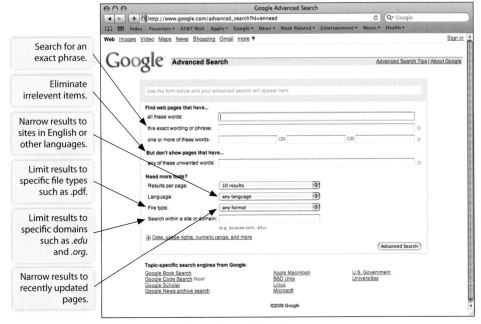

FIGURE 6.2 An Advanced *Google* Search

Quick Reference **Metasearch Engines**

Clusty <clusty.com>

Copernic Agent <www.copernic.com>

Dogpile <www.dogpile.com>

Info.com <www.info.com>

Ixquick <ixquick.com>

MetaCrawler <www.metacrawler.com>

Search.com <www.search.com>

Surf Wax <www.surfwax.com>

Vivisimo <vivisimo.com/>

Webcrawler <www.webcrawler.com>

However, the number of results returned by metasearch engines is limited—they usually take only the first few sets of results from each engine. The result is streamlined but incomplete. Particularly if your topic is obscure, you may find that searching a few comprehensive search engines, such as *Ask, Google,* and *Yahoo!,* one by one is more effective.

Searching the invisible Web

A wide variety of information sources exist on the Web but are not routinely turned up by a keyword search on a search engine. These gaps in web searches occur because of the inability of some search engines to find the following:

- Data within a database
- Files that are dynamically created in response to a user typing a keyword into a search box
- Files that require a password or login information
- Files that are not in HTML format (like blogs and news feeds, which are usually in XML format)
- File names (URLs) that contain question marks
- Image, sound, and video files

Because these kinds of sites are not always flagged by search engines, they make up what is sometimes called the invisible (or dark) Web. Finding information on the invisible Web requires the use not just of simple searches on search engines but the use of databases, subject directories (p. 74), and search engines that go beyond HTML files.

Using subject directories

Subject directories are hierarchically arranged collections of websites, organized into groups by topic and frequently annotated. Their organization—from general to specific—provides an effective overview of a topic and allows you to drill down to increasingly specific levels. The annotations provide information about a site before you navigate to it. For these reasons a subject directory can be an effective tool for discovering and narrowing (or expanding) a topic as well as a good starting point for conducting research.

Two types of subject directories are available: commercial directories and academic ones. Commercial directories rarely scrutinize their listings as carefully as the academic directories do, and because they cater to a general audience, they do not emphasize academic topics or links. Academic directories, on the other hand, may offer a smaller number of links, but the links are evaluated carefully and the categories are chosen to be of use to an academic audience. So, while commercial directories like *Yahoo!* <dir.yahoo.com> and *About.com* <www.about.com> can be useful for helping you devise a topic, you should use an academic directory to locate useful sources.

More about ▸▸▸
Devising a topic, 24–31
Narrowing a topic, 32–33
Expanding a topic, 34

Quick Reference — Academic Subject Directories

Academic Info <www.academicinfo.net>
BUBL LINK <bubl.ac.uk/link>
CompletePlanet <www.completeplanet.com>
INFOMINE <infomine.ucr.edu>
The Internet Public Library <www.ipl.org>
Librarians' Index to the Internet <www.lii.org>
Resource Discovery Network <www.rdn.ac.uk>

Tech

Using *Google Scholar*

Google Scholar <scholar.google.com> allows users to search the Web exclusively for scholarly materials—articles in academic journals, theses, books, and abstracts.

Pros

- *Google Scholar* can help you locate material that you would otherwise need both your library's catalog and its subscription databases to find.
- It can link to your own library's digital holdings (see the Preferences setting in *Google Scholar*).
- It indicates how many online sites have cited the source and provides links to those citations; a source heavily cited in scholarly journals is likely to be reputable.

Cons

- *Google* does not define "scholarly," so your instructor may not consider some listed works appropriate.
- You may be shifted to sites where you will be asked to pay for full-text versions of the text. (Check your library's holdings or interlibrary loan before paying.)
- Recent sources are often not included, or they appear at the end of the list. (You can include a date range in Advanced Scholar Search.)
- Bibliographic data cannot be imported to bibliographic software.

More about ▸▸▸
Evaluating sources, 80–92
Interlibrary loan, 57

EXERCISE 6.1 Search Engines

Using one of the search engines listed on p. 68, conduct a keyword search on your topic. Follow these steps in your search:

1. Compile a list of keywords for your topic.
2. Enter a single keyword, and conduct a simple search.

3. Enter two or more keywords with Boolean operators or search engine math to conduct a more complex search.
4. Use Advanced Search options to limit your results to items posted after 2002 with a noncommercial domain.

How do the results differ at each step in terms of effectiveness, efficiency, and accuracy in coming up with relevant information? Which step returns sites that are most useful in academic research?

6b Finding Other Electronic Sources

In addition to conventional websites, a variety of other electronic sources, including weblogs ("blogs"), discussion lists, and news alerts, can offer insight into your topic.

Finding blogs

An increasing number of people maintain weblogs in which they write informally about their hobbies, interests, and special areas of knowledge. For this reason, blogs have become an important source for news, in politics as well as in academic disciplines.

To find a blog on your topic, try visiting a search engine that seeks out blogs. *Google,* for example, offers a special blog search page <blogsearch.google.com>.

More about ▶▶▶
Evaluating reliability of a blog, 86–90
Citing a blog,
MLA style, 261–62
APA style, 314
Chicago style, 348
CSE style, 373

CAUTION Not all blogs are reliable; they can be generated by anyone. Evaluate them carefully before using the information they provide.

Quick Reference **Blog Search Engines**

Blogarama <www.blogarama.com>
Blogdex <www.blogdex.net>
Blogdigger <www.blogdigger.com>
Bloglines <www.bloglines.com>
Blogsearch <www.blogsearchengine.com>
Blogstreet <www.blogstreet.com>
Eatonweb Portal <portal.eatonweb.com>
GlobeofBlogs <www.globeofblogs.com>
Google Blogs <blogsearch.google.com>
Readablog <www.readablog.com>
Technorati <www.technorati.com>

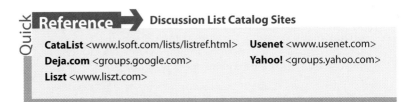

Quick Reference → **Discussion List Catalog Sites**

CataList <www.lsoft.com/lists/listref.html>
Deja.com <groups.google.com>
Liszt <www.liszt.com>
Usenet <www.usenet.com>
Yahoo! <groups.yahoo.com>

Finding discussion lists

Discussion lists—email discussion lists, newsgroups, and chat rooms—allow people with common interests to carry on electronic discussions. *Email discussion lists* allow members of a group to send email messages to all other subscribers. *Newsgroups* are web-based bulletin boards on which members can read or respond to postings. Both email discussion lists and newsgroups require participants to subscribe. *Chat rooms* are informal, drop-in forums. To participate in a chat room, users simply click on a link from a web page. Because chat rooms may have a number of "conversations" going on simultaneously, be careful when you post that you are contributing to the "chat" that you have been reading.

More about ▸▸▸
Search engines that find dynamic websites, 68
Citing email discussion lists, newsgroups, and chat rooms,
MLA style, 261
APA style, 313–14
Chicago style, 348
CSE style, 373–74

To find an email discussion list or a newsgroup pertinent to your topic, enter your search terms in one of the email discussion list or group catalog sites listed in the Quick Reference box above.

You can also enter your keyword plus "email discussion list," "newsgroup," or "chat room" in a search engine that finds dynamic websites. You will have the best results if you begin with very general keywords. As with weblogs, always keep in mind that the information you gain from discussion groups will have to be verified, and write down the information you will need later for citing any post you refer to as a source.

Using news alerts

News alerts help you track media coverage of current events and are an invaluable resource for research. To register for news alerts, go to *Google* <www.google.com/newsalerts> or a news outlet such as *CNN* <www.cnn.com/EMAIL/> and register for the service. You will then receive daily email updates on the topics you have chosen.

Finding online reference works

Because online resources are fairly easily updatable, web formats are suited to reference works. Entries can be added and adjusted as information becomes available. Furthermore, reference works online are often quite searchable. Thus, online reference works are great places to start a search, particularly when you do not know much about your subject. Some, such as the *Concise Columbia Electronic Encyclopedia* <www.bartleby.com/reference>, are available online to all users. Others, such as the *Oxford English Dictionary* (*OED*), require a subscription for access.

Subject librarians at your school may have filtered the Web for the best reference works in their areas, and the library may even have a subscription to give you access to restricted works. Check your library website for "subject librarians" or "research guides." From these locations on the library website, you will be able to choose subject areas in which you are interested (Figure 6.3). The lists created by your school's research librarians will include a range of resource types including online reference works.

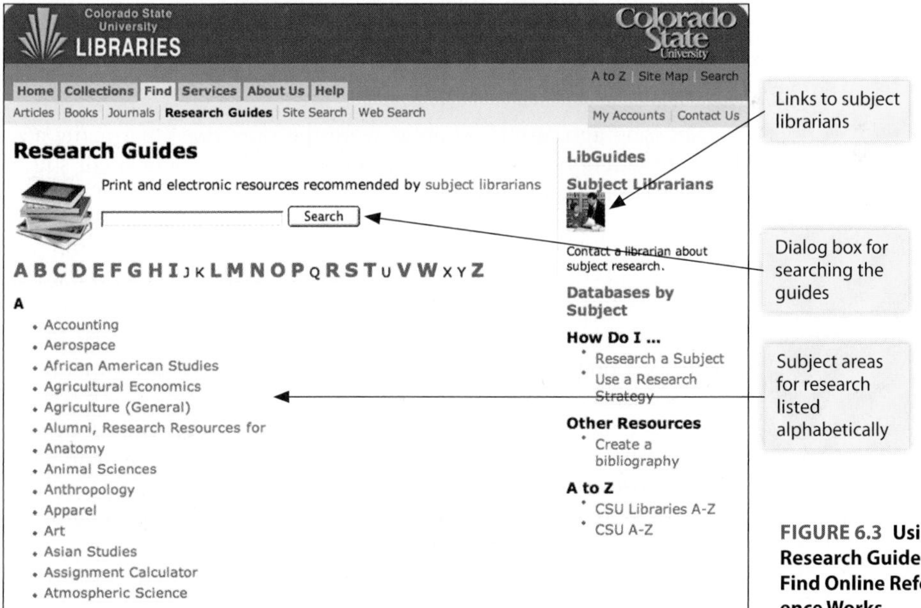

FIGURE 6.3 Using Research Guides to Find Online Reference Works

Find Out **More . . . Online Government Statistics**

Much of the statistical data found in yearbooks and almanacs can be accessed online from the following government agencies:

Bureau of Economic Analysis <www.bea.doc.gov/>

Central Intelligence Agency (CIA) <www.odci.gov/cia/publications/factbook/>

USA.gov <www.usa.gov/Topics/Reference_Shelf/Data.shtml>

US Census Bureau <www.census.gov>

US Department of Justice <www.usdoj.gov/eoir/statspub/syb2000main.htm>

Some almanacs and yearbooks, too, are now available online. Check your library's catalog or its list of databases.

6c Finding Multimedia Sources Online

More about ▶▶▶
Finding multimedia sources in the library, 66

Photographs, graphs, charts, and drawings have long been a staple of research papers in disciplines such as art history, film studies, history, geography, geology, political science, psychology, and sociology. With research in all disciplines now being shared through multimedia presentations and websites, the demand for multimedia resources has also grown.

Not long ago, print resources were the only ones that many academic researchers were expected to consult. That might seem still to be the case for some research topics, such as the poetry of William Blake (1757–1827) or the early writings of feminist anarchist Emma Goldman (1869–1940). Now, though, there are many impressive and reliable online sources: The Berkeley Digital Library, for example, offers an invaluable source on Goldman, *Emma Goldman: A Guide to Her Life and Documentary Sources.* And multimedia sites abound: The Library of Congress, for example, maintains a useful hypermedia archive of Blake's works.

When conducting research for an academic project, do not neglect online and multimedia sources, but be sure you evaluate them carefully and use multimedia sources only when they help you make your point. Many multimedia resources can be located through search engines that index non-HTML files.

In addition to finding multimedia materials in a library's collection or online, you can create your own graphics (tables, charts, and graphs) by putting data from a government website, an almanac, a yearbook, or your own research into a spreadsheet program to create a table, chart, or graph.

More about ▸▸▸
Using visuals as support, 177–79
Formatting papers, 272–89, 317–32, 352–60, 375–85

A Final Thought

The Web does not have to be an impenetrable Library of Babel. Nor should you approach it as though everything you find when you search is true and reliable. With the right search tools and techniques, however, research online can be rewarding.

7 Evaluating Information

IN THIS CHAPTER

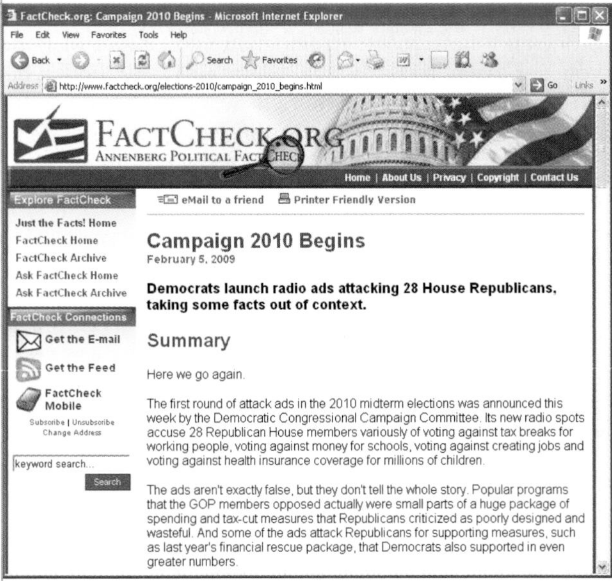

You hear an advertisement on the radio about a political candidate in your district who voted to "bail out big banks" but who "opposed tax breaks for 95 percent of American workers."* Can you take these statements at face value? Might the official have opposed tax-cut measures for other reasons, such as tax cuts for the remaining 5 percent that were also included in the bill? Might the official have supported a bank bailout for fear that failing banks would adversely affect citizens? Relying on irrelevant, biased, or manipulative information could mislead you into throwing your support behind a candidate whose platform

*FactCheck.org assessed the truthfulness of an advertisement on this theme sponsored by the Democratic Congressional Campaign Committee.

you do not support. Worse, you could pass along this information, undermining your own credibility. Whether in your personal life, your professional life, or your academic life, critically assessing sources of information is a crucial skill.

Evaluating sources means assessing how *relevant,* or useful, a source is to your research; determining the source's *reliability*—how much you can trust it; and checking *logic,* the ways the authors build an argument. This chapter will help you build the skills you need to evaluate your sources critically.

7a Evaluating Relevance

When considering a potential source, first consider its relevance: Does the source offer information that could enrich your understanding of your topic, provide background information or evidence for your claims, or suggest alternative perspectives? Before reading the entire text, determine its relevance by *previewing* it:

More about ▸▸▸
Previewing, 12–13

- **Read the title and subtitle.** These elements can often give you a sense of the contents.
- **Check the publication date.** Recently published works are most likely to be of the greatest relevance, as they will probably provide the most up-to-date information. Be alert, though, for classics; they contain information or ideas on which researchers still rely. Classics will be cited frequently by other reliable sources, and your instructor can help you identify them.
- **Read the abstract, foreword, introduction, or lead (first paragraph in a newspaper article).** These sections usually provide a summary, an overview, or key facts detailed in the source.
- **Read the headings and subheadings.** These elements provide an outline of the work.
- **Scan figures and illustrations.** These visuals might signal important ideas and explain complex processes.
- **Read the conclusion.** The conclusion—the last few paragraphs in a journal or magazine article or in the final chapter of a book—often reiterates the central idea and argument, important questions, and major findings of the entire text.
- **Consult the index.** If the potential source is a book with an index, check it for key terms in your research.

Writing Responsibly **Keeping an Open Mind**

As a writer, you also have a responsibility to avoid bias: Read sources with an open mind, use reliable sources, consider evidence that undermines your position, avoid exaggerated claims, and criticize unreasonable or poorly supported conclusions but not the people who hold them. Sound research considers all sides of an argument. Be especially careful as you evaluate sources that you immediately agree or disagree with: Just because you agree with them does not mean they are reliable sources, nor does your disagreement invalidate them.

7b Evaluating Reliability

Judging reliability is not a simple, yes-or-no litmus test. Instead, rate the source on a variety of criteria. The more criteria on which you can rate the source highly, the more reliable it is likely to be:

- **Is the source scholarly or popular?** Scholarly texts are written by subject matter experts for academic journals and presses as a contribution to knowledge, and they are reviewed by other experts before being published. Articles in magazines and books published by the popular press are commercial; they were selected by an editor who believes an audience will buy the material. Popular sources are not reviewed by experts and thus are generally less reliable (Figure 7.1).
- **Is the author an expert on the topic?** Does the author have special knowledge or experience of the subject? You can answer this question by reading about the author in a biographical note or a biographical reference work, by finding other works the author has published, by considering the author's academic background, and by determining whether the author has been cited in the footnotes or bibliographies of other reliable sources.
- **Does the source seem objective?** Does the author use an objective tone, make reasonable claims supported by logical reasons and solid evidence, recognize alternative perspectives, and treat opponents with respect? Or does the author use emotionally loaded language, make exaggerated claims, or support those claims with faulty logic and questionable or scanty evidence?

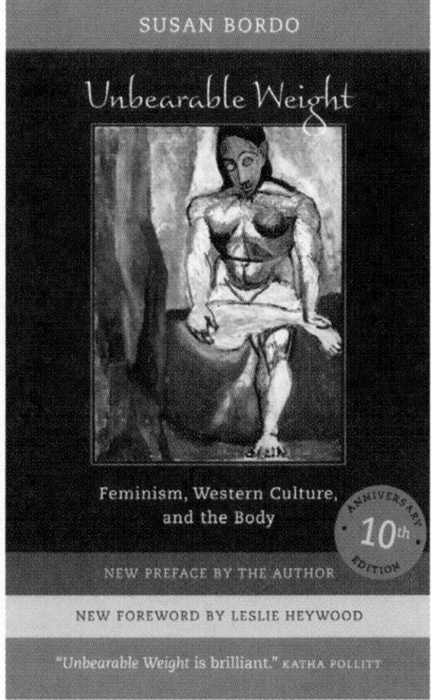

FIGURE 7.1 Popular versus Scholarly Books *The South Beach Diet,* published originally by Rodale Publishing, is a popular-press book aimed at a segment of the general public: people wanting to lose weight. *Unbearable Weight: Feminism, Western Culture, and the Body* (University of California Press), on the other hand, is a scholarly book about our culture's obsession with women's weight; its target audience is scholars in fields such as women's studies and cultural studies.

- **Does the author or publisher have a vested interest?** Consider whether or how the author stands to benefit from the work other than just through sales of the book or through prestige in publishing. Is the author promoting a product or process from which she or he will benefit financially? Will the author or publisher gain adherents to a political position? Check the author's or publisher's website for biographical information, advertisements, and a mission statement to see whether one of these items reveals an agenda.
- **Does the text cite its sources?** Most scholarly articles and books and some popular books include a bibliography, and some journal databases list the articles' sources in the citation. Reputable newspapers and magazines check a writer's sources, though those sources are often identified only as a "White House source" or a "source close to the investigation."
- **Do other scholars cite the text?** Also important is the number of times a source has been cited by other scholarly works (Figure 7.2, p. 84). Some journal databases indicate the

More about ▸▸▸
Citing sources:
MLA style, 230–89
APA style, 290–332
Chicago style, 333–60
CSE style, 361–85
Choosing a citation style, 223

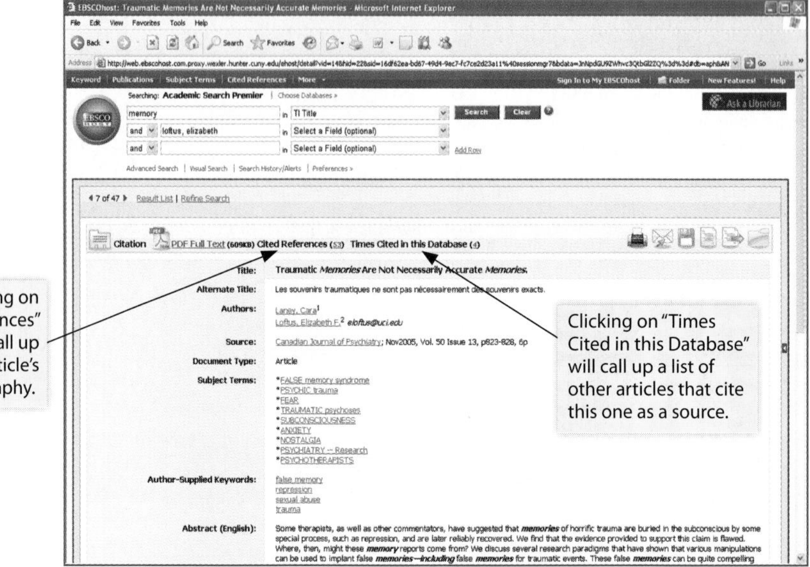

FIGURE 7.2 Determining Reliability by Assessing Citations Both the number of times an article has been cited and the citations in the article itself are useful ways of determining an article's reliability.

number of times an article has been cited by other articles indexed by that database. Citation indexes, such as *Web of Science* and *Google Scholar,* also provide this information.

> ***More about*** ▸▸▸
> Choosing research sources strategically, 51–52

- **How did you find the source?** Sources located through your college library are more likely to be reliable than sources located through a *Google* search because library sources are selected in consultation with subject matter experts, in response to reviews, or after considering where the source was published. A source published solely on the Web (unless in a scholarly journal published online) is not likely to have been subjected to the same level of scrutiny.

> ***More about*** ▸▸▸
> Editing and proofreading, 196–201
> Designing, 204–217

- **Is the source well written and edited?** Has the writer approached the task with a sense of responsibility, writing, organizing, editing, and proofreading the material carefully?

7c Evaluating Logic: Claims, Grounds, and Warrants

The philosopher Stephen Toulmin says that people make *claims* (main points or theses); we support our claims with *grounds,* or evidence; and we tie the grounds to the claims with *warrants,* or assumptions. When analyzing an argument, begin by assessing the strength of the main claim; then evaluate the grounds supporting that claim and examine the assumptions underlying it. Start your critical evaluation by identifying and classifying the argument's main claim. Is it a claim of *fact, opinion,* or *belief*? Or is it simply a *superstition* or *prejudice*?

Next, evaluate the grounds, or evidence, supplied to support the claim. Writers use various types of evidence to support their claims. Some types of evidence—like stories—are *qualitative,* using examples to show relationships and patterns; other types of evidence—like statistics—are *quantitative,* using empirical data and numbers to show how many and to what extent. Regardless of its type, good evidence must be all of the following:

- **Accurate.** *Is the evidence true?* If evidence is exaggerated, distorted, or just plain false, it is inaccurate.
- **Reliable.** *How consistently does the evidence support the claim?* If the evidence supports the claim only in certain circumstances, it may be unreliable.
- **Balanced.** *Does the evidence represent all credible angles of the issue?* The principle of balance in evidence suggests that a writer weigh all of the alternatives and give them equal consideration.
- **Sufficient.** *Has enough evidence been gathered to support the claim?* Scanty evidence does not prove an argument.
- **Relevant.** *Does the evidence have logical connections to the claim?* If the evidence proves something different than the claim—if the evidence and claim do not match—then the evidence is irrelevant.
- **Untainted by stakeholders' investments.** *Who are the stakeholders, and how did they influence the process or result?* If the author, publisher, or other stakeholders are biased, the evidence may skew the argument.

As you read a text critically, look for the underlying warrants, or assumptions, unstated claims for which no evidence is offered. If the argument is to succeed, what must both writer and audience agree is true? Identifying a text's assumptions will help you decide whether you agree with its claims; it will also help you identify the writer's audience. When Martin Luther King, Jr., said, "The nations of Asia and Africa are moving with jetlike speed toward gaining political independence, but we still creep at horse-and-buggy pace toward gaining a cup of coffee at a lunch counter," he relied on the assumption that American progress should not lag behind that of Africa and Asia. Is this assumption *correct*? That depends on whether you share it; Dr. King knew that most people in his audience—US citizens—would. An African or Asian audience, on the other hand, might be less likely to share this assumption about American progress.

Make It **Your Own**

Using the criteria in the section above (summarized in the Quick Reference box at the end of the chapter), write a paragraph evaluating three print sources that are in your working bibliography or that you plan to consult for a research project in this or another class.

7d Evaluating Online Texts: Websites, Blogs, Wikis, and Web Forums

More about ▸▸▸
Meeting the challenges of online research, 67–79

Anyone can create a website, post a blog, or contribute to an open wiki. This freedom makes the Web exciting, and it also requires researchers to evaluate online sources with special care. In addition to the general criteria listed above for evaluating sources, consider these other factors when evaluating websites: URL, site sponsor, whether the site is open or moderated, and number of links to the site.

URL

A site's URL (short for *uniform resource locator,* its Web address) appears at the top of the browser window (Figure 7.3). Every item on the Web has a URL, and all URLs end with an extension that indicates the site type. The most common URL extensions are these:

- ***.com*** (commercial): sites sponsored by businesses.
- ***.edu*** (educational): sites sponsored by colleges and universities, including administration, faculty, and students. Note that

US primary and secondary schools typically have *.k12* in their URLs and end in *.us*.

- ***.gov*** (government): sites sponsored by departments within branches of federal, state, or local governments.
- ***.net*** (network): typically, sites sponsored by businesses selling internet infrastructure services (such as internet service providers), but this extension is also sometimes chosen by businesses that want to appear technologically sophisticated.
- ***.org*** (organization): usually sites sponsored by nonprofit groups (though sometimes the nonprofit status of these groups may be questionable).

Sites sponsored by educational, government, and nonprofit organizations are likely to be reliable, but your evaluation of websites

> **Tech**
>
> **Identifying Personal Websites**
>
> A URL that includes a personal name (jsmith) plus a tilde (~) or a percent sign (%) or words like "users" or "members" indicates that the site is likely to be *personal* (not sponsored by a larger organization). Before using information from a personal site, investigate the author's credentials carefully.

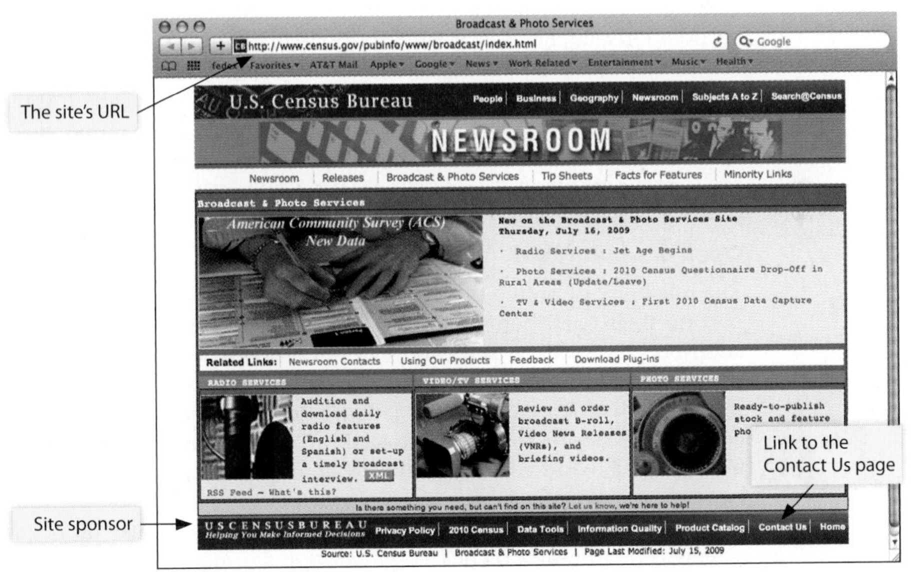

FIGURE 7.3 A Web Page The URL appears at the top of the browser window. Note that the page displays the sponsoring organization prominently and provides links to the sponsor's home page and to a page providing contact information.

should not end with their URLs. Businesses usually offer information intended to sell products or services, yet commercial sites can nevertheless be highly informative. A site ending in *.edu* may just as easily have been constructed and posted by a student as by a faculty or staff member, and much of the information posted on university websites is designed to entice new students (which is a type of advertising). Although not trying to sell a product, nonprofit organizations are usually seeking support. And government sites, while usually highly reliable, are unlikely to publish information that would undermine the administration's agenda. Carefully scrutinize the reliability of information from all sites (and, indeed, all texts).

Site sponsor

As with any publication, the credentials of a website's creator are an important factor in assessing reliability. You may be able to research the owner of a blog, the contributors to an email discussion list, or visitors to a chat room, and you can *lurk* (read online discussions without contributing) to get a sense of the quality of a discussion. But websites frequently lack a single author. Instead, they have *sponsors*—corporations, agencies, and organizations that are responsible for creating and posting the site's content. To determine who sponsors a site, navigate to the home page (see Figure 7.3), link to pages called About Us or Contact Us, or click on the website's logo. If the website yields little information, try conducting a web search on the site's title. If the site is secretive about its sponsor, be especially wary of its content.

Open or moderated

The reliability of online discussion forums and wikis depends in large part on their contributors. Open sources (those to which anyone can contribute) should be screened carefully; nonexpert enthusiasts can post inaccurate information, and people can deliberately insert distorted "truths." For example, in January 2006 *Wikipedia* had to block certain web addresses on Capitol Hill to keep congressional staffers from altering—and falsifying—the biographies of their bosses or their bosses' political opponents.

Wikis and web forums in which prospective contributors are screened by the site's owner, or *moderator,* are more likely to be reliable. The wiki *Encyclopedia of Life,* for example, promises to provide reliable information because it will be created and moderated by a

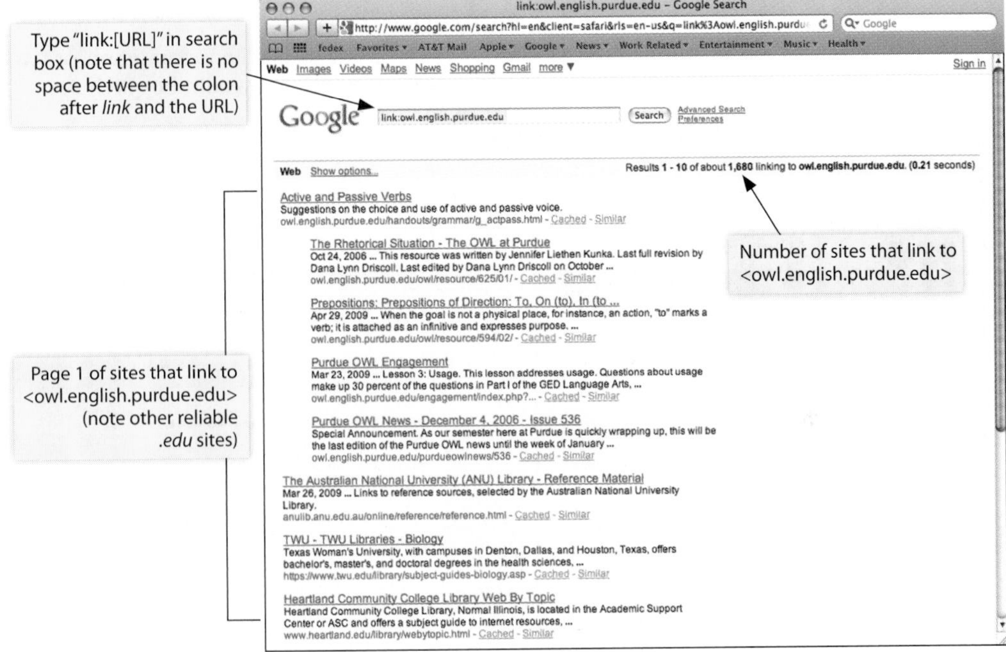

FIGURE 7.4 Weighing Source Reliability Use the number of links to a page to assess reliability.

consortium of highly regarded scientific institutions. Some scholars are even writing wiki textbooks to which they invite other experts to contribute.

Links

An additional step in assessing the reliability of a website or blog is to determine the number and type of sites that link to it. From the *Google* search page, you can determine the number of times a site has been linked to and review the linked sites: Type "link:" followed by the URL in the search box, and click on "Search" or hit Return (Figure 7.4).

Popularity does *not* guarantee reliability—the site may be fun to read or authored by a celebrity—but when coupled with other criteria, it can be one indication of reliability.

EXERCISE 7.1 Evaluating Web Pages

Using the criteria discussed on pp. 86–89, write a paragraph or two evaluating the two web pages below. Which would be the more reliable source on plagiarism, and why?

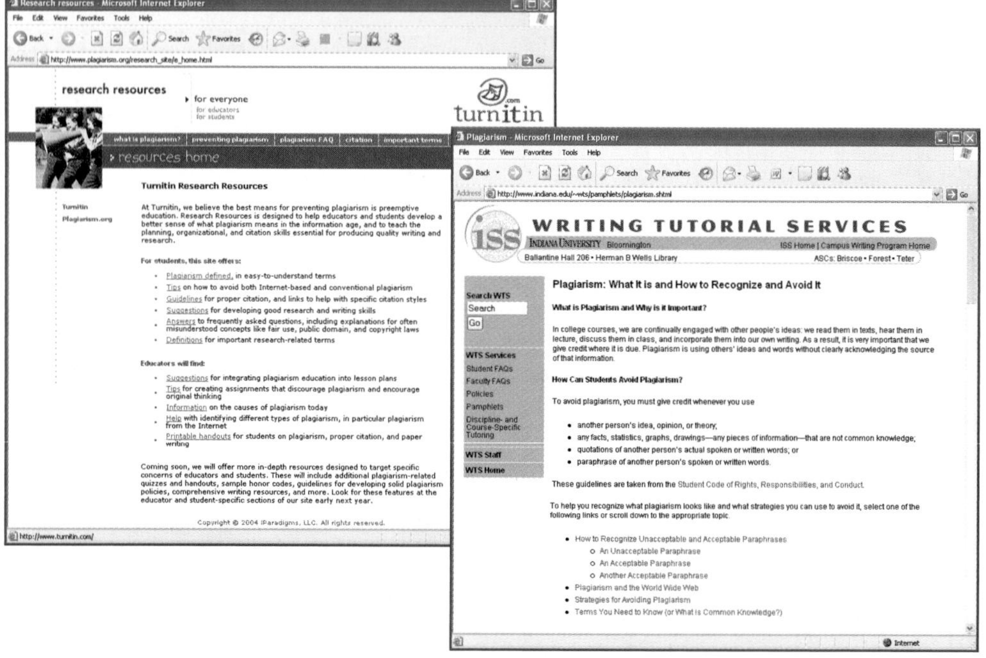

7e Evaluating Visual Sources

More about ▸▸▸
Evaluating visuals, 90–91

Visual texts, such as information graphics (tables, graphs, flowcharts), photographs, drawings, maps, comics, and even video or film sources, convey their messages powerfully yet sometimes so subtly that uncritical viewers may accept their claims without even realizing that a claim is being made. The image of a hungry child, for example, has long been a staple of humanitarian fund-raising. One hungry child looking at you plaintively can be far more persuasive than whole paragraphs of logical claims and evidence. As with printed texts, researchers need to evaluate visual texts carefully.

To determine the relevance and reliability of graphics and photographs, ask these questions:

- What purpose(s) does the image serve? Is it to entertain, to inform, or to persuade?
- What is the overall message the visual sends?
- Who is the item's intended audience?
- How authoritative is the source in which the visual appears?
- On what date was the visual created?
- What are the credentials of the visual's creator?
- How accurate are the title, headings, labels, and any other text that appears with the visual? How does the text influence how you "read" the visual? How relevant is the visual to the accompanying text?

For graphics, also consider the following:

- What do the data represent?
- What relationships does the graphic show?
- How up-to-date is the information in the graphic?
- Are the data complete? Are there any gaps in years covered or groups represented?
- Are the data presented fairly?
- Is the source of the data unbiased?
- How were the data gathered? If there is no explanation of the data-gathering process, question the information further.

For photographs, also consider the following:

- What is in the foreground and background, and what is your eye drawn to?
- To what social, ethnic, or national groups do the subjects belong, and is this relevant?
- What emotions does the photograph depict? What emotions does it elicit from you or other viewers?
- Has the photograph been manipulated or cropped to omit or distort information (Figure 7.5)?
- What is the point of view or angle of the photo? The photographer's position in relation to the object establishes the viewer's relationship to it, as well.

FIGURE 7.5 President Franklin D. Roosevelt in a Wheelchair, 1945 Although many Americans knew that President Roosevelt had been partially paralyzed by polio, only two photographs were taken of the President in a wheelchair. Were photographers protecting FDR's privacy or suppressing important information? FDR at Hilltop Cottage, in Hyde Park, NY, Franklin D. Roosevelt Presidential Library and Museum

Quick Reference → Judging Reliability

All Sources

Scholarly work. Was the source published in a scholarly journal or book or in a popular magazine, newspaper, or book?

Expertise. Is the author an authority on the subject?

Objectivity. Does the author seem unbiased (based on tone, logic, quality of evidence, treatment of opposition)?

Citations. Does the text cite sources, and is it cited by others?

Scrutiny. Did someone else subject the text to scrutiny before you saw it? For example, was it selected by the library, reviewed by another scholar, or fact-checked for accuracy?

Presentation. Is the text clearly written, well organized, and carefully edited and proofread?

Logic. Does the evidence match the claims, and is the evidence reliable?

Web Sources

URL extension. Does the main portion of the URL end in *.edu* or *.org,* suggesting a noncommercial purpose, or does it end with *.com* or *.net,* suggestion a commercial purpose?

Site sponsor. Is the site's host identified? Does the host promote a specific viewpoint or position?

Number of links or hits. Is the source visited often and frequently linked?

Visual Sources

Graphics. Is the graphic based on recent data with no groups/years omitted and not misleadingly drawn?

Photographs. Is the image accurate and not misleadingly presented?

A Final Thought

In school and in life you will be expected over and over again to be able to critically filter sources, to not take them at face value. Without skills in this area, you risk being manipulated and misinformed at precisely those moments when you wish to be most in control of the information before you. The flip side of this coin is that you will also want to be able to evaluate your own claims, evidence, and other rhetorical moves so that you can responsibly offer information to *your* readers.

8 Taking Notes and Keeping Records

IN THIS CHAPTER

A stunning innovation, cuneiform, the world's first written symbol system, was used by the Sumerians primarily to keep records. This ancient civilization pressed its symbols into clay, allowing some of its records to survive for 5,000 years or more. The ability to keep track of things, such as how much grain was sold, facilitated trade.

Records help modern researchers, too. Writing effective research projects always involves more information than the writer can commit to memory. Good notes and records provide an intellectual trail; they allow you to put your reading into context; they give you opportunities to step away from the information and return to it with fresh eyes. Perhaps your records will not survive for 5,000 years, but they should last through the duration of your project and beyond.

8a Choosing an Organizer to Fit Your Work Style

Note taking is best done on note cards, in computer files, or on weblogs or wikis. If you prefer using a notebook, equip yourself with an array of multicolored stick-on notes to help you sort ideas and themes.

Tech

Filing with Folders and Subfolders

If you typically save everything as a separate file with no folders, use this research project as a motivator to try folders. Here is a sample saving strategy:

- Start with a folder titled something like your project title: Obscenity_Defs.
- Create subfolders: Notes, Outlines, Drafts.
- Save files with the date they were last altered (Obscenity_Defs_Outline 080709) as part of the title, or save them by adding v1, v2, v3 so that you can keep a record of your changes.

Taking notes on index cards

Do you enjoy the tactile feel of pen and paper? Do you like to spread things out in front of you to see what you have to work with? While they are harder to back up and therefore easier to misplace, note cards may fit your work style best.

Taking notes on a computer

Increasingly, writers do most of their work directly on a computer because typing is faster than handwriting and the text is easy to copy, move, reorganize, and save. You can even save your notes in outline order to create a skeleton of your essay.

If you maintain your notes on a computer, always make a backup in a separate place: on another computer, on a thumb drive, on an iPod, or even printed out. Finally, notes on a computer are useful only if you can find them. When taking notes on a computer, decide where your notes will "live," and name files in a way that will be meaningful to you later.

A *double-entry journal* uses two columns for two different types of entries, inviting writers to engage in critical reading. You can divide reading responses into any two of the following categories:

- A record of new vocabulary
- A summary of main points
- Freewriting on the topic
- Your responses to the text

More about ▶▶▶
Keeping a reading journal, 14–15
Freewriting to explore a research topic, 25–26
Summarizing, 18, 181–82

The following student's double-entry journal response refers to Wray Herbert's "Why Uncertainty May Be Bad for Your Health" (*Newsweek,* 19 Sept. 2006).

Vocabulary

deep-seated (par. 3) – firmly established, rooted, ingrained. [Always thought this was "deep-seeded" – never saw it written down before.]

qualifiers (par. 5) – words that modify or specify the meaning of other words. [Par. 8 uses the examples "possibly" and "likely."]

untoward (par. 5) – unfortunate, hard to control. [Also means "improper," but that doesn't seem to fit in this context.]

euphemisms (par. 5) – indirect, innocuous terms or phrases used instead of direct ones to avoid seeming harsh or offensive. [Example: "She's in a better place." Yet, when used in talking to patients and their families, euphemisms may cause more damage in the long run! Sometimes direct is better.]

unambiguous (par. 7) – without uncertainty, clear, straightforward. [I guessed what this meant from context and the word "ambiguous," then looked it up to double-check.]

nebulous (par. 8) – indistinct, vague. [Qualifiers and euphemisms are also nebulous. There are many precise kinds of "uncertainty."]

Response

- The opening story (a meteorologist predicting a "chance" of rain while it pours outside) made me laugh. It was a great way to introduce a key point: Language can often confuse what we mean instead of making it clearer. Herbert shifts the tone and raises the stakes effectively when he points out that doctors use these same inexact phrases—like "possible" or "unlikely"—to refer to patients' conditions and chances of recovery. That's not just annoying, like an imprecise weather report; that's someone's life. (pars. 1–3)
- What does "possibly" mean? The insomnia/deafness test and the estimated percentages (10%–100%) support a "severity bias," another misleading factor. The results of Bonnefon's study are good evidence for Wray's point: that under-informed patients can suffer severe distress by assuming their situation is more dire or less severe than it actually is. (pars. 6–7)
- Wray makes a case for more specificity when doctors talk to patients. I agree 100%. (pars. 8–9)
- This relates to my research question about patients' responsibilities in their own health care because it suggests patients should be asking questions and demanding more precision in the doctors' language.

Taking notes in a weblog

Much like a journal, a *blog* (short for *weblog*) is a website created by an individual or group to chronicle thoughts and collect sources.

When you take notes in a blog, you can create an entry for each source, insert links to online texts, and sort sources by category ("tagging") (Figure 8.1). You can post to your blog from any computer that has internet access.

Taking notes on a wiki

A *wiki* is an online collaborative environment that typically mimics word processing. Wikis are best for collaborative research projects because multiple users can make changes to them, but they can also be very useful to the independent writer because they are accessible through the Web.

As with a blog, you will need to do a little advance setup to use a wiki for your note taking. *Google Documents* <docs.google.com>, *wikispaces* <wikispaces.com>, and *Wetpaint* <wetpaint.com> offer free wiki services.

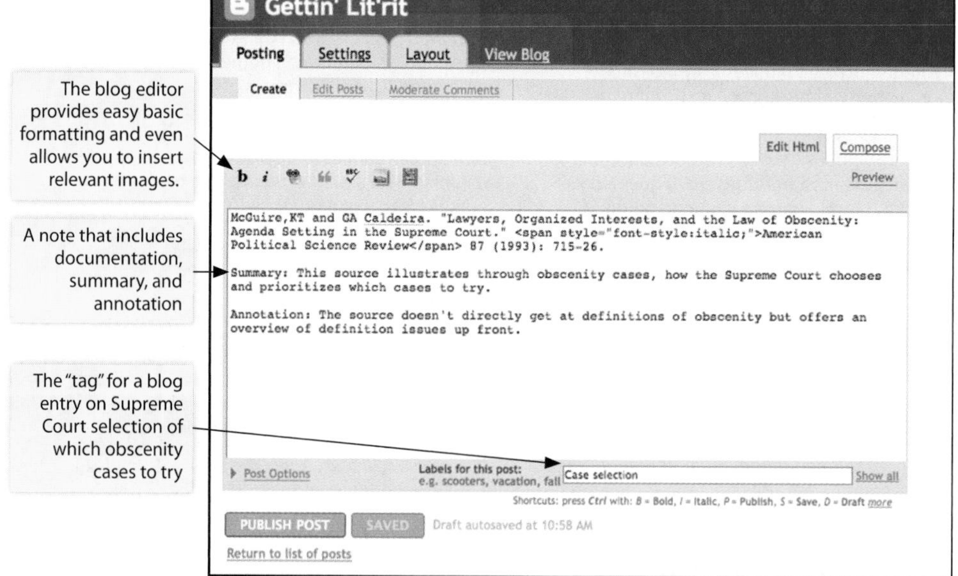

FIGURE 8.1 Sample Research Blog Entry This entry is for a project on arts, obscenity, and the First Amendment.

8b Keeping the Trail: Your Search Notes

Because few researchers find what they are looking for with their very first search, you can keep from doing the same work twice or forgetting where you left off by creating a simple table on paper, in a computer file, or even on the research blog you have started to keep track of your work. Such a chart would *not* include content notes, but only information on the search: search date, search location (the database, search engine, catalog), search terms and strategies (including search engine math and Boolean operators), and your notes on what you have found. Then, if you are not finding the information you need, show your search record to a librarian. He or she can help you quickly develop more effective strategies.

8c What to Include in Research Notes

Research note taking involves five essential activities:

- Documenting
- Summarizing
- Paraphrasing
- Recording quotations
- Writing your own comments

More about ▶▶▶
Annotating your working bibliography, 45, 48
Writing an annotated bibliography, 120–27
Quoting, paraphrasing, and summarizing, 181–86
Sample annotated bibliography, 123–27

8d Taking Content Notes

When taking content notes, you have to decide two things:

1. What is worth recording?
2. How should I record the information: as a summary, a direct quotation, or a paraphrase?

What is worth recording?

Decide what is worth recording based on the principles you would use for overall education of a source, including relevance to your topic, accuracy, reliability, balance, and bias. Be selective; recording anything and everything can lead to accumulation of useless data. Ask yourself this question: What are the main points you need to convey to get your argument across without suppressing critical portions of the conversation?

More about ▶▶▶
Evaluating information, 80–92

Quick Reference: What to Include in Your Research Notes

Bibliographic Information (Documentation).

- **Books:** author(s), title and subtitle, edition, publisher, place and date of publication, and page numbers.
- **Articles:** author(s); title of article; title of periodical; volume and number of issue; date of publication; page numbers; if accessed through a database, name of library, name of subscription database (e.g., *EBSCO* or *ProQuest*), URL of subscription service home page, and date of access.
- **Website:** name of organization sponsoring site, title of web page, author's name, date updated, date of access, and URL.

Summary.
A brief restatement capturing the gist of the source's main argument. Use fresh words (except key terms).

Paraphrase.
A restatement at approximately the same length of a source's main points and examples. Use fresh words (except key terms).

Quotations.
An exact (word-for-word) restatement of a passage from a source (useful for capturing an idea expressed with special complexity, verve, or power); enclose it in quotation marks or use a block indent.

Commentary.
Your analysis of the source or your synthesis of ideas from the source with your own ideas or ideas from other sources.

More about ▶▶▶
Documenting sources:
MLA, 230–89
APA, 290–332
Chicago, 332–60
CSE, 361–85

More about ▶▶▶
Synthesis, 179–81

Summarize, quote, or paraphrase?

When to summarize You should *summarize* a source when you want to convey its basic argument to your audience in an abbreviated form, omitting specific details and examples. Most of your content notes will summarize your sources. You will typically *synthesize* these summaries with your argument, comparing and contrasting them.

When to quote You should *quote* from sources under the following circumstances:

- When your source uses particularly vivid or engaging language
- When you want to reproduce a subtle idea that might be difficult to paraphrase or summarize without distortion
- When your source uses specialized language that is difficult to paraphrase (but resist quoting just because you do not yet understand the material)

- When you want to *analyze* the specific language used in the source
- When you want to emphasize an important point
- When you are working with primary sources, such as interviews and surveys that you have conducted

More about ▶▶▶
Analysis, 20, 179–81

More about ▶▶▶
Conducting interviews, 131–35
Surveying, 137–40
Primary versus secondary sources, 129

When to paraphrase You should paraphrase your sources when you want to do the following:

- Understand the logic of complex passages (paraphrasing a source helps you understand it)
- Mention examples and details from the source so that readers can better follow your generalizations

8e Taking Notes to Avoid Plagiarizing and Patchwriting

Even with the best intentions, you will have trouble effectively paraphrasing, summarizing, quoting, citing, and documenting your sources if you do not take good notes throughout your research process.

Working to avoid plagiarism and patchwriting: Paraphrasing

Writers who are inexperienced with paraphrasing often *patchwrite:* They replace some key terms with synonyms, delete a few words, or alter the grammar slightly, but they do not put the passage fully into fresh words and sentences. Some people consider patchwriting a form of plagiarism, and nobody considers it good writing.

To paraphrase without patchwriting, follow these steps:

1. Read the source until you feel you understand it. Make sure you think about the overall meaning of the passage. Figure out whether there are any key terms that should be retained in your paraphrase.
2. Close the book and walk away. Do something else for a few minutes or a few hours.
3. Come back to your desk and write what you remember. If you cannot remember anything, repeat steps 1 and 2.
4. Check your paraphrase against the source to make sure you have correctly represented what it says. If you have closely

More about ▶▶▶
Avoiding patchwriting, 19
Defining patchwriting, 107
Drafting to avoid plagiarism and patchwriting, 114–15
Paraphrasing, 181–86

followed any of the source language or even its sentence structures, either copy it exactly and include quotation marks, or repeat steps 1 and 2.

When your paraphrase is complete, check to be sure that you have done *all* of the following:

- Quoted key terms exactly, placing them in quotation marks the first time you use them but not thereafter.
- Used synonyms rather than the source language for the remainder of your paraphrase.
- Freely rearranged the ideas of the source so that they make sense in your own text. For example, if the author presents a cause and its effects, you might present the effects first and the causes second.
- Provided transition words to clarify relationships among ideas.
- Used different sentence structures from those in the original passage. If you find yourself mirroring the source's sentence structure, try dividing or combining sentences or varying their length and structure to alter their rhythm.
- Omitted details that are not relevant to *your* main point. Make sure, though, that your deletions do not alter or distort the meaning of the source text.

The following example illustrates techniques for revising passages to avoid patchwriting:

Passage from Source

> Until recently, the Church was one of the least studied aspects of the Cuban revolution, almost as if it were a voiceless part of Cuban society, an institution and faith that had little impact on the course of events." —Super, John C. "Interpretations of Church and State in Cuba, 1959–1961." *The Catholic Historical Review* 89.3 (2003): 511–29. Print.

The following first-draft paraphrase contains patchwriting: Despite some minor changes in word order and some synonym substitutions, the paraphrase follows the original, phrase by phrase. Even with a citation, this would be a misuse of the source.

Note (with Patchwriting)

Super 511

The Catholic Church until recently was not much studied as an aspect of the Cuban revolution. It was as if the Church was voiceless in Cuban culture, as if it had little influence on events.

Note (Revised to Avoid Patchwriting)

Super 511

Scholarship on the Cuban revolution is only beginning

~~The Catholic Church until recently was not much studied as an aspect~~

to recognize the influential role of the Church.

~~of the Cuban revolution. It was as if the Church was voiceless in~~

~~Cuban culture, as if it had little influence on events.~~

The revised note still retains a version of a word from the source: "influence" has been changed to "influential." And of course the identifying terms "Cuban revolution" and "Church" are in both the original passage and the revised note. But the passage no longer draws heavily on the source's sentence structure, organization, or word choices.

EXERCISE 8.1 Recognizing Patchwriting

Study the following source text, as well as the first draft of a paraphrase that follows. Identify the ways in which the draft is patchwriting rather than paraphrasing. Then revise the note, correcting the patchwriting.

PASSAGE FROM SOURCE

Washington has posed a special problem for Wikipedia, which is monitored by 800 to 1,000 active editor-volunteers. In the recent flare-up, a community of Wikipedia editors read a story in the *Lowell Sun* newspaper in which staffers for [Representative Marty] Meehan acknowledged replacing an entry on him [in Wikipedia] with more flattering verbiage. That prompted last week's Capitol Hill Wikipedia blackout; all computers connected to servers at the House of Representatives, identified by a numerical Web address, were denied access. —Yuki Noguchi, "On Capitol Hill, Playing WikiPolitics." *Washington Post* 4 Feb. 2006: A1. Print.

DRAFT NOTE

> Noguchi A1
>
> Wikipedia and its active editor-volunteers have a special problem with Washington. Recently the editors read a *Lowell Sun* newspaper story about Meehan's staffers having acknowledged that they had replaced an entry on him with more flattering words. That resulted in last week's Wikipedia blackout on Capitol Hill computers, which were denied access.

Working to avoid plagiarism and patchwriting: Summarizing

More about ▸▸▸ Summarizing, 181–82

To achieve the best results in your summaries, follow this process:

1. Annotate the source and then close the book.
2. On a clean sheet of paper (or a new document on your computer), try to repeat the main ideas of the source.
3. Check the text to make sure you have conveyed the main idea and the major supporting points without distortion and without recycling the source's words.

Check your summary carefully and revise as necessary. Summaries, too, should convey the main idea of the source, not merely identify the topic. The note below illustrates this problem, and the second example shows a solution.

Note (Summary That Merely Identifies Topic)

The verbs in the draft note are neutral and do not convey DuBois's argument.

> DuBois
>
> In "The Hampton Idea," a 1906 speech, W. E. B. DuBois explains how African Americans should be educated and talks about the Tuskegee model.

Solution

DuBois

In "The Hampton Idea," an essay from a 1906 speech, W. E. B. DuBois argues that college education for African Americans should not just be ~~explains how African Americans should be educated and argues against~~ vocational but should instead prepare teachers, thinkers, and leaders. ~~the Tuskegee model~~.

Verbs lead into claims.

Note does not just list topics but states claim as well.

Working to avoid plagiarism and patchwriting: Quoting

A *quotation* is someone else's words transcribed exactly, with quotation marks or block indention (for long quotes) to signal that it is from a source. When taking notes, copy quotations exactly, word for word, and check them against the source. To avoid any confusion later put quotation marks around each selection that you copy. In your writing project, you can—and should—adjust quotations when writing your paper, but you must use ellipses for signaling cuts and brackets for indicating words you have added or changed. But in your notes, the quotation should appear exactly as it did in the source.

When working with primary sources such as interviews and surveys that you have conducted, you are likely to use quotations extensively. In contrast, secondary sources such as newspaper articles and scholarly books are already quoting, summarizing, and paraphrasing their sources, so you should limit the number of direct quotations you copy from them.

More about ▸▸▸
Primary versus secondary sources, 129

If you find that you are copying a lot of quotations and paraphrasing or summarizing very little, it could be that you do not fully understand what you are reading. Try the following:

More about ▸▸▸
Using quotation marks, 108–109
Quoting, 181–86
Reading your sources, 11–23

- Read the source again.
- Look up words you do not understand.
- Consult reference sources that can provide background knowledge.
- Discuss the source with your instructor, classmates, or friends.

The following reading notes on Claudia Milne's article "On the Grounds of the Fresh Water Pond: The Free-Black Community at Five

Points, 1810–1834" in the *International Journal of Historical Archaeology* (June 2002) correctly use quotation marks to signal material taken word for word from the source. Yet they also signal that the note taker does not fully understand what he is writing about.

Draft

> Milne 140
>
> The "free-black community . . . of Five Points" is not reflected in "the areas of Block 160 that were excavated." "All that survived . . . were the remains of their ancestors interred in the mostly forgotten burying ground, a few intriguing and unusual items discarded in the defunct privies and cisterns, and a handful of church addresses." But "it is probable that many members of this community remained in the neighborhood, living 'off-the-grid.'. . ."

These notes are merely a string of quotations, sewn together with a few of the note taker's own words. A research paper based on these notes would similarly be a mosaic of quotation, difficult to read and lacking the researcher's critical judgment. The following revision is better:

Revision

> Milne 140
>
> Very few items belonging to members of the African American population in Five Points have been excavated, most likely because members of this community were not part of mainstream society, not because they had all moved away.

Quick Reference **Avoiding Common Errors in Note Taking**

Some of the most common errors note takers make include the following. As you take notes, ask yourself:

- Have I cut and pasted chunks of what should be quoted materials without using quotation marks?
- Have I taken a note without a page number (print sources) or enough information to find the internet source again quickly (precise URL and/or full title of the page where I found the information)?
- Have I taken a note that looks like a paraphrase or a summary but that only changes a word here or there and does not exactly and carefully quote the source?
- Have I indicated the topic in my note without recording the source's argument or main point?

A Final Thought

In many ways it is easier than ever to keep good records while doing research. Cell phones allow writers to text a note to their email accounts when they do not have the relevant research folder in their bags. Wikis allow collaborative groups to share and keep track of notes that they update collectively. Databases allow users to save citations to folders and email citations and whole documents to themselves. Databases even generate perfectly formatted citations in virtually any discipline's style. Yet all of these good tools are only as effective as their users. Develop a note and record keeping system that works for you and with your technological strengths and weaknesses.

9 Citing Your Sources and Avoiding Plagiarism

IN THIS CHAPTER

Louis Bloomfield

In 2001, physics professor Louis Bloomfield (University of Virginia) accused more than a hundred students of plagiarism. Many were found guilty and expelled from the university.[1]

In January 2008, Mounir Errami and Harold Garner (University of Texas, Southwestern Medical Center) published a report in the journal *Nature* on duplicate articles in the *Medline* database. They tested a portion of the abstracts in *Medline* using text-matching software, coming up with some 420 potential duplicates. Of these, they found 73 that were written by different authors, leading them to suspect plagiarism. What they worry most about is the publication of plagiarized drug-safety studies, since these can give practitioners a false sense of the safety or efficacy of the drugs tested.[2]

Harold Garner

Ibrahim al-Marashi

In 2003 the British government "borrowed" information from a student's doctoral thesis to make its case for war against Iraq—without citing Ibrahim al-Marashi, the author of the thesis.[3]

[1]Hansen, Brian. "Combating Plagiarism: The Issues." *CQ Researcher* 13.32 (19 Sept. 2003): 775–96. Print.

[2]Errami, Mounir, and Harold Garner. "Commentary: A Tale of Two Citations." *Nature* 451 (2008): 397–99. Web. 30 March 2009.

[3]Hinsliff, Gaby, Martin Bright, Peter Beaumont, and Ed Vulliamy. "First Casualties in the Propaganda Firefight." *Observer.* Guardian News and Media, 9 Feb. 2003. Web. 26 June 2009. "The Plagiarism Plague." *BBC News.* BBC, 7 Feb. 2003. Web. 26 June 2009.

Plagiarism, at least in an academic setting, involves the presentation of another person's work—a paper or story, a photograph or graphic, a speech or song, a web page or email message—without indicating that it came from a source. Buying a paper from a website or borrowing one from a fraternity's file and presenting it as one's own work would be plagiarism; so would pretending to have written someone else's song or copying material from a website without acknowledging the site's creator. College writers need to take plagiarism seriously.

Also be alert to the possibility of *patchwriting,* copying and only partially changing the language of a source. The National Council of Writing Program Administrators defines patchwriting as a misuse of sources. Sometimes, though, instructors and college policies categorize it as plagiarism. In either case, patchwriting is not good writing. It often results not from an intention to present another's words and ideas as one's own but, rather, from inaccurate note taking, misunderstanding the source, incorrect use of or omitting quotation marks, or incomplete paraphrasing.

More about ▸▸▸
Taking notes to avoid plagiarism and patchwriting, 99–105

Inform yourself in detail about what your instructor and your college (or your employer) define as ethical writing; although everyone rejects plagiarism, the definition of what constitutes plagiarism can vary subtly from one discipline or profession to another. Still, following the guidelines for writing described in this chapter (and throughout this book), you can be confident that the work you produce represents its sources responsibly.

9a Developing Responsibility: Why Use Sources Carefully?

Never has it been more important to think of writing in terms of *responsibilities.* Part of your responsibility as a writer is to your audience and your topic. You owe it to your audience to offer a complete, accurate representation of your material and to write so that the audience can fully comprehend what you are saying.

You have responsibilities to yourself, as well. You may have come to college to obtain a credential that will get you a job. If, however, you arrive at that position without the skills you need to do it, you will not last long in the job, and most jobs in an information society require communication skills. You have the responsibility to acquire not just a credential but also an education. You owe that to yourself.

You also have a responsibility to other writers. In most of the writing you do for college and the workplace, you will be working from texts that others have written, whether they are business reports, websites, or scholarly articles. You owe it to these other writers to acknowledge the contributions they have made to your thinking on your topic.

The practice of acknowledging sources has another benefit: It places you *in conversation* with your sources. Although avoiding plagiarism is a compelling reason for citing sources, this other reason may be more important: When you acknowledge sources, you position yourself, not as a copier or an amateur, but as a scholar, a thinker, a member of a community of people interested in this topic. You gain credibility.

Make It **Your Own**

Write three to five paragraphs describing and reflecting on your attempts to write responsibly and ethically. What is most difficult for you about using sources? What do you worry about the most? How might you address your concerns?

9b Acknowledging Sources: What Does It Involve?

People often say that writers should "cite" their sources. In academic writing, however, there are actually three components of acknowledging sources—quotation, citation, and documentation—and *all three are essential.*

More about ▸▸▸
Using quotation marks, 109–10, 185
Citing sources:
MLA style, 230–89
APA style, 290–332
Chicago style, 333–60
CSE style, 361–85

- **Quotation.** When you copy the language of a source exactly, you must mark the copied passage as a quotation. Usually you do this by putting quotation marks at the beginning and end of the copied passage. If the passage is lengthy, it should be indented as a *block quotation.*
- **Citation.** At the place in your text where you borrow language or ideas from a source, you must *cite* that source. How you cite depends on the style sheet you are using, but most style sheets require that you name the author and the relevant page number. How you cite a source, then, depends on the *documentation* (or *citation*) *style* you use. Check with your instructor about which style is most appropriate for your course.

Quick Reference Documentation Styles

Discipline	Style Manual	Abbreviation/Covered in Chapter . . .
Literature and foreign languages	*MLA Handbook for Writers of Research Papers,* 7th edition	MLA / 19
Psychology and other social sciences	*Publication Manual of the American Psychological Association,* 6th edition	APA / 20
Other humanities, such as history, art history, and philosophy	*The Chicago Manual of Style,* 15th edition	*Chicago* / 21
Sciences, such as biology, chemistry, and physics	*Scientific Style and Format: The CSE Manual for Authors, Editors, and Publishers,* 7th edition	CSE / 22

More about ▸▸▸
Conducting research in the disciplines, 222–29

The most popular styles for academic writers are listed in the Quick Reference box above.

- **Documentation.** In academic writing you are expected to conclude your text with a list of the works that have contributed to your text—depending on the discipline, this may be called a list of works cited, a reference list, or a bibliography. Even though you have placed quotation marks around passages that you copied exactly and even though in your text you have provided authors' names and page numbers for quotations, paraphrases, summaries, and ideas, you also need to provide full publication information for all those sources at the end of your paper. Complete documentation ensures that your readers (and you) will be able to find your sources quickly and easily for further investigation.

9c Understanding What You *Must* Cite: Quotations, Paraphrases, Summaries, *Un*common Knowledge

You must document quotations, paraphrases, summaries, and information that nonexperts are unlikely to know.

- **Quotations.** A *quotation* is an exact transcription of someone else's words, with quotation marks or block indentation

More about ▸▸▸
Signal phrases, 182
Integrating quotations, 184–85

to signal that the passage is from another source. Name the author either in a signal phrase (*Jones argues)* or in a parenthetical citation, and include the page number. (In some styles, you may include this information in a footnote or endnote.) Then document the source in your list of works cited, reference list, or bibliography.

Chicago Style Example

Signal phrase

Quotations in quotation marks

In-text citation (page reference in parentheses)

Williams describes as "distinctly American" the decision not to have national oversight over the state universities that emerged in the nineteenth century: "George Washington had proposed a national university in 1790 . . . but the idea languished in part because of lack of federal funds and in part because it went against the American idea of states' rights" (191).

Documentation (complete source information in a list at the end of the paper)

Bibliography

Williams, Jeffrey J. "The Post-Welfare State University." *American Literary History* 18, no. 1 (2006): 190–216.

More about ▸▸▸
Summarizing, 18, 98, 181–86
Paraphrasing, 98, 181–86

- **Paraphrases and summaries.** A *paraphrase* restates someone else's ideas in fresh words. A *summary* conveys a source's main ideas in fewer words and in fresh language. Cite all sources used, even when you are not quoting. As with quotations, cite the author and page number in the text, and include full source information in your list of works cited, reference list, or bibliography.

MLA Style Example

Paraphrase

In-text citation (author's last name and page reference in parentheses)

The University of Missouri is one example of universities whose opening was delayed for lack of adequate funding (Williams 191).

Works Cited

Williams, Jeffrey J. "The Post-Welfare State University." *American Literary History* 18.1 (Spring 2006): 190–216. Print.

- **Ideas and information that are *not* common knowledge.** Whenever you provide information from a source that is *not* common knowledge, acknowledge that source in your text and provide full source information in your list of works cited, reference list, or bibliography. If you are in doubt about what is considered common knowledge, see the list on p. 112 and check with your instructor. Remember that an interview with an expert needs to be cited just as much as information found in an article or a book does.

APA Style Example

When a college has an honor code, its faculty are more likely to regard cheating as a serious matter (McCabe, Butterfield, and Treviño, 2003, p. 391).

Summary

In-text citation (authors' last names—not mentioned in text—and page reference in parentheses)

References

McCabe, D. L., Butterfield, K. D., & Treviño, L. K. (2003). Faculty and academic integrity: The influence of current honor codes and past honor code experiences. *Research in Higher Education, 44*(3), 367–385.

9d Knowing What You *Need Not* Cite: Common Knowledge (facts, dates, events, cultural knowledge)

You need not acknowledge your source for common knowledge (unless the information is included in a quotation). *Common knowledge* is general information that is available in a number of different sources and that is considered factual and incontestable (such as the height of the Empire State Building or the characteristic markings of the red wolf).

Whether an idea is widely known and accepted depends on who your readers are. Experts in the field may be aggravated by unnecessary and distracting citations to what they consider common knowledge. On the other hand, your instructor may assign a high priority to source citation and may be concerned about absence of a citation for material that is new to you (however well known it may be to experts in the field).

Common knowledge usually refers to ideas, but it can sometimes refer to a particular expression. When you say, "A rose by any other name would smell as sweet," you need not cite Shakespeare's *Romeo and Juliet,* because in English-speaking countries this expression is part of common knowledge. Nor is it necessary to get the language exactly correct: "A rose by any other name would smell as sweet" is an approximation of the passage in Shakespeare, sufficient to bring it to mind. Here are more examples:

Facts

- The earth is 91 million miles from the sun.
- Labor organizer "Mother" Jones worked on behalf of the United Mine Workers of America.

Dates

- The spring equinox occurred on March 20 in 2006.
- U.S. women won the right to vote on August 26, 1920, when the Nineteenth Amendment was passed.

Events

- Francis Crick, James Watson, and Maurice Wilkins are credited with discovering the structure of DNA.
- The Stonewall Rebellion occurred in a Greenwich Village bar in New York City, when its gay patrons violently resisted a police raid.

Cultural Knowledge

- The composer Wolfgang Amadeus Mozart was a child prodigy.
- Elvis Presley made the song "Hound Dog" a smash hit, although he did not write it.

Even if you are learning such information for the first time, you do not need to cite your source. Everything else, though, should be cited in the text of your project and documented in a footnote or in your bibliography, reference list, or list of works cited.

Writing Responsibly **Visuals and Common Knowledge**

Images, including maps, are not considered common knowledge. You may know that the capital of Nebraska is Lincoln, but if you include a map of Nebraska (that you did not draw) in a paper, you must credit the creator of that map, even if you downloaded it from a website. Unless you made the image yourself, you must credit your source for all images that you talk about or reproduce in your paper.

More about ▶▶▶
Using visuals as support, 177–79

9e Understanding Why There Are So Many Ways to Cite

As you go about your research, you may find one source that puts page numbers in parentheses at the end of a sentence while another seems to have no page numbers in the text. The former is probably an academic source using MLA style, while the latter might be an article from a newspaper. When you download PDF articles from a scholarly database, too, you will find a range of citation and documentation styles.

These differences reflect a range of disciplinary and professional values. While in the sciences the date is one of the most important pieces of information a reader needs to know about a source (because timely information is key in these fields), in the humanities the date is far less important because old information is often just as credible as new.

More about ▶▶▶
Conducting research in the disciplines, 222–29

Each of these documentation styles is summarized in detail in this book, but you should consult the style manual itself—your college library is likely to have copies in its reference collection—for more examples or to cite types of sources not included here.

More about ▶▶▶
MLA style, 230–89
APA style, 290–33
Chicago style, 333–60
CSE style, 361–85

Once you know which documentation style sheet to follow, do not forget to convert citations you find from their found form to the right form for the style sheet you are following. The entry in the first example appears as formatted in *EBSCO*'s search results list; this is what it would look like if you simply copied and pasted it from the list. While it includes all of the information necessary to find the source again, it needs to be altered significantly to conform to APA documentation style.

Found Bibliographic Entry

Visual hallucinations in schizophrenia: Confusion between imagination and perception. Brébion, Gildas; Ohlsen, Ruth I.; Pilowsky, Lyn S.; Neuropsychology, Vol 22(3), May 2008. pp. 383-389. [Journal Article]

Revised Bibliographic Entry

References [APA style—see chapter 20]

Brébion, G., Ohlsen, R. I., & Pilowsky, L. S. (2008). Visual hallucinations in schizophrenia: Confusion between imagination and perception. *Neuropsychology, 22,* 383–389.

9f Drafting to Avoid Plagiarizing and Patchwriting

More about ▶▶▶
Taking notes, 93–105
Drafting, 161–72

From notes to first drafts, many of the techniques for avoiding plagiarizing and patchwriting are similar. If you have taken effective notes with attention to how each source might be useful to your study and with care to preserve quotations where appropriate and alter them fully where useful, you should have little trouble avoiding plagiarism. However, all writers make mistakes sometimes. As a result, it is a good idea to do some double-checking when you get to the drafting stage. When you expose your document to readers, your responsibilities to others become particularly critical.

To continue best practices for using sources at the drafting stage, take the same care as you move your notes into the document that you took when you made them initially:

- If you have a quotation in your note, include the quotation marks in your draft.
- Always include page numbers for quotations and paraphrases.
- As you integrate sources into your draft, transfer the documentation information immediately into your list of works cited, reference list, or bibliography. One approach is to use a page break (Insert, Page Break) to separate the documentation from the draft text.

- Always proceed with a sense of your purpose and the argument that has emerged from your research. You should be making claims that are informed by the sources you have found, even while you stand slightly independent of them.
- Paraphrase and adapt information carefully from a note to your draft, to make everything in your final document coherent. This may mean that, after you have altered your paraphrase, you will need to return to the original source to make sure the source language has not slipped back in.

Each time you integrate a note from a source, look at the balance between source information and your interpretation and contextualization of that information. Did you *talk about* the source as much as you *quoted it*? Maintaining balance helps prevent source misuse.

If you feel overwhelmed by drafting *and* paying close attention to citation and documentation, build in a separate stage—an evening, perhaps—when you can check all of your citations as part of your editing and proofreading process.

As part of this proofreading, read through your draft aloud. Anything that feels strange coming out of your mouth might signal that you have adopted the form or language of a source. If you do not find instances of plagiarism or patchwriting, you may at least identify awkward sentences that would be better if rewritten.

More about ▸▸▸
Proofreading, 191–203

9g Getting Permissions

Plagiarism and copyright violation are two separate things. Plagiarism is a matter of local customs and guidelines. Each college, for example, writes its own plagiarism policy and sets its own penalties for violation of that policy. Plagiarism is concerned with *acknowledgment* of the sources for ideas or language.

Copyright law, in contrast, is unconcerned with source acknowledgment. Instead, it focuses on source *use* and authors' *permissions.* When a writer takes a substantial portion of another writer's text, acknowledging the source is not enough: The writer must obtain the original author's permission, often in exchange for payment.

Copyright law is also unconcerned with small copyings from a source. If a writer copies an entire paragraph from a book without obtaining the author's permission, that writer is not in violation of copyright law because a paragraph is only a small portion of a book. (If the borrowing is not acknowledged, that writer will, however, be subject to ridicule for having plagiarized. And the writer's local community—his or her college, employer, or professional society—may penalize the infraction.)

As a student, your use of sources is covered under the *fair use* provision of copyright law. Your use of source material for educational purposes—for your own education—cannot violate copyright. If, however, you publish your work for others to read (and a web page is a publication), your text is no longer exclusively for educational purposes, so you have to think not only about avoiding plagiarism but also about observing copyright law. In this situation, you need to ask for permission to use images, music, and video, and any text that is more extensive than a short quotation.

When you publish work on a website or elsewhere that contains chunks of text longer than a quotation or when you use images, audio, or video that you did not create, you need to seek permission to use those items. To gain permission, you will want to write a letter or an email to the copyright owner that includes the following information:

- A specific reference to the work that you would like to use: "I am writing to request use of your photo 'Afghan hound,' which appears on the Pet Planet website in a research report on dog training."
- A clear statement of how you will use this work (will it be published on a website? in a research proposal sent to a particular audience?): "This report is primarily for educational purposes and will be published on my student website."
- A statement regarding whether you will profit from using this material (for a student these occasions are rare, and copyright owners are much more likely to grant rights to use when there is no profit involved): "Because I am completing this report for a research writing course, I will not profit in any way from using your photo, and my website should not compete in any way with your pet resource."
- How long the item will be public, and to how broad an audience: "I do not anticipate keeping the website active beyond 2011, when I will complete my undergraduate course work. The audience for this work will be my instructor and anyone who happens to find my site."
- The date by which you need a response: "The project completion date is October 30; therefore, I appreciate in advance your

quick response to my query." It would not be reasonable to make a request such as this with less than a week remaining in your project cycle. If your time is this tight, you will need to instead seek a resource that is part of the *cultural commons,* a resource free for anyone to use within reasonable guidelines.

- Your contact information.

Do your best to determine the copyright owner based on what you can find on the source itself. It is also a good idea to pursue more than one option simultaneously, as permissions often take time to acquire.

9h Collaborating and Source Citation

More about ▸▸▸ Collaboration, 9–10, 93–95, 171–72, 197–200

Collaboration adds new dimensions to source use and citation. Many effective groups initially divide the labor and then work in the drafting and revising stages to create a unified document. What this means is that, somewhere in the process, you or one of your teammates could introduce a plagiarized bit of writing. As with any plagiarism or unethical source use, this could come from inaccurate notes, a misunderstanding of citation standards, or a deliberate misrepresentation of work. As a team, you will probably all share equal responsibility for a piece of collaboratively written work handed in.

How, then, can you make sure that what you sign your name to embodies responsible citation and documentation practices? You may be tempted to block off chunks of the work and then not touch something someone else drafted, to keep the work effectively singular, planning an "I-never-touched-that-part" defense. The danger is that, if the goal is to create a coherent document, the work may not read fluidly. Instead, use good project management, note-taking, and editing strategies *as a team:*

- Make sure all members of the team keep copies of sources they have used in sections on which they work.
- Plan in advance as a team the form you want notes and materials to be in, and ask that teammates follow the outlined procedures.
- Read closely for anything that seems suspicious in the final draft. Does a passage sound too technical to have been written by one of your partners? Are there any uncited data? This close reading should be a part of your copyediting process.

Quick Reference **Avoiding Plagiarism**

- Have you used another person's work (text, image, media resource) without indicating that it came from a source?
- Have you used a string of the same words as your source without enclosing them in quotation marks and including the author's name and a page number in the text, as well as an entry for the source in your list of works cited, reference list, or bibliography?
- Have you used even one word that is distinctive and central to someone else's argument without using quotation marks, a name and page number, and a source citation in your list of works cited, reference list, or bibliography?
- Have you paraphrased (put into your own words) a sentence without including a citation?
- Have you summarized a key idea such as an argument without including citation and documentation?
- Have you patchwritten—that is, altered a word or phrase in what would otherwise be a quotation rather than quoting it directly or paraphrasing it more fully?
- Does your list of works cited, reference list, or bibliography contain an entry for every source you quote, paraphrase, summarize, or reproduce (images, etc.) in your project?
- Do you cite all kinds of sources, from interviews to surveys, from photographs to book chapters?

- Assign a member of the team to be a quotation checker. Provide that person with copies of all cited sources against which to compare quotes and information in the text.

Good source citation practices throughout the project will help you avoid plagiarism and fulfill your responsibilities to yourself, your sources, your teammates, and your readers.

EXERCISE 9.1 Plagiarism and Source Use

After reading this chapter, test your knowledge using one of the many online quizzes on source use and plagiarism. Here are three possibilities:

- "How to Recognize Plagiarism"
  <www.indiana.edu/~istd/plagiarism_test.html>
  This quiz uses APA style, which is primarily used by the social sciences, as its base style sheet.

- "Plagiarism Quiz"
  <www.dsa.csupomona.edu/judicialaffairs/plagquiz.asp>
  This quiz tests your general knowledge about plagiarism scenarios.

- "Plagiarism Quiz Flash File" <www.esc.edu/esconline/across_esc/library.nsf/3cc42a422514347a8525671d0049f395/4310c8138928493a85256dda0056880b?OpenDocument> Like the previous quiz, this one tests your knowledge of scenarios.

About which aspects of plagiarism and source use were you still unclear? Write down any questions that taking the quiz raised, and direct them to your instructor. This will help to ensure that you understand what is expected in terms of citation.

A Final Thought

In "The Day the Violence Died," an episode of the *Simpsons,* Bart and Lisa discover their favorite cartoon, "Itchy and Scratchy" was an idea stolen from its rightful originator. The real creator, having lost all benefits of his good idea, ends up on the street, and is forced ultimately to sue for his idea. While not citing your sources may not leave authors on the street or you in a courtroom, not citing can hurt your credibility and the effectiveness of your document, not to mention possibly leading to more extreme outcomes such as punishment in school and your professional life. Instead, develop your skills of source integration; it is likely you would want other writers to do the same for you.

10 Writing an Annotated Bibliography

IN THIS CHAPTER

Annotated Bibliography of Writings in Feminism and Aesthetics

JOSHUA SHAW

This is a selective annotated bibliogra[...] thetics from 1990 to 2003. It is inte[...] by Linda Krumholz and Estella Laut[...]

Annotated Bibliography on Musician Wellness

COMPILED AND ANNOTATED BY LINDA COCKEY WITH KATHRYN KALMANSON

The items marked with this symbol can be ordered via the MTNA website through our affiliation with Amazon.com. Go to www.mtna.org and choose Member Services from the Membership option in the main menu bar for more information.

Introduction

The annual Annotated Bibliography on Musician Wellness has been researched and compiled annually for more than 15 years now, first for the National Keyboard Pedagogy Conference and the last 10 years for MTNA. The publication of new wellness resources for musicians is currently slowing down a bit; therefore, this year's review will also devote a portion to discussing and recapitulating the most useful resources out there for the purpose of giving readers a list of what they might really utilize and want to own in their own personal libraries. New updates will also be included as issues. Topics include prevention of medical problems, meditation, performance anxiety, performance preparation, healthy practicing techniques, learning theories and physiological and psychological issues related to overall musicianship.

Update

Smith, Brenda, and Robert T. Sataloff. (2006) *Choral Pedagogy, 2nd edition.* Plural Publishing, 5521 Ruffin Rd., San Diego, CA 92123;

Have you ever had a great conversation in which you really debated ideas? Research conversations can be like that. Kenneth Burke, something of a Renaissance thinker, said the research conversation is like a parlor where lots of people are talking and we, as researchers, enter in.* We need to listen to the people already talking before we can catch the drift of the conversation and consider joining in ourselves. Our own thinking will be affected by those who preceded us. And after we

*Burke, Kenneth. *The Philosophy of Literary Form.* Berkeley: U of California P, 1941. 110–11. Print.

contribute to the conversation, that conversation will also be affected by us, so we should contribute with care. The annotated bibliography allows researchers to listen carefully and start testing ideas before they contribute to the conversation surrounding a topic.

10a Understanding What an Annotated Bibliography Is and Why You Should Write One

An annotated bibliography provides brief summaries of selected sources on a research topic, with the sources arranged in alphabetical order. It can also include your evaluations of and responses to these sources. Annotated bibliographies are common college assignments, and they can be freestanding published works (journal articles or even books) because they are very useful to readers who want a quick understanding of a research conversation. The images that open this chapter illustrate two such publications.

One of the greatest benefits of preparing an annotated bibliography is processing your sources so you can represent them ethically and effectively. Preparing an annotated bibliography helps you consider these issues: Who are the key thinkers on the topic? What are their basic stances? Who is in conversation with whom?

Other benefits include:

- Slowing down your reading process enough that you do not miss anything important in your sources.
- Giving you practice with summary, a difficult and important writing technique.
- Placing you and your ideas among the other thinkers and writers on the topic without demanding that you immediately synthesize all of the information.
- Allowing an instructor or other readers to help you identify gaps in the research.

More about ▶▶▶
Summary, 14–19, 98, 109–11
Synthesis, 14–19, 20–23, 179–81

Students who write annotated bibliographies sometimes initially feel that they are labor-intensive, but when they begin to write their research projects (from essays to commentaries to proposals), they remark how much easier the projects are to write after having prepared an annotated bibliography. Even when an annotated bibliography is not part of the assignment, you may find it useful to write one as you prepare a major research project.

10b Preparing the Citation

More about ▸▸▸
Acknowledging sources, 108–09
Preparing an MLA-style list of works cited, 246–71
Preparing an APA-style reference list, 302–16
Creating *Chicago*-style notes and bibliography entries, 334–50
Preparing a CSE-style reference list, 363–75

Each entry in the annotated bibliography begins with full source information, presented as if it were in a list of works cited or a reference list at the end of a researched essay. (*Note:* The examples in this chapter follow Modern Language Association [MLA] style; for other documentation styles, see chapters 19–22.)

Hudson-Williams, Harri Llwyd. "Political Speeches in Athens." *Classical Quarterly* ns 1 (1951): 68–73. Print.

The entries are arranged in alphabetical order by author. If any entries do not have an author, use the first word (except *a, an,* or *the*) of the title to determine the alphabetical location of the entry.

10c Writing the Annotation

More about ▸▸▸
Summary, 14–19, 98, 109–11

In an annotated bibliography, each citation is followed by an annotation that summarizes the source. Usually these annotations are two

Writing Responsibly — Dealing with Abstracts

Many published texts begin with a one-paragraph abstract of the source. Source abstracts can also be found in many databases, such as *ProQuest* and *EBSCO.* When you are assigned to write an annotated bibliography, you are expected to read the sources and write your own summaries. Copying abstracts that others have written and representing them as your own work is plagiarism. Even paraphrasing the abstracts that others have written is unacceptable, especially if it means that you have not read the sources yourself.

But how do you avoid being overly influenced by abstracts? One option is to put them out of sight where they cannot tempt you. A better option is to read them; they are extremely useful in helping you anticipate what you will read in the article. Read the abstract, and then read the article, taking notes that you can use to write your annotation. To ensure that you use your own language in your annotation, try not to return to the abstract again, except after drafting your annotation.

to five sentences long. Sometimes this *abstract*—this very condensed summary of the source—is introduced by a sentence or two that offers information about or evaluation of the author or the publisher. You can see this approach in the selection from Dan Long's annotated bibliography at the end of this chapter.

If the annotated bibliography is part of a larger research project, you may want to conclude each annotation with a one-sentence indication of how you will use the source in your project, as Long did in his. Another alternative is to have one summary paragraph followed by a full evaluation paragraph that suggests how you will use the source.

More about ▶▶▶
Evaluation and critique, 14–19, 179–81

10d Formatting the Annotated Bibliography

Your annotated bibliography should include your name, a title, a brief explanation of why you have read these sources, full bibliographic information for each source, and annotations for each source. Unless your instructor gives you different instructions, follow the format and layout of Dan Long's annotated bibliography in section 10e.

10e Sample Student Annotated Bibliography (in MLA style)

Following is a selection of four entries from Dan Long's annotated bibliography, which originally contained ten entries.

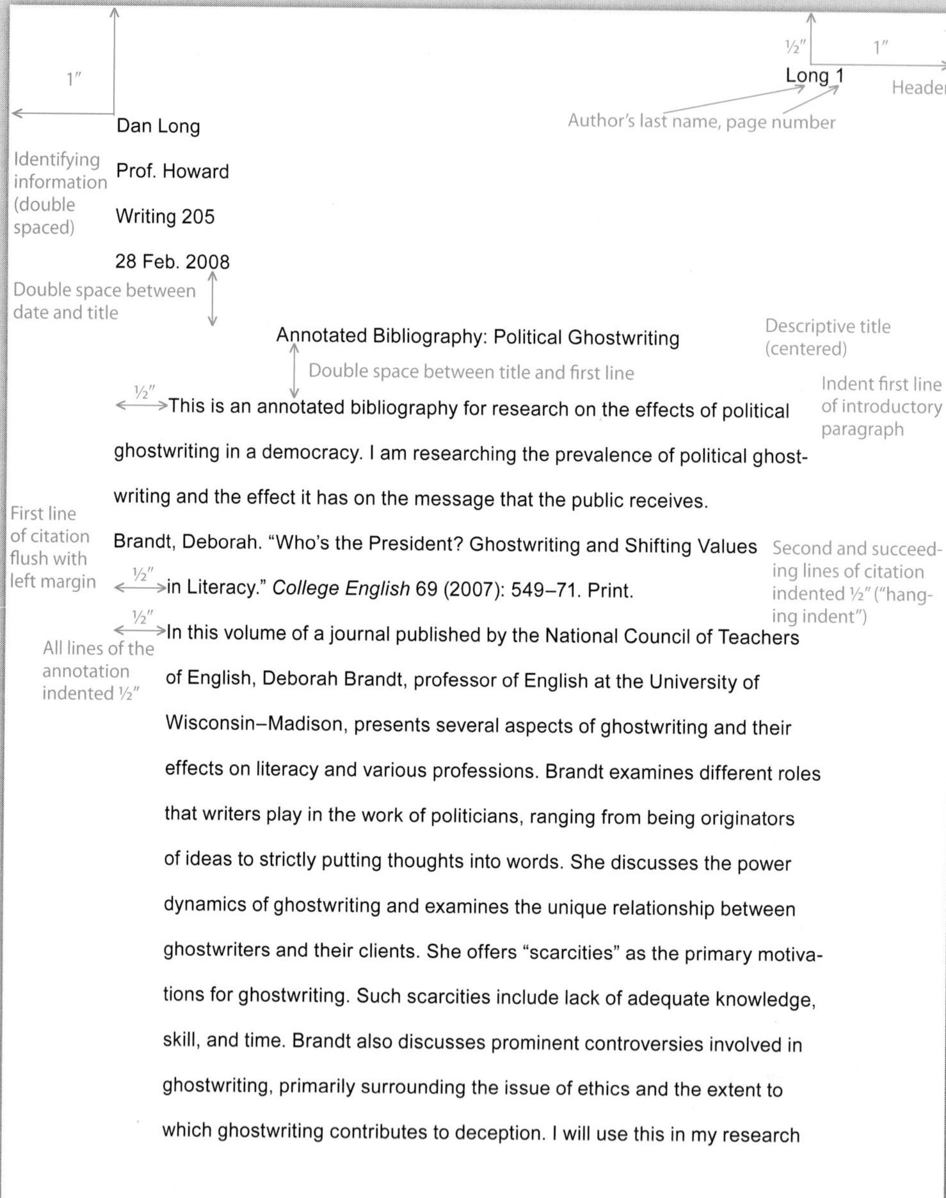

1″
½″
1″
Long 1
Header
Author's last name, page number
Dan Long
Identifying information (double spaced)
Prof. Howard
Writing 205
28 Feb. 2008
Double space between date and title
Annotated Bibliography: Political Ghostwriting
Descriptive title (centered)
Double space between title and first line
½″
Indent first line of introductory paragraph
This is an annotated bibliography for research on the effects of political
ghostwriting in a democracy. I am researching the prevalence of political ghost-
writing and the effect it has on the message that the public receives.
First line of citation flush with left margin
Brandt, Deborah. "Who's the President? Ghostwriting and Shifting Values
½″
in Literacy." College English 69 (2007): 549–71. Print.
Second and succeeding lines of citation indented ½″ ("hanging indent")
½″
In this volume of a journal published by the National Council of Teachers
All lines of the annotation indented ½″
of English, Deborah Brandt, professor of English at the University of
Wisconsin–Madison, presents several aspects of ghostwriting and their
effects on literacy and various professions. Brandt examines different roles
that writers play in the work of politicians, ranging from being originators
of ideas to strictly putting thoughts into words. She discusses the power
dynamics of ghostwriting and examines the unique relationship between
ghostwriters and their clients. She offers "scarcities" as the primary motivations for ghostwriting. Such scarcities include lack of adequate knowledge,
skill, and time. Brandt also discusses prominent controversies involved in
ghostwriting, primarily surrounding the issue of ethics and the extent to
which ghostwriting contributes to deception. I will use this in my research

as a scholarly evaluation of the ethics and a controversy surrounding ghost-writing's effect on various professions.

Dille, Brian. "The Prepared and Spontaneous Remarks of Presidents Reagan and Bush: A Validity Comparison for At-a-Distance Measurements." *Political Psychology* 21 (2000): 573–85. Print.

Brian Dille's research is focused on how differences between prepared and spontaneous remarks reflect psychological characteristics. His primary hypothesis is that the psychological scores for spontaneous remarks would be significantly different from the scores of prepared remarks. He tested his hypothesis on prepared and spontaneous remarks from President Reagan and President Bush. His findings showed that there was a significant difference between prepared and unprepared speech in relation to the respective presidents' operational code and policy implementation. There was a difference in the measurement of conceptual complexity in the speeches for President Reagan, which could reflect slightly different ideologies between President Reagan and his writers. I will use this study in my research to provide quantitative evidence for discrepancies between ideologies reflected by prepared speeches and spontaneous speeches.

Hudson-Williams, Harri Llwyd. "Political Speeches in Athens." *Classical Quarterly* ns 1 (1951): 68–73. Print.

In this volume of the peer-reviewed *Classical Quarterly,* Harri Llwyd Hudson-Williams of the University of Liverpool focuses on written speeches in ancient Greece. Hudson-Williams uses the work of Alsidamas and Isocrates to analyze the role of written speech as opposed to extempore speech in Greece. The philosophers viewed written speeches as a necessary evil but held reservations against their role in politics. In ancient Greece it was common for legal and forensic speeches to be written, but political speeches were primarily spontaneous. Many felt that specific preparation of political speeches interfered with truth. The philosophers largely felt that it was acceptable to outline specific points and arguments before the speech but that the delivery of the speech should be extempore. Hudson-Williams effectively addresses ancient philosophical thought about speechwriting but could have elaborated further on its role in Greek politics. I will use this in my research as a source of philosophical thinking on the ethics of political speechwriting. It will be particularly useful as an indication of how famous philosophers viewed the role of political speechwriting in society.

Hult, Karen, and Charles Walcott. "Policymakers and Wordsmiths: Writing for the President under Johnson and Nixon." *Polity* 30 (1998): 465–87. Print.

This article addresses the increasing gap between administrative policies and written presidential statements, and the beginning of contemporary political ghostwriting starting with the Lyndon Johnson and Richard Nixon presidential administrations. Hult and Walcott find that speechwriters are aloof from policymakers and don't have enough knowledge about specific policies to effectively write about them. Due to both an increased demand for writers and disorder within President Johnson's administration, speechwriters became less specialized and wrote about many different topics. Nixon

Long 4

established an Office of Speechwriting and Research in his first term, effectively expanding the number of writers and their duties. His writers were often invited to policy meetings, but only to become more in-tune with how the policymakers thought of ideas. In Nixon's abbreviated second term, writers didn't have as much guidance and became further separated from the ideas behind the policies about which they were writing. This study will be useful in my research because it gives me a transition from a time when writers were well connected with politicians to a time when they were disconnected. It gives me reasons for the shift and how it has affected political ghostwriting.

Quick Reference **What to Include in Your Annotated Bibliography**

1. A title indicating the topic of the annotated bibliography
2. A one-paragraph introduction to the topic
3. The source citation in the appropriate documentation style (MLA, APA, *Chicago*, CSE) for your class, discipline, or task
4. A summary of the source, representing its main argument in new language, usually one paragraph long
5. Often, an evaluation of or response to the source, indicating how reliable you think the source is and/or how you will use it in your research project

A Final Thought

Responsible communicators listen carefully so they do not misunderstand or misrepresent what others have said and so they do not sound foolish when they contribute. The same is true when the communication is written. Writers can learn from those who have written before them, and they too, can add to the discussion. An annotated bibliography is one of the best tools for sorting out and comprehending the conversation you hope to enter.

11 Developing New Information

IN THIS CHAPTER

This ancient Egyptian wall painting depicts smiths refining ore to produce gold. Like these goldsmiths, writers engaged in primary research produce valuable nuggets of information from firsthand research in archives as well as by conducting interviews, observational studies, and surveys.

11a Using Archives and Primary Documents

One mode of primary research is the study of primary documents. This research may include analyzing any of the following:

- A novel, story, play, or poem for a literature class
- A famous speech for a political science or speech class

Quick Reference → Primary Sources versus Secondary Sources

Primary Sources	**Secondary Sources**
Eyewitness accounts of events, experiments, or studies; accounts that have not been interpreted by other researchers	Works that interpret firsthand accounts or works of literature or art; may include both primary and secondary research
Examples	**Examples**
■ The data recorded in a laboratory notebook ■ A work of literature or art ■ A letter home from a soldier about a battle she or he has fought in	■ A laboratory report that analyzes the data from an experiment ■ An interpretation of a work of literature or art ■ A historian's analysis of a battle based on soldiers' letters, the general's battle plans, and other sources

- A historical document, such as the Magna Carta or the Emancipation Proclamation, for a history class
- A painting, sculpture, or drawing for an art history class
- A radio show, television show, or advertisement for a media studies class

More about ▸▸▸
Evaluating visual sources, 90–92
Using visuals as support, 177–79

You may also gather information from archives or special collections, which may include any of the following:

- Written records, such as diaries and letters (Figure 11.1).
- Statistical data, such as the average income of residents in a particular zip code or the average SAT score of college applicants in the United States. This information might be collected by the US Census Bureau or the National Center for Education Statistics.

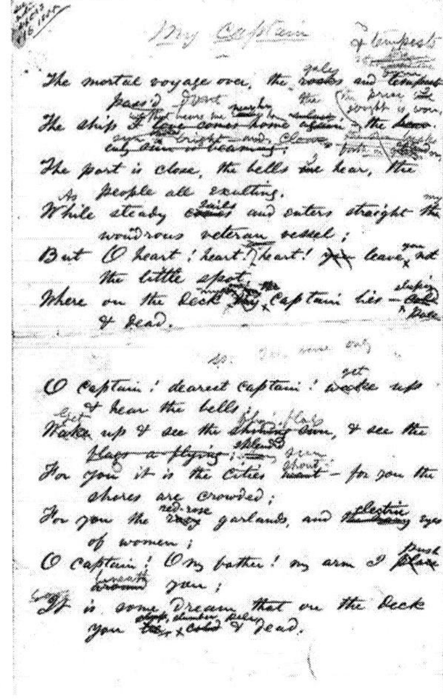

FIGURE 11.1 An Early Draft of Walt Whitman's "O Captain, My Captain" A study of Whitman's early draft could shed light on how the poem developed. Courtesy Library of Congress, Manuscript Collection <http://www.loc.gov/rr/mss/guide/ms04355a.jpg>

- Survey archives that record, for example, the popularity ratings of politicians over their term in office. This type of information is collected by organizations such as Gallup and CNN.

Worthwhile research on primary documents requires

- Creative analysis to determine the type of information that will help you answer your research questions
- Perseverance to retrieve the archival data, which may take several trips to the archive if the materials have not been digitized and cannot be removed for study
- Comparison of data from different sources to reach a reliable conclusion

More about ▸▸▸ Evaluating for reliability, 82–84

Contacting the archive

Archives have many rules to protect documents and monitor access. To use your time efficiently, find out before you visit how the archive operates:

- Where is the facility, and what are its operating hours?
- Can you make an appointment with an archivist or librarian to get advice on finding information about your topic?
- Do you need special permission or a letter of introduction from a professor or reference librarian?
- Are the materials you want to examine restricted? Do you need to request materials in advance? (Not all archives store files onsite, and it can take several days to retrieve them from storage.)
- Will you need to bring money (for a locker, to make photocopies), and can you get change if you need it?
- What will you be able to bring into the archive to take notes (a laptop? A pencil and notepad?)

In short, ask about anything you are not sure of, and request that the archive or special collections personnel tell you anything you might have forgotten to ask.

Making use of online tools

Many archives and special collections now offer electronic catalogs online. If the archive or special collection you want to visit does so,

Find Out **More . . . Multimedia Materials in Archives and Special Collections**

Be alert to possibilities for multimedia archives that might enrich your topic. These archives contain such sources as maps, photographs, recorded speeches, music, videos, and even scanned documents. A few such archives are listed here:

African Studies Center, University of Pennsylvania	<www.africa.upenn.edu/Home_Page/GIF_Images.html>
Kennedy Space Center's Media Gallery	<mediaarchive.ksc.nasa.gov/index.cfm>
Library of Congress	
Moving Image Collection	<mic.loc.gov/>
Rare Books and Special Collections	<www.loc.gov/rr/rarebook/>
Recorded Sound Reference Center	<www.loc.gov/rr/record/>
Miller Center of Public Affairs, University of Virginia, Scripps Library and Multimedia Archive	<millercenter.virginia.edu/scripps/>
The Newberry Library, Chicago	<www.newberry.org/general/generalinfo.html>
Smithsonian Institution	<www.si.edu/>
Viet Nam Multimedia Archives	<www.ibiblio.org/vietnam/canhg.html>

take advantage and search the catalog before your visit. This will help you determine which artifacts you want to examine and will save you time when you get there. Some archives and special collections may also allow you to email research questions to the staff. Answers you receive in advance can help you tailor your on-site search.

11b Conducting Interviews

While much information can be acquired by studying documents, interviews can sometimes be the only way to tap expert insight and get the "inside scoop." You can draw on expert information differently in an interview than through reading articles: Interviews let you shape the questions and follow up the responses.

Selecting an interview type

Interviews take three primary forms: informal, semistructured, and structured. An *informal interview* involves a very casual question-and-answer structure and may be conducted early in the research process to get a general idea about a topic. A *semistructured interview* involves prepared questions in a preplanned order from which you might deviate slightly as you respond to the interviewee. Semistructured interviews allow you to follow an idea and ask for more information, even skipping or adding a question when it seems appropriate. Finally, a *structured interview* is similar to a survey or questionnaire; you might use it to interview more than one person in a standard way, always asking the questions in the same way and in the same order.

Media such as email, instant messaging, and even the telephone extend your range of possible interviewees, but face-to-face interviews give you an opportunity to "read" the other person's body language—facial expressions and gestures. Still, conducting interviews online offers benefits of its own:

- A written record of responses
- Time for your interviewee to consider each response

However, try to ensure that the interviewee is comfortable with the email interview, as it will probably demand more of the respondent's time.

Choosing and contacting interviewees

When looking for an expert to interview, start with your college campus and local community: Are there instructors or local professionals with special expertise in your subject? Many organizations can connect you to experts who work or volunteer for the group, and government employees may provide insight into the workings of their

Writing Responsibly **Conducting Interviews**

When interviewing an expert to gather information, be fair to the interviewee:

- Ask about available times, and work around the interviewee's schedule.
- Show up for the interview on time and prepared.
- Ask for information that you need the interviewer to provide, not for information you can easily gather on your own.
- Tell the interviewee at the outset how you plan to use the information you gather, and get his or her consent.
- Stay within the allotted time.
- Confirm any quotations you may want to use.
- Offer the interviewee an opportunity to review your notes or your draft document. (You need not change your notes or document in response, but you should acknowledge to your reader(s) any difference of opinion.)

departments. When researching cultural or historical events, consider interviewing participants—the attorneys in a legal case, your soldier-cousin for her experience in Iraq, and so forth.

Connect your choice directly to your question. If you want to learn about student behaviors in dormitories, residence hall directors and residence assistants are appropriate interview subjects.

Preparing for the interview

Your interview will be only as good as the preparation you put into it:

- Consider your purpose, and shape your questions accordingly.
- Conduct background research on the topic and on the person you want to interview.
- Contact the potential interviewee, letting the subject know who you are, what you are researching, why you selected her or him, and the date by which you will need responses.
- Develop preliminary questions. Avoid asking yes/no, either/or questions (often called "closed" questions). Instead of asking, "Is the president of the student senate doing a good job?" (a closed question), ask "How would you rate the job the president of the student senate is doing and why?" (an open question). Open questions prompt more than a "yes" or "no" response from your interviewee.
- Have your teacher, a writing center consultant, or a classmate review your questions. Ask reviewers to add any they feel are missing, suggest a more logical order, remove any that are beyond the scope of your study, or reword any that are too narrow or too vague.

Conducting the interview

A good semistructured interview (the type you are most likely to conduct) is like a good conversation. There should be some give-and-take, and your questions should lead the interviewee to elaborate. The following guidelines will help you to conduct an effective interview:

- Remind the interviewee of the purpose of the interview and the way you plan to use the information you receive.
- Have the interviewee sign your informed consent form. (See Figure 11.2 on p. 134 for a model.)

Consent for Using Interview Results

I am conducting this interview for my _______________ course on __________ topic. I believe your knowledge and expertise will shed important light on the topic; therefore, I request the right to use your responses to my interview questions as a component of my research, which is part of my academic scholarship. Please consider signing the following statement, indicating that you give me consent to use these responses:

I agree to allow ______________________ to use my responses as part of his or her academic scholarship. I understand that I may be quoted at length and carefully paraphrased.

Name (please print):

____

Address:

____

____

Signature:

____

Date:

____

FIGURE 11.2 Interview Consent Form

- Put the interviewee at ease by leading off with some easy questions and assuring the subject that you are interested in his or her perspective.
- Use your prepared questions, but also listen for surprise responses and ask follow-up questions. Those surprises may shed new light and become central to your research project.

- Affirm the interviewee's responses. Nodding, maintaining eye contact, even saying "uh-huh" or "that's interesting" can encourage an interviewee to say more.
- Ask the interviewee to repeat important points so that you can document them accurately.
- Take extensive notes or make a recording (with permission) so that you can represent the interview faithfully when you are ready to write.

Wrapping up and processing the information

The interview is not complete when you leave the interviewee. There is still much to be done:

- Send a thank-you note within twenty-four hours of your interview acknowledging your gratitude for the interviewee's time, restating how you will use the information from the interview, offering to provide a copy of your research project when it is completed, and repeating your contact information.
- Make a transcript of the interview to which you can refer as you write up your results, and send a copy to your interviewee for comment or confirmation. (You are not obliged to accept the interviewee's revisions, but you may gain deeper insight by considering his or her comments.)
- Ask any additional questions, or request clarification of earlier responses, via email or phone.
- Send the interviewee a copy of your finished project.

11c Making Observations

Observational studies allow researchers to pay attention to people's activities and behaviors in action.

Preparing to observe

To prepare for observation-based research, consider the following:

- **Your purpose.** What do you hope to learn? Write down a hypothesis before you begin your observations. Plan to refine it as your observations progress.

Hypothesis A tentative explanation for a phenomenon

- **Your role.** Will you participate in the group or observe it from outside? Consider how your experiences and perspectives will affect your observations. Take steps to minimize bias.
- **Your methods.** Establish categories for the observations you expect, and adjust them in response to your actual observations. Take notes diligently—do not trust your memory.

The table that follows shows how one student prepared to observe a computer gaming party to learn about the ways games bring people together and the kinds of behaviors associated with group gaming.

Preparing to Observe Student Gaming and Group Behavior

Purpose	Discover the way games can bring people together by observing gamers in action.
Hypothesis	Games bring people together through socializing, problem solving, and the building of common experiences and languages.
Role	Participate (participant researcher role) to experience what goes on in the networked environment as well as in the room itself.
Methods	Categories: socializing in pairs or small groups, group-specific language, problem solving, other.*

*Use the "other" category to note things that do not seem to fit my predetermined categories. Afterward, build one or two new categories based on what shows up in the "other" column.

For observations of organized groups, ask permission from the group's leader (the pastor of a church congregation, the president of a student organization, the counselor of a self-help group), and let the leader decide whether the larger group should be informed. For unorganized groups (users of your dorm's laundry room or patrons of a game arcade, for example), inform the manager of the facility, and reveal your purpose to patrons when asked directly.

Conducting an observation

While conducting an observation, avoid disrupting the normal flow of activity as much as possible. This is true even when you are a participant observer. Drawing attention to the fact that you are conducting research can cause the people you are observing to behave differently. We might call it the Big Brother factor: If people know they are being observed, they are likely to be guarded or on their best behavior, and neither is good for researching real life. How, then, can you reduce your impact on the research environment?

- Sit out of others' line of sight.
- Try to blend in. Find out, for instance, how people will be dressed and dress similarly. If laptops are not common in the situation you are observing, avoid using one for note taking (even though doing so can be very handy).

Processing the information

The hard work of observation often occurs after the observation is over. You need to decide how to interpret, analyze, and evaluate what you saw.

More about ▸▸▸
Interpreting, analyzing, and evaluating information, 20–23

- Review the notes you made, developing new categories for any actions that do not fit neatly into your preestablished categories. Consider any patterns that emerged within your observation data: What kinds of things occurred repeatedly and similarly? What seemed surprising?
- Write some reflections on what you are seeing in the data. What is the significance of the patterns? Do they reinforce, enhance, or change your hypothesis?
- Compare the information you found to existing research. Has other research confirmed what you saw? Is what you saw different from other researchers' observations?

11d Developing and Conducting Surveys

Surveys collect information from people about their beliefs, experiences, opinions, and behaviors. Designing surveys that fairly and accurately represent a population is an advanced technical skill: Arlene Fink's guide to conducting surveys—*The Survey Kit,* 2nd ed. (2003)—

Writing Responsibly **Avoiding Bias When Conducting Surveys**

To avoid bias when developing and conducting surveys:

- Frame your questions carefully to avoid leading respondents. Asking "Don't you think we should have a new parking lot?" prompts respondents to agree.
- Select a representative sample of the population you are studying, not just those who are easy to locate or who you believe will support your hypothesis.
- Draw only the conclusions that the data you collect support.
- Never falsify data to support a predetermined conclusion.
- Alert your readers to the limitations of your research: Be candid about what your research does and does not demonstrate.

for example, is a ten-volume work. Most surveys conducted for a college research project cannot meet the high standards of statistical accuracy, but if designed with care, they can provide tentative insights into local situations.

Preparing to survey

When developing a survey, consider these issues:

- **Your purpose.** What do you hope to learn from your survey? Write down a hypothesis before you design your survey.
- **Your target population.** What group will you try to reach, and how will you contact them? Strive to include a broad and representative range of respondents.
- **Your survey.** What type of questions will you ask, how many questions will you include, and how will you administer the survey? Most surveys provide a fixed number of responses (as in a multiple-choice test) because it is easier to administer and analyze surveys of this type, but be sure that your answer options are fair and offer an adequate range of responses. Because respondents are not likely to spend more than a few minutes answering questions, surveys should be brief: Two pages is a reasonable limit.

The table below shows an example of one student's preparation for a survey to study student gaming and group behavior:

Preparing to Survey: Student Gaming and Group Behavior

Purpose	To determine whether gaming affects students' schoolwork or is a higher priority to some students than homework.
Hypothesis	A minority of students spend significant amounts of time (more than ten hours) gaming each week, and those students are more likely to be doing badly in school than are those who do not play games as frequently. I suspect the type of games students play also matters.
Target Population	All college students

Sample Questions	• How much time each week do you spend playing computer or video games (including card games, Wii, online games, etc.)?
	• Which type of game do you play most frequently?
	  • Shooter games
	  • Exercise games
	  • Card games
	  • Immersive world games
	  • Other (write in type) ______
	• What is your GPA?
	• How many hours a week do you typically spend doing homework?

Distributing and collecting surveys

There are several things to keep in mind about distributing and collecting surveys:

- The more surveys you distribute and collect, the more confident you can be about your findings.

- Distribute your surveys where you will get a good representation of your target population. To answer a question about the general student population, for example, look for a distribution location *all* students use, such as the Union. Alternatively, use a resource such as Survey Monkey to create your survey online; then distribute the survey link via email to a campus list.
- Be sure those surveyed know the survey will be anonymous; consider providing a box into which respondents can drop the survey. Again, using an online survey service is ideal because you never see participants, making it easier to maintain anonymity.

Processing the information

Responses to many survey questions can be tabulated as percentages: What percentage of those surveyed answered in a specific way? If you have included an open question or two in your survey, you will have to analyze the responses for patterns. As with other kinds of research, it is useful to verify your findings against those of other research.

A Final Thought

Developing new information can be an exciting and rewarding experience. You may find that, in its archives, your school has documents that shed light on your regional culture, giving you insight into your grandparents' and great-grandparents' lives. Interviews allow you to access expert knowledge firsthand. Observing can give you a clearer idea of people's interactions and the use of spaces. Surveys can produce timely information that is focused on your question. Building these kinds of hands-on research skills will help to develop your critical mind and your problem-solving skills.

12 Writing and Refining Your Thesis

IN THIS CHAPTER

The process of answering research questions is a little like blazing trails in the wilderness. It can be hard work, surprise you, and lead you places you have never been. Typically, when the trail is completed, at its head stands a signpost that signals what to expect and the direction the trail takes. Through the written product of your research, then, you invite readers to travel with you along the intellectual trails you have blazed, and the signpost is the thesis statement.

A *thesis statement* is one or two sentences indicating the main idea of your paper, the idea that each body paragraph and all the reasons and evidence in those body paragraphs support. Your thesis should grow out of your research hypothesis (or hypotheses), revised in light of what you learned through the research process. A good thesis interests readers, gives them a clear sense of what will follow, and is well supported. The path to the conclusion will be clear of obstacles because you, as the writer, have thought through what your readers will need to believe your main claim.

12a Drafting a Thesis Statement

More about ▸▸▸
Exploring topics, 24–31
Developing your research question, 34–35
Drafting research questions and hypotheses, 40–41

As you began your research, you chose and defined a *topic* that would be appropriate to your purpose and of interest to your reader. You then framed *research questions* and turned them into a *hypothesis* that you tried to confirm or refute through your research. Now, with research data in hand, you are ready to draft a *thesis statement.*

A well-crafted thesis statement should do all of the following:

- **Make an assertion**, or claim, that you will explain in the essay. "I will talk about global warming" does not express a claim, while "Citizens should be more aware of soft (bituminous) coal's impact on the environment and what they can do to lobby against its use" makes a strong claim.
- **Reflect your findings** by forecasting what you learned through your research.
- **Indicate the specific topic** you will address.
- **Express your purpose.** You need not say specifically, "I will persuade" or "I will inform," but your purpose should be clear nonetheless. For example, the writer of the earlier thesis about citizens becoming aware of the effects of soft coal seeks to persuade readers. If, instead, the writer's purpose were to inform, the thesis could be rewritten in this way: "Soft (bituminous) coal is a major contributor to pollution and acid rain, burning less cleanly than hard coal and other fuels."
- **Convey your point of view.** You can, of course, agree with one of your sources, but always try to add your perspective on that position. Otherwise, why should someone read your paper instead of one of the sources you consulted?
- **Use concrete language.** Weed out vague words such as *good* and *interesting.*
- **Suggest the topic's significance or relevance.** For example, the thesis "Green architecture methods typically used in urban areas need to be adapted to rural settings for maximum impact" suggests that readers should care about architecture's impact on the environment and signals the existence of ways to decrease its negative impact.
- **Achieve a balanced and reasonable tone.** Extreme positions can be difficult to support and can alienate readers. Considering counterarguments can help you achieve a reasonable tone.

- **Fit the assignment and genre.** Do you need to propose a plan for change? Comment on a trend? Analyze a situation? Persuade someone to change his or her mind on a subject? Go back to the assignment to make sure your thesis suits both its rhetorical and learning goals.

Lydia Nichols's research question, hypothesis, and thesis statement for her student research essay on underground comics illustrate the process of developing a thesis statement:

▶▶▶Sample student paper: "Holy Underground Comics, Batman! Moving Away from the Mainstream" by Lydia Nichols, 278–89

Research question: What are the characteristics of underground comics?

Hypothesis answers research question by listing three distinguishing traits

Hypothesis: The characteristics of underground comics are a ❶ focus on topics that challenge social mores, an author or author ❷ team that has creative control, and an adult readership. ❸

Thesis places underground comics in context familiar to readers

Thesis: While far less well-known than their superhero counterparts, underground comics offer an innovative and sophisticated alternative to mainstream titles.

Thesis transforms specifics into a broader, more engaging claim

Purpose is both informative and persuasive: compares types of comics (informative) to convince readers that underground comics are more innovative and sophisticated (persuasive)

The thesis statement grows out of the hypothesis, but it is broader: It offers to explain how underground comics differ from mainstream comics, but it leaves the exact ways in which they differ for the body of the essay. The thesis conveys the essay's dual purpose—it uses comparison to persuade readers that underground comics are more innovative and sophisticated than their superhero cousins—and it clearly announces the position the writer is taking.

Make It **Your Own**

For a research paper that you are working on, draft (or revise) a thesis statement. Does the thesis statement concisely assert your central idea? Will it appeal to your readers? Does it convey your purpose? If your paper is making an argument, do you clearly indicate your position? Be sure to refer to the criteria for an effective thesis statement on pp. 142–44.

Writing Responsibly **Acknowledging Counterevidence**

While sorting your notes, be sure to retain *counterevidence*—evidence that *undermines* your claims. Do not suppress this counterevidence. Instead, revise your thesis or supporting reasons with it in mind, or acknowledge the counterevidence and explain why the support for believing your thesis is more convincing than the challenges to it. Your readers will appreciate your presentation of multiple perspectives.

12b Refining Your Thesis

More about ▶▶▶ Reasons and evidence, 174–77

Most writers revise their thesis statement repeatedly as they draft, sharpening it so that it reflects their developing ideas. In the section that follows, look carefully at how Erin Buksbaum's and Tom Hackman's thesis statements evolved from dull and general to interesting and specific.

Purpose: Informative

More about ▶▶▶ Purpose in the project proposal, 38–40

The thesis of an informative document makes a claim of fact—it makes a claim about something that can be verified—and the balance of the essay provides the verification. To be engaging, an informative thesis must make a claim of fact that is not yet widely known to or accepted by the audience.

Draft Thesis

This paper is about using social networking sites.

This draft thesis statement makes a claim of fact, but it is far too general, doing nothing more than identifying the paper's general topic.

Revision 1

While social networking sites allow for new forms of social communication, they can also be dangerous.

This thesis statement is more specific but still too general: Because it does not specify the types of dangers social networking sites represent, it commits the writer to discussing *all* the ways in which social networking sites can be dangerous (physically, psychologically, financially; for users, families and friends of users, companies).

Revision 2

While social networking sites allow for new forms of communication, they also open new avenues for privacy violations.

This thesis statement narrows the scope: The writer is responsible only for reporting on privacy violations. Because the thesis suggests that the paper will discuss a current topic about which many students know far more than their instructors, it is also likely to spark the instructor's interest.

Purpose: Argumentative/Persuasive

The thesis of a persuasive text must make a claim of judgment rather than a claim of fact. It must offer an opinion, a provisional judgment, that is not widely shared and that can be explained with reasons and evidence.

More about ►►► Positioning your argument in relation to others, 173–90

Draft Thesis

There are many types of plagiarism.

This is a simple claim of fact; it is insufficient for an essay with a persuasive purpose.

Revision 1

Plagiarism has many motivations, which, I believe, makes a single punishment inappropriate.

This draft makes a claim of judgment, but the first half of the statement remains overly general (it would take many pages to discuss the motivations of *all* writers), and it announces a claim ("I believe"), that is unnecessary.

Revision 2

Reducing the incidence of plagiarism among college students will be difficult without understanding its causes. This requires going beyond the simplistic explanations that are frequently offered.

The thesis now focuses on a much smaller group (college students), and it no longer unnecessarily announces its claim.

Although you can revise your thesis statement at any stage of the writing process, you are most likely to revise it at two points:

1. After collecting and processing your information
2. After writing your first draft and beginning your revisions

Quick Reference → Revising the Thesis Statement

Use this checklist as you revise and refine your thesis statement to make it as strong as possible. The goal is to check off each item in the checklist. Before you revise ask an outside reader to check off the items he or she feels your thesis satisfies.

- ☐ Does the thesis answer your research question?
- ☐ Does the thesis make a debatable claim, one with which some readers might disagree until convinced otherwise?
- ☐ Does the thesis express the main topic by using the key terms of your study?
- ☐ Does the thesis use precise terms instead of broad and general ones?
- ☐ Is your thesis supported by your research?
- ☐ Does the thesis express your take on the topic, rather than simply repeating what one of your sources has said?
- ☐ Does the thesis take a balanced and reasonable stance, not overstating the case? (Watch for "all," "never," "always," and other absolutes, and revise where the absolute is unsupportable.)
- ☐ Does the thesis suggest the significance or relevance of the topic?
- ☐ Does the thesis make your purpose (to inform, persuade, analyze, or interpret) clear?
- ☐ Do you feel excited by and engaged with the claim you are making?

When first drafting and revising your thesis statement, focus on making sure it satisfies the criteria listed on pp. 142–44. You may also use the checklist in the Quick Reference box above. When revising your thesis statement after writing a draft, check your thesis against those criteria and also make sure your reasons and evidence support your claim. If they do not, either replace the irrelevant reasons and evidence, or revise your thesis so that the support you offer is pertinent.

Work **Together**

Using the thesis statement you have developed based on your research, pair up with a classmate to debate your claims. One person should play the role of the investigative reporter and the other, the role of the researcher defending his or her research. The reporter should try to poke holes in the researcher's argument by asking probing questions. Then, switch roles. After each round, take a few moments to jot down information you need to find that will strengthen your argument, and note ways you need to refine your claim. Which questions did your partner ask that you could not answer adequately?

A Final Thought

Most writing has a central claim, and all persuasive writing does. How well your readers comprehend your central claim depends on the clarity and strength of your thesis statement. All other parts of your writing hinge on these one or two sentences, supporting, enhancing, and elaborating on the thesis. From the reader's perspective, the thesis offers a sense of what is to come. From the writer's perspective, a strong thesis is about getting your voice heard. It should be neither a shout nor a whisper. Your audience should know what your primary claim is and why they, too, should believe as you do on the topic.

13 Organizing Your Project

IN THIS CHAPTER

Home improvement shows often depict organization as a way to improve the look and feel of household spaces. Messy, disorganized rooms are almost unlivable and unusable. Writing benefits similarly from attention to its structure and order. Most documents need attention to organization both *before* and *after* drafting. Organizing beforehand makes drafting easier and more effective. Reviewing the structure after you have written a draft can show you where you need more support, whether the document is logically organized, and whether any of the evidence you have included is irrelevant.

More about ▶▶▶
Reorganizing a draft, 191–95

13a Reviewing Your Prewriting

Start organizing by reviewing all the preparatory writing you have done: your research log, any freewriting, brainstormed lists, clusters in progress, and so on. Your materials should be fresh in your mind as you outline and draft.

Ask yourself whether reading through all of your prewriting has given you any new insight into your topic. If so, adjust your thesis statement. Then write your preliminary thesis statement at the top of a new electronic document or a clean sheet of paper. If you are working as a team, you might want to make a new wiki page. Below the thesis statement, list all the ideas that might be relevant to it, looking especially for supporting evidence or counterevidence.

More about ▸▸▸
Keeping a journal or blog, 14–19, 93–97
Freewriting, 24–31
Brainstorming, 24–31
Clustering, 24–31
Hypothesis development, 35, 41
Thesis statements, 141–47

13b Grouping Your Ideas

As you read through and develop your list, group ideas into subtopics. For instance, Erin Buksbaum noticed three different types of subtopic groupings she could use for her notes on social networking: positive aspects versus dangers, profiles and photos, and violations and dangers.

▸▸▸Student sample essay by Erin Buksbaum:
Early draft, "Is Social Networking a Serious Danger?" 170–171

There are many grouping methods that will help you get closer to an outline of your project. If you are working with an electronic document, you can cut and paste your ideas into logical groups using *subheadings* (these subheadings might be functional parts of the final document or might disappear altogether as you write) or display all related ideas in the *same font color*. If you have been using a blog and tagging your entries, the *tags* serve as functioning groups you can refine. If you are working with pen and paper, you can highlight related ideas with the *same color highlighting marker* or write each group of ideas on a *separate sheet* of paper. If you favor note cards, you can create *piles* that represent each subtopic or potential section of your research project. You might also want to create a *cluster diagram* based on your subtopics or sections.

Do you have an item that does not seem to fit your categories? Anything that must be forced into a group either might not be relevant or might reveal information you still need to gather.

13c Arranging Your Ideas from General to Specific

Within each group, arrange ideas from most general to most specific. Grouping general and specific ideas on the same topic can help you determine whether you have enough specific reasons, evidence, and examples for each major point.

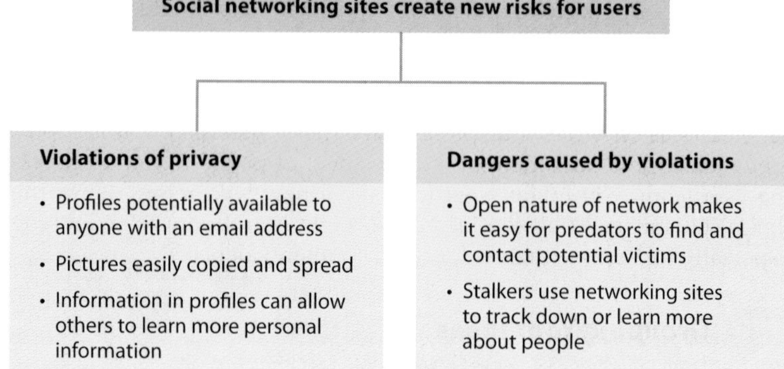

FIGURE 13.1 Tree Diagram A tree diagram can help you organize your thoughts before you begin writing.

At this stage, you might also find it helpful to create a *tree diagram,* in which you place the most general information at the top and increasingly specific information on branches below. The tree diagram in Figure 13.1 shows the preliminary organization for Erin Buksbaum's essay.

13d Considering Your Project's Overall Shape

The typical academic research essay has three basic parts: introduction, body, and conclusion. In its simplest form, the essay has a "five-paragraph" structure: one paragraph for the introduction, three for the body, and one for the conclusion. Of course, college writing seldom takes such a tidy form. Instead, it is more likely to unfold as described below.

Introduction

More about ▶▶▶ Conducting research in the disciplines, 222–29

More about ▶▶▶ Drafting the introduction, 165–66
Revising the introduction, 193–94

The introduction is typically brief: one to three paragraphs, depending on the length of the project. Often, the thesis statement appears in the introduction, where it can shape the reader's expectations, but it may also appear in the conclusion (more common in the social sciences). What goes into the introduction depends on the document's purpose, audience, context, and genre. In most cases, though, the introduction should do the following:

- Identify the topic
- Entice readers to read on
- Provide a thesis statement or a research question
- Prepare readers for what follows, in some cases by forecasting the project's main points

Body

The body is the longest portion of a text, with its length depending on the complexity of the ideas being expressed and the quantity of support needed to convince the audience. Each paragraph in the body should make one point, expressed in a topic sentence; the body paragraphs should supply reasons and evidence supporting the topic sentence; and each topic sentence should support the thesis. Evidence may include the following:

More about ▶▶▶
Developing paragraphs, 166–67
Reasons and evidence, 161–64
Counterevidence, 145, 161–64

- Facts
- Statistics
- Expert testimony
- Observations
- Examples
- Case studies
- Anecdotes

The one major deviation from this pattern is the introduction of *counterevidence*—alternative or contrasting points of view on your topic. Introduce counterevidence either early or at the very end of the body, acknowledging that there are other positions on the topic than the one you have taken but explaining why the evidence you present is more compelling.

Conclusion

Like the introduction, the conclusion is usually rather brief (one to three paragraphs, depending on the length of the project). Just as the introduction should entice readers, so the conclusion should convince them that they have spent their time well. An effective conclusion might do one of the following:

More about ▶▶▶
Drafting the conclusion, 168–69

- Point to further avenues for research
- Offer a personal reflection
- Explain why readers should follow your recommendations
- Suggest the broader significance of your findings

An effective conclusion should not introduce reasons to doubt your argument, nor should it offer new supporting material or repeat your thesis word for word ("In my paper, I have shown . . .").

13e Choosing an Organizational Strategy

Once you have collected and organized your notes, choose an organizational pattern that best fits your thesis and supporting materials. Some organizational patterns include the following:

- **General-to-specific/specific-to-general order.** Probably the most common organizational scheme for academic essays begins with a general statement—the thesis—and then proceeds to the body of the essay, where specific reasons and evidence are provided. With indifferent or even hostile readers, consider reversing this order: Begin with something specific—an engaging anecdote, some dramatic statistics, a provocative illustration—that will gain your audience's interest, attention, or sympathy, and then move on to the general conclusion.
- **Familiar-to-unfamiliar/unfamiliar-to-familiar order.** If you are writing for an audience likely to balk when faced with new ideas, especially ones that challenge their beliefs, lead with what you believe your readers already know and accept, and move gradually toward what they do not. To startle your readers into seeing a familiar issue in a new light, use unfamiliar-to-familiar order: Begin with surprising issues or information, and then move on to familiar ground.
- **Problem-to-solution organization.** Much research is aimed at solving problems. Such projects typically begin by defining the problem and offering an informed rationale for a particular solution. This structure is typical of proposals for change.
- **Cause-and-effect organization.** Research often helps us to understand how things came to occur and what the impacts of those causes have been. Historians are often interested in what led people to war, for instance.
- **Climactic organization.** You may choose to organize your body paragraphs from least to most exciting. You might even save your thesis until the conclusion.

- **Chronological organization.** Use *chronological* (or *time*) order to tell a story (*narrative*) or explain a process (*process analysis*). For instance, to explain how to snowboard, you might start with how to strap on the board, move on to how to adopt the right position when you first start down the hill, and conclude with how to get up after you fall.
- **Spatial organization.** When your findings are descriptive, organize spatially, from left to right, inside to outside, top to bottom. To describe the sedimentary layers in a mountainside for an assignment in your geology course, for example, you might begin your description with the top layer and move downward into the earth. This structure is best suited to observation-based field research.

Make It Your Own

Revisit a research project you wrote recently. What organizational strategy or strategies did you use? What organizational changes would you make now? Why?

13f Choosing an Outlining Technique

Outlines, whether "scratch" or formal, not only guide you as you draft, but also allow you to experiment with ways to sequence your supporting paragraphs. Perhaps most importantly, they allow you to check whether all your evidence really supports your thesis.

An informal (scratch) outline

An *informal,* or *scratch, outline* is simply a list of ideas in the order you want to present them. You can jot down your ideas in words, phrases, complete sentences, even pictures—whatever jogs your memory about what to put next. You can present the ideas in a simple series, or you can cluster them in groups—introduction, body, conclusion. Below is a sample scratch outline for Erin Buksbaum's essay on social networking sites.

▸▸▸Student sample essay by Erin Buksbaum:
Early draft, "Is Social Networking a Serious Danger?" 170–71

Intro:
Social networking sites = new pathways of communication.
Benefits: Way to communicate with friends, make new friends, promote movies, shows, bands.
Thesis: While social networking sites allow for exciting new forms of communication, they also open new avenues for privacy violations and even danger.

Body:
Background: User profiles and the kind of information/ elements they include, how information is accessed
Dangers: Pictures—some inappropriate or misused (ruin reputation, lose jobs); Profiles—information available too widely (teachers, parents, criminals, perverts), lying about who you are

Conclusion:
Be cautious; don't post info you wouldn't want to see in the newspaper.

If the organization of your project is likely to be straightforward, a tree diagram (see Figure 13.1, p. 150) may provide all the structure you need. Since tree diagrams do not suggest the order in which ideas will appear in the paper, however, you might number the branches or work from left to right to keep your document growing in the right shape.

A formal outline (topic or sentence)

A *formal outline* uses roman numerals (I, II, III), capital letters (A, B, C), arabic numerals (1, 2, 3), lowercase letters (a, b, c), and indentions of five spaces (or half an inch) to indicate level of generality, with roman numeral headings being the most general to lowercase letters the most specific. Each level of your outline should include at least two entries. Each subsidiary point must support the idea at the level above it, and each heading must unify the subsidiary points in the level below. To use a simple example, if the first-level heading is *I. Types of Cheese,* the next-level headings could be

A. Muenster

B. Swiss

C. Cheddar

They should not be

A. Methods of Making Cheese

B. Aging the Cheese

C. Using the Right Feed Grain

because all the headings at each level must be *parallel,* or follow the same pattern. Thus, the sequence

A. Muenster

B. Swiss

C. Cheddar

is fine (all are adjectives describing a type of cheese), whereas the sequence

A. Methods of Making Cheese

B. Aging the Cheese

C. Using the Right Feed Grain

is not. (You would have to change *Methods of Making Cheese* to *Making the Cheese* to make the first heading parallel with the others.)

The examples above are from a *topic outline:* They use words and phrases to indicate the ideas to be discussed. Some writers prefer to create a *sentence outline* because it provides a starting point from which to draft. Compare the first two sections of a topic outline and a sentence outline for Erin Buksbaum's essay:

Thesis: While social networking sites allow for exciting new forms of communication, they also open new avenues for privacy violations and other social dangers.

Topic Outline

I. User profiles
   A. Typical components
      1. Basic personal information: name, age, school
      2. Favorite music, movies, books
      3. Animations, videos, Flash movies, banners
   B. Dangers they create
      1. Make personal info available to anyone with an account
      2. Children may post details that make them easy to find and harm

II. Photographs
   A. Popularity of posting on profiles
      1. Most profiles usually have numerous photographs
      2. Users enjoy posting pictures of themselves, friends, pets
   B. Dangers of prevalence of photographs
      1. Children may see inappropriate images
      2. Photos could be downloaded and misused

Sentence Outline

I. The center of the social networking experience is the user's profile.
   A. These profiles can be thought of as personalized web pages.
      1. Profiles usually include basic personal information such as a user's name, age, and school.
      2. Most users also post lists of their favorite books, bands, and songs.
      3. More sophisticated users post animations, videos, and Flash movies.
   B. While it sounds like harmless fun, what people post in their profiles can be extremely dangerous.
      1. User profiles allow any other member of the social network to learn personal details about that user.
      2. Many children may foolishly post details that make it easy for others to track them down offline.

II. Photographs are another key feature of social networking sites.
   A. Photographs are an extremely popular element of user profiles.
      1. Most profiles include many, many pictures.
      2. Usually, users post photographs of themselves, their friends, or their pets.
   B. The prevalence of photographs creates its own set of complications.
      1. Children may see images that are not appropriate for their age group.
      2. Photographs can be easily downloaded and hence easily misused.

Though Buksbaum has not referred directly to sources in these outlines, when drafting you should cite any sources to which you refer within your outline, not only when you include a full quotation but also when you paraphrase an idea.

A storyboard or a site map

For a multimedia research project or if you are a visual thinker, you will want a more visual kind of outline such as a storyboard or a site map. *Storyboards* are analogous to cartoon frames. Each square of the storyboard usually has both a visual and a textual component, and the storyboard moves from the beginning to the end of the project. This allows you to employ visual and verbal evidence where appropriate. A *site map* is an outline of a website or hyperlinked project, allowing you to indicate the relationships among pages. Figure 13.2 on p. 158 shows a sample site map of a research project on Plato's *Phaedrus* and a storyboard of a multimedia project on underground comics.

If you are writing up your research collaboratively, decide as a group which outline style will work for all of you. Once you have made that decision, you will be able to use a wiki (an online, editable document) so that all can contribute to the outline. You might also divide the project into general sections as a group and then ask individuals to fill out the specifics of a single section, putting the whole outline together later for all to tweak.

More about ▶▶▶
Collaborating on research, 9–10, 117–19, 171–72
Wikis, 93–96

13g Checking Your Outline for Unity and Coherence

More about ▶▶▶
Developing paragraphs, 166–67

Once you have completed your outline, review it critically for unity and coherence. You have achieved *unity* when all the supporting paragraphs are relevant to the thesis and all the examples, reasons, and evidence are relevant to the main idea of the supporting paragraph. You have achieved *coherence* when the supporting paragraphs, with all their reasons, evidence, and examples, are organized logically, so that readers can move from idea to idea without having to pause to consider the relationship among the parts.

When reviewing your outline, ask yourself the following questions:

- Are all the reasons, evidence, and examples relevant to the main idea?
- Do all the ideas reinforce the thesis statement?

Web Site on Implications of Plato's *Phaedrus* for Modern Writers, Site Map

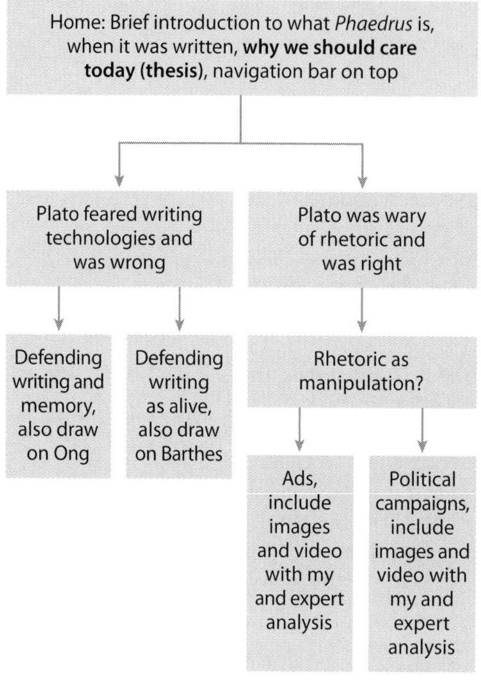

Sample Storyboard: *PowerPoint* Video on Underground Comics (first four frames)

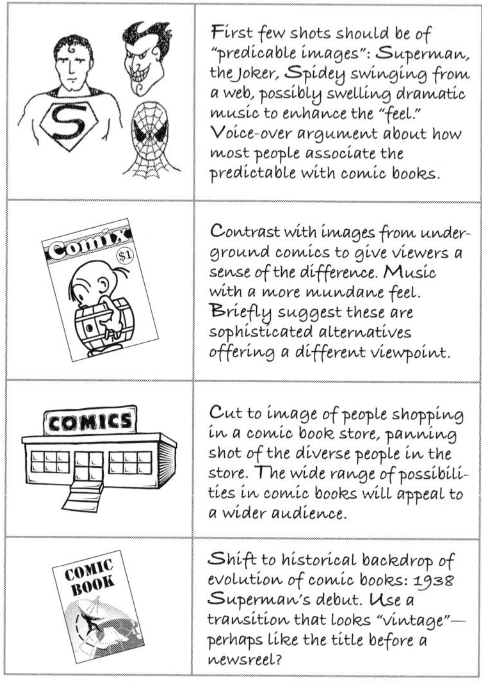

FIGURE 13.2 Site Map and Storyboard A site map can help you visualize the organization of research presented across multiple web pages. www.conceptdraw.com/en/sampletour/web/

- Are all the ideas organized logically?
- What is the connection between point one and point two? (This connection will become your transition when you begin drafting.)

EXERCISE 13.1 Outlining Informally

Arrange the ideas below this thesis statement into an informal outline for an essay. Write a brief rationale for the order you have chosen.

Thesis (informative): The first modern people lived in Africa.

List of ideas:

- Populations with the greatest genetic diversity have been established for the longest time.
- Scientists today can study genetic code—the "genome"—of people alive today to learn about where their ancestors lived.
- All humans alive today share 99.9 percent of their genetic code with all other humans.
- Until the mid-1980s, scientists could learn about humans only from bones and cultural artifacts.
- When random mutations occur in the remaining 0.01 percent of a person's genetic code, they are passed on to his or her descendants.
- Mutations occur at a fairly steady rate.
- The greatest genetic diversity occurs in women of African descent.

EXERCISE 13.2 Outlining Formally

Using the ideas in Exercise 13.1 or your own research, create a formal topic outline.

Work Together

Exchange your project outline with a classmate, and assess your classmate's outline for unity and coherence. Explain your observations to your classmate. Then, using whatever useful ideas you gained from your classmate's response to your outline, revise it.

Quick Reference Getting Organized

- Review your prewriting for patterns.
- Group your ideas logically.
- Arrange your ideas from general to specific.
- Consider your project's overall shape (introduction, body, conclusion).
- Choose an organizational strategy.
- Choose an outlining technique and develop the outline.
- Check your outline for unity and coherence.

A Final Thought

The classic Tetris video game is all about seeing how visual objects fit together, planning quickly and effectively as one plays. While it is very satisfying to see pieces lock into place with no gaps in between, one of the great challenges of the game is having to plan, organize, and execute virtually all at once. Fortunately, most researched writing does not have to proceed that way; writers get the opportunity to make plan through a proposal, sketch the plan more specifically through outlining, and return and revise the organization throughout the drafting and revising stages. And seeing claims and evidence lock into place to build knowledge and inform and persuade an audience of readers can be much more satisfying than the fleeting pleasure of virtual block stacking.

14 Drafting Your Project

IN THIS CHAPTER

Before producing a new line of clothing or an automobile, designers sketch the product, drafting and arranging the shapes before dressing them in colors and textures. Writers, too, begin with a draft: They sketch their ideas in words and arrange them in topics, sentences, and paragraphs. Both artists and writers sometimes erase initial ideas, reconceive preliminary thoughts, and revise early efforts. That first sketch is an important step forward to a satisfying finished work.

14a Preparing to Draft

When the moment comes to draft, setting aside some time and finding a place where you can concentrate are essential. Even in the best circumstances, you may encounter writer's block, but by using the appropriate techniques, you will be able to get past it.

Getting ready

Ideally, reserve a substantial block of time for writing your first draft. How you define *substantial* depends on how long or complex your essay will be: An hour or two might be enough for a first draft of a three- to five-page essay; a longer text will probably require more time. If you are unable to set aside a large block of time, work in smaller segments over several days. Do not delay starting just because you can cobble together only a half hour at a time.

Next, consider what place is best for you. For some this means a study carrel in the library; for others, it is a table for one at a noisy street-side café. Whatever your preference, focus on the task at hand by turning off your cell phone and exiting from instant messenger, email, and your internet browser. It is a common misconception that people can multitask effectively.

Starting to write

More about ▶▶▶
Analyzing the rhetorical situation, 38–40
Exploring a topic, 24–31
Drafting a thesis, 141–44
Organizing your project, 148–59

The writing you have done while analyzing your rhetorical situation (audience, context, purpose, genre, and tone or style), exploring your topic, drafting your thesis, and organizing your ideas will provide a starting point. Begin by reviewing this material, and then try one of the following drafting methods (or a combination of them):

- **Method 1: Fill in your outline.** Start a new computer document and type or paste your outline into it, or save your outline file with a new name. Then, use your outline as scaffolding, filling it in and fleshing it out until it becomes a first draft.
- **Method 2: Start anywhere.** Instead of beginning at the beginning, start writing whatever parts of the essay you feel confident about—an engaging example or a descriptive passage in support of one of your ideas, even just a sentence or phrase that captures a relevant thought. Continue writing out-of-order thoughts until you can begin stitching them together, filling in the gaps.
- **Method 3: Write straight from your brain.** Place your thesis statement at the top of a sheet of paper or the beginning of a computer file, and then just start writing. This may produce a very brief, general first draft, but it will be one that speaks your message. You can supplement later.

Make It **Your Own**

For a paper that you are working on, produce a first draft using one of the methods of drafting described on p. 162.

Whatever method of drafting you choose, do not worry about the language you use to present your ideas. You can smooth out the kinks later, when you revise, edit, and proofread.

***More about* ▸▸▸**
Revising, editing, and proofreading, 191–203

Overcoming writer's block

Gene Fowler, a newspaper columnist, novelist, and screenwriter, once said that "[w]riting is easy: All you do is sit staring at a blank sheet of paper until drops of blood form on your forehead." Fortunately, there are techniques to help you avoid writing trauma:

- **Write something else.** Write a journal or blog entry about the problems you are having with the paper. Write about another topic you know well or care passionately about. Just the act of writing can help unblock you.
- **Write what you can.** Write the parts you *can* write, even if you cannot yet string them together.
- **Do not start from scratch.** Use your outline, brainstorming, and other notes to jump-start your writing.

***More about* ▸▸▸**
Idea-generating techniques, 24–31

Tech

Protecting Your Work

Because terrible things often happen to computer files, it is important to take these steps:

- **Save early and often.** Adjust your computer to save your file automatically every five or ten minutes. Also, each time you pause, manually save your file.
- **Save your file in multiple locations.** After each writing session, burn your file to a CD or DVD; save it on a USB flash drive, your school's network drive, or a web-based backup service; or send a copy to your email account.
- **Do not delete.** When you reject something you have written, do not delete it. Instead, cut and paste it to a file for discards. You may want to restore something later that you cut.
- **Use your word processor's Undo function.** If you delete a paragraph by mistake or make a change you do not like, use "Undo" to go back a step.

- **Write a message to yourself.** For some writers, the idea of an audience can be inhibiting, so try writing a note to yourself: "What I want to say is . . . ," and then finish the sentence.
- **Talk.** Tell a tutor, instructor, classmate, or family member what your paper will be about. Get your listener to take notes as you talk. Then use those notes as a starting point for writing.
- **Use technology.** Instead of talking with someone face-to-face, use Web communication tools such as email, Twitter, or *Facebook*. Explain your topic to jump-start your writing.
- **Return to research.** Perhaps you are stuck because you do not yet know enough to continue writing. If this is the case, do some more research, but be alert for when you *do* know enough to return to writing.
- **Change your situation.** Switch the medium—from pencil and paper to word processing, or vice versa—or change the setting in which you are writing, by shutting off (or turning on) some background music or by moving from a study carrel to a table in the cafeteria.
- **Do not expect perfection.** It is the rare writer who produces a masterpiece on the first try, and trying to be that rare writer can be inhibiting. If you cannot avoid focusing on errors, try turning off your computer screen so you cannot see what you have written until it is time to start revising.

***More about* ▸▸▸**
Gathering information, 50–66
Meeting the challenges of online research, 67–79
Developing new information, 128–40

14b Developing a Title

A project title might at first seem like an afterthought or unimportant because it is so small. For some writers, though, developing a good title can help focus the drafting and remind them of their thesis. Drafting a title can also let you introduce a bit of play or cleverness.

To develop a draft title, return to your thesis and the key terms you used to search for information. Pull out the most specific, clearest, or most provocative key terms from the thesis and your search. Using your list of the terms, develop multiple possible titles, playing with word combinations until you have something you believe suggests your main point and might catch a reader's attention. Remember that titles are the first clue readers have about your text and may encourage them to read on—or may confuse or turn them off. These approaches can help you write a good title:

- Ask a question (your research question, perhaps) to which your reader will want to learn the answer. For example, Erin Buksbaum titled her first draft "Is Social Networking a Serious Danger?"
- Create a two-part title divided by a semicolon or other punctuation. You might make half the title funny or playful and the other half more serious and directly expressive of your main point. For example, Lydia Nichols titled her project "Holy Underground Comics, Batman! Moving Away from the Mainstream." Heather DeGroot used this structure to create a serious two-part title: "The Power of Wardrobe: Male Stereotype Influences."
- Create a descriptive one-part title. For example, an alternate title for Heather DeGroot's project might be "Wardrobe's Influence on Male Stereotypes."

Avoid uninspiring or overly general titles like "Essay 1" or "Global Warming."

14c Drafting the Introduction

Introductory paragraphs shape readers' attitudes toward the rest of the text. Many writers find it helpful to draft the body of the essay before tackling the introduction.

Whether you write the introduction first or last, keep in mind that it should prepare readers for the essay that follows. In many cases, this means including the thesis. Providing the thesis at the beginning of the paper helps guide readers and keeps novice writers focused.

More about ▸▸▸
Writing and refining your thesis, 141–47

A common placement for the thesis statement is at the end of the introduction—this is the *funnel* introduction. Another possibility is to hold the thesis until the end of the essay so that the essay leads readers inductively from evidence to main claim.

One or more of the following strategies can help you write an introduction that will make your audience want to read on:

- Begin with a vivid quotation, a compelling question, or some interesting data.
- Start with an engaging—and relevant—anecdote.
- Offer a surprising but apt definition of a key term.
- Provide needed (not obvious) background information.

- State a commonly held belief and then challenge it.
- Explain what interesting, conflicting, difficult, or misunderstood territory the essay will explore.

In the introductory paragraph that follows, the writer uses several effective strategies: She begins with a question that challenges the audience to examine some common assumptions about the topic. Then she provides background information that her readers may lack. She concludes with a thesis statement that explains why reading her text should be important to the audience.

Opening question

Answer that provides background information

Thesis

> Many people enjoy sitting down to a nice seafood dinner, but how many of those people actually stop to think about where the fish on their plate came from? With many species of wild fish disappearing because of overfishing, increasingly the answer will be a fish farm. But while fish farming can help to supply the demand, it can threaten the environment and cause problems with wild fish. It can also threaten the health of consumers by increasing the risk of disease and increasing the quantity of antibiotics consumed. In fact, as a careful and conscientious consumer, you would do well to learn the risks involved in buying and eating farm-raised fish before one winds up on your dinner plate.
>
> —Adrianne Anderson, Texas Christian University, "Aquaculture: Booming Business Fraught with Controversy"

One additional thing to note about introductions: Although brief essays may require only a one-paragraph introduction, longer texts often need more than one paragraph. While there are no hard-and-fast rules about the length of an introduction, it should be in proportion to the essay's length.

14d Developing Paragraphs

As you draft, you will develop paragraphs that are structured like mini-essays. While at first you should concentrate on getting ideas on paper (virtual or real), ultimately each paragraph should be an organic part of the whole text. A paragraph will be effective when it is all of the following:

- **Relevant.** It should support the main idea of the paper (your *thesis*) and, when possible, remind readers of what that thesis is.

- **Unified.** It should have a clear point (*topic*) and include only material that explains that point.
- **Coherent.** It should include connections among sentences so that readers will understand the relationships among your ideas.
- **Well developed.** It should supply the information your readers need to be persuaded of your point.
- **Connected.** It should begin and end in a way that shows readers its relationship to the paragraphs that precede and follow it.
- **Interesting.** It should make your readers want to move on to the next paragraph.

14e Transitioning within and between Paragraphs

Coherent paragraphs provide guideposts that point readers from one sentence to the next. These *transitional words and phrases* alert readers to the significance of what you are saying and point up the relationships among your ideas. Make sure you choose the appropriate transition for the job (a number of transitions appear in the Quick Reference box below), and vary your selection to avoid ineffective repetition.

Quick Reference — Sample Transitional Expressions

To add to an idea: again, also, and then, besides, further, furthermore, in addition, incidentally, likewise, moreover, next, still, too

To compare: alike, in the same way, like, likewise, resembling, similarly

To concede: certainly, granted, of course

To conclude: finally, in brief, in conclusion, in other words, in short, in sum, in summary, that is, to summarize

To contrast: after all, although, and yet, but, conversely, despite, difference, dissimilar, even so, even though, granted, however, in contrast, in spite of, instead, nevertheless, nonetheless, notwithstanding, on the contrary, on the other hand, otherwise, regardless, still, though, unlike, while this may be true, yet

To emphasize: after all, certainly, clearly, even, indeed, in fact, in other words, in truth, it is true, moreover, of course, undoubtedly

To indicate cause or effect: accordingly, as a result, because, consequently, hence, since, then, therefore, thus

To offer an example: as an example, for example, for instance, in other words, namely, that is, thus, to exemplify, to illustrate, specifically

14f Drafting the Conclusion

The shape of the conclusion is often what might be called an *inverted funnel:* While the introduction often starts general and then narrows to the thesis, a common strategy for the conclusion is to start out specific and then broaden out.

The purpose of the conclusion is twofold: to provide readers with a sense of closure and also a sense that reading the text was worthwhile. To achieve closure and convey the importance of the essay, try one or more of these strategies:

- Refer to the anecdote, question, or quotation with which you began.
- Summarize your findings (in long or technical projects).
- Discuss how what you have learned has changed your thinking.
- Suggest a possible solution (or solutions) to the problems raised in the text.
- Indicate additional research that needs to be conducted.
- Suggest what the reader can do.
- Leave readers with a vivid image, quotation, or anecdote.

The concluding paragraphs that follow exemplify some of the options available. Note the widely differing tones of these two conclusions.

Thesis: Although America's farmers have declined in number and importance, their philosophy and ideals live on today in the American dream.

Makes reader feel time reading was well spent by showing importance of American dream

Restates thesis (American dream = hope for greater security, opportunity)

Achieves closure by referring to introduction with mention of American dream

> The farmers of nineteenth-century America could afford to do here what they had not dared to do in the Old World: hope. This hope—for greater economic security, for more opportunity for themselves, their children, and their grandchildren—is the optimism and idealism that has carried our country forward and that, indeed, still carries us forward. Although the American dream has evolved across the centuries, it survives today and is a cornerstone of American philosophy. It is what underlies our Constitution and our laws, and it is a testimony to the vision of the farmers who founded this nation.
>
> —Leonard Lin, University of Southern California, "The Middle Class Farmers and the American Philosophy"

All the same, if a cure were found, would I take it? In a minute. I may be a cripple, but I'm only occasionally a loony and never a saint. Anyway, in my brand of theology God doesn't give bonus points for a limp. I'd take a cure; I just don't need one. A friend who also has MS startled me once by asking, "Do you ever say to yourself, 'Why me, Lord?'" "No, Michael, I don't," I told him, "because whenever I try, the only response I can think of is 'Why not?'" If I could make a cosmic deal, who would I put in my place? What in my life would I give up in exchange for sound limbs and a thrilling rush of energy? No one. Nothing. I might as well do the job myself. Now that I'm getting the hang of it.

Ends with a series of questions (one embedded in a quotation)

Achieves closure by answering questions

—Nancy Mairs, "On Being a Cripple"
(*Plain Text: Essays,* Tucson: U Arizona P, 1986)

14g Drafting Responsibly

One more aspect of writing to keep in mind while you are drafting is *writing responsibly*. Because writing is so challenging and because so much is often riding on the success of writing projects, it is easy for other objectives (getting an A, impressing the boss, looking clever to friends, finishing the task quickly) to get in the way of fulfilling your responsibilities as a writer. At the drafting stage, ask yourself the following questions to make sure you have worked responsibly so far:

- Have I done enough research to answer my research question without making too many assumptions?
- Have I acknowledged any counterevidence in my draft?
- Have I documented any sources I have referred to in my draft, whether quoted, paraphrased, summarized, or reproduced (images and other media)?
- Have I avoided misrepresenting my sources?

More about ▸▸▸
Introducing counter-evidence, 150–52, 174–77
Citing your sources and avoiding plagiarism, 106–19

Sample Student Essay: First Draft

The first draft of Erin Buksbaum's essay on social networking sites follows. Note that in this draft Buksbaum does not worry about polished writing or even perfect grammar and spelling. She knows she can make necessary alterations as she revises. For now, her focus is on getting her ideas down in a logical order and on supporting her thesis

▸▸▸Additional samples from Erin Buksbaum:
Freewriting, 24–31
Revised thesis, 144–47
Outlines, 153–57

More about ▸▸▸
Integrating visuals, 207–15

with evidence. Note, too, that Buksbaum includes a place for a screen capture from a social networking site. Although she has not selected the particular capture she will use, she wisely builds a place for this major element into her earliest draft.

Is Social Networking a Serious Danger?

The internet has changed the way people communicate and interact with each other forever. Social networking sites let users create a personalized web profile, meet new people with common interests, organize clubs, plan gatherings, promote bands or movies—the possibilities for communication are nearly endless. But there are risks involved. The immediate access of these sites are easily exploited. (Remember the teenage girl who killed herself because of a mean message from a boy she liked—really from a friend's mom?) While social networking sites allow for exciting new forms of communication, they also open new avenues for privacy violations and other social mischief.

The center of the social networking experience is the user's profile. The user's profile can be thought of as personalized web pages. Profiles usually include basic personal information such as a user's name, age, current school, and Zodiac sign. They also usually include lists of the user's "favorites": favorite books, songs, bands, and movies. More sophisticated users also post animations, videos, and Flash movies on their profiles. People really push the technical envelope in their profiles, and it's very impressive.

[INSERT SCREENCAPTURE HERE.]

While it sounds like harmless fun, what people post in their profiles can be extremly dangerous. User profiles allow any other member of the social network to learn personal details of that user. In other words: If you have a profile, anyone else in the network can see what you are like. That's fine for users who are experienced using the internet, and know to keep certain key details hidden. However, many children post details that make it easy for others to track them down offline. Considering how open a site like MySpace.com is, this is a serious problem.

Photographs are another key feature of social networking sites. Photographs are an extremely popular element in most user profiles. The internet is a visual medium, after all. Hence, most profiles include many, many pictures. Usually, users post photographs of themselves, their friends, or their pets. But the prevalence of photographs creates its own set of problems. Children may see images that are not appropriate for their age group. Also, photographs can be easily downloaded and hence easily misused. When you post your face on the internet, you lose all control over what happens to it.

Perhaps the most powerful part of social networking sites, though, is their capacity for user interaction. Using a "Search" feature, you can find a user who likes the same band, or who lives in the same area, or who is the same age. Then you can send them a message or post a note on their profile. It's that easy. But while most users are just looking for new friends, some might have darker purposes. Criminals like stalkers and pedophiles have been known to use social networking sites to track down targets.

There is no way to reverse the internet revolution, even if we wanted to. MySpace, Facebook, and other such sites are here to stay. So, users need to be careful. A good rule of thumb is to never post something online you wouldn't to appear in a major newspaper. While you might not realize it, the internet offers that level of access to the outside world. While social networking sites offer exciting new paths of communication between people the world over, these new rewards also come with new risks.

14h Drafting Collaboratively

Drafting collaboratively can be a difficult process to manage, but it can also be rewarding and creative. The following principles will help keep the experience a positive one:

- If possible, limit group size to three or four participants. Smaller groups can reach the "critical mass" needed for creativity without as many management difficulties (such as finding a time to meet) that larger groups face.
- Each member of the group should have an opportunity to contribute to the draft. Make an effort to restrain overbearing members and to encourage reluctant participants.

More about ▸▸▸
Developing topics collaboratively, 9–10
Using wikis to take notes, 93–96
Collaboration and source citation, 117–19
Outlining collaboratively, 153–57

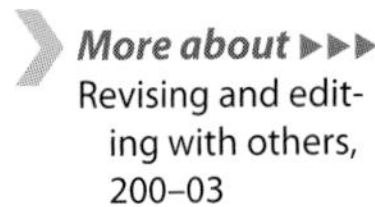
More about ▶▶▶
Revising and editing with others, 200–03

- Treat everyone's writing (and the writers themselves) respectfully. Some group members may be more skilled than others, but insightful ideas can be coaxed from initially unimpressive material.
- Make sure everyone has a copy of the latest draft, the current schedule, and a to-do list following each session.

A Final Thought

All writers, even professionals, write first drafts that do not quite come together. Recognizing this fact and continuing to write in spite of a first draft's shortcomings can prepare you to identify what is valuable when you revise and edit.

15 Entering Conversations and Supporting Your Claims

IN THIS CHAPTER

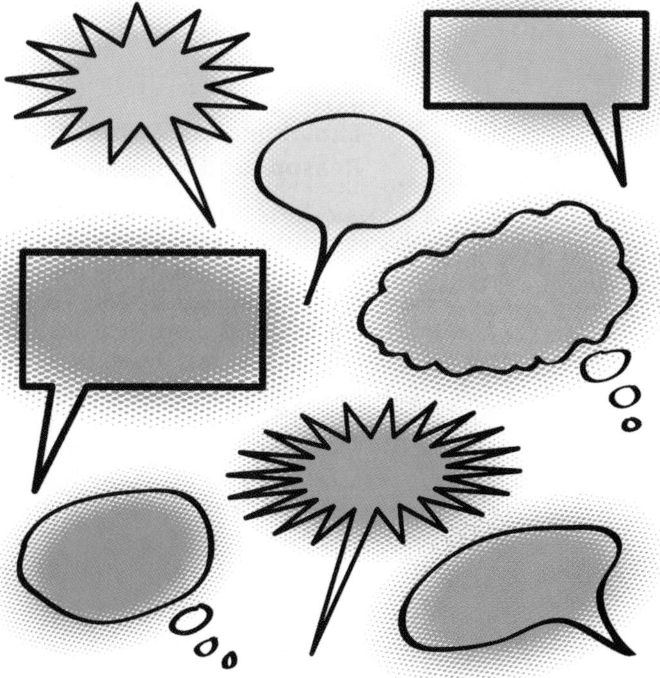

People often speak of "proving" an argument they are making: "I need evidence to prove my thesis." You may already have written an argument to prove a belief you held. Most of the research assignments you receive in college, however, have a different objective: They are intended to help you *explore a topic* and then, based on what you learn, *make a claim*. In this model of forming an argument, you do not know what your claim is until you have studied the evidence.

More about ▸▸▸
Exploring your topic, 24–31
Evidence, 174–77
Counterevidence, 150–52, 174–77

Writers of the first type of argument look only for evidence that supports their claim, and that is usually all they present. This model is familiar in advertising, politics, and propaganda. Writers of the second type of argument include both evidence and counterevidence for their claims. Exploring their topics means including all perspectives and then explaining why, despite mixed evidence, their claim is believable. In this model, writers are not solely persuaders but are also participants in a conversation. They explore with others—with their sources and their audience—the issues and possible answers surrounding their topics.

15a Explaining and Supporting Your Ideas: Reasons and Evidence

If popes or presidents say something is true, many people believe them, even if they offer no explanation, because people trust these speakers. Popes and presidents (and many others, as well) carry great authority among large groups of people.

Your authority is probably much more limited. Your friends, family, and co-workers may respect you and consider you very knowledgeable, but even they may want some explanation for what you claim is true. Even presidents and popes provide evidence for their claims when they want to be especially persuasive.

Such explanations are at the heart of researched arguments. It is not enough to say that something is true; you must also explain its truth to your readers by offering *reasons* and *evidence.*

Offering reasons for your thesis

More about ▸▸▸
Thesis, 141–47

Why do you believe your thesis and the other claims you make in your researched writing? You may not be able to answer this question easily; it may require reflection. Write down your reasons as you think of them. Make as long a list as possible, even if you think some of your answers are trivial. "I believe we should invest more money in diabetes research because my uncle has been diagnosed with the disease" may not be very persuasive to others, but it is to you. It is one of the reasons for your claim, so write it down. You may be able to use it as an illustration or anecdote in your paper.

Providing evidence to support your claims

To support the claim that your thesis makes, you will need to supply not only reasons but also evidence that will make your claims persuasive to others. There are many types of evidence; here are some of the most common:

- Facts
- Statistics
- Expert testimony
- Observations
- Examples
- Case studies
- Anecdotes
- Textual passages

Tailor the type of evidence you offer to the reasons you supply, as well as to the rhetorical situation (purpose, audience, context, and genre) of the text you are writing. The outline for Erin Buksbaum's essay in chapter 13, for example, indicates that while social networking sites have a lot of enjoyable components, they also carry with them some significant risks for users. By highlighting the issue of risk, Buksbaum takes into consideration the possibility that her audience might also use *Facebook* and be unaware of the dangers.

More about ▸▸▸
Analyzing the rhetorical situation, 38–40

In support of her claim, Buksbaum includes a discussion of user profiles, the central component of social networking sites like *MySpace,* and how these profiles open the door for privacy violations. The evidence she selected was a series of facts about what profiles commonly reveal: the user's name, age, school, and other personal details that could be ill-used. Later in her paper, she notes that criminals have often used social networking sites to identify potential victims. As evidence, she cites the existence of *MyCrimeSpace.com,* a website dedicated to documenting crimes that involve social networking sites.

More about ▸▸▸
Writing in the social, natural, and physical sciences, 226–29
Writing in the humanities, 222–26

▸▸▸Samples from Erin Buksbaum:
Freewriting, 24–31
Revised thesis, 144–47
Outlines, 149–50, 153–57
First draft, 170–71

In a laboratory report for a science class (a quite different disciplinary context than Buksbaum's English course), you are likely to use evidence from your own observations, as well as the observations others have made in their research. In a paper for an economics course, you will probably use statistics, as well as expert testimony, examples, and case studies to show relationships among economic forces. In an analysis of a work of literature, you would use excerpts from the literary work to support your claims, as well as quotations from experts on that work or on the literary theory you are using as the basis of your analysis.

Writing Responsibly **Made-up "Evidence"**

In May 2005, a stem cell expert resigned his position at Seoul National University following revelations by the journal *Nature* that his laboratory had falsified data. Hwang Woo Suk's case is not an isolated one: In 2002, for example, Bell Laboratories fired star researcher Jan Hendrik Schon for falsifying data. Commentators have noted that competition was a factor in these cases: The desire for acclaim and advancement had become more important than the desire for truth.

The highly competitive academic environment may tempt you, too, to make up "facts" to support a thesis in a paper. It is easy to alter data, invent statistics or quotations, or manipulate an image so that it "shows" what you want it to. Resist the temptation: the short-term benefits are not worth it. Not only are you likely to get caught—fabricated evidence often *sounds* fake—but you would also be sacrificing the opportunity to learn something about your topic and about the writing process.

Incorporating the counterevidence to your claims

More about ▶▶▶ Counterevidence, 150–52

Advertising almost always suppresses counterevidence. Shampoo ads, for example, tell you the benefits of the product, but not its shortcomings. The shampoo may eliminate dandruff, but it may also make your hair dry and brittle—you are likely to find only the positive information in the ad. In recent years, government regulations and public pressure have brought counterevidence into ads for potentially dangerous products such as tobacco and alcohol.

Academic writing, on the other hand, usually benefits from the inclusion of counterevidence. The purpose of most academic writing is not to sell products but to explore and explain ideas. Demonstrating that you have considered all sides of a thorny problem and have come to a reasonable resolution of it requires that you include counterevidence.

To develop the counterevidence for a researched argument, ask what doubts you have about your thesis. Have you included these doubts in your project? Reasons for including counterevidence in an academic argument are to demonstrate the complexity of the issue you are addressing and to allow your audience to form its own well-informed opinions. For example, Amy Ehret offers this paragraph of counterevidence, assessing the possible shortcomings of her research:

> Limitations of this study include the small sample size (n = 54) with the majority of participants being white female college students. The

> study is not an equal representation of the university's population or the general population. There are very few native English speaking minorities present in the study. Because the sample is quite young (college students), it is difficult to generalize these findings with those from an older and more varied sample. Results containing older participants may be dramatically different from those of this study. In general, students may have more experience and access to computers and internet-related activities.
>
> —Amy Ehret, Illinois State University, "Navigational Layout and User Preferences in Internet Privacy Notice Design"

Do not worry that your counterevidence will overwhelm your evidence. You can deal with that concern in two ways. First, be sure that you not only offer both evidence and counterevidence but also explain why you believe the evidence to be more persuasive than the counterevidence. You need not give counterevidence the same amount of space as evidence within the project.

More about ▸▸▸ Organizing your project, 148–59

Second, think about the organization of your material. If you place counterevidence at the end of your project, that is what your audience will have in mind as they reflect on what you have written. Instead, place the counterevidence toward the beginning of the project. At the beginning, it follows your introduction, which identifies your topic and suggests the position you are taking on that topic (your thesis). Immediately after the introduction, acknowledge that there are other perspectives on this topic that the audience should take into account. Then explain the counterevidence. Finally, say that you nevertheless believe your thesis because . . .—and begin to present your evidence.

15b Using Visuals as Support

More about ▸▸▸ Designing your project, 204–17

Visuals can offer crucial support in college research projects as examples, explanations of processes, or displays of factual or statistical data. Remember that in academic writing, all visuals must contribute to your argument, not merely ornament the text.

Information graphics, such as *tables, bar graphs, pie charts, line graphs, flowcharts, timelines,* and *maps,* convey complex data efficiently. Each type of information graphic has certain advantages in conveying specific types of data or relationships among data. Information and concepts that require long passages of text to explain

Quick Reference: Matching Visual Evidence to Claims

- **Tables** are most effective at displaying large amounts of data that readers may want to examine in detail.
- **Pie charts** convey divisions in a single entity that add up to 100 percent.
- **Bar graphs** compare two or more variables.
- **Line graphs** show changes among variables over time.
- **Diagrams** help readers visualize something difficult to describe in words.
- **Maps** represent geographic locations and spatial data.
- **Drawings** can capture a setting, and they can portray your idea of possible scenarios.
- **Cartoons** can simplify a concept or can ridicule a person or situation.
- **Photographs** can offer concrete illustrations, provide readers with a reference point, or show change over time.
- **Screenshots** can offer illustrations of electronic resources like websites and software.
- **Movie stills** can capture a moment for discussion and analysis, offer a concrete example, or, in a series, show a process.

If you are using multiple media to present your research, the types of illustrations you can use expand to include the following:

- **Animations,** which can bring your graphics to life.
- **Video clips,** which can illustrate a process, offer an example, or document a performance.
- **Sound files,** which can make musical notation come alive, provide an example in an analysis of a musical work, or document a performance.

Writing Responsibly: Exploitative Images

When using images in your academic work, refrain from including images that may be seen as emotionally manipulative of the reader, as well as those that might be emotionally exploitative of those whom they depict. As you review the images you have selected, think about whether they respectfully depict their subjects and how those subjects might feel about the use of the images.

can often be conveyed quickly through information graphics. Other types of visuals—such as *drawings, cartoons, photographs, screenshots,* and *movie stills*—capture and evoke emotion, image, and relationship. When drafting visuals, consider which types best suit your purposes. For instance, a project on body language and presidential speeches would benefit greatly from photos illustrating the differences in body language between presidents delivering bad news and presidents offering strategic plans. Use the Quick Reference box above to determine which kinds of visuals might enhance your project.

EXERCISE 15.1 Thinking about Visuals as Evidence

For your research project, gather or create possible visuals. How would you use these visuals—as ornament or as evidence for your claims? What kinds of evidence does each visual provide?

15c Weaving It All Together like an Expert

When you have figured out your thesis, reasons for believing it, and evidence for it, you still have the challenge of weaving everything together. Evaluation, analysis, and synthesis are the tools you will need for that job. *Evaluation* is your own assessment of a source—its credibility, originality, and relevance to your research. *Analysis* is your dissection of a text into its component parts and interpretation of its meaning. *Synthesis* is the integration of the ideas you have gleaned from sources with your own insights or with ideas from other sources.

Evaluating

Before you begin taking notes, evaluate your sources to determine whether they are likely to be reliable and pertinent to your research. Evaluation involves identifying and judging the credibility of the author or authors, identifying and examining who published the source, and assessing how much of the source is pertinent to your research. Are you drawing only from a small portion of the source, or is the entire source relevant to your work? The difference is important to both you and your readers. It is all right to draw on sources in which only small passages are pertinent to your research. But you also want sources that centrally address what you are investigating; otherwise, your research becomes a collection of "sound bites"—tiny snippets—on the topic. Your readers, too, will want to know whether you (and your text) are in a substantial conversation with a source or whether you are drawing on only a small portion of that source.

More about ▸▸▸
Evaluating sources, 20–23
Evaluating information, 80–92

Analyzing

Analyze your sources carefully, figuring out what they are saying, how they support their position, and whether their position is reasonable. Be alert for logical fallacies. Think, too, about how much a source is in conversation with other sources. Does the author seem well read on the topic?

More about ▸▸▸
Analyzing sources, 20–23

Synthesizing ideas and information

More about ▶▶▶ Synthesizing sources, 20–23

As you conduct research, you may notice that information in one source supports ideas in another source. You may also recognize areas of agreement (or disagreement) among sources and draw conclusions of your own about which sources are more persuasive, and why. This is synthesis, and it is the crucial step in moving from simply reciting other writers' ideas to writing a research project.

▶▶▶Sample student research project: "Holy Underground Comics, Batman!" by Lydia Nichols, 278–89

When Lydia Nichols was writing her research paper comparing conventional comics with underground comics, she found the Comic Book Code in one source, and examples of comics that adhered to the code or that suffered as a result of the code in others. She synthesized that information to write her text. In the paragraph below, she weaves together evidence from two sources with her own ideas to support her claim:

Nichol's claim | Signal phrase (identifies credentials) | Supporting evidence (paraphrase) | Source citation | Signal phrase (identifies credentials) | Signal phrase (quote introduction and paraphrase) | Supporting evidence (quotation) | Supporting evidence (analysis of illustration) | Supporting evidence (illustration)

> Underground artists not only push the envelope in terms of content—they also employ innovative and experimental visual devices, earning critical praise for breaking away from traditional comic layouts in favor of more experimental, cinematic perspectives. Artists such as Daniel Clowes have suggested that in some senses, comic art can be more evocative than film, especially in the use of nonlinear storytelling techniques (Hignite 18). *New York Times* columnist John Hodgman agrees: Discussing a moment of existential crisis in Kevin Huizenga's *Ganges #1,* he writes, "I have never seen any film . . . that gets at that frozen moment when we suddenly feel our mortality, when God is seen or denied, as effectively as a comic panel" ("Comics Chronicle"). Artist Chris Ware manipulates the borders and frames in his comics so extensively that even reading his works can feel like an art to be mastered (see Fig. 5). The demands his comics place on the reader create a powerful interactive dynamic between viewer and artist, one that is rarely found outside of a museum—and even more rarely in the pages of superhero titles.

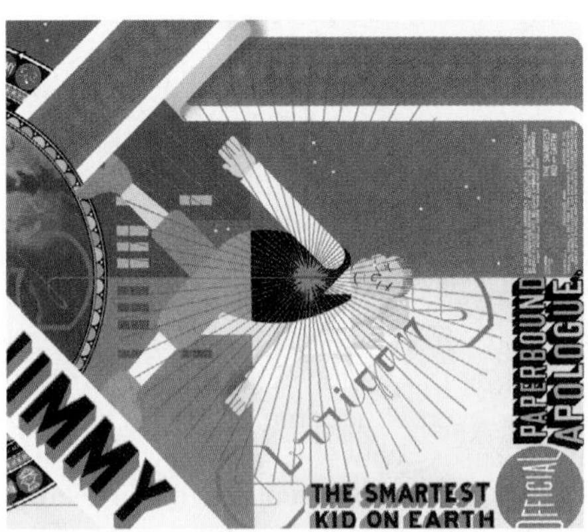

Fig. 5. Cover from Chris Ware's *Jimmy Corrigan: The Smartest Kid on Earth* (New York: Pantheon, 2000). Critically acclaimed *Jimmy Corrigan* comics experiment boldly with visual storytelling techniques, pushing the genre's limitations and making the reader work to achieve understanding.

Figure number

Figure title (including source information)

Figure caption

When synthesizing sources, ask yourself what your sources have in common and how they differ, using your thesis as a lens. Pay attention, too, to your reactions to your sources: Your prior reading and knowledge are an integral part of the equation. Synthesis is a process of connecting the dots: establishing connections among the sources you have consulted and placing them in conversation with each other and with your own thoughts.

15d Quoting, Paraphrasing, and Summarizing

Notice that in the sample paragraph on p. 180, Lydia Nichols uses a combination of quotation, paraphrase, and her own ideas. She *quotes* Hodgman because the passage is especially vivid. She *paraphrases* Hignite because she wants to borrow his argument and reasons and because it is easier to incorporate the information after she has put it

More about ▸▸▸
Quoting, paraphrasing, or summarizing, 109–11

into her own words. Had she wanted to briefly relate another source's argument, she would have used *summary*.

Signaling sources

More about ▶▶▶ Signal phrases, 109–11

To incorporate borrowed material smoothly into your prose, introduce it with a signal phrase. A *signal phrase* couples the name of the writer from whom you are borrowing with a verb that conveys your sense of the writer's intent. (A list of sample signal verbs appears in the Quick Reference box on p. 183.)

In choosing your signal verb, consider the *attitude* or *position* of the writer you are quoting. Is the writer making a claim? Is she or he agreeing or disagreeing, or even conceding a point? Or is the writer's position neutral? In most cases, you will probably choose a neutral verb, such as "writes," "says," or "comments." (In the example paragraph above, Nichols uses "have suggested" and "agrees.")

Where possible, go beyond these neutral verbs to indicate the writer's attitude:

> Oscar Wilde quipped, "A poet can survive everything but a misprint."

For the Wilde quotation above, "quipped" (which means "uttered a witty remark") is clearly appropriate, given the cleverness of the sentence quoted. "Snarled," on the other hand, would not be appropriate: Although Wilde's quip may have an edge to it, few would agree that the comment conveys the anger or viciousness associated with the verb "snarl." Avoid ascribing intentions to a writer that cannot clearly be inferred from the text.

To maintain your reader's interest, vary the signal words you use. You may also vary your placement of the signal phrase:

> E. M. Forster asked, "How do I know what I think until I see what I say?"
>
> "How do I know what I think," E. M. Forster asked, "until I see what I say?"
>
> "How do I know what I think until I see what I say?" E. M. Forster asked.

Not only should you identify the source (through a signal phrase or in-text citation, and an entry in your list of works cited or reference list), but you also have a responsibility to contextualize the borrowed information. Briefly indicate the source's authority and the role the quotation, example, or statistic plays in the original source. In the ex-

Quick Reference — Signal Verbs

Neutral Signal Verbs

Analyzes	Interprets
Comments	Introduces
Compares	Notes
Concludes	Observes
Contrasts	Records
Describes	Remarks
Discusses	Reports
Explains	Says
Expresses	Shows
Focuses on	States
Illustrates	Thinks
Indicates	Writes

Signal Verbs That Indicate:

Claim/Argument

Alleges	Demonstrates
Argues	Finds
Asserts	Holds
Assumes	Maintains
Believes	Points out
Charges	Proposes
Claims	Recommends
Confirms	Suggests
Contends	

Concession

Acknowledges
Admits
Concedes
Grants

Agreement

Agrees
Concurs
Confirms
Supports

Disagreement

Complains	Disputes
Contradicts	Questions
Criticizes	Refutes
Denies	Rejects
Disagrees	Warns

cerpt from her paper that follows, Lydia Nichols not only indicates the credentials of her source but also places the quotation in context:

> Artists such as Scott McCloud have changed this perception of comic books by offering a broader definition of what a comic is. According to McCloud, comics are "juxtaposed pictorial and other images in a deliberate sequence" (12). This definition includes not only what one might find in the latest Spider-Man comic, but also all the experimental work that McCloud and his underground colleagues are creating.

Indicates source's purpose

Establishes McCloud's authority

Integrating quotations

In some cases, a sentence you want to quote may contain some content that is irrelevant to your essay. In the example on p. 180, Nichols omits a few words from the Hodgman quotation because they do not help her make her point. She uses ellipses to signal where the deletion occurred. As long as the omission does not significantly change the meaning of the passage and is indicated with ellipses, such cuts are acceptable. In fact, as long as writers do not significantly change the source's meaning, they may do any of the following to fit the borrowed material more fluidly into their prose:

- Add or change words for clarity
- Change capitalization
- Change grammar
- Remove nonessential words
- Indicate by inserting "sic" that the original writer made a mistake

All changes, with the exception of replacing words with ellipses, should be placed in square brackets.

Consider this example:

▶▶▶Sample student research project: "Holy Underground Comics, Batman!" by Lydia Nichols, 278–89

Quotation integrated into student text	Original quotation
Certain portions of the code were incredibly specific and controlling, such as the rule that forbade "[t]he letters of the word 'crime' on a comics magazine . . . [to] be appreciably greater in dimension than the other words contained in the title" (qtd. in "Good Shall Triumph over Evil").	"The letters of the word 'crime' on a comics magazine shall never be appreciably greater in dimension than the other words contained in the title."

In this passage, Nichols changes a capital letter to a lowercase letter, adds a word ("[to]"), and omits a couple of words ("shall never") to fit the quotation into her sentence structure. But the overall meaning of the passage remains the same.

Imagine, however, that Nichols had made these changes instead:

Quotation integrated into student text	**Original quotation**
Certain portions of the code allowed some flexibility. Consider, for example, the rule that allowed "[t]he letters of the word 'crime' on a comics magazine . . . [to] be appreciably greater in dimension than the other words contained in the title" (qtd. in "Good Shall Triumph over Evil").	"The letters of the word 'crime' on a comics magazine shall never be appreciably greater in dimension than the other words contained in the title."

Clearly this alteration of the quotation is *not* acceptable because it changes the sense of the quotation by leaving out the word "never."

EXERCISE **15.2** Altering Quotations

Read the passage below and the quotations that follow it. Then, circle the numbers of those that alter the original material fairly, and cross through the numbers of those that change the meaning of the original material.

> Paul Revere was half French and half English, and always entirely American. He was second-generation American on one side, and old-stock American on the other, and cherished both beginnings. He was the product of a Puritan City on a Hill and a lusty, brawling Atlantic seaport, both in the same American town. He thought of himself as an artisan and a gentleman without the slightest sense of contradiction—a new American attitude toward class.
>
> —David Hackett Fischer, *Paul Revere's Ride* (New York: Oxford, 1994, p. 5)

1. Because Revere was "half French and half English," he was troubled, asserts Fischer, by being born an American.
2. Fischer comments that Revere "was the product of [both] a Puritan City on a Hill and a lusty, brawling Atlantic seaport."
3. Although "[h]e thought of himself as an artisan," explains Fischer, Revere aspired to the status of gentleman.
4. Fischer points out that Revere embodied "a new American attitude toward class."
5. Being "second-generation American on one side" was not sufficient for most old-stock Americans to trust Revere's loyalty, suggests Fischer.

Make It Your Own

For a research paper that you have drafted, show how you have integrated supporting evidence from sources by listing:

1. Three different sentences in your paper that demonstrate how you varied your choice of signal words
2. Three other sentences in your paper that demonstrate how you provided context and identified source authors
3. Three other sentences in your paper that demonstrate how you incorporated quotations fairly into your own prose by adding, deleting, or changing words

Did you find all nine sentences in your paper? If not, consider revising to integrate supporting evidence from sources into your prose more effectively.

More about ▸▸▸
In-text citation:
MLA style, 231–45
APA style, 291–301
Chicago style, 334–51
CSE style, 361–63
Quotation, 97, 97–99, 99–105, 108–09, 109–11, 181–86
Documentation:
MLA style, 246–71
APA style, 302–16
Chicago style, 334–51
CSE style, 363–75

15e Creating Transparent, Elegant Citations

A citation names the source that you are talking with, and the other cues you provide reveal the nature of that conversation. To cite well—to go beyond simply naming the source—is to make your conversation "transparent." Your goal should be not only to name your sources, but also to make obvious how you are using them.

By breaking up your citation, putting a signal phrase at the beginning and a page citation at the end, you can show *how much* and *which parts* of your text are derived from the source. In the following example, it is clear that the first sentence is the writer's statement of her own ideas, the second is a paraphrase from the Rosenfeld source, and the third is a quotation from Rosenfeld:

The last name of the author of the source (or, in the absence of an author, the first words of the title) is identified.

Quotation marks enclose exact copying from the source.

The page from which the quotation comes is identified.

> The effects of music go beyond mere entertainment. Rosenfeld asserts that music not only brings pleasure to the soul but can also heal the body. "There may be, as yet, no empirical evidence that the cosmos sings, but the belief that music heals is old and ubiquitous" (89).

Especially if your use of a source is paraphrase without quotation, you need to show where your use of the source *ends*. The page citation in the previous example accomplishes this, but when you are using an unpaginated source, such as a web page, you have no page numbers to cite; you can provide only the author's name (or, in an anonymous source, an abbreviated title of the source). The following example clearly identifies the sources used, and it also makes clear that the last sentence is the writer's own ideas. But the parenthetical citations make the paragraph difficult to read:

> More and more people are visiting emergency rooms ("Hospital Admissions"), and more and more are receiving poor treatment (Miesel and Pines). Part of the problem is the economics of hospital admissions: Patients who are admitted through the E.R. are highly likely to be uninsured and thus a financial liability to the hospital (Miesel and Pines). Without universal health insurance, this situation is likely to continue, and with it the neglect of an increasing number of E.R. patients.

Signal phrases (source acknowledgments integrated into the sentence) make the paragraph easier to read:

More about ▶▶▶ Signal phrases, 109–111

> Statistics published on the web page "Hospital Admissions" make it clear that more and more people are visiting emergency rooms. In Miesel and Pines's description, more and more of these people are receiving poor treatment. Part of the problem is the economics of hospital admissions: Miesel and Pines explain that patients who are admitted through the E.R. are highly likely to be uninsured and thus a financial liability to the hospital. Without universal health insurance, this situation is likely to continue, and with it the neglect of an increasing number of E.R. patients.

However, in the example above it is no longer clear where the writer stops relating information from his sources and begins to state his own ideas. That problem can be remedied with phrases such as *I believe* or *in my opinion:*

> Statistics published on the web page "Hospital Admissions" make it clear that more and more people are visiting emergency rooms. In Miesel and Pines's description, more and more of these people are receiving poor treatment. Part of the problem is the economics of hospital admissions: Miesel and Pines explain that patients who are admitted through the E.R. are highly likely to be uninsured and thus a financial liability to the hospital. It is my opinion that without universal health insurance, this situation is likely to continue, and with it the neglect of an increasing number of E.R. patients.

There are more sophisticated ways to accomplish the task. You might, for example, refer to your research rather than yourself:

> Statistics published on the web page "Hospital Admissions" make it clear that more and more people are visiting emergency rooms. In Miesel and Pines's description, more and more of these people are receiving poor treatment. Part of the problem is the economics of hospital admissions: Miesel and Pines explain that patients who are admitted through the E.R. are highly likely to be uninsured and thus a financial liability to the hospital. My research convinces me that without universal health insurance, this situation is likely to continue, and with it the neglect of an increasing number of E.R. patients.

Or you might speak in the first person plural, drawing your reader into the argument:

> Statistics published on the web page "Hospital Admissions" make it clear that more and more people are visiting emergency rooms. In Miesel and Pines's description, more and more of these people are receiving poor treatment. Part of the problem is the economics of hospital admissions: Miesel and Pines explain that patients who are admitted through the E.R. are highly likely to be uninsured and thus a financial liability to the hospital. We cannot escape the conclusion that without universal health insurance, this situation is likely to continue, and with it the neglect of an increasing number of E.R. patients.

You could also comment on the source or its information:

> Statistics published on the web page "Hospital Admissions" make it clear that more and more people are visiting emergency rooms. In Miesel and Pines's description, more and more of these people are receiving poor treatment. Part of the problem is the economics of hospital admissions: Miesel and Pines explain that patients who are admitted through the E.R. are highly likely to be uninsured and thus a financial liability to the hospital. Such information makes it clear that without universal health insurance, this situation is likely to continue, and with it the neglect of an increasing number of E.R. patients.

A Final Thought

Elegant citation goes beyond source transparency. It also invites the source and the reader into the conversation by providing information about the source or the writer, or both.

This chapter began with the notion that research writers should be open to hearing what sources on their topics have to say—that the conversation is worth having. Through signaling, citing, quoting, synthesizing, and documenting, you can ethically convey this conversation and situate yourself within it. By relating traces of the conversation you have had with your sources, you can create a sophisticated, readable document that readers are likely to trust.

16 Revising, Editing, and Proofreading

As writers chisel meaning from their first words and sentences, they erase and redraw parts of the broad outline, carve out details to craft meaning, and refine their workmanship by sanding down rough edges. Only through revising, editing, and proofreading carefully can a writer transform a rough-hewn draft into a polished work.

REVISING GLOBALLY: LEARNING TO RE-SEE

Revising globally means looking at the big picture to address issues such as purpose, audience, context, genre, and ethical responsibilities. The first step toward assessing these aspects of your writing is to gain perspective by distancing yourself from your work.

16a Gaining Perspective

Writers feel a sense of ownership toward the texts they compose. Ownership helps writers develop a commitment to the ideas they express. But during revision, too much ownership can keep a writer from making necessary changes. To gain objectivity in your writing, draw on techniques like these:

- **Allow time between drafts.** A few days or even a few hours between drafts can give you perspective.

Quick Reference **Revising Globally**

	Focus (topic/thesis/purpose)	Audience
Introduction	Does my introduction identify my topic? Does it indicate my purpose and attitude toward my topic? Does it convey my main claim or research question?	Does my introduction provide needed background information? Will my readers find my introduction engaging or compelling?
Body Paragraphs	Is each body paragraph relevant to my thesis? Is the evidence in each paragraph relevant to the paragraph's topic?	Will my readers need more (or less) information? Will my readers be receptive, or, if not, how can I win them over? Is my language at the right level and tone?
Conclusion	Does my conclusion make my topic's importance clear? Does my thesis statement appear in my conclusion if it is *not* in the introduction?	Does my conclusion give readers something to think about or supply a necessary summary? Does my conclusion provide readers with a satisfying feeling of completion?

- **Clear your mind.** If you cannot allow much time between completing your first draft and beginning to revise, do something to clear your mind—go for a run, play a quick game, or read something unrelated to your topic.
- **Learn from other readers.** Having others read and react to your draft will give you a sense of what your text is (and is not) communicating.
- **Analyze the work of a fellow writer.** Most tutors and teachers will tell you that they learn as much from the coaching experience as do the people whom they coach.
- **Listen to your draft being read aloud.** Every time your reader stumbles, pauses, or has to reread a passage, mark the spot. Then, figure out what caused the interruption, and revise accordingly.
- **Reverse-outline your draft.** Locate the main idea and key supporting points of each drafted paragraph and arrange them

More about ▸▸▸
Organizing your project, 148–59
Genre, 38–40
Context, 38–40

	Organization (cohesion/unity)	Development (reasons/support)
Introduction	Is my thesis statement or research question placed so that readers will recognize it? Does my introduction prepare readers for what follows?	Does my introduction hint at the reasons I will offer to support my thesis?
Body Paragraphs	Does my organizational pattern suit my reasons and evidence? Does each paragraph lead logically to the next? Have I provided logical transitions between paragraphs?	Are the reasons and evidence I supply relevant? Do I provide enough evidence? Is the evidence compelling? Do I credit my sources?
Conclusion	Is my conclusion logically organized? Do all the sentences fit together and support the topic sentence? Does my conclusion grow logically out of my introduction and body paragraphs?	Do I avoid introducing new supporting evidence in my conclusion?

into an outline. If any sections seem unconnected to the thesis or to the sections before or after, reorganize.

- **Compare texts in the target context and genre.** When writing in an unfamiliar context or genre, reading professional texts can help you see what does and does not work in your own writing.

16b Revising Your Draft

Once you have gained some perspective, you are ready to start revising. Work through each paragraph considering issues of *focus, audience, organization,* and *development.* Be sure to read through to the end before making any changes, and remember to revise before editing. Avoid the temptation to look at your spelling, grammar, and mechanics before adding, cutting, reorganizing, and making other big-picture, or global, changes.

Focus: Is your thesis the consistent focus of your draft, and does your draft fulfill your purpose and assignment?

More about ▶▶▶
Drafting a thesis, 142–44
Refining your thesis, 144–47

After rereading your text, make sure that the points you make support your thesis. Because writers often discover and develop their ideas as they draft, the draft thesis may not describe the project's real main idea (often, the true thesis appears in the conclusion of the first draft). This might mean you should adjust your reasons and evidence to your thesis. More frequently it means you should revise your thesis to match the reasons and evidence you offer in your draft.

When revising, make sure, too, that your draft fulfills the assignment. If you were asked to analyze a work of literature, check to see that you have not merely summarized it; if you were instructed to argue for or against corporal punishment in elementary school, be sure you have adopted a clear position and not merely repeated the arguments on both sides.

Audience: Is your draft appropriate for your readers?

More about ▶▶▶
Audience, 38–40
Reasons and evidence, 174–77

Consider how your readers will react to your text. Will they be receptive to your topic and your approach to it? If not, how can you win them over?

More about ▶▶▶
Drafting the introduction, 165–66
Developing paragraphs, 166–67
Transitioning within and between paragraphs, 167
Drafting the conclusion, 168–69

Think about your *introduction.* Will it draw your readers into your text? Next, consider the *reasons* and *evidence* you supply in your body paragraphs. Are they likely to persuade your readers, given their background, interest level, and attitude toward your topic? Is the *language* appropriate to your audience? An academic or business audience will expect a more formal tone but will not need you to define specialized terms; a general audience, however, may be more engaged by a casual tone and may need specialized terms clearly defined. Finally, consider your *conclusion.* A conclusion should leave readers with a feeling of closure. For a long or complex text, readers may need you to summarize your findings in your concluding paragraphs. If you want your readers to take action, offer them a plan.

Organization: Is your draft coherent and unified?

More about ▶▶▶
Unity and coherence, 158–60
Transitions, 167

Rereading your text may have alerted you to problems with organization. When revising, make sure that your essay is both unified and coherent. In a *unified* essay, all the paragraphs support the thesis, and all the details in each paragraph support the paragraph's main idea. When revising, be prepared to delete ideas, facts, and even whole paragraphs—no matter how much you like them—if they do not support your thesis.

In a *coherent* essay, the relationship among the paragraphs is clear and logical. A text may lack coherence because the writer has not included transitional words and phrases that signal the relationships among ideas. Other texts lack coherence because the writer has omitted a step in the argument. Be sure to clarify the relationships among your paragraphs by adding or changing transitions, by tightening the logic of your argument, or both.

Development: Did you explore and support your ideas fully?

More about ▸▸▸
Relevance, 81–82
Generating ideas, 24–31
Developing paragraphs, 166–67
Finding information, 50–66, 67–79, 128–40

In rereading your text, you may have had concerns about the reasons or evidence you offered in support of your thesis. Perhaps you noticed that one of your reasons was weak or irrelevant, that you did not offer enough reasons, that the evidence you supplied was overly general, or that you just did not supply enough evidence. If you need more or better reasons or more relevant, more specific, or just more evidence, go back to the idea-generating stage or return to the library to do additional research.

You may find it possible to revise for focus, audience, organization, and development simultaneously. Most writers, though, focus on only one issue at a time.

16c Reconsidering Your Title

More about ▸▸▸
Developing a title, 164–65

Once you have revised your draft globally, revisit your title. If your thesis has changed, you will probably need to change your title. Your title should prepare your audience for what follows. In most college

> **Writing Responsibly** **The Big Picture**
>
> Another way to think about revising is to focus on your responsibilities to your *audience,* your *topic, other writers,* and *yourself:*
>
> - Have you provided your *audience* with a worthwhile reading experience?
> - Have you covered your *topic* fully and ethically?
> - Have you represented borrowed ideas accurately and acknowledged all your *sources,* whether you have quoted, summarized, or paraphrased?
> - Have you developed a voice that readers will find credible, represented your ideas clearly and powerfully, and written in a voice that reflects *your best self?*

projects, your title should accurately reflect not only the topic, but also your approach to the topic and possibly your main claim:

Note how many of these titles hint at their main claims (highlighted in blue).

Note how many of these titles use a descriptive phrase (underlined) to make their titles more specific.

Note how these titles indicate their approach (highlighted in yellow) in their titles.

- The Power of Wardrobe: An Analysis of Male Stereotype Influences
- Transcending Stereotypes in Hurston's *Their Eyes Were Watching God*
- Holy Underground Comics, Batman! Moving Away from the Mainstream
- My View from the Sidelines: A Close Reading of Gary Snyder's "Front Lines"

Here are additional tests of a title's effectiveness:

- Would you pick up this piece and read it based on its title?
- Can someone else anticipate what you will argue by reading the title? The closer the reader can come to identifying your argument based on your title, the more effective the title. Also, will readers find the title interesting?

Make It Your Own

Revise a current draft or past writing assignment considering the global issues outlined in the Quick Reference box on p. 193 or the Writing Responsibly box on p. 195.

REVISING LOCALLY: EDITING WORDS AND SENTENCES

Your writing is a reflection of you—your ideas and your attitude toward your topic and audience. Revise locally to make sure that your words and sentences convey your meaning and that together they create a persona (the writer's personality conveyed through tone and style) that is appropriate for your purpose, audience, context, and genre.

16d Choosing Your Words with Care

When revising, reconsider your word choices. Each word should reflect your intended meaning (the right *denotation*). In a project on graphic novels, for instance, "comics" would not be accurate and specific enough to discuss the subgenre of the graphic novel, and "picture books" would be inaccurate and misleading. Readers may sometimes guess your intent, but you cannot count on it, and you should not expect them to be charitable.

In addition to denotations, words carry emotional associations, or *connotations,* that color meaning and indicate the writer's attitude. When writing, think carefully about the connotations of your words. Be particularly careful with words describing groups (religious, ethnic, gender, age, sexual orientation). For example, while it may be acceptable among your friends to refer to young women as "girls" or "ladies," many women find these terms condescending. It is also inappropriate to refer to experts by their first name. Use their full names instead: Martin Luther King, Jr., instead of "Martin." Because word connotations reveal biases, writers must choose their words carefully to avoid alienating their readers.

Finally, there are three basic formality levels: formal, mid-level, and informal. Formal style is that of specialized professionals communicating in the highly specific language of their work. Mid-level formality signals professionalism without being inaccessible; some specialized jargon might be used but usually is defined. Finally, informal style is accessible to everyone. The appropriate level of formality depends on audience, context, and genre: Traditional academic research essays typically aim for mid-level formality, while a researched commentary might adopt a less formal tone, even employing slang when it helps to make a point. One of the questions to ask your instructor or to note in any models is whether it is appropriate to speak in the first ("I") or third ("this project," "the research") person.

16e Crafting Grammatically Correct, Varied, and Concise Sentences

When revising, reconsider the structure of your sentences:

1. Are they grammatically correct?
2. Are they varied in length and structure, and do they emphasize the most important information?
3. Are they as concise as they can be without sacrificing meaning or affecting style?

Writing grammatically correct sentences

In most contexts (academic and business, in particular), readers expect sentences to be formed according to the conventions of English grammar. Nongrammatical sentences may confuse, distract, or even annoy readers, so it is important to edit your prose to conform to standard written English. Handbooks and online resources can help you with editing for correctness.

Writing varied sentences

Once you are sure that your sentences are clear and correct, shape them to reflect your emphases. A good way to begin editing for style is to read your draft aloud—or better still, get a friend to read it to you. Listen to the rhythm of your sentences. Do they all sound alike? If so, your sentences probably use the same sentence structure, begin the same way, or are the same length.

To correct this problem, consider the information in your sentences. Combine related information in a single sentence, putting the most important information in the independent clause and additional information in the subordinate or dependent clause (created by using such connectors as *while, because, since, when,* and *although*). If the information is of equal weight, use compound sentence structure (connected by *and, or, nor, for, yet, but,* or *so*) to emphasize this balance. Where appropriate, use questions, commands, and exclamations for variety or emphasis.

Writing concise sentences

In addition to writing varied sentences, work to eliminate clutter. Try these strategies to revise for wordiness:

- Eliminate empty expressions (*to all intents and purposes*), intensifiers (*actually*), roundabout expressions (*due to the fact that*), and redundancies (*future plans*).
- Eliminate ineffective repetition (*Global warming threatens the world's ~~aquatic~~ fisheries.*).
- Favor the active voice (*The* [tornado completely destroyed] *~~destruction of~~ the town ~~by the tornado was complete.~~* [.]).

Writing concisely for the Web is particularly important because most users prefer pages that are easy to scan.

You may be tempted to pad a paper that is not long enough, but doing so will make it harder for your audience to finish. Instead of adding "fluff," expand your piece by searching out additional relevant information and fully explaining the significance of your evidence.

Find Out **More . . . Revising Globally and Locally**

For a different view of the revision process, visit one or more of the following sites:

Attending to Grammar, Dartmouth College
<www.dartmouth.edu/~writing/materials/student/ac_paper/grammar.shtml>

Revision: Cultivating a Critical Eye, Dartmouth College
<www.dartmouth.edu/~writing/materials/student/ac_paper/revise.shtml>

Steps for Revising Your Paper, The OWL at Purdue
<owl.english.purdue.edu/owl/resource/561/05/>

Making a personalized editing checklist

Writers make a variety of mistakes, so a personalized editing checklist can come in handy. To create one, try the following:

1. Review the last five texts that you have written, looking for errors and less-than-effective choices.
2. List the issues you found (or that your instructor marked).
3. Reorganize the list, arranging items from most to least frequent mistake.

The next time you have to produce a document, use the top five items on the list to guide your local revision. Over time, you are likely to find that you make fewer of these errors and can focus on some of your less common mistakes.

Make It **Your Own**

Create your own personalized editing checklist. Then, revise a writing project, focusing on your words and sentences.

REVISING WITH OTHERS

Writers can be touchy. We pour ourselves into our texts and worry that others might not understand or appreciate what we have written. Little wonder, then, that we often feel defensive when others read our work. Yet paradoxically, getting feedback from a real, live audience is one of the best ways to make sure readers will understand your writing, be

More about ▸▸▸
Audience, 38–40

convinced by your evidence, be persuaded by your conclusion, and form a high opinion of you as a responsible, authoritative writer.

16f Receiving Feedback

Feedback can come in many forms. In business, feedback might mean sharing your text with co-workers online or through email. In school, it usually means sharing your draft with your classmates, a consultant at a writing center, or an instructor. Whether in a business or academic context, the roles of writer and respondent carry their own responsibilities.

Understanding the writer's role

When readers respond to your text, adopt a stance that is both engaged and receptive:

- **Prepare.** Before requesting feedback, look over your project and develop specific questions and concerns for your readers to address.
- **Talk, or write in the margins.** Explain orally—or, even better, in writing directly on your text—what your goals are for the text and what problems you encountered. What are you trying to accomplish in this project, and what would you like help with?
- **Be open.** As others respond to your draft, listen instead of arguing, defending, or dismissing. If readers seem clueless or careless, figure out how you can revise the text so that even a clueless or careless reader can understand what you are trying to say.
- **Question.** If your readers are not addressing your concerns or are speaking in generalities, ask them to point to specific passages. Ask yourself what underlying issue they are trying to get at. Do not settle for a disappointing response.
- **Record.** Take notes as your readers talk. What they say may be vivid at the time, but you may be surprised by how quickly you forget the details.
- **Evaluate.** You are the person who must make the final decision about your writing. Be open to advice, but consider whether there may be a better way of solving the problem.

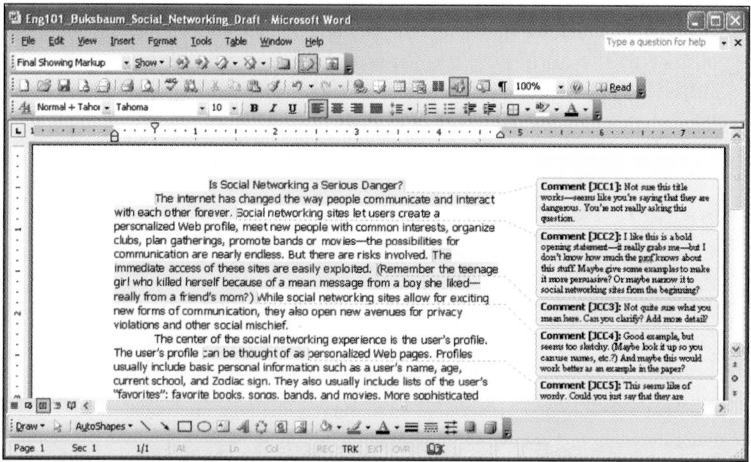

FIGURE 16.1 Electronic Peer Review If you are reviewing a peer's work electronically, remember that there is a person on the receiving end of your comments. Keep them positive, helpful, and friendly, and link them to something specific in the text, as Buksbaum's respondent has done using the Comment feature.

Understanding the reader's role

As a respondent, keep the following guidelines in mind:

- **Stay positive.** Tell the writer what is working well, along with what could be improved (Figure 16.1).
- **Talk to the writer.** Listen and respond to the writer's concerns, whether replying face-to-face or electronically.
- **Look at the big picture, but be specific.** Focus on what the writer is trying to achieve, and help her or him think about alternative strategies for achieving those ends. But back up general comments by pointing to specific passages in the text and explaining as best you can why they do or do not work for you.
- **Be a reader and a fellow writer—not a teacher, editor, or critic.** Your job is not to judge the text or rewrite it, but to provide the writer with one reader's responses to it and offer suggestions for improvements.

Work **Together**

In groups of three or four, read through a group member's draft, and use the questions in the Writing Responsibly box on p. 195 to focus on whether the writer has shown responsibility to the audience, the topic, other writers, and her- or himself. Discuss how the writer could improve the draft globally. Save editing comments for a later stage.

Make It **Your Own**

Using comments you received from a respondent, revise your draft. After completing the process, write a paragraph discussing which suggestions made the biggest difference in your revision, and why. If you did not find the review process helpful, what might you or the reader have done to make it more productive?

PROOFREADING

When you revise and edit, you concentrate on your ideas and how you have expressed them. When you proofread, you pull back from the content of the essay to concentrate on finding and correcting errors.

To proofread effectively, print out your draft, and read the hard copy sentence by sentence from the bottom up. (This will keep you from focusing on the meaning.) Placing a ruler under each line as you read it will help you catch even more errors. Mark your corrections on the printout as you read, enter them one by one, and then check to make sure that you have made each correction without introducing additional errors.

Writing **Responsibly** Beware Spelling Checkers!

While spell-check software can be very helpful in catching typos, it cannot distinguish between homonyms (*they're, there, their; it's, its*) or other frequently confused words (*lay, lie; affect, effect*). Spelling checkers may even lead you astray, suggesting words that are close to the word you mistyped (*defiant* for the misspelled *definate*) but worlds away from the word you intended (*definite*). Do not merely run your computer's spell-check software; also use a dictionary, and proofread your text carefully yourself. Only you know what you *meant* to say!

Quick Reference → A Checklist for Proofreading

Spelling

- Spell-check your project using your word processing software.
- Read through the text carefully, looking for misused words.
- Check for words you frequently confuse or misspell.

Punctuation

- Check punctuation, especially use of the comma and the apostrophe.
- Double-check that all quotations have opening and closing quotation marks and that end punctuation is correctly placed (end-punctuation placement may depend on the style guide you are using).
- Check for punctuation errors you commonly make.

Documentation

- Check that you have included in-text citations where needed (for summaries, paraphrases, quotations, or ideas you have borrowed).
- Check in-text citations against the list of works cited, reference list, or bibliography to ensure that you have included entries for all citations.
- Double-check the format of all entries in the list of works cited/reference list/bibliography against models from the style guide you are using.

More about ▸▸▸
Style guides:
MLA, 230–89
APA, 290–32
Chicago, 333–60
CSE, 361–85

A Final Thought

Taking the time to revise, edit, and proofread as three separate activities will allow you to be responsible to your readers, the topic itself, the writers of your sources, and your own writer's persona. Readers will see the traces of this work. Like good craftsmanship in other fields, the best writing happens over time with continued attention to detail.

17 Designing and Presenting Your Project

IN THIS CHAPTER

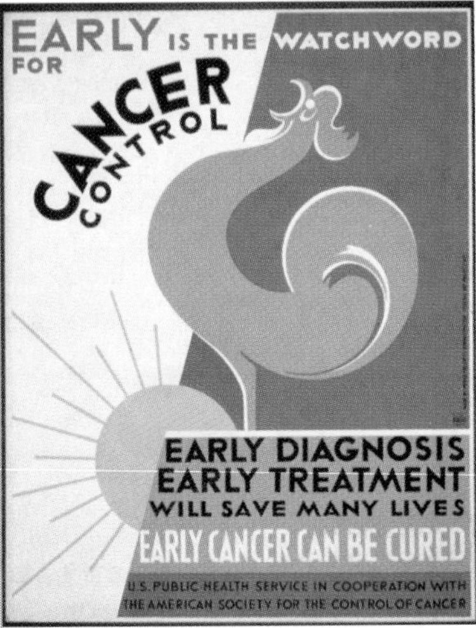

Posters like this one from 1938 rely on striking visual design for impact and meaning. To convey the idea that cancer treatment rests on early detection, its creators used strong color *contrast* to make the black text of "cancer control" stand out against its white background and the contrast of straight and curved text to add emphasis. They used *proximity* and the *repetition* of curves to pull the image of the rooster (the "early bird"), the idea of cancer control, and the positive symbol of the sun together. They used *alignment* to draw readers' eyes down the angled line, and *repetition* of the word "early" to drive home the main point of the poster. According to renowned graphic designer Robin Williams, these four principles—proximity, alignment, repetition, and contrast—are the pillars on which effective design rests.

17a Understanding Design Principles: Proximity, Alignment, Repetition, and Contrast

Williams explains how the four principles of design work:

- **Proximity** (nearness or grouping) suggests that content is related; lack of proximity (distance) suggests that content is unrelated.

Find Out **More . . . Robin Williams on Design**

For more design advice, as well as before and after makeovers for newsletters, brochures, flyers, websites, and other media, see Williams's

Robin Williams Design Workshop, 2nd ed. (with John Tollett) (Berkeley, CA: Peachpit, 2006)

Two earlier books by Williams may also prove helpful:

The Non-Designer's Design Book (Berkeley: Peachpit, 2003)

The Non-Designer's Web Book, 3rd ed. (with John Tollett) (Berkeley: Peachpit, 2005)

- **Alignment,** the arrangement of objects in a straight line (vertical, horizontal, or diagonal), creates invisible lines of connection. Centered alignment feels more conservative than left or right alignment, even dull.
- **Repetition** of a design element lends unity (oneness).
- **Contrast** among design elements calls attention through difference, highlighting one element among others.

Effective design exemplifies the four principles, directing readers to the most important information and highlighting relationships among the elements on the page or screen. Consider how the web page in Figure 17.1 uses Williams's design principles to highlight important elements and link related content.

17b Planning Your Design Project

To figure out how best to apply the four principles of design to your project, you must first plan and then organize the information you want to convey.

Purpose, audience, tone, context, and genre

As with writing your project, begin planning the design of your project by carefully considering purpose, audience, tone context, and genre:

More about ▸▸▸ Purpose, audience, tone, context, and genre, 38–40

- **Purpose.** How can you reflect your purpose (to inform, persuade, interpret, or analyze) in your design?
- **Audience.** Who is your audience, what kind of expectations do they bring with them, and what kind of relationship do you have (or want to have) with them? Will they be drawn to

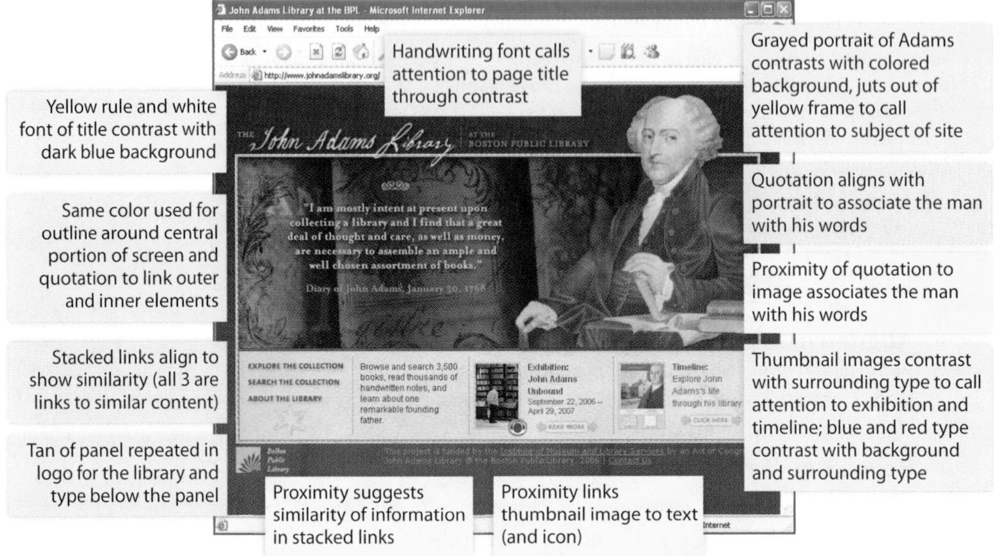
Handwriting font calls attention to page title through contrast
Grayed portrait of Adams contrasts with colored background, juts out of yellow frame to call attention to subject of site
Yellow rule and white font of title contrast with dark blue background
Quotation aligns with portrait to associate the man with his words
Same color used for outline around central portion of screen and quotation to link outer and inner elements
Proximity of quotation to image associates the man with his words
Stacked links align to show similarity (all 3 are links to similar content)
Thumbnail images contrast with surrounding type to call attention to exhibition and timeline; blue and red type contrast with background and surrounding type
Tan of panel repeated in logo for the library and type below the panel
Proximity suggests similarity of information in stacked links
Proximity links thumbnail image to text (and icon)

FIGURE 17.1 A Web Page from the Boston Public Library's Website

a conservative academic design; a bolder, more artistic design; or something else entirely?

- **Tone.** What kind of attitude do you want your design to convey? Seriousness? Playfulness? Professionalism?
- **Context.** In what context (academic, business, public) or setting (over the internet, in person) will your project be "consumed," and how will this affect its design?
- **Genre.** What category does your project fall into: Is it a résumé or a business letter? an essay or a lab report? a newsletter, brochure, flyer, or website? What design conventions are associated with that genre?

Organization

More about ▶▶▶
Organizing, 148–59
Claims and evidence, 173–90

Before you can apply the principles of design, you must determine how the pieces of information you want to convey relate to one another:

- What information is most (and least) important?
- Is the information evidence, or does it represent the main claim?
- How can the information be grouped?

17c Applying the Principles of Design

Once you have categorized the content you plan to convey, you are ready to begin designing your project.

Creating an overall impression

Start by considering the overall impression you want to give the reader: Should the design be conservative or trendy? serious or playful? contemporary, classic, or historic? Your decision about the style of your project will guide your choice of colors, fonts, and visuals.

More about ▸▸▸ Storyboards and site maps, 153–57

Creating the layout

Next consider your project's overall *layout,* the visual arrangement of text and images. An effective layout should use proximity, alignment, repetition, and contrast to make the relationships among the elements clear. Keep your layout simple, and use it to direct the reader's eye to the most important pieces of information. Create white space around elements you wish to emphasize. Making a sketch, or *mock-up,* of your layout (such as the one in Figure 17.2 for a flyer) can help you decide where to place elements on the page.

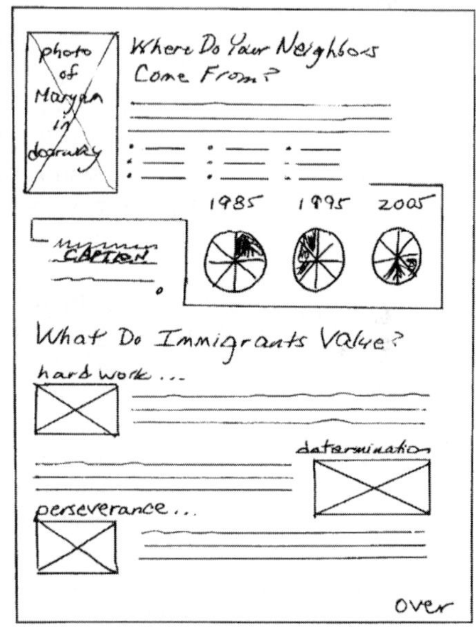

FIGURE 17.2 Sketch for Front of Flyer on Immigrants The persuasive purpose of this flyer is evident in its invitation to view immigrants as neighbors. The three subheadings in the second section emphasize that immigrants and citizens share the same values.

Designing the document

Once you have sketched your layout, you are ready to create the actual document. Use the following elements to create a cohesive and attractive design.

Fonts Word processors give writers a wide range of fonts (or typefaces) to choose from. Selections range from Arial and Courier to Palatino and Verdana, with many, many choices in between. Generally, serif fonts (fonts with a little tail on the ends of letters, such as Courier and Palatino) are easier to read when printed on paper, while sans serif fonts (fonts with no

Quick Reference → Fonts

Serif fonts	Have curled or flat tops and bottoms of letters. Use for long sections of print text.	Times New Roman Book Antiqua
Sans serif fonts	Have no curls, tops, or bottoms to finish the letters. Use for online texts.	Helvetica Arial
Decorative fonts	Evoke a distinctive style. Use sparingly for emphasis.	BANK GOTHIC Cracked

letter tails or tops, such as Arial and Verdana) are easier to read onscreen. Decorative fonts (distinctive in character, such as **Jazz LET** and Marker Felt) should be used very sparingly, yet boldly. All-capital letters should almost never be used because words set in all caps look like yelling on the page.

In addition to selecting a font family, you can choose from a variety of styles, including **boldface,** *italics,* underlining, or **color**. Use color or boldface for emphasis and contrast, but do so consistently and sparingly: The more these emphasis styles are used, the less attention they call to themselves. Since italics and underlining often have specific meanings, use them only when required.

When choosing a font, make sure it is easy to read, especially if you are using it for the *body* (the main text) of your project. Most readers find a 10- or 12-point type to be legible, but print out a page of text to check the size: 10-point type in one font may look larger than 12-point in another.

Choose fonts to add contrast or, through repetition, to group items. If you choose a serif font for most of your text, consider calling attention to headings by using a sans serif font (or the serif font in bold, a different color, and/or a larger size) for them. When designing multimedia, web, or other public writing, emphasize contrasts more than you would for an academic essay.

Keep in mind, too, that the fonts you use (especially in headings) can reinforce the overall impression you are trying to create. A typeface such as **Old English,** for example, might be appropriate in a poster announcing the first meeting of the Shakespeare Society. But be careful: For a document that is mainly text, legibility is more important than drama. More than a few words in a decorative font like *Edwardian Script* or **Haettenschweiler** will be hard to read.

> **Writing Responsibly** **Selecting Fonts with Readers in Mind**
>
> Not all readers have perfect vision. If your audience includes members over forty (or under twelve), use a font size of at least 12 points to make the reading experience easier and more pleasant. If individuals with visual impairments will make up a portion of your audience, increase your font size even more.

White Space White space is the portion of a page or screen with no text or images—it does not literally have to be white. The margins at the top, bottom, left, and right of this page provide white space, as does the extra space before a paragraph or around a heading or a visual. Extra white space above or around text or a visual can group elements into sections (Figure 17.3). Using the same amount of white space around all headings of the same level or visuals of the same type lends consistency to your layout; adding extra white space lends emphasis through contrast.

Ample white space makes a page inviting and easy to read (Figure 17.4). Without it, the page looks crowded, and your eye has difficulty knowing where to focus.

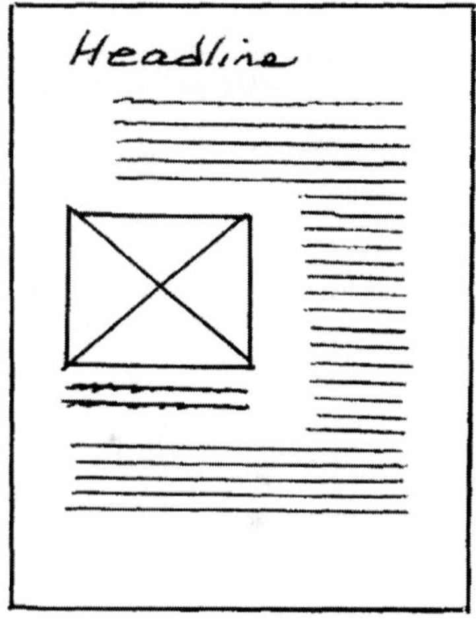

FIGURE 17.3 Using White Space to Group Elements Adding white space above a heading or around a figure and its caption groups them into a unit for readers.

Lists Another strategy for grouping related items (and for adding white space) is to use lists (see Figure 17.4). List entries should be written succinctly so that readers can skim them for information. When creating lists, remember to:

- Keep list items parallel (all phrases or all sentences).
- Limit the number of items in the list.
- Begin list items with a dot, diamond, square, or number, and align all items.
- Use numbered lists to indicate steps in a process and bulleted lists to group related pieces of information.

Keep in mind that while lists are common in business writing (in résumés and presentations, for example), they should be used sparingly in most academic writing.

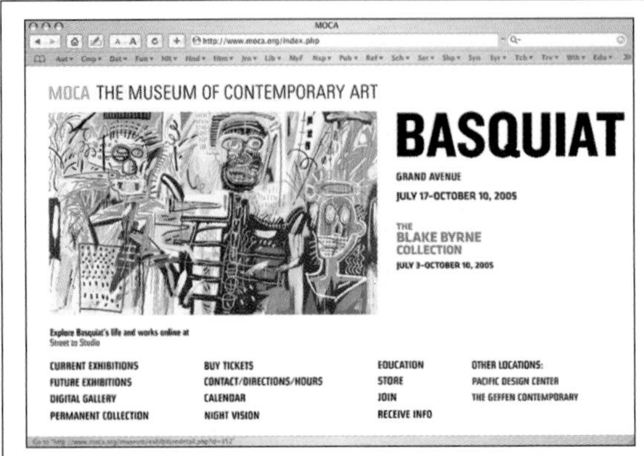

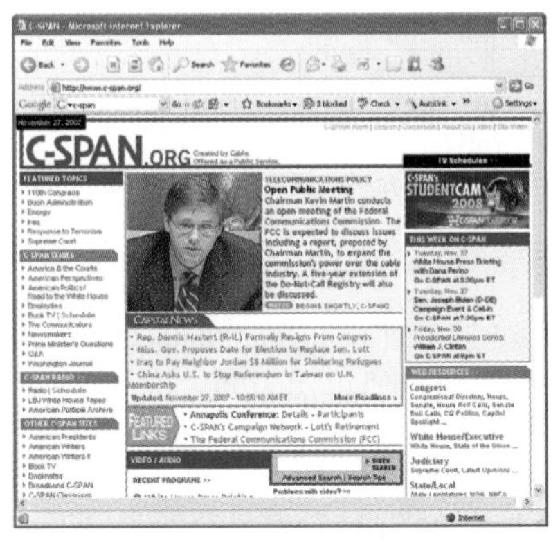

FIGURE 17.4 Use of Color and White Space in Web Pages The *C-Span* web page (*right*) is crowded with information, so the designer has used headings and colored panels to group information and make the page easier to navigate. The web page from the Museum of Contemporary Art (*left*) contains far less text, so the designer has used headings and white space to group information and make the page attractive (crucial given the sponsoring organization's mission). Both pages make use of lists and columns, common design features of website home pages, to organize information.

Color Color, through contrast, calls the reader's attention to what is important in the text: Headings; bullets, or numbers in lists; boxes, charts, and graphs, or illustrations often appear in color so that readers will notice them. But use color judiciously:

- **Use a limited color palette.** Too many colors displayed together create a hodgepodge effect.
- **Use complementary colors.** Analogous colors, those adjacent to each other on the color wheel (Figure 17.5), create a harmonious look. Complementary colors, those opposite each other on the color wheel, contrast with each other, each making the other color look brighter.
- **Use legible colors and color combinations.** Make sure colors contrast enough with their background that they are legible—yellow type on a white background may sound attractive but is hard to read.
- **Use appropriate colors.** Colors and combinations of colors carry associations: pastels for new babies, bright yellow and black for warnings, green for nature. Warm colors, such as red and orange, are seen as more aggressive than cool colors,

such as green and blue, which are considered calming. When selecting a color scheme, choose colors that reinforce your topic and purpose.

- **Use colors consistently.** To group items of the same type, display them in the same color. For example, set all headings of the same level in the same color, and use the same background color for boxes of the same type.

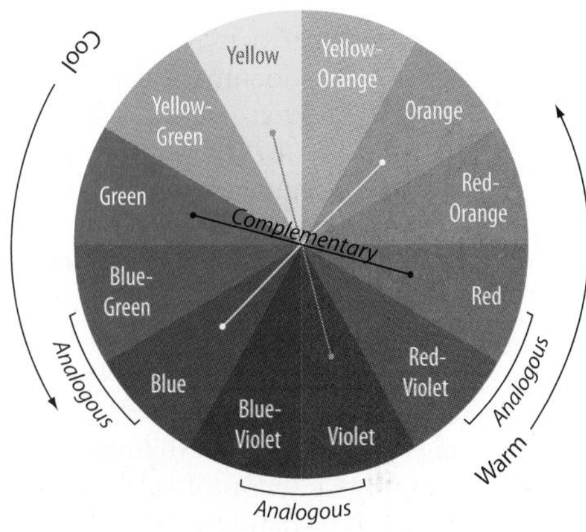

FIGURE 17.5 The Color Wheel Colors on opposite sides of the wheel are complementary; colors next to each other are analogous. <http://wgu.educommons.net/liberal-arts/visual-and-performing-arts-after-11-30-2007/color-wheel/image_view_fullscreen>

Headings Most texts use headings and subheadings to group text and guide readers; headings make long documents far easier to read. They can help readers find information quickly and comprehend a text's structure at a glance. The principles of repetition and contrast are crucial with headings:

More about ▸▸▸
Headings, 153–57

- Set all headings that are at the same level in the same font, style, and color; and position each level the same way (at left, centered) on the page:

  First-level heading

  Second-level heading

  Third-level heading

- Use the same grammatical structure for all headings of the same level. For example, use all *-ing phrases* (Containing the Economic Downturn, Bailing Out Wall Street) or all *noun phrases* (Economic Downturn, Wall Street Bailout).

The more complex your layout, the more elements you will need to vary to help readers distinguish among heading levels.

Headers and Footers Headers and footers are located at the top and bottom of a page, respectively. They are set off from the main text by white space and/or a rule (see the example on p. 217 in Figure 17.7) and generally include information that is repeated from page to page, such as the author's last name, the page number, and sometimes a portion of the title or chapter information. This repeated information is particularly important for navigating long documents.

Text Boxes Text boxes can hold pull quotes, sidebars, and explanations of images. *Pull quotes* are key quotations from the document text itself, "pulled" out and made larger so that readers scanning the document can get a sense of the main argument before reading the text. *Sidebars* add related information alongside a text. Text boxes are also helpful for *image annotation,* drawing attention to parts of the image for analysis or illustration.

Alignment, Justification, and Columns You can choose from three types of *alignment* for different parts of your document: left, right, and centered. Centered text sends a conservative message. Left-aligned text (in which the left margin is straight while the right margin is uneven, or unjustified) is typical in academic projects and for large segments of text. Aligning text at the right draws attention to it. *Justification* (addition of space between words to create text with even right- and left-hand margins) gives text a boxy, solid feel but is not recommended by most style guides for academic writing. You can also use *columns* to create a more journalistic feel and increase the white space on a page for readability.

LEFT ALIGNED

The quick, brown fox jumped over the lazy dog.

RIGHT ALIGNED

The quick, brown fox jumped over the lazy dog.

CENTERED

The quick, brown fox jumped over the lazy dog.

JUSTIFIED

The quick, brown fox jumped over the lazy dog. The quick, brown fox jumped over the lazy dog. The quick, brown fox jumped over the lazy dog. The quick, brown fox jumped over the lazy dog. The quick, brown fox jumped over the lazy dog.

TWO COLUMNS

The quick, brown fox jumped over the lazy dog. The quick, brown fox jumped over the lazy dog. The quick, brown fox jumped over the lazy dog. The quick, brown fox jumped over the lazy dog. The quick, brown fox jumped over the lazy dog. The quick, brown fox jumped over the lazy dog.

FIGURE 17.6 Use of Lines (Rules) and Borders *CNN.com* uses a thick red line to draw attention to its masthead, which is repeated consistently on each page of the site. Subtle gray borders segment the page into units.

Lines and Borders Lines, or rules, and borders can be used to define document sections (through proximity); draw attention to what is above, below, or beside them (through contrast); provide a repeating feature (for continuity); and create clear vertical or horizontal alignment (Figure 17.6).

Visuals Visuals are the first thing readers notice when they look at a text. For this reason, they are integral to documents intended for the general public, such as websites, newsletters, brochures, and flyers that must catch the eye of potential readers. Ideally, any visuals you include in a document should be visually arresting. But this does not mean that you should choose images just because they will capture a reader's attention. To be effective, images must be compelling and expand readers' understanding of your text.

More about ▶▶▶
Evaluating visual sources, 90–92
Visuals and common knowledge, 111–13
Using visuals as support, 177–79

First consider the types of visuals that will be appropriate for your text:

- **Images.** Photographs, sketches, drawings, and screenshots of websites (among other images) can be used to depict or explain an event or a process, illustrate a concept, summarize a discussion, or analyze for deeper understanding. In some writing contexts, you can use images to reinforce or even to make an argument. But in most academic and business contexts, you should avoid using images to persuade without making your argument explicit in your text.

- **Graphics.** Tables, bar graphs, pie charts, timelines, and maps (among other graphics) are useful in all contexts and genres as tools for making large amounts of data readily accessible to readers. Be sure to avoid graphics that will mislead your readers.

Position visuals as close as possible to, but *after*, the text discussion of them. In academic and business writing, include a reference to each figure or table in your text, numbered in order of appearance (Figure 1, Table 2, for example). Provide a title (for tables) or a caption (for figures) that identifies the image and, when possible, adds information that is not included in the text. Place the caption adjacent to the visual: For tables, generally place the title immediately above the visual; for figures, generally place captions immediately below or beside the image. Also be sure to provide a source for any visual you did not create yourself.

EXERCISE 17.1 Learning Design from Models

Find a document you think is in the spirit of the project you are writing, with a similar audience, context, purpose, and genre. Analyze its layout and design, answering these questions:

- What overall impression does the document give (for example, trendy, conservative, playful, serious)?
- What kind of font variation is there?
- How are white space, lists, color, headings, and text boxes used to create proximity, alignment, repetition, and contrast?
- What kinds of visuals does the document include, and how do they function: Do they, for example, reinforce product identity, provide an example, offer additional information, further the argument, or demonstrate a process?

Finally, consider the overall effect of the document. Did your assessment of its purpose, audience, context, and genre change as you studied it more closely?

Tech

Inserting Images and Text Boxes

To insert an image into a word-processed document, you can click on the image file on your desktop and drag it to the document. Or in the word processing program, you can choose "Insert" and then "Picture" from the drop-down menu. Then, choose "Clip Art" to select from your word processor's stock art or "From File" to select an image from your hard drive. Finally, if you want to adjust the size of the image, click on it, then click on a corner, hold down the mouse, and drag to resize.

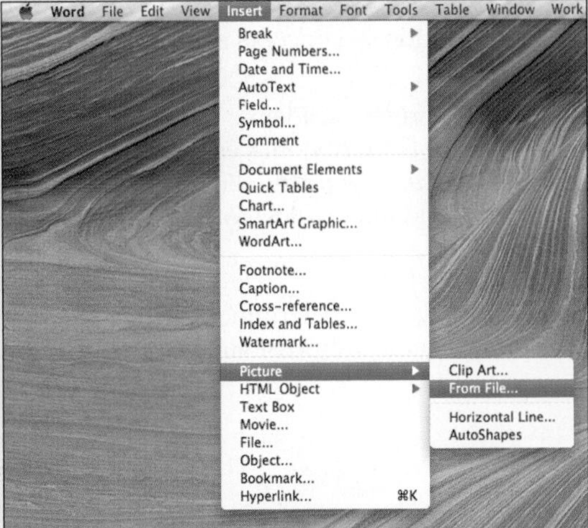

To insert a text box, follow a similar procedure: Choose "Insert" and then "Text Box." Then click in your text where you would like to place the text box. An outlined box will appear. Click inside the box to place your cursor and start typing.

To insert an image into a web page, place the image file in your server folder. Then insert the tag <img src = "*"> in your document. Replace the asterisk with the file name of your image, including its file extension (e.g., *jpg, gif,* or *tiff*).

17d Designing an Academic Research Essay

Printed academic writing is typically designed conservatively, and you can use your style guide's instructions on formatting as a baseline. Typical design features for academic writing include:

More about ▶▶▶
Formatting a paper in MLA style, 272–77
Sample paper formatted in MLA style, 278–89
Formatting a paper in APA style, 317–20
Sample paper formatted in APA style, 321–32
Formatting a paper in *Chicago* style, 352–53
Sample paper formatted in *Chicago* style, 354–60
Formatting a paper in CSE style, 375–76
Sample paper formatted in CSE style, 377–85

- 12-point fonts for paragraph text
- 1-inch margins
- Either a cover page or a header on page one indicating title, author, and contextual information such as course and date
- Headers after page one showing author's last name and the page number (sometimes the page number appears in a footer instead)
- Boldface type for subheadings
- Figures for visual illustration of concepts and information discussed in the text

Sometimes, however, even printed academic writing deviates from these norms in terms of design. Lindsay Bohl's essay, published in the *Vanderbilt Undergraduate Research Journal* (Figure 17.7), illustrates the use of columns, boldface, and lines (rules) for clean, readable, and scholarly design.

Be sure to ask your instructor which style guide is appropriate for the assignment and course. Also determine whether alternative designs, formats, genres, and media are possibilities for your research project.

Quick Reference **Checklist for Good Design**

Use these guidelines to determine whether you have achieved a good design for your document:

- Is my color scheme consistent and harmonious?
- Have I thought about the meanings of my color choices? Do they match and enhance the meaning of my text?
- Have I provided enough white space for my readers' eyes to rest, and have I placed it where it will draw attention to important information?
- Have I avoided using too many different fonts?
- Are the fonts I have chosen readable?
- Have I created a consistent pattern among my headings and subheadings?
- Have I chosen images and graphics that add value, not just visual impact?
- Have I aligned like items consistently?
- Have I avoided using all capital letters, except in one- or two-word instances?
- Have I created enough contrast to lead readers through my text?
- Do my choices convey the tone I need to achieve, whether playful, professional, serious, or other?

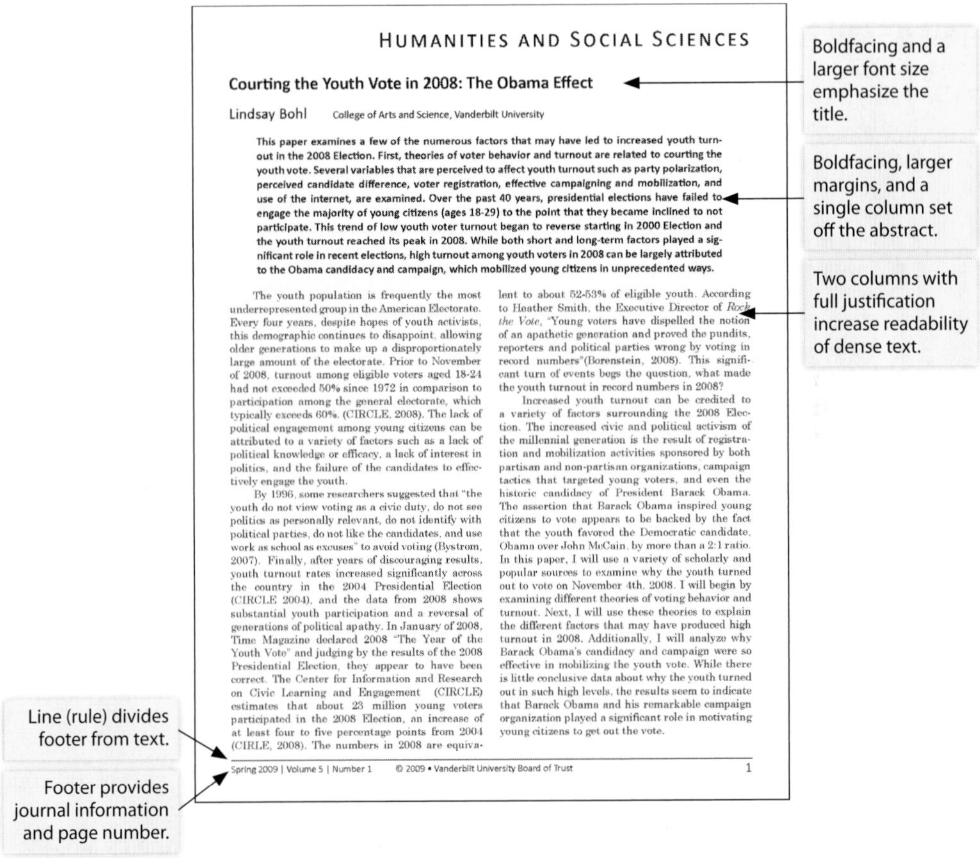

HUMANITIES AND SOCIAL SCIENCES

Courting the Youth Vote in 2008: The Obama Effect

Lindsay Bohl College of Arts and Science, Vanderbilt University

This paper examines a few of the numerous factors that may have led to increased youth turnout in the 2008 Election. First, theories of voter behavior and turnout are related to courting the youth vote. Several variables that are perceived to affect youth turnout such as party polarization, perceived candidate difference, voter registration, effective campaigning and mobilization, and use of the internet, are examined. Over the past 40 years, presidential elections have failed to engage the majority of young citizens (ages 18-29) to the point that they became inclined to not participate. This trend of low youth voter turnout began to reverse starting in 2000 Election and the youth turnout reached its peak in 2008. While both short and long-term factors played a significant role in recent elections, high turnout among youth voters in 2008 can be largely attributed to the Obama candidacy and campaign, which mobilized young citizens in unprecedented ways.

The youth population is frequently the most underrepresented group in the American Electorate. Every four years, despite hopes of youth activists, this demographic continues to disappoint, allowing older generations to make up a disproportionately large amount of the electorate. Prior to November of 2008, turnout among eligible voters aged 18-24 had not exceeded 50% since 1972 in comparison to participation among the general electorate, which typically exceeds 60%. (CIRCLE, 2008). The lack of political engagement among young citizens can be attributed to a variety of factors such as a lack of political knowledge or efficacy, a lack of interest in politics, and the failure of the candidates to effectively engage the youth.

By 1996, some researchers suggested that "the youth do not view voting as a civic duty, do not see politics as personally relevant, do not identify with political parties, do not like the candidates, and use work as school as excuses" to avoid voting (Bystrom, 2007). Finally, after years of discouraging results, youth turnout rates increased significantly across the country in the 2004 Presidential Election (CIRCLE 2004), and the data from 2008 shows substantial youth participation and a reversal of generations of political apathy. In January of 2008, Time Magazine declared 2008 "The Year of the Youth Vote" and judging by the results of the 2008 Presidential Election, they appear to have been correct. The Center for Information and Research on Civic Learning and Engagement (CIRCLE) estimates that about 23 million young voters participated in the 2008 Election, an increase of at least four to five percentage points from 2004 (CIRLE, 2008). The numbers in 2008 are equivalent to about 52-53% of eligible youth. According to Heather Smith, the Executive Director of *Rock the Vote*, "Young voters have dispelled the notion of an apathetic generation and proved the pundits, reporters and political parties wrong by voting in record numbers"(Borenstein, 2008). This significant turn of events begs the question, what made the youth turnout in record numbers in 2008?

Increased youth turnout can be credited to a variety of factors surrounding the 2008 Election. The increased civic and political activism of the millennial generation is the result of registration and mobilization activities sponsored by both partisan and non-partisan organizations, campaign tactics that targeted young voters, and even the historic candidacy of President Barack Obama. The assertion that Barack Obama inspired young citizens to vote appears to be backed by the fact that the youth favored the Democratic candidate, Obama over John McCain, by more than a 2:1 ratio. In this paper, I will use a variety of scholarly and popular sources to examine why the youth turned out to vote on November 4th, 2008. I will begin by examining different theories of voting behavior and turnout. Next, I will use these theories to explain the different factors that may have produced high turnout in 2008. Additionally, I will analyze why Barack Obama's candidacy and campaign were so effective in mobilizing the youth vote. While there is little conclusive data about why the youth turned out in such high levels, the results seem to indicate that Barack Obama and his remarkable campaign organization played a significant role in motivating young citizens to get out the vote.

Spring 2009 | Volume 5 | Number 1 © 2009 • Vanderbilt University Board of Trust 1

Boldfacing and a larger font size emphasize the title.

Boldfacing, larger margins, and a single column set off the abstract.

Two columns with full justification increase readability of dense text.

Line (rule) divides footer from text.

Footer provides journal information and page number.

FIGURE 17.7 First Page of a Research Essay Designed for an Undergraduate Journal

17e Presenting Your Research

Research is often transmitted in more than one form, in print and then verbally before a live audience, as a podcast, or in another multimedia format. Translating your research from written to oral presentation means adjusting for a new audience, context, purpose, and genre, and it may alter your tone. It also often requires drawing on your design skills.

Quick Reference → Overcoming Presentation Anxiety

Rehearsing in front of a live audience of friends or family is a good way to overcome stage fright. These techniques may also help:

- Work hard on your presentation (especially your introduction) so that you can have well-founded confidence in yourself and your material.
- Envision success. Picture yourself calm and relaxed at the podium. Imagine your sense of accomplishment when the presentation is over.
- Get a good night's sleep the night before, and eat something an hour or two before the presentation.
- Take several slow, deep breaths, or tighten and relax your muscles just before you take the podium.
- Ignore your racing heart or clammy hands. Instead, use the adrenaline surge to fill your presentation with energy.
- Focus on your message. Conveying excitement about what you have to say will draw the audience into your presentation.
- Accept the fact that you may stumble, and be prepared to go on.

Organizing your presentation

People have more trouble understanding and retaining ideas presented orally than they do ideas presented in writing. To help your audience hold your main points in memory while your presentation unfolds, you will need to organize your talk carefully.

Introduction During your brief introduction (10–15 percent of your presentation), try to accomplish the following three things:

1. **Get your audience to relate to your topic.** An engaging anecdote, startling statistics, or an apt quotation are all good opening gambits.
2. **Establish your credentials.** Why should the audience listen to you? What special expertise do you offer? Knowledge, experience, or the research you have conducted all give you special expertise.
3. **Briefly summarize your main points.** Let listeners know in advance what they should be listening for.

Body The body (75–85 percent of your presentation) should develop the points you previewed in your introduction. Ideally, present only three to five main supporting points, regardless of the length of your presentation. The audience might have trouble keeping track of more than that.

Conclusion Keep your conclusion brief (5–10 percent of your presentation). Use it to reinforce the main point of your presentation. This can mean repeating your main idea and key supporting points for listeners to take away with them. But it can also mean reiterating your main point with a brief but powerful statement or quotation or returning to the anecdote, example, or statistics you opened with.

Creating visual, audio, and multimedia aids

When using visual or multimedia aids during a presentation, make sure of the following:

- You use only relevant visual and multimedia aids.
- You explain each aid clearly and succinctly.
- You are selective, limiting the number of aids so that the audience pays attention to you rather than to them.
- You speak to your audience, not to your visual aids.

Designing your visual, audio, and multimedia aids well is essential to a successful presentation:

- Keep your aids simple: Audience members should be able to absorb their contents quickly and then return their attention to you.
- Be sure your aids are clearly visible, audible, and legible from all parts of the space in which you are speaking.
- Use simple fonts that are large enough to be read easily.
- Choose a limited number of colors, and use them consistently or to highlight key points.
- Keep the contrast between background and foreground sharp: A light background with dark type works best in a well-lit room; a dark background with light type works best in a dark room.

Tech

Ten Steps to Making an Effective *PowerPoint* Presentation

1. **Review your outline to determine where slides would enhance your presentation.** Do not overwhelm your presentation by creating a slide for every moment.
2. **Create a title slide.** Begin with a slide that includes the title of your presentation, your name, and any other useful identifying information.
3. **Use templates and slide layouts to create a uniform design, but vary slide content.** In general, slides are most effective when the text component is brief (the audience should be listening to you, not reading your slides) and the other components (images, sound clips, etc.) are varied.
4. **Add blank slides.** Blank slides let you display a blank screen when you move on to a part of your presentation that is not illustrated.
5. **Make sure your slides are visually pleasing.** Keep slides uncluttered (use only a few fonts; limit text to what the audience can take in quickly), balanced, consistently designed, and with few animations.
6. **Proofread your slides carefully.** Check for both clarity and correctness.
7. **Learn *PowerPoint* commands so that you can move smoothly through your presentation.** Keystroke commands allow you to advance or return to slides, use the animation effects, and end the slide show.
8. **Practice your presentation in advance.** Use animations to bring information forward. Do not continue to display a slide after you have moved on to the next topic.
9. **Check the equipment; make sure it will function properly in the presentation space.** Make sure, for example, that the cord linking your computer to the projector is long enough, that you have needed extension cords, and that you know how to lower the lights and can cover the windows to darken the room.
10. **Be prepared to give your presentation *without PowerPoint.*** If the power fails or your computer dies, you should be able to go on with the show.

A Final Thought

Developing skill in design and presenting, like most aspects of writing, takes attention and practice. Start paying attention to the good designs you encounter as you read. Notice the contrasting colors on covers as you browse the magazine rack. Pay attention to how elements align—vertically, horizontally, and diagonally—on flyers and brochures you encounter. Become aware of repeated features in textbooks you read for school. And consider how authors in various contexts group and divide information with white space, columns, boxes, lines, and borders. Do the same with presentations. Pay attention to effective presenters: How do they open, hold their audience's attention, use graphics and media, pace their presentations, and close? Then, apply good design and presentation strategies in your own work.

18 Conducting Research in the Disciplines

IN THIS CHAPTER

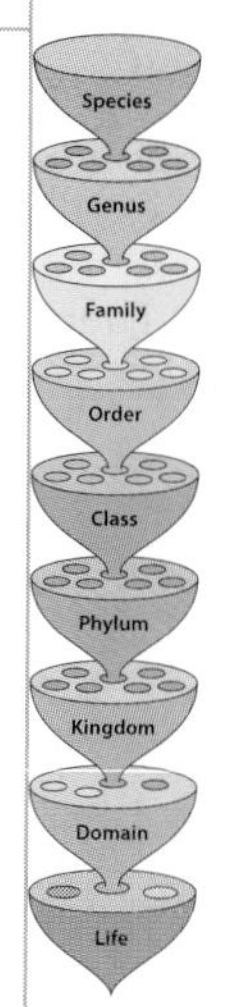

To understand the range of animal behaviors, characteristics, and relationships, scientists have divided the animal kingdom into groups: kingdom, phylum, class, order, family, genus, species. Academic studies, too, are classified into groups, or *disciplines:* communities of scholars who share a subject, approaches, and resources (types of evidence) for answering questions. The traditional disciplines are the humanities, the social sciences, the physical and natural sciences, and mathematics. (The Quick Reference box on p. 223 identifies the subject matter, approaches, and usual style guide for each of these disciplines.)

Success in college requires that you understand the approach, the tools used to conduct research and answer questions, the language, and the formats that are specific to the disciplines in which you take classes.

18a Conducting Research and Writing in the Humanities

More about ▶▶▶
Archival research, 128–31

More about ▶▶▶
Interpretation, 20–23
Analysis, 20–23
Synthesis, 20–23
Critique, 20–23

The *humanities* focus on the meaning and value of human experience by studying *texts* (including works of literature, art, and music; films; philosophical works; historical artifacts, documents, and events; speeches; and so on), as well as the conditions under which these texts are made and used. Students in the humanities read not just to comprehend but also to *engage with* texts: to ask difficult questions about them and to explore a range of possible answers.

Quick Reference → The Liberal Arts Disciplines

Discipline	Humanities	Social Sciences	Natural Sciences and Mathematics
Areas of study within the discipline	Art history, history, languages, literature, philosophy, religion, theater	Anthropology, communications, economics, geography, political science, psychology, sociology	Astronomy, biology, chemistry, geology, physics; algebra, calculus, geometry
Subject matter	Works of art, music, literature; cultural phenomena; abstract ideas	Human behavior (individual and group)	Natural phenomena
Primary sources	A painting or sculpture; a poem, novel, or play; manuscripts and diaries; legal cases and government documents	Data from observational studies, surveys, or interviews	Data from laboratory and field research
Secondary sources	Books or articles about a primary source	Books or articles describing primary research	Books or articles describing primary research
Typical assignments	Interpretation, analysis, and critique	Reports on field and experimental research; reviews and analyses of such research	Reports on experimental and field research; reviews and analyses of such research
Style guide	**Literature and languages:** *MLA Handbook for Writers of Research Papers*, 7th ed. **Other subjects:** *Chicago Manual of Style*, 15th ed.; *A Manual for Writers of Research Papers, Theses, and Dissertations*, 7th ed.	**Psychology and communications:** *Publication Manual of the American Psychological Association*, 6th ed. **Other subjects:** *Style Manual for Political Science* (American Political Science Association); *ASA (American Sociological Association) Style Guide*, 2nd ed.; *Chicago Manual of Style*, 15th ed.	**General:** *Scientific Style and Format: The CSE (Council of Science Editors) Manual for Authors, Editors, and Publishers*, 7th ed. **Specific fields:** *AMA (American Medical Association) Manual of Style*, 10th ed.; *IAU (International Astronomers Union) Style Manual; Mathematics into Type*, updated ed.

More about ▶▶▶
Documentation:
MLA style, 230–89
APA style, 290–332
Chicago style, 333–60
CSE style, 361–85
Formatting:
MLA style, 272–89
APA style, 317–32
Chicago style, 352–60
CSE style, 375–85

Street artist Moose decorates a tunnel in Leeds, England, by removing dirt to create a pattern. Alex Coley © Symbollix 2003

Adopting the approaches of the humanities

More about ▶▶▶
Primary versus secondary sources, 129
Developing new information, 128–40

In most humanities courses, you are likely to be required to study *primary sources.* For instance, in art history, a painting (such as an image of St. Cecilia) or a video of a reverse-graffiti artist like Moose at work would be considered primary sources.

More about ▶▶▶
Scholarly and popular sources, 82–84
Finding reference works, 59–60

You will also draw on *secondary sources* to find out what others have said about the work or to learn about a critical framework that can provide the scaffolding for your interpretation. Of those secondary sources, *scholarly works,* like peer-reviewed articles in a scholarly journal or books published by a university press, are likely to be deemed more reliable by your instructor than are more accessible *popular sources,* like magazine or newspaper articles. You may also draw on *specialized reference works* to get an overview of your topic.

Using the language of the humanities

Learning the language of a discipline (both the vocabulary and the way words are used) is crucial to academic success. When writing in the humanities, pay particular attention to these issues:

- **Past versus present tense.** Writers in the humanities generally use the past tense to discuss actual events that have happened and the present tense to discuss the work being studied, the elements or events within the work being studied, and the ideas of other scholars.

- **First person** (*I, we*) **versus third person** (*he, she, they, it*). Use of the first- or third-person pronoun varies from one humanities discipline to another. In part, this reflects a difference in emphasis: Is the focus the writer's own argument (first person) or the evidence on which the argument is based (third person)? When writing for a class, ask your instructor about the preferred style, or read samples of writing from the discipline to figure out current practice.
- **Active versus passive voice.** In general in the humanities, writers use the active voice because it is likely to result in clearer, less wordy writing. Consider these two sentences:

  ACTIVE VOICE Jonas Salk invented the vaccine for polio in 1955.

  PASSIVE VOICE The vaccine for polio was invented in 1955.

  The first provides more information than the second, clearly indicating who did what. Of course, some circumstances may require the passive voice, as when the "who" is unknown or when you want to emphasize the action rather than the actor.

Writing assignments in the humanities

Assignments in the humanities frequently call on students to include the following:

- **Summary/description.** An interpretive analysis, critique, review, or bibliographic essay often includes a summary or description for readers who are unfamiliar with the text, event, or object being discussed.
- **Synthesis.** A synthesis connects one text to another, explaining how the works relate and what new understandings might be derived from their combination. Frequently, writing in the humanities begins with a review of other works (a literature review).
- **Interpretation.** Even when writing a research paper, writers in the humanities are usually expected to offer their own interpretation of primary texts, explaining what meaning they found in the text and what features of the text prompted their interpretation.

More about ▶▶▶
Summary, 14–19, 98, 109–11
Synthesis, 14–19, 178–80
Analysis, 14–19, 178–80
Interpretation, 14–19
Evaluation and critique, 14–19, 178–80
Literature review, 48

- **Evaluation.** An evaluation involves judging a text's quality or plausibility, offering a rationale for the judgment, and considering possible objections.

18b Conducting Research and Writing in the Social, Physical, and Natural Sciences

Social scientists focus on the behavior of people, as individuals and in groups. Physical and natural scientists focus on the characteristics, systems, and processes of the natural world. What unites the social sciences with the physical and natural sciences, though, is reliance on the scientific method.

More about ▸▸▸
Developing new information, 128–40
Developing hypotheses, 142–43

Adopting the approaches of the social, physical, and natural sciences

The search for verifiable evidence anchors the writing produced by all scientists. Verifiable evidence comes from *empirical research*: experiments, observations, surveys, questionnaires, and interviews.

To conduct empirical research, social, physical, and natural scientists first develop *hypotheses*—predictions that can be proved true or false—and then they test these hypotheses. A hypothesis that successfully explains or predicts other phenomena and that is consistently confirmed by research becomes a *theory*.

Quick Reference — The Scientific Method

Four major elements comprise the scientific method:

- **Descriptions** delineate the object of a study. Description relies on systematically observing, measuring, and quantifying and requires keeping careful records of observations in a laboratory notebook.
- **Hypotheses** offer a prediction about the object of a study. A hypothesis should be "elegant": clear, simple, and based on established facts.
- **Experiments** involve testing to determine the accuracy of a hypothesis. You will need to be able to explain, step by step, how you conducted an experiment so that others who repeat the experiment can obtain identical results.
- **Theories** draw on hypotheses and experimentation to explain the behavior of the object of a study.

Using the language of the social, physical, and natural sciences

Pay particular attention to these language issues when writing in the social, physical, and natural sciences:

- **Specialized terminology.** Even at the introductory level, most writing in the social, physical, and natural sciences requires that you learn some specialized terminology and use it with precision. You will learn much of this terminology from textbooks and your instructors.
- **Third person and passive voice.** Since (in principle) the individual conducting the research is unimportant, researchers in the sciences generally use the third person and passive voice to describe how research was conducted. Some social scientists use the first person (*I, we*) when discussing observations they made as a participant or the conclusions they drew from their research. Check with your instructor about what is customary in your discipline.
- **Past versus present tense.** Use the past tense to discuss methods and the present tense to discuss implications.

Writing assignments in the social, physical, and natural sciences

The most common types of writing projects in the social, physical, and natural sciences include the following:

- **Literature reviews** summarize research on a specific topic, analyze and evaluate the sources and the research on which these studies were based, and synthesize sources to develop a thorough understanding of the topic.
- **Research or laboratory notebooks** record in precise detail (1) the materials you used in the order you used them; (2) a chronological list of the procedures you followed; and (3) your results (raw data, clearly labeled and logically organized), including any graphs or calculations you made.
- **Research or laboratory reports** provide a detailed description of your research, including your methods, your results, and the conclusions you drew from those results. (See the following detailed discussion of how to write a research report.)

More about ▸▸▸
Summary, 14–19, 98, 109–11
Analysis, 14–19, 178–80
Evaluating sources and information, 80–92
Synthesis, 14–19, 178–80
Literature review, 48

Unlike a humanities research paper, a research or laboratory report in the social, physical, or natural sciences usually follows a standard format, which is outlined below.

Title Page The title page should include the following information: title of the report, instructor, date of submission, author of the report, and author's affiliation.

Abstract A brief (150-word) summary of the report, the abstract may include a one-sentence summary of the most important points in each section of the report.

Introduction The report introduction should provide necessary background, such as a brief review of other, closely related studies; indicate your purpose in conducting the research; and introduce the limits of your research.

Methods The methods section should provide information about participants and describe the methods you used to collect information and record data. Describe your methods in enough detail that others could repeat your study or experiment.

More about ▶▶▶
Matching visual evidence to claims, 177
Integrating visuals, 206–14

Results The results section should provide details of your outcome. Use information graphics to convey results succinctly.

Discussion The discussion section of your report offers readers an interpretation of your results, showing how the data you collected support your hypothesis, recognizing the limitations of your data, and relating your results to those of earlier researchers.

Conclusions The conclusions section summarizes your findings and explains the implications of your research.

More about ▶▶▶
Creating an APA-style reference list, 302–17
Creating a CSE-style reference list, 363–75

References For the social sciences, typically use American Psychological Association (APA) style; for the physical and natural sciences, use the Council of Science Editors (CSE) style guide. However, individual disciplines may have their own preferred style (for example, the American Sociological Association [ASA] also publishes its own style guide), so check with your instructor.

Appendices Place in an appendix any figures, tables, photographs, and other materials that amplify but are not directly relevant to the discussion. Appendices should be mentioned in the main body of your text so that readers know to consult them. Each appendix should have a succinct, descriptive title, such as "Appendix C: Interview Questions."

A Final Thought

College-level discourse can seem mysterious and complicated. Part of the mystery is that researched writing in college is simply not all the same. From discipline to discipline, differing practices have arisen to deal with studying and talking about different kinds of problems. To dispel the mystery, pay attention, ask questions, and observe patterns in the disciplines.

19 Documenting Sources: MLA Style

IN THIS CHAPTER

More about ▶▶▶
Popular academic styles per discipline, 222
APA style, 290–332
Chicago style, 333–60
CSE style, 361–85

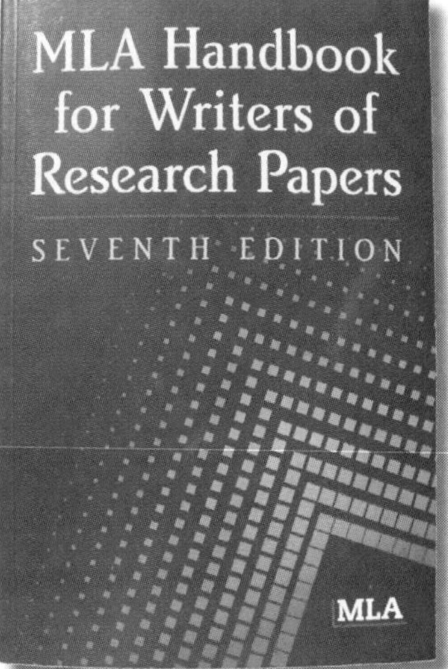

MLA Handbook for Writers of Research Papers
SEVENTH EDITION
MLA

Developed by the Modern Language Association (MLA), MLA style guidelines are used by many researchers in the humanities—especially in languages and literature—to cite and document sources and to format papers in a uniform way. The MLA requires that sources be acknowledged in two ways:

- **Citation:** Provide an in-text citation for each source used in the body of your project.
- **Documentation:** Provide a list of all works cited at the project's end.

Writing Responsibly | **Citing and Documenting Sources**

When you cite and document sources, you acknowledge any material that you have borrowed from a source, and you join the conversation on your topic by adding your own interpretation. Simultaneously, you give interested readers (including your instructor) a way to join the conversation: Accurate entries in the text and list of works cited allow your audience to find and read your sources so that they can evaluate your interpretation and learn more about the subject themselves. Accurate entries also demonstrate the care with which you have written your research project, and they reinforce your reputation as a sound scholar.

19a Creating MLA-Style In-Text Citations

In-text citations appear in the body of your paper. They mark each use you make of a source, regardless of whether you are quoting, paraphrasing, summarizing, or drawing on an idea from the source. They also alert readers to a shift between *your* ideas and those borrowed from a source.

You can cite a source in your text by using a signal phrase, a parenthetical note, or both:

- **Signal phrase.** Include the author's name (the full name in the first reference and then just the surname in all references that follow) and an appropriate verb in your sentence; put the page numbers from which the borrowed material comes in parentheses.

  While encouraging writers to use figurative language, journalist Constance Hale cautions [signal phrase] that "a metaphor has the shelf life of a fresh vegetable" (224), [page no.] illustrating the warning with her own lively metaphor.

  Signal phrases often make it easier for readers to determine where your ideas end and borrowed material begins. They also allow you to integrate the borrowed material into your sentence and to put the source in context by adding your own interpretation and describing the qualifications of the source author. For these reasons, most summaries, paraphrases, and quotations should be introduced by a signal phrase.

- **Parenthetical note.** Include the author's surname plus the page number(s) from which the borrowed material comes, all in parentheses:

  While figurative language can make a passage come alive, be aware that metaphors have "the shelf life of a fresh vegetable" (Hale 224). [parenthetical note]

  Parenthetical notes are most appropriate when readers can tell from the context where borrowed material begins and ends, as in the example above. They are also useful when you are citing more than one source, when you are establishing facts,

More about ▸▸▸
What you must cite, 109–11
What you need not cite, 111–13
Signal phrases, 111–13, 180–89
Parenthetical notes, 109–11, 185–89

or when the author is not especially important to the point you are making.

NOTE The entry in the list of works cited is the same whether you use a signal phrase or a parenthetical note:

author / title / publication info. / medium

Hale, Constance. *Sin and Syntax.* New York: Broadway, 2001. Print.

---

1. Include enough information to lead readers to the source in the list of works cited.

Whether using a signal phrase or a parenthetical note, provide enough information for readers to locate the source in the *list of works cited.* In most cases, providing the author's surname and a page reference is enough to guide readers to the correct source. Occasionally, however, you may need to provide more information:

Example 6, 238–39

- If you cite more than one source by the same author, mention the title of the work in the text or include a shortened form of the title in the in-text citation. (You may also want to mention the title of the work if it is relevant to the point you are making.)

Example 7, 239

- If you refer to sources by two different authors with the same surname, mention the authors' first names as well as the surname in the text, or include the authors' first initials with the surname in the in-text citation.

Tech

Page References and Web Pages

Despite the term *web page,* most websites do not have page numbers in the sense that printed books do. Your browser may number the pages when you print a web page from a website, but this numbering only appears on your printed copy. Different computers and printers break pages differently, so your printed page 5 might be someone else's page 4 or 6. For this reason, citations of most web pages include only the author's name. If a website numbers its paragraphs, provide that information instead of a page reference.

Occasionally, you may need to include less information. For example, you would omit a page number in these cases:

- When you are summarizing an entire source
- When your source is just one page long
- When your source, such as a web page, is not paginated

Example 14a, 244

2. Place in-text citations so readers know where borrowed material starts and stops.

When you incorporate a quotation, paraphrase, summary, or idea from a source into your own text, carefully consider the placement of the in-text citation, keeping the following goals in mind:

- To make clear exactly which material is drawn from the source
- To avoid distracting your reader

Signal Phrase When using a signal phrase, bookend the borrowed information: Insert the author's name *before,* and the page number *after,* the cited material.

> Daniels, who has written several books about DC Comics' creations, notes that underground comic artists are not controlled by corporate interests that discourage "daring" material that might not sell (165, 180).

Parenthetical Note When using a parenthetical note, place the note at a natural pause in a sentence—at the end of a phrase, clause, or sentence—right after the borrowed material and before any punctuation.

Following a sentence

> Underground comic artists are not controlled by corporate interests that discourage "daring" material (Daniels 165, 180).

Following a clause

> While underground comic artists are not constrained by the conservatism of large corporations (Daniels 165), they are beholden to a different set of standards—those of their loyal and opinionated readers, who may balk at experimental shifts in style or story.

Following a phrase

> Free from the control of large corporations (Daniels 165), underground comic artists are still beholden to their readers' standards.

Multiple Sources When you use different sources for different pieces of information within a sentence, give separate citations in the appropriate places.

Example

> from Daniels
>
> Other common themes in underground comics include sex and sexual identity, politics, and social issues (Daniels 165), as shown in Crumb's
>
> from Heller
>
> work, which is well known for its satirical approach to countercultural topics (Heller).

When the information you are drawing on comes from more than one source, follow the borrowed material with a list of all relevant sources, separated by semicolons:

Example

> Jamestown was once described as a failed colony populated by failed colonists, but new findings suggest that the colonists were resourceful survivors (Howard; Lepore 43).

Block Quotations When the text you are quoting runs to more than four lines of your project, indent the borrowed material as a block, and place the parenthetical note one space *after* the closing punctuation mark.

More about ▶▶▶
Block quotations, 99–105, 108–11, 274, 279

Example

signal phrase

Howard and Kennedy assert that parents and school officials tend to ignore hazing until an incident becomes public knowledge. They describe a concrete incident that demonstrates their claims:

> In general, the Bredvik school community (parents, teachers, coaches, and students) condoned or ignored behaviors that could be called "hazing" or "sexual harassment." However, when the incident was formally brought to the attention of the larger, public audience of the community, a conflict erupted in the community over how to frame, understand, and react to the event. (347–48)

3. Adjust in-text citations to different types of sources.

The exact form of an in-text citation depends on the type of source you are citing. The examples below cover the most common types. For more unusual sources, study the general principles as outlined here and in the *MLA Handbook for Writers of Research Papers,* 7th ed. (available in any library), and adapt them to your special circumstances.

MLA In-Text Citations

1. One author

a. Signal phrase

Cahill cautions responsible historians against disparaging the Middle Ages; medieval Europe's reputation as a time of darkness, ignorance, and blind faith is "largely (if not wholly) undeserved" (310).

page no.

Quick Reference MLA Style In-Text Citations

MLA In-Text Citations

1. One author
2. **Two or three authors**
3. More than three authors
4. Group or corporate author

b. Parenthetical note

> The Middle Ages are often unjustly characterized as a time of darkness, ignorance, and blind faith (Cahill 310).

2. Two or three authors Include the surnames of all the authors in your signal phrase or parenthetical note; use *and,* not an ampersand (&), in the parenthetical note.

> To write successfully about their families, authors must have motives—and perspective—beyond merely exposing secret histories (Miller and Paola 72).

3. More than three authors For sources with more than three authors, you may either list each author by surname (follow the order in the text) or insert the abbreviation *et al.* (which stands for the Latin phrase *et alii,* "and others") following the first author's surname.

NOTE *al.* is an abbreviation, so it requires a period; *et* is a complete word, so it does not. There should be no punctuation between the author's name and *et al.*

all authors in signal phrase

Visonà, Poynor, Cole, Harris, Abiodun, and Blier stress that symbols used in African art are not intended to be iconic but instead to suggest a wide variety of meanings; the authors liken this complexity to "a telephone line that carries multiple messages simultaneously" (19).

Symbols used in African art are not intended to be iconic; rather, the artist's goal is to suggest a complex range of meanings to different viewers (Visonà et al. 19).

1st author + et al.

Whichever you choose, do the same in your entry in the list of works cited.

Example 3, 248

4. Group or corporate author When a government agency, corporation, or other organization is listed as the author, use that organization's name in your in-text citation.

government agency as author

The Federal Emergency Management Agency indicates that Kansas City is located in a region of frequent and intense tornadic activity (4).

MLA In-Text Citations

3. More than three authors
4. Group or corporate author
5. **Unnamed author**
6. **Two or more sources by the same author**
7. Two or more authors with the same surname
8. Selection from an anthology

The MLA suggests incorporating names into your sentence in a signal phrase to avoid long parenthetical notes. If a parenthetical note makes more sense in the context, use common abbreviations ("U.S." for *United States,* "Corp." for *Corporation*) to shorten the name where you can.

5. Unnamed author If the author is unnamed and the work is alphabetized by title in the list of works cited, use the title in your in-text citation. Abbreviate long titles in parenthetical citations.

> One nineteenth-century children's book vows that "when examined by the microscope, the flea is a pleasant object," and the author's vivid description of this sight—a body "curiously adorned with a suit of polished armor, neatly jointed, and beset with a great number of sharp pins almost like the quills of a porcupine"—may win readers' curiosity, if not their sympathy (*Insects* 8).
>
> [title]

If you do abbreviate the title, start your abbreviation with the word by which the title will be alphabetized in your list of works cited. Only if the author is listed specifically as "Anonymous" should you use that designation.

6. Two or more sources by the same author When you draw on two or more sources by the same author, differentiate between these sources by including titles.

> [book title]
>
> In her book *Nickel and Dimed,* social critic Barbara Ehrenreich demonstrates that people cannot live on the then-current minimum wage (60). Perhaps, as she notes in her blog entry "'Values' Voters Raise Minimum Wages," people will be a little better able to hold their own in the six states (Arizona, Colorado, Montana, Missouri, Nevada, Ohio) that have recently raised their minimum wage.
>
> [blog entry title]

If you use a signal phrase, use the full title; if you use a parenthetical citation, abbreviate it ("'Values' Voters").

7. Two or more authors with the same surname When your paper includes sources by two different authors with the same surname, differentiate them by including their first names (the first time you mention them in a signal phrase) or by including their first initials (in a parenthetical reference or subsequent text references).

> Including citations is important not only because they give credit but also because they "organize a field of inquiry, create order, and allow for accountability" (S. Rose 243). This concern for acknowledging original sources dates back to the early eighteenth century: Joseph Addison was one of the first to argue for "the superiority of original to imitative composition" (M. Rose 114).

8. Selection from an anthology If your source is a work included in an anthology, reader, or other collection, your citation should name the author of your source—not the editor of the anthology.

> Southern fiction often explores the marked curiosity that women of stature and mystery inspire in their communities. Faulkner's [author of story] "A Rose for Emily," for example, describes the title character as "a tradition, a duty, and a care; a sort of hereditary obligation upon the town . . ." (79).

9. Multivolume source If you use information from more than one volume of a multivolume work, your in-text citation must indicate both the volume and page from which you are borrowing. (This information can be omitted if you use only one volume of the work, since your works-cited entry will indicate which volume you used.)

MLA In-Text Citations

author
Tarbell writes that in 1847 Abraham Lincoln was a popular man of "simple, sincere friendliness" who was an enthusiastic—though awkward—bowler (1: 210).
vol. no. pg. no.

The words *volume* and *page* (or their abbreviations) are not used.

10. Literary source Because many classics of literature—novels, poems, plays—are published in a number of editions (printed and digital) with pagination that varies widely, your citation should provide your readers with the information they will need to find the passage, regardless of which edition they are reading.

a. Novel Include the chapter number (with the abbreviation *ch.*) after the page number for your edition:

Joyce shows his protagonist's dissatisfaction with family, faith, and country through the adolescent Stephen Daedalus's first dinner at the adult table, an evening filled with political and religious discord (274; ch. 1).
pg. no. ch. no.

Use arabic (*2, 9, 103*), not roman (*ii, ix, ciii*), numerals, regardless of what your source uses.

If the novel has chapters grouped into parts or books, include both the part number and the chapter number, using the appropriate abbreviation (*pt.* for *part* or *bk.* for *book*).

Even though New York society declares the Countess Olenska beyond her prime, Newland Archer sees in her a "mysterious authority of beauty" (Wharton 58; bk. 1, ch. 8).

If the source has no pagination, a chapter number might be the only information you can include.

b. Play When citing plays, use act, scene, and line numbers (in that order), not page numbers. Do not label the parts; instead, separate them with periods.

When the ghost of Hamlet's father cries, "Adieu, adieu, adieu! remember me," Hamlet wonders if he must "remember" his father through vengeance (1.5.91).

No spaces

c. Poem For poetry, use line numbers, rather than page or location numbers. With the first reference to line numbers, use the word *line* or *lines;* omit it thereafter.

In Audre Lorde's poem "Hanging Fire," her fourteen-year-old frets, "What if I die / before morning" (lines 7–8), making me remember my own teenage worries of just a few years ago. Each of the three stanzas ends with "and momma's in the bedroom / with the door closed" (9–10, 20–21, 32–33), bringing me back to my "now": I am that mother who does not understand.

1st ref.

later refs.

For long poems that are divided into sections (books, parts, numbered stanzas), provide that information as well, omitting the section name (or abbreviation) and separating section number from line number(s) with a period.

David Mason's *Ludlow* (2007) begins with a description that captures Luisa's life:

Down below
the mesa, smells of cooking rose from shacks
in rows, and there Luisa scrubbed the pot
as if she were some miner's wife and not
a sapper's daughter, scrawny, barely twelve. (1.5–8)

No spaces

MLA In-Text Citations

11. Sacred text Cite sacred texts (such as the Bhagavad-Gita, the Talmud, the Qur'an, and the Bible) not by page number but by book title (abbreviated), chapter number, and verse number(s); and separate each section with a period. Do not italicize book titles or put them in quotation marks, and do not italicize the name of the sacred text, unless you are referring to a specific edition.

sacred text

In the Bible's timeless love poetry, the female speaker concludes her description of her lover with this proclamation: "This is my beloved and this is my friend, / O daughters of Jerusalem" (Song Sol. 5.16).

book ch.verse

No space

specific edition

The *New Oxford Annotated Bible* offers a moving translation of the timeless love poetry in the Song of Solomon. The female speaker concludes her description of her lover with this proclamation: "This is my beloved and this is my friend, / O daughters of Jerusalem" (5.16).

MLA In-Text Citations

12. Indirect source When you can, avoid quoting from a secondhand source because it *may* misquote or misrepresent the original and it *will* provide a limited sense of the original. When you cannot locate the original source, mention the name of the person you are quoting in your sentence; in your parenthetical note, include *qtd. in* (for *quoted in*) plus the name of the author of the source in which you found the quote.

Handel's stock among opera-goers rose considerably over the course of the twentieth century. In 1912, an English music critic, H. C. Colles, maintained that "it would be difficult, if not impossible, to make any one of Handel's operas tolerable to a modern audience" (qtd. in Orrey 62). Today, however, Handel's operas are performed around the world.

author quoted

source of quotation

In your list of works cited, include the *indirect* source (*Orrey*), not the source being quoted (*H. C. Colles*).

13. Dictionary or encyclopedia entry In the citation of a dictionary or encyclopedia entry, omit the page number on which you found the item. For a dictionary entry, place the defined word in quotation marks, followed by the abbreviation *def.;* follow this with the letter or number of the definition you wish to reference.

> Another definition of *honest* is "respectable" ("Honest," def. 6), but what, if anything, does truth have to do with respectability?

In the parenthetical note for an encyclopedia entry, include the entry's full title in quotation marks.

> The study of ethics is not limited to philosophers, as its "all-embracing practical nature" makes it an applicable or even necessary course of study in a wide variety of disciplines, from biology to business ("Ethics").

If you are citing two entries with the same name from different reference sources, add an abbreviated form of the reference work's title to each entry.

> While the word *ethics* is commonly understood to mean "moral principles" ("Ethics," def. 4, *Random House Webster's*), to philosophers it is "the evaluation of human conduct" ("Ethics," *Philosophical Dict.*).

14. Website or other electronic source Cite electronic sources such as websites, online articles, e-books, and emails as you would cite comparable print sources, but note that many online sources do not use page numbers.

MLA In-Text Citations

11. Sacred text
12. Indirect source
13. Dictionary or encyclopedia entry
14. Website or other electronic source
15. Personal communication
16. Table or figure

More about ▶▶▶
Evaluating online texts, 86–90

MLA In-Text Citations

a. Without page, paragraph, or screen numbers Unless there is another numbering system at work (such as a reference to a location or numbered paragraphs or screens), cite the author without a page reference.

> When first published in 1986, Alan Moore's *Watchmen* revolutionized the comic book; today, even its harshest critics acknowledge the book's landmark status (Shone).
>
> author only

You may credit your source more elegantly by mentioning the author in a signal phrase and omitting the parenthetical citation altogether.

> signal phrase
>
> Reading Alan Moore's *Watchmen* in 2005, critic Tom Shone found it "underwhelming," but he admitted that in 1986, the comic book was "unquestionably a landmark work."

b. With paragraph, screen, or slide numbers If an electronic source numbers its paragraphs, screens, or slides, you can reference these numbers as you would pages (with an appropriate identifying abbreviation—*par.* or *pars., screen* or *screens, slide* or *slides*).

> The internet has also become an outlet for direct distribution through artist websites, making independent titles not only more accessible to consumers but also more affordable for individual artists to produce and market (Fenty, Houp, and Taylor, par. 1).

c. In a PDF file Most documents saved as PDFs (portable document format) are formatted just as a print document would be, with clearly numbered and consistent pagination. Therefore, you can and should cite page numbers for PDFs.

15. Personal communication As with other unpaginated sources, when citing information from a letter, email message, interview, or other personal communication, you should include the author's name in a signal phrase or parenthetical citation. Also indicate the type of source you are citing.

> Many people have asked why teachers cannot do more to prevent school shootings; in an email [source type] to this author, one instructor responds: "As creative writing teachers untrained in psychology, can we really determine from a student's poetry whether he or she is emotionally disturbed—even a threat to others?" (Fox) [author of email].

16. Table or figure If the visual you are discussing is *not* included in your paper, include the name of the artist, the work of art, and any other relevant information in the text, and include an entry in your list of works cited.

> . . . There is no experience quite like standing in front of a full-size painting by Jackson Pollock; they have an irresistible sense of movement to them, the particular quality of which is unique to his work. This is especially evident in *One Number 31, 1950*, which currently hangs on the fourth floor of New York's Museum of Modern Art. . . .

More about ▸▸▸
Using visuals as support, 177–79

If the visual *is* included in your project, include the source information in a table's source note (see Figure 19.1) or in a figure's caption (for figures, see the figure on p. 281 in the model student project at the end of this chapter).

TABLE 1 | THE DEMISE OF THE THREE-DECKER NOVEL

Year	No. of 3-deckers published
1894	184
1895	52
1896	—
1897	4
1898	0

Source: Information from John Feather, *A History of British Publishing* (Clarendon: Crown Helm, 1988), quoted in Kelly J. Mays

FIGURE 19.1 Table in MLA Style

19b Preparing an MLA-Style List of Works Cited

The list of works cited, which comes at the end of your research project, includes information about the sources you have cited in your text. (A bibliography that includes sources you read but did not cite in your research project is called a list of works consulted.) Your list of works cited provides readers with the information they need for locating the material you drew on in your paper. The format of each entry depends in part on the type of source it is.

Quick Reference → MLA Works-Cited Entries

Books—Printed and Electronic

In a printed book, most or all of the information you need for creating an entry in the list of works cited appears on the title and copyright pages. In an online or e-book, print and electronic publication information often appears at the top or bottom of the first page or is available through a link.

▸▸▸Annotated visual of where to find author, title, publication, and other information, on foldout following p. 385

MLA Works-Cited Entries

1. One author

a. Printed The basic entry for a printed book looks like this:

Author's surname, First name. *Title: Subtitle.* Place of publication: Publisher (shortened), date of publication. Medium of publication.

Here is an example of an actual entry in the list of works cited:

author — title — publication information — medium

Morrison, Toni. *A Mercy.* New York: Knopf, 2008. Print.

place — pub. — date

b. Database When you are documenting a book you accessed through a database, add the name of the database and change the medium of publication from *Print* to *Web.* Also, add the date (day, month, year) on which you accessed the work.

Wharton, Edith. *The Age of Innocence.* New York: Appleton, 1920.
database — date accessed
Bartleby.com. Web. 5 July 2007.
medium

c. E-book The citation for an electronic version of a book is the same as for a printed book except that the medium of publication changes from *Print* to the specific type of e-book file you read: *Gemstar e-book file, Microsoft Reader e-book file, Kindle e-book file,* and so on.

medium
Morrison, Toni. *A Mercy.* New York: Knopf, 2008. Kindle e-book file.

2. Two or three authors List authors in the order in which they appear on the title page. Only the first author should be listed with surname first.

author 1 — author 2
Miller, Brenda, and Suzanne Paola. *Tell It Slant.* New York: McGraw, 2004. Print.

author 1 — author 2 — author 3
Fleming, Robert L., Jr., Dorje Tsering, and Liu Wulin. *Across the Tibetan Plateau: Ecosystems, Wildlife, and Conservation.* New York: Norton, 2008. Print.

More about ▸▸▸ *et al.,* 237

3. More than three authors Either list all the authors, or just list the first and add *et al.* Whichever you choose, do the same in your in-text citation.

Visonà, Monica Blackmun, et al. *A History of Art in Africa.* New York: Abrams, 2001. Print.

Example 3, 237

Visonà, Monica Blackmun, Robin Poynor, Herbert M. Cole, Michael D. Harris, Rowland Abiodun, and Suzanne Preston Blier. *A History of Art in Africa.* New York: Abrams, 2001. Print.

4. Unnamed (anonymous) author Start the entry with the title.

title

Terrorist Hunter: The Extraordinary Story of a Woman Who Went Undercover to Infiltrate the Radical Islamic Groups Operating in America. New York: Ecco-HarperCollins, 2003. Print.

Alphabetize the entry in your list of works cited using the first significant word of the title (not an article, like *a, an,* or *the*). Only if the author is listed specifically as "Anonymous" should you use that designation in the entry.

Anonymous. *Go Ask Alice.* Englewood Cliffs: Prentice, 1971. Print.

5. Two or more works by the same author Alphabetize the entries by the first important word in each title. Supply the author's name only with the first entry; for subsequent works, replace the author's name with three hyphens.

Chabon, Michael. *The Final Solution: A Story of Detection.* New York: Fourth Estate, 2004. Print.

---. *The Yiddish Policeman's Union: A Novel.* New York: HarperCollins, 2007. Print.

6. Group or corporate author Treat the sponsoring organization as the author.

corporate author

Blackfoot Gallery Committee. *The Story of the Blackfoot People: Nitsitapiisinni.* Richmond Hill: Firefly, 2002. Print.

MLA Works-Cited Entries

5. Two or more works by the same author
6. Group or corporate author
7. **Author and editor or translator**
8. **Edited book or anthology as a whole**
9. **One or more selections from an edited book or anthology**
10. Edition other than the first
11. Imprint (division) of a larger publishing company

7. Author and editor or translator List the author first; after the title, include the abbreviation *Ed.* or *Trans.* (as appropriate) and the editor's or translator's name.

NOTE When the abbreviation appears before the editor's or translator's name, it means *edited by* or *translated by,* so use the same abbreviation whether there is one editor or translator or many.

Larsson, Asa. *Sun Storm.* Trans. Marlaine Delargy. New York: Delacorte, 2006. Print.

8. Edited book or anthology as a whole If you are citing the work as a whole, treat the editor as the author.

Furman, Laura, ed. *The O. Henry Prize Stories: The Best Stories of the Year.* New York: Anchor, 2008. Print.

If there is more than one editor, use *eds.* (for *editors*).

Delbanco, Nicholas, and Alan Cheuse, eds. *Literature: Craft and Voice.* New York: McGraw, 2009. Print.

9. One or more selections from an edited book or anthology If you are citing a selection from an edited book or anthology, start the entry with the selection's author and title. Include the page numbers for the entire selection (even if you used only part).

author — title (selection)

Faulkner, William. "A Rose for Emily." *Literature: Reading Fiction, Poetry, and Drama.* Ed. Robert DiYanni. 6th ed. New York: McGraw, 2009. 79–84. Print.

pages

Example 8, 250

If you are citing more than one selection in the anthology or collection, include an entry for the collection as a whole. For each selection you use, include the author and title of the selection, followed by the surname of the editor and the page numbers of the selection.

Faulkner, William. "A Rose for Emily." DiYanni. 79–84. Print.

For a scholarly article included in an edited book, include the article's original publication information first, the abbreviation *Rpt. in* for *reprinted in,* and then the publication information for the anthology.

Example 23 (a–c), 256–57

original publication info.

Stock, A. G. "Yeats and Achebe." *Journal of Commonwealth Literature* 5 (1968): 105–11. Rpt. in *Things Fall Apart.* By Chinua Achebe. Ed. Francis Abiola Irele. New York: Norton, 2008. 271–77. Print.

reprint publication info.

10. Edition other than the first Insert the edition number (*2nd ed., 3rd ed.*) or edition name (*Rev. ed.* for "revised edition") after the book's title. The edition number or name should appear on the title page.

Rosebury, Brian. *Tolkien: A Literary Phenomenon.* 2nd ed. New York: Palgrave, 2004. Print.

If there is an editor or translator, insert the edition number or name after the editor's or translator's name.

11. Imprint (division) of a larger publishing company Name both the imprint and publisher, separating them with a hyphen.

Betcherman, Lita-Rose. *Court Lady and Country Wife: Two Noble Sisters in Seventeenth-Century England.* New York: Morrow-HarperCollins, 2005. Print.

imprint publisher

12. Introduction, preface, foreword, or afterword Begin with the name of the person who wrote this section of the text. Then provide a descriptive label (such as *Introduction* or *Preface*), followed by the title of the book, the word *by,* and the name of the book's author. (If the author of the section and the author of the book are the same person, use only the author's surname after the title.) Include the page numbers for the section.

author of intro. label title of book author of book

Barrett, Michèle. Introduction. *The Origin of the Family, Private Property and the State.* By Friedrich Engels. New York: Penguin, 1986. 7–30. Print.

MLA Works-Cited Entries

If this section has a title, include it before the descriptive label.

afterword's title

Burton, Larry W. "Countering the Naysayers: Independent Writing Programs as Successful Experiments in American Education." Afterword. *A Field of Dreams: Independent Writing Programs and the Future of Composition Studies.* Ed. Peggy O'Neill, Angela Crow, and Larry W. Burton. Logan: Utah State UP, 2002. 295–300. Print.

label

13. Entry in a reference work Format an entry in a dictionary or encyclopedia as you would a selection from an edited book or anthology. For signed articles, include the author's name. (Articles in reference works often carry the author's initials only, so you may need to cross-reference the initials with a list of contributors in the front or back of the book.) If an article is unsigned, begin with its title.

a. Printed For familiar reference works, omit publication information other than the edition and year of publication; for all other reference works, include full publication information. If the entries are arranged alphabetically, omit a page reference.

"Culture." *Oxford English Dictionary.* Compact 2nd ed. 1991. Print.

Green, Michael. "Cultural Studies." *A Dictionary of Cultural and Critical Theory.* Cambridge: Blackwell, 1996. Print.

b. Online For online reference works, add the site's sponsor, change the medium of publication to *Web,* and add the date you accessed the site.

sponsor

"Culture." *Merriam-Webster Online Dictionary.* Merriam-Webster Online, 2008. Web. 1 Dec. 2008.

medium access date

c. CD-ROM or DVD-ROM Although CD-ROMs and DVD-ROMs have largely been replaced by the internet, you may still need to use them. If the CD-ROM or DVD-ROM is published in versions rather than editions, use the abbreviation *Vers.* and include the version number after the title or editor's name. Change the medium of publication to *CD-ROM* or *DVD-ROM.*

Cooley, Marianne. "Alphabet." *World Book Multimedia Encyclopedia.* Vers. 6.0.2. Chicago: World Book, 2002. CD-ROM.

(version: Vers. 6.0.2.; medium: CD-ROM.)

14. Multivolume work

a. Multiple volumes Indicate the total number of volumes, followed by the abbreviation *vols.,* and indicate the span of years in which the volumes were published. Specify the volume from which you borrowed a particular passage or idea in your text citation.

Example 9, 239–40

Tarbell, Ida M. *The Life of Abraham Lincoln.* 2 vols. New York: Lincoln Memorial Association, 1895–1900. Print.

(no. of vols.: 2 vols.; pub. date: 1895–1900.)

b. One volume If you used only one volume, include the number of the volume you used before the publication information, and give only the publication date of that volume.

Tarbell, Ida M. *The Life of Abraham Lincoln.* Vol. 1. New York: Lincoln Memorial Association, 1895. Print.

(vol. used: Vol. 1.; pub. date: 1895.)

15. Book in a series If the book you are citing is part of a series, the series title will usually be noted on the book's title page or on the page before the title page. Insert the series title (with no quotation marks or italics) after the medium of publication. If books in the series are numbered, include the number following the series title.

Todorov, Tzvetan. *Mikhail Bakhtin: The Dialogical Principle.* Trans. Wlad Godzich. Minneapolis: U Minnesota P, 1995. Print. Theory and History of Literature 13.

(series title: Theory and History of Literature; no.: 13.)

16. Republished book A republished book is one that has been published by a new publisher or in a new form (for example, in paperback after having been published originally in hardcover). Include the original publication date (which will appear on the book's copyright page) before publication information for the version you consulted.

Mallon, Thomas. *Stolen Words.* 1989. New York: Harvest, 2001. Print.

(orig. pub. date: 1989.; repub. info.: New York: Harvest, 2001.)

If material such as an introduction has been added, include that information (e.g., *Introd. Declan Kiberd*) between the original date of publication and the republication information.

17. Title within a title Omit italics from any title that would normally be italicized when it falls within the main title of a book.

book title — title within title

Blamires, Harry. *The New Bloomsbury Book: A Guide Through* Ulysses. 3rd ed. London: Routledge, 2006. Print.

If the title within the title appears in quotation marks, retain the quotation marks and italicize both titles.

18. Sacred text Italicize the title only when you are documenting a particular edition. Editors' and translators' names generally follow the title.

The Holy Qur'an. Ed. and trans. Abdullah Yusuf Ali. 10th ed. Beltsville: Amana, 1997. Print.

19. Missing publication information Replace missing information with an appropriate abbreviation, such as *n.d.* for *no date* or *n.p.* for *no publisher* or *no place of publication.*

Barrett, Edgar, ed. *Football West Virginia 1960.* N.p.: West Virginia U, n.d. Print.

Examples 1–7, 248–50

20. Pamphlet, brochure, or press release Follow the format for book entries. For a press release, include day and month of publication, if available.

"Family Teams Key to March for Babies." Fargo: March of Dimes, 17 Jan. 2008. Print.

Example 1, 248

If emailed or published online, document as you would a book published online.

21. Conference proceedings Include the name of the conference, the sponsoring organization, and the year the conference was held, if that information is not already conveyed by the book's title.

Bizzell, Patricia, ed. *Rhetorical Agendas: Political, Ethical, Spiritual.*

conference/sponsor date

Proc. of the Rhetoric Society of America, 2004. Mahwah:

Erlbaum, 2005. Print.

For a paper delivered at a conference, follow the format for a lecture.

Example 46, 267

22. Dissertation Include the abbreviation *Diss.*, the school to which the dissertation was submitted (abbreviate *University* to *U*), and the year it was submitted. For published dissertations, set the title in italics.

Agopsowicz, William Joseph. *In Praise of Fantasy: A Study of the Nineteenth Century American Short Story (Poe, Hawthorne, Irving, Melville, Bierce, James).* Diss. Arizona State U, 1992. Ann Arbor: UMI, 1992. Print.

For unpublished dissertations, put the title in quotation marks.

Brommer, Stephanie. "We Walk with Them: South Asian Women's Organizations in Northern California Confront Domestic

diss. submission info

Abuse." Diss. U of California–Santa Barbara, 2004. Print.

MLA Works-Cited Entries

Periodicals—Printed and Electronic

A periodical is a publication issued at regular intervals—newspapers are generally published every day, magazines every week or month, and scholarly journals four times a year. For all periodicals, include not only the title of the article (in quotation marks) but also the title of the periodical (in italics). The other publication information you include depends on the type of periodical you are documenting.

▶▶▶Annotated visual of where to find author, title, publication, and other information, on foldout following p. 385

23. Article in a scholarly journal The information you need to create an entry for a printed journal article is on the cover or table of contents of the journal and the first and last page of the article. For articles downloaded from a database, the information you need appears on the screen listing the articles that fit your search terms or on the first (and last) page of the file you download. For articles that appear in journals published solely online, you may find the information you need on the website's home page, in the journal's table of contents, or on the first screen of the article.

a. Printed The basic entry for an article in a printed journal looks like this:

> Surname, First name. "Article Title." *Journal Title* volume.issue (year):
>
> pages. Medium of publication.

Here is an example of an actual entry:

> Cantor, Nancy, and Steve Schomberg. "What We Want Students to Learn: Cultivating Playfulness and Responsibility in a Liberal Education." *Change* 34.6 (2002): 47–49. Print.

MLA Works-Cited Entries

b. Accessed through a database When you document an article from a scholarly journal that you accessed through an online database, add the name of the database (in italics), change the medium of publication to *Web,* and add the date (day, month, year) on which you accessed the work.

> Cantor, Nancy, and Steve Schomberg. "What We Want Students to Learn: Cultivating Playfulness and Responsibility in a Liberal Education." *Change* 34.6 (2002): 47–49. *Academic Search Premier.* Web. 2 Dec. 2008.

c. Online

To document an online journal article, follow the model for a printed journal article; at the end of the entry, add the date on which you accessed the article. Although many journals that are published only online do not provide all the information that is available for printed journals, your entry should include as much of that information as possible. If the article you are documenting omits page numbers, use *n. pag.* in their place. Include the article's URL only if readers will not be able to find the article by searching for the author or title. (The parts that are different from a printed journal article are highlighted below.)

Lohnes, Sarah, and Charles Kinzer. "Questioning Assumptions about Students' Expectations for Technology in College Classrooms." *Innovate* 3.5 (2007): n. pag. Web. 28 June 2007.

(medium: Web.; access date: 28 June 2007.)

24. Article in a magazine

a. Printed Provide the issue's publication date (month and year; or day, month, and year) and the page range for the article, but not the magazine's volume or issue number, even when they are available.

Samuels, David. "Shooting Britney." *Atlantic Monthly* Apr. 2008: 36–51. Print.

(pub. date: Apr. 2008:; pgs.: 36–51.)

b. Accessed through a database

Samuels, David. "Shooting Britney." *Atlantic Monthly* Apr. 2008: 36–51. *Academic Search Premier.* Web. 25 Apr. 2008.

(database: *Academic Search Premier.*; medium: Web.; access date: 25 Apr. 2008.)

c. Online Very few online magazines include page or paragraph numbers; use *n. pag.* instead.

Stevenson, Seth. "Ads We Hate." *Slate* 26 Dec. 2006: n. pag. Web. 3 Jan. 2007.

(pgs.: n. pag.; medium: Web.; access date: 3 Jan. 2007.)

If you are documenting the online edition of a print magazine, provide the site name (usually a variation on the print title, such as *Progressive .org* or *Vanity Fair Online*), the publisher of the site, the publication date, and the date you accessed the material.

Carr, Nicholas. "Is Google Making Us Stupid?" *The Atlantic.com.* Atlantic Monthly Group, July/Aug. 2008. Web. 2 Dec. 2008.

(site name: *The Atlantic.com.*; sponsor: Atlantic Monthly Group)

25. Article in a newspaper The information you need to create an entry for a printed newspaper article is on the masthead of the newspaper (at the top of the first page) and on the first and last page of the

MLA Works-Cited Entries

article. For newspaper articles downloaded from a database, the information you need appears on the screen listing the articles that fit your search terms or on the first (and last) page of the article itself. Articles that appear in online versions of the newspaper usually contain all the information you need at the top of the first screen.

a. Printed For an article in a daily newspaper, include the date (day, month, year). If the paper paginates sections separately, include the section number, letter, or name immediately before the page number.

> Bolanos, Enrique. "Facing Down the Sandinistas." *Washington Times* 12 May 2005: A20. Print.
>
> [date: 12 May 2005; sec. & pg.: A20]

If the section number or letter is not part of the page number, add the abbreviation *sec.* and the section name, number, or letter. If the section is named, add the section name before the abbreviation *sec.* If no author is listed, begin the entry with the title of the article. If the article continues on a nonconsecutive page, add a plus sign after the first page number (*A20+*). If the newspaper's masthead specifies an edition (such as late edition or national edition), include that information after the date.

> Keller, Julia. "Viral Villainy." *Chicago Tribune* 22 Mar. 2009, final ed., sec. 6: 1+. Print.

If the name of the city in which the newspaper is published does not appear in the newspaper's title, include it in brackets after the title.

> Willman, David. "NIH Calls Actions of Senior Researcher 'Serious Misconduct.'" *Plain Dealer* [Cleveland] 10 Sept. 2006: A15. Print.
>
> [newspaper: *Plain Dealer*; city: [Cleveland]]

For well-known national newspapers (such as the *Christian Science Monitor*, *USA Today*, and the *Wall Street Journal*), no city or state is needed. If you are unsure whether the newspaper is well known, consult your instructor or a reference librarian.

b. Accessed through a database For a newspaper article accessed through a database, add the database name, change the medium, and add the access date.

Bolanos, Enrique. "Facing Down the Sandinistas." *Washington Times*

date sec. & pg. database medium access date

12 May 2005: A20. *LexisNexis.* Web. 2 Dec. 2008.

c. Online For an online newspaper article, provide the title and publisher of the online publication, and include your date of access.

Woo, Elaine. "Edna Parker Dies at 115; Former Teacher Was World's

site name sponsor

Oldest Person." *LATimes.com.* Los Angeles Times, 28 Nov. 2008.

access date

Web. 2 Dec. 2008.

26. Article on microform Many libraries still store some back issues of periodicals on microform, a photograph of a periodical printed on plastic and viewed through a special microform reader. Your entry for a source stored on microform is the same as if you had accessed the source in print.

Example 23a, 256
Example 24a, 257
Example 25a, 258

If your source is preserved on microform in a reference source such as *NewsBank,* change the medium of publication to *Microform* and add the title of the reference source and any access numbers (such as fiche and grid numbers) following the medium of publication.

27. Review Begin with the reviewer's name (if provided), followed by the title of the review (if any) and the label *Rev. of* (for *Review of*). Then include the title and author of the work being reviewed. Finally, include the title of the periodical and its publication information. If the review was accessed online, add information as shown in item 23b–c, 24b–c, or 25b–c.

Grover, Jan. "Unreliable Narrator." Rev. of *Love Works Like This: Opening One's Life to a Child,* by Lauren Slater. *Women's Review of Books* 19.10–11 (2002): 40. Print.

28. Editorial Often editorials are unsigned; when that is the case, begin with the title of the editorial (if any). Then insert the label *Editorial* and follow with the periodical's publication information.

"Expanding the Horizon: OSU President Seeks to Give Students a New View of Their Place in the World." Editorial. *Columbus Dispatch* 12 Mar. 2009: A8. Print.

MLA Works-Cited Entries

25. Article in a newspaper
26. Article on microform
27. Review
28. Editorial
29. Letter to the editor
30. Website

MLA Works-Cited Entries

If the editorial was accessed online, add information as shown in item 23b–c, 24b–c, or 25b–c.

29. Letter to the editor Begin with the author's name, followed by the label *Letter* and the periodical's publication information.

> Pritchett, Laura. Letter. *Poets & Writers Magazine* Jan.–Feb. 2004: 7. Print.

If the letter to the editor has a title, add it after the author's name (in quotation marks). If the letter to the editor was accessed online, add information as shown in item 23b–c, 24b–c, or 25b–c.

Other Electronic Sources

While it is usually easy to find the information you need to create a complete entry for a book or an article in a periodical, websites can be a bit trickier. Most of the information you need will appear on the site's home page, usually at the bottom or top of the page, or on the web page you are documenting. Sometimes you may need to look further: Click on links such as "About us" or "More information." Frequently, websites will not provide complete information, so provide as much as you can.

▶▶▶Annotated visual of where to find author, title, publication, and other information, on foldout following p. 385

30. Website The basic entry for a website looks like this:

> Author's surname, First name. *Website Title.* Copyright date or date last updated. Sponsor. Medium. Access date.

Here is an example of an actual entry:

editor / title (website) / update / sponsor / medium / access date

> McGann, Jerome J., ed. *The Complete Writings and Pictures of Dante Gabriel Rossetti: A Hypermedia Archive.* 2008. Institute for Advanced Technology in the Humanities, U of Virginia, and Networked Infrastructure for Nineteenth-Century Electronic Scholarship. Web. 30 Jan. 2007.

If no author or editor is listed, begin with the website's title.

31. Web page Add the title of the web page to the entry for a website.

page title

Bahri, Deepika. "Yehuda Amichai." *Postcolonial Studies.* Dept. of English, Emory U. 13 Nov. 2002. Web. 7 Feb. 2007.

Personal websites often do not provide all the information needed to create a complete entry. If the site does not have a title, include the identifier *Home page* or *Website;* if the title includes the author's name, do not restate it.

32. Home page (academic)

a. Course

instructor / course title / label / term & year

Gray, David. *Introduction to Ethics.* Course home page. Spring 2006.

department / school / medium / access date

Dept. of Philosophy. Carnegie Mellon U. Web. 17 Apr. 2007.

b. Department

dept. / label

English. Dept. home page. U of California–Santa Barbara. 2005. Web. 20 July 2007.

33. Discussion list posting Treat the subject line as the title, and include the label *Online posting,* the date of the posting (if available), and the name of the list or sponsoring group.

subj. line / label / date posted

Tucker, Mieke Koppen. "Grammar Study." Online posting. 7 Oct. 1995.

list name

Writing Program Administration Discussion List. Web. 2 Jan. 2004.

34. Article on a wiki Since wikis are written and edited collaboratively, there is no author to cite; begin the entry with the article title.

sponsor/host

"The Knife of Never Letting Go." *ChildLitWiki.* Created and maintained by Mat Berman. 14 Sept. 2008. Web. 17 Sept. 2008.

35. Blog, blog posting, or comment on a blog posting

a. Blog

blogger / blog / label / medium / access date

Walker, Jill. *Jill/txt.* N.p. Web. 10 June 2007.

b. Blog posting

post author / post title

Bartow, Ann. "Why Are There So Many Academic Books Out There That Would Be Better as Longish Articles?" *Sivacracy.net.* Institute for the Future of the Book, 26 Dec. 2006. Web. 30 Dec. 2006.

sponsor/host / post date

c. Comment on a blog posting

comment author / title of entry commented on

Bailey, Jonathan. Comment on "Content Theft / Blog Plagiarism," by Ryan McCue. *Ryan McCue's Blog.* 18 Nov. 2004. Web. 19 Nov. 2004.

If the comment's author uses a screen name, use that; if the actual name is available and of interest to readers, provide that as well, following the screen name, in square brackets.

MLA Works-Cited Entries

36. *Second Life* If the author/speaker uses an avatar with a different name than the writer's actual name, use the avatar's name, but if the writer's actual name is available and of interest to readers (it may lend credibility, for example), provide it in square brackets following the avatar name.

avatar / actual name

Reuters, Eric [Eric Krangel]. "*Second Life* on *The Daily Show.*" *Second Life News Center/Reuters.* Linden Lab, 8 Apr. 2007. Web. 10 Feb. 2008.

sponsor/host

37. Source published in more than one medium Some sources may include multiple media; for example, a printed book may come with a supplementary website or CD-ROM. In the entry in your list of works cited, follow the entry format for the part of the source that you mainly used, but list all the media you consulted in alphabetical order.

Davis, Robert L., H. Jay Siskin, and Alicia Ramos. *Entrevistas: An Introduction to Language and Culture.* 2nd ed. New York: McGraw, 2005. CD-ROM, print, website.

list of media

38. Computer software

title / vendor / release date / medium / download date

PowerResearcher. Atlanta: Uniting Networks, 2004. Digital file. 8 June 2004.

39. Video game

game / publisher / release date / medium

Rock Band 2. Redmond: Nintendo, 2008. Wii video game.

Audio and Visual Sources

The information you need to create an entry for most audio and visual sources will appear on the cover, label, or program of the work or in the credits at the end of a film. The person you list in the "author" position—the director, performer, artist, or composer—will vary depending on what you have emphasized in the body of your research project. If you are writing about a director's body of work, put the director's name first; if you are writing about a performance, put the performer's name first. If it is the work itself that you are writing about, put the title of the work first. However you choose to organize the entry, indicate the role of those whom you list, using abbreviations such as *perf.* (*performer*), *dir.* (*director*), and *cond.* (*conductor*).

As with any other entry, italicize the titles of complete or longer works (such as albums, films, operas, and original works of art) and place quotation marks around the titles of shorter works or works published as part of a larger whole (such as songs on a CD or a single episode of a television show). Publication information includes the name of the distributor, production company, or network, as well as the date on which the audio or visual was created, recorded, or broadcast and the medium through which you accessed it. If you found the audio or visual source online, also include the date on which you last accessed it.

40. Motion picture

a. Film

title / director / distributor / release date / medium

King of Kong. Dir. Seth Gordon. PictureHouse Entertainment, 2007. Film.

If other artists besides the director are relevant to your project, list them between the director and the distributor.

MLA Works-Cited Entries

performers

King of Kong. Dir. Seth Gordon. Perf. Steve Wiebe and Billy Mitchell. PictureHouse Entertainment, 2007. Film.

If your project stresses the director, performer, or other contributor, place that information at the beginning of the citation.

Gordon, Seth, dir. *King of Kong.* Perf. Steve Wiebe and Billy Mitchell. PictureHouse Entertainment, 2007. Film.

b. Video or DVD Include the original release date, when relevant, before the distributor, and include the medium through which you accessed it.

orig. release — medium

The Lady Eve. Dir. Preston Sturges. Perf. Barbara Stanwyck and Henry Fonda. 1941. Universal Home Entertainment, 2006. DVD.

c. Internet download Include the date on which you accessed the film.

access date

Juno. Screenplay by Diablo Cody. Dir. Jason Reitman. Perf. Ellen Page, Michael Cera, Jennifer Garner, Jason Bateman, J. K. Simmons, and Alison Janney. 20th Century Fox, 2007. Digital file. 19 Jan. 2009.

41. DVD extras Add the title of the extra (in quotation marks).

DVD extra

"Making *Capote:* Concept to Script." *Capote.* Dir. Bennett Miller. Perf. Philip Seymour Hoffman and Catherine Keener. 2005. Sony Pictures, 2006. DVD.

42. Television or radio broadcast In most cases, begin with the title of the series or episode. Follow that with a list of the relevant contributors and information about the local station that broadcast the program. Because the director may change from episode to episode, other contributors, such as the creator or producer, may be more relevant. Next, include the date of the program and the medium through which you accessed it. If your project emphasizes an individual, begin with that person's name. Add any supplementary information at the end of the entry.

MLA Works-Cited Entries

a. Series

series
Lost. Creat. and exec. prod. J. A. Abrams, Jeffrey Lieber, and Damon Lindelof. Perf. Naveen Andrews, Matthew Fox, Jorge Garcia, Josh Holloway, Daniel Dae Kim, Yunjun Kim, Evangeline Lilly, and Terry O'Quinn. ABC. KNXV, Phoenix, 22 Sept. 2004–29 May 2008. Television.

network — city of local station — broadcast dates — medium — call letters

Bridging the Morphine Gap. Host Mukti Jain Campion. BBC. Radio 4, London, 3 Mar. 2008. Radio.

b. Episode

"In Buddy's Eyes." *Desperate Housewives.* Perf. Teri Hatcher, Felicity Huffman, Marcia Cross, Eva Longoria Parker, and Nicollette Sheridan. ABC. KNXV, Phoenix, 20 Apr. 2008. Digital file, television. *iTunes,* 2008.

supplementary info.

c. Single program

Persuasion. By Jane Austen. Adapt. Simon Burke. Perf. Julia Davis and Rupert Penry-Jones. PBS. WGBH, Boston, 13 Jan. 2008. Television.

d. Podcast For a podcast, replace the original medium of publication with the word *Podcast* and the date on which you accessed the file.

"The Giant Pool of Money." Narr. Ira Glass. *This American Life.* Natl. Public Radio. WBEZ, Chicago, 27 Sept. 2008. Podcast. 3 Oct. 2008.

medium — access date

43. Musical or other audio recording Begin with whichever part of the entry is most relevant to your project—the name of the composer or performer, or the title of the CD or song. Song titles are placed in quotation marks, and album titles are italicized even when the composition itself may not usually be italicized (like long musical compositions identified only by form, number, and key, such as Bruckner's Symphony no. 8).

a. CD, LP, audiobook

Adamo, Mark. *Little Women.* Perf. Stephanie Novacek, Chad Shelton, Margaret Lloyd, and Stacey Tappan. Cond. Patrick Summers. Houston Grand Opera. Ondine, 2001. CD.

prod. co. & release date — medium

Bruckner, Anton. *Symphony No. 8.* Vienna Philharmonic Orchestra. Cond. Herbert von Karajan. Deutsche Grammophon, 1989. CD.

b. Song or selection from a CD, LP, or audiobook

Los Campesinos. "My Year in Lists." *Hold on Now, Youngster. . . .* Arts & Crafts, 2008. CD.

c. Compressed music file (MP3, MP4)

Los Campesinos. "My Year in Lists." *Hold on Now, Youngster. . . .* Arts & Crafts, 2008. MP3. *iTunes,* 2008. 16 Dec. 2008.

supplementary info. — download date

d. Online sound file or clip For a sound recording accessed online, combine the format for a web page with the format for a sound recording.

Example 31, 261

Chaucer, Geoffrey. "'The Miller's Tale': Nicholas Seduces Alisoun." Perf. Alfred David. *The Canterbury Tales. "The Criyng and the Soun": The Chaucer Metapage Audio Files.* VA Military Inst. Dept. of Eng. and Fine Arts. 11 Dec. 2006. Web. 20 July 2007.

author — selection title — title of work — website — sponsor — date posted — medium — date accessed

44. Live performance The entry for a performance is similar to that for a film. Instead of the distributor, year of release, and medium of publication, include the group (if any), the venue and city of the performance, the date of the performance you attended, and the word *Performance.* If your project emphasizes the composer, writer, or performer, begin the entry with that information. If the performance is untitled, include a descriptive label.

a. Ensemble

Macbeth. By William Shakespeare. Dir. Christopher Carter Sanderson. Perf. Natasha Badillo, Ambjorn Elder, and Frances You. Gorilla Repertory Theatre Company. Fort Tryon Park, New York. 17 May 2002. Performance.

(group: Gorilla Repertory Theatre Company; venue: Fort Tryon Park; city: New York; perf. date: 17 May 2002)

b. Individual

Stinespring, Marjorie M. Piano recital. Chicago State University. 2 Mar. 2004. Performance.

(performer: Stinespring, Marjorie M.; label: Piano recital.)

45. Musical composition To document a musical composition itself rather than a specific performance or recording, include the composer and the title of the work. Complete the citation as you would for a book.

Mozart, Wolfgang Amadeus. *Don Giovanni.* New York: G. Schirmer, 1961. Print.

(composer: Mozart, Wolfgang Amadeus.; title: *Don Giovanni.*)

Schumann, Robert. *Symphony no. 1 in B-flat major, op. 38.* London: Eulenburg, 1986. Print.

(composer: Schumann, Robert.; title: *Symphony no. 1 in B-flat major, op. 38.*)

46. Lecture, speech, or debate Treat the speaker as the author; place the title in quotation marks (if there is one); and indicate the occasion and sponsoring organization (if relevant), location, date, and mode of delivery. If the lecture, speech, or debate is untitled, replace the title with a brief descriptive label.

Biden, Joseph, and Sarah Palin. "Vice Presidential Debate 2008." Washington University, St. Louis. 9 Oct. 2008. Debate.

(speakers: Biden, Joseph, and Sarah Palin.; title: "Vice Presidential Debate 2008."; sponsor: Washington University,; location: St. Louis.; date: 9 Oct. 2008.; medium: Debate.)

47. Table For a table included in your paper, place a source note below the table. For a table that you are discussing but that does not appear in your paper, follow the model below:

author / title / label / medium / access date

U.S. Senate. "Senate Salaries since 1789." Chart. 7 June 2004. Web.

48. Work of art For a work of art included in your paper, place source information in the figure caption. For a work that you discuss but that does not appear in your project, follow the model below:

a. Original work

artist / title / date of production / medium / location

Pollock, Jackson. *One Number 31, 1950*. 1950. Acrylic on canvas. Museum of Modern Art, New York.

b. Reproduction of a work of art

Lichtenstein, Roy. *Whaam!* 1963. Acrylic on canvas. Tate Gallery, London. *Responding to Art: Form, Content, and Context.* By Robert Bersson. New York: McGraw, 2004. Print.

49. Comic or cartoon For a cartoon reproduced in your project, provide source information in the caption. For cartoons that you discuss but that do not appear in your project, follow the models below:

a. Cartoon or comic strip

artist / title / label / publication information / medium

Wright, Larry. "Kit 'n' Carlyle." Cartoon. *Evening Sun* [Norwich] 28 Dec. 2006: 8. Print.

b. Comic book or graphic novel

authors / title / pub. info. / medium

Pekar, Harvey, and Joyce Brabner. *Our Cancer Year.* Illus. Frank Stack. Philadelphia: Running Press, 1994. Print.

50. Map or chart For a map or chart reproduced in your project, provide source information in the caption. For a map or chart discussed but not included in your project, follow the model on the next page:

MLA Works-Cited Entries

"The Invasion of Sicily: Allied Advance to Messina (23 July–17 August 1943." Map. *The West Point Atlas of American Wars.* Ed. Vincent J. Esposito. Vol. 2. New York: Praeger, 1959. Print.

(label: Map.)

51. Advertisement For an advertisement reproduced in your project, provide source information in the caption. For an advertisement discussed but not included in your project, follow the models below:

Earthlink Cable Internet. Advertisement. *Metro* 17 Apr. 2007: 11. Print.

(label: Advertisement.)

Infiniti. Advertisement. *Yahoo.com.* Web. 20 Apr. 2007.

(date accessed: 20 Apr. 2007.)

Domino's Pizza. Advertisement. Comedy Central. 2 Aug. 2006. Television.

(date viewed: 2 Aug. 2006.)

Miscellaneous Sources

52. Government publication If no author is listed, use the name of the governing nation and the government agency or department that produced the document as you would for a work with a corporate author. Abbreviate Government Printing Office as *GPO.*

Example 6, 249

United States. War Department. *Advanced Map and Aerial Photograph Reading.* Washington: GPO, 1941. Print.

(nation: United States. department: War Department.)

For Congressional documents, include the number and session of Congress and the number and type of document. Common abbreviations in U.S. government documents include the following:

HR	House of Representatives	**Res.**	Resolution
S	Senate	**Doc.**	Document
Sess.	Session	**GPO**	Government Printing Office
Rept.	Report		

a. Printed

United States. Cong. House. *Combat Bonus Act.* 110th Cong., 2nd sess. HR 6760. Washington: GPO, 2008. Print.

b. Online

United States. Cong. House. *Combat Bonus Act.* 110th Cong., 2nd sess. HR 6760. 2008. *Govtrack.05.* Web. 16 Dec. 2008.

53. Legal case

legal case — case number — court — decision yr

Gideon v. Wainwright. 372 US 335. Supreme Court of the US. 1963. *FindLaw.* Web. 16 Dec. 2008.

website

Example 9, 250

54. Letter (published)

a. Single letter Cite a single letter as you would a selection from an edited book or anthology, but add the recipient's name, the date the letter was written, and the letter number (if there is one).

author — recipient — date written

Brooks, Phillips. "To Agnes." 24 Sept. 1882. *Children's Letters: A Collection of Letters Written to Children by Famous Men and Women.* Ed. Elizabeth Colson and Anna Gauseroot Chittenden. New York: Hinds, 1905. 3–4. Print.

Example 8, 250

b. Collection of letters Cite a collection of letters as you would an edited book or anthology.

Examples 23–25, 255–59

Example 42, 264–65

55. Interview Treat a published interview as you would an article in a periodical. Treat an interview broadcast on radio or television or podcasted as you would a broadcast. In either case, if there is no title, use the label Interview, and include the interviewer's name.

person interviewed — host — site name — sponsor

Saberi, Roxana. Interview with Melissa Block. *NPR.org.* National Public Radio, 28 May 2009. Web. 29 May 2009.

date posted

For an unpublished interview you conducted, include the name of the person interviewed, the label *Personal interview, Telephone interview,* or *Email interview,* and the date on which the interview took place.

person interviewed — label — date

Freund, Deborah. Personal interview. 11 Feb. 2003.

56. Personal correspondence To document personal correspondence, such as a letter or email message you received, include a descriptive label such as *Letter to the author* or *Message to the author,* as well as the medium (*MS* for "manuscript"; *Email; Memo; Instant Message*).

a. Letter

letter writer / label / date written / medium

Gould, Stephen Jay. Letter to the author. 13 Nov. 1986. MS.

b. Email Treat the subject line as the title; include the descriptive label *Message to the author* and the date the email message was sent. Change the medium to *Email.*

email author / subject line / label / date sent / medium

Elbow, Peter. "Re: bibliography about resistance." Message to the author. 12 Apr. 2004. Email.

A mass email or electronic memo should include a label describing recipients such as *Email to faculty and staff at Cal State–Chico* or *Email to ENG 204 students.*

c. Memorandum Very few institutions send out printed memos anymore, but if you need to document one, treat it like an email message, replacing the word *email* with the word *memo* at the end of your entry.

d. Instant message (IM)

label

White, Rose. Message to the author. 14 June 2007. Instant Message.

57. Diary or journal entry

a. Single entry, published Treat an entry in a published diary or journal like an article in an edited book or anthology, but include a descriptive label (*Diary entry*) and the date of composition after the entry title.

Example 9, 250

b. Single entry, unpublished

writer / title / label / entry date / medium

Zook, Aaron. "Sketches for *Aesop's Foibles* (new musical)." Journal entry. 1 May 2007. MS.

c. Diary or journal, published Treat a complete diary or journal as you would an edited book or anthology.

Example 8, 250

MLA Works-Cited Entries

19c Using MLA Style for Content and Bibliographic Notes

In addition to in-text citations, MLA style allows for content notes and bibliographic notes. These provide information that is useful to the reader but that might be distracting if incorporated into the body of the text. The MLA recommends the use of endnotes for this purpose. Number the notes sequentially, using arabic numerals, and insert the numbers in the text, in superscript (above the line), immediately after the material they comment on. Type the notes, double spaced, on a new page labeled "Note" or "Notes" and insert it between the last page of your paper and your list of works cited.

Sample content note, 287

Use *content notes* to provide information that clarifies or justifies a point in your text, but avoid notes that include interesting digressions that could distract your readers. Lydia Nichols's essay at the end of this chapter includes a content note. You can also use content notes to acknowledge the contributions of others (tutors, classmates, etc.) to the preparation of your paper.

Sample bibliographic note, 287

Bibliographic notes can add information about a source or point readers to other sources on the topic. If several sources provide the same information, cite the most valuable source in your text, and list the others in a bibliographic note. Then include the full citation of all these sources in your list of works cited.

19d Formatting a Paper in MLA Style

Sample student research paper, MLA style, 278–89

If you are writing for English or foreign language classes (or if your instructor asks you to), format your project using MLA style. Lydia Nichols's paper, at the end of this chapter, provides a model.

1. Margins and spacing

Set one-inch margins at the top, bottom, and sides of your paper. Indent the first line of each paragraph one-half inch. Double-space the entire paper, including long quotations, the list of works cited, and any endnotes. Use a hanging indent for each entry in the list of works cited: The first line should be flush with the left margin with subsequent lines indented half an inch.

Creating a Header

Most word processing programs allow you to insert a header. In Microsoft *Word,* select "Header and Footer" under the View menu. A box for the header will appear at the top of your page, and a box for the footer at the bottom. Any information you type into these boxes will then appear on every page of your manuscript. From the menu bar, you can choose to insert page numbers into the header or footer to paginate your project automatically.

2. Typeface

Choose a standard typeface, such as Times New Roman or Arial, in a readable size (usually 12-point).

More about ▸▸▸
Choosing a typeface and type size, 206–14

3. Header

MLA style requires that each page of the essay include a header, consisting of the student's surname and page number. Place the header in the upper right-hand corner, a half inch from the upper edge and one inch from the right edge of the page.

4. Identifying information

The following identifying information should be included in the upper left-hand corner of the first page of your research project, one inch from the top and left edges of the paper:

- Your name
- Your instructor's name
- The number of the course in which you are submitting the paper
- The date

MLA style does not require a title page, but some instructors may request one, especially if you are including additional items, such as an outline or a previous draft, with the final draft of your project. If you are required to provide a title page, Figure 19.2 provides a model.

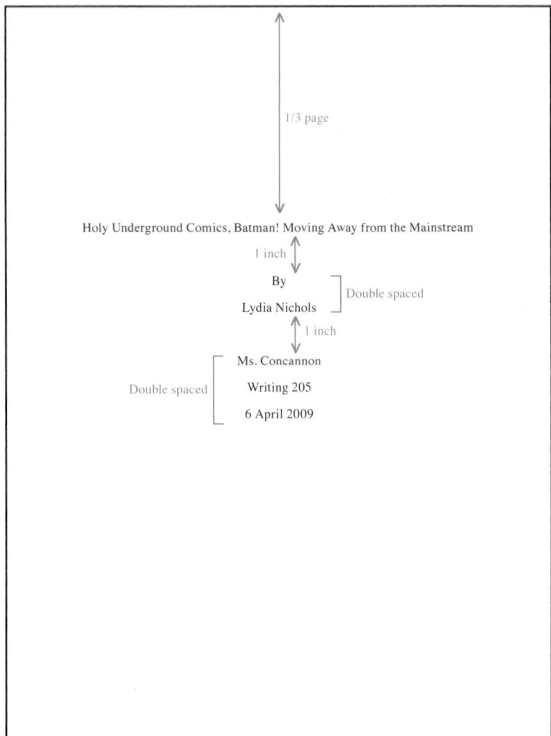

1/3 page
Holy Underground Comics, Batman! Moving Away from the Mainstream
1 inch
By
Lydia Nichols
Double spaced
1 inch
Ms. Concannon
Writing 205
6 April 2009
Double spaced

FIGURE 19.2 A Sample Title Page Note that the title precedes the identifying information from the heading and that the title page does not include a header.

5. Title

More about ▸▸▸
Developing a title, 163–64, 194–95

Center the title of your project and insert it two lines (one double space) below the date. Do not put quotation marks around your title or set it in italics. Drop down two more lines (one double space) before beginning to type the first paragraph of your research project.

6. Long quotations

More about ▸▸▸
Block quotations, 99–105, 108–11
Example block quotation, 235, 279

Set quotations of prose longer than four lines of your text as a block: Omit the quotation marks, and indent the quotation one inch from the left margin of your text. When quoting four or more lines of poetry, indent the lines one inch from the left margin, break lines in the same places as in the original poem, and include the line numbers of the passage quoted. If a line of the poem is too long to fit, indent the continuation by another quarter of an inch.

7. Tables and figures

Tables and figures (photographs, cartoons, graphs, and charts) will be most effective when they appear as close as possible after the text in which they are first discussed. (If placing figures and tables appropriately is awkward, consider including them in an appendix at the end of your project.) Labeling your tables and figures, both in the text and in your caption, will help readers connect your discussion with the illustration:

- Refer to the visual in your text using the word *table* or the abbreviation *fig.*, and number figures and tables in a separate sequence using arabic numerals (table 1, table 2; fig. 1, fig. 2). MLA style uses lowercase for in-text references to tables and figures unless they begin a sentence: "Table 1 presents 2005 data, and table 2 presents 2009 data."
- Accompany each illustration with the word *Table* or the abbreviation *Fig.*, the appropriate number, and a brief, explanatory title. Customarily, table numbers and titles precede the table, and figure numbers and titles follow the figure. Generally, they use the same margins as the rest of the paper.
- If additional information is needed, provide an explanatory caption after the label, number, and title. (This information should not repeat what is in the text.)
- If you borrow the illustration or borrow information needed to create the illustration, cite your source. Any photographs or drawings you create yourself should identify the subject but do not need a citation. Citations usually appear below the table in a source note or in the figure caption. If you document the illustration in a figure caption or source note, you do not need to include an entry in your list of works cited.

8. Printing and binding

If you are submitting a hard copy of your project, print it using a high-quality printer (make sure it has plenty of ink), on opaque, 8½ × 11–inch white paper. Most instructors do not want you to enclose

Writing Responsibly **Of Deadlines and Paper Clips**

Instructors expect students to turn in thoughtful, carefully proofread, and neatly formatted papers on time—usually in class on the due date. Another assumption is that the writer will clip (or staple) the pages of the paper *before* it is submitted. Do justice to yourself by being fully prepared: Do not hand in a stack of loose sheets or expect your instructor to provide a paper clip.

your paper in a binder. Unless your instructor tells you otherwise, clip the pages together in the upper left-hand corner with a paper clip.

More about ▸▸▸
Portfolio, 43–44
Research notes, 93–105
Working bibliography, 44–45, 46–47
Annotated bibliography, 45, 48, 120–27
Outlining and sample outlines, 148–59

9. Portfolios

Many instructors ask students to submit the final draft of the research paper in a portfolio, which may include a research log, an outline, preliminary notes and drafts, a working or annotated bibliography, and a personal statement describing your writing process and what you have learned from the experience (Figure 19.3).

Student Research Project: MLA Style

In the sample student research project that follows, Lydia Nichols explores the world of underground comics. She uses comparison-contrast to support her claim that underground comics are more innovative than their mainstream cousins, and she provides a historical overview to fill in the background her readers lack. Her research draws on a variety of print and online sources, and she uses visuals to support some of her points.

More about ▸▸▸
Gathering information, 50–66
Online research, 67–79
Using visuals as support, 177–79

FIGURE 19.3 Page 1 of Lydia Nichols's Personal Statement Nichols created a visual personal statement to explain how her interest in underground comics developed.

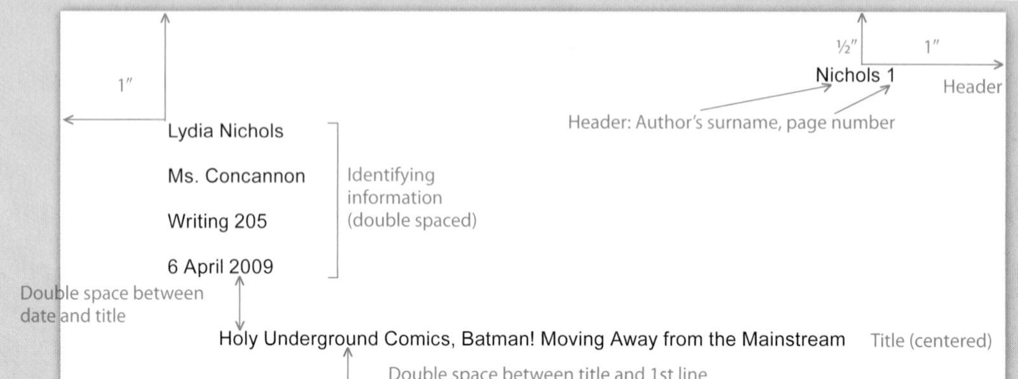

½″ 1″ 1″

Nichols 1

Header

Header: Author's surname, page number

Lydia Nichols

Ms. Concannon

Writing 205

6 April 2009

Identifying information (double spaced)

Double space between date and title

Holy Underground Comics, Batman! Moving Away from the Mainstream

Title (centered)

Double space between title and 1st line

½″

When most people think of comic books, predictable images usually come to mind: caped heroes, maniacal villains, deeds of incredible strength, and other typical elements of super-powered adventures. Undeniably, characters like Batman, Superman, and Spider-Man are the most prominent features of the comic book landscape, in terms of both popularity and revenue (Wright xiv). However, there is more to comic books than superpowers and secret identities. Underground comics (also known as *comix*), printed by small publishers or by individual artists, are very different from what is usually expected in the genre. While far less well-known than their superhero counterparts, underground comics often offer an innovative and more sophisticated alternative to mainstream titles.

Funnel introduction: Initiates contrast, moves from familiar to unfamiliar, concludes with thesis

In-text citation—book

Thesis: Establishes topic, purpose, and author's position

Almost from the beginning, comic books were associated with superheroes. The first comic books appeared in the early 1930s, nearly four decades after comic strips such as *Yellow Boy* began appearing in the major newspapers. Yet comic books did not gain widespread popularity until June of 1938, when writer Jerry Siegel and artist Joe Shuster debuted their character Superman in *Action Comics* #1 (Daniels 9). Superman was an immediate success, and he quickly inspired the creation of copycat superheroes in other comic books. The

Topic sentence: Prepares reader for historical overview

Body: Begins with historical overview

1″

protagonists of these comics each had their own strengths and vulnerabilities, but the stories all shared a basic formula: individuals with extraordinary abilities battling against evil and struggling to maintain a secret identity. These superhero comics, though similar to each other, set the comic book industry on its feet, paving the way to profits and sustained success (Daniels 9). Over the decades and even today, the best-selling comics have typically been in the superhero genre.

While artists and writers over the years have certainly done inventive work in superhero comics, some similarity in mainstream titles was for many years unavoidable. This was due to the creation in 1954 of the Comics Code Authority (CCA), an organization formed by a number of the leading comic publishers to regulate the content of comics (Heller 101). It set very explicit standards, dictating what content was allowed in comic books and what content was expected. Some parts of the code are incredibly specific and controlling:

Block indention for long quotes

> The letters of the word "crime" on a comics magazine shall never be appreciably greater in dimension than the other words contained in the title. The word "crime" shall never appear alone on a cover. . . . Restraint in the use of the word "crime" in titles or subtitles shall be exercised. (qtd. in "Good Shall Triumph over Evil")

Indirect source: Author unknown, so title used

Other rules were more general—vague enough to allow the CCA a free hand in shaping content. One read, "Respect for parents, the moral code, and for honorable behavior shall be fostered" (qtd. in "Good Shall Triumph over Evil"). The CCA also regulated the presentation of criminals and criminal acts, themes of religion and race, and dialogue, especially profanity. While the CCA had no legal authority,

Quotation marks for brief quotation

major magazine distributors refused comics that did not have CCA approval. Many comic publishers, such as EC Comics (*Vault of Horror, Tales from the Crypt*), were virtually forced out of business as a result of the CCA, though the banned titles would eventually gain the appreciation of collectors and aspiring comic artists such as Art Spiegelman, author of the graphic novel *Maus* (1986) ("Comic Book Code"). Other publishers, including DC Comics, made their artists abide by CCA rules in order to continue selling to a wide audience. The result was that the comics with the largest distribution were those that conformed to the CCA's strict rules about appropriate language, subjects, and tone ("Good Shall Triumph over Evil").

Website: no page numbers

In the 1960s, in contrast to mainstream CCA-approved superhero comics (fig. 1, left), alternatives (fig. 1, right) began to appear. Robert Crumb's *Zap,* first released in 1968, initiated the "underground comix revolution" (Heller 101). Crumb and other like-minded artists did not submit their comics for CCA approval. Though this limited the distribution of their work, it allowed them artistic freedom. From its first issue, *Zap* satirized mainstream, conservative beliefs and did not shy away from sexual or political content (Heller 101–02). Beneath the crude humor of *Zap* and similar comics lay insightful commentary on society and its principles, which many readers found to be a refreshing change from mainstream superhero titles.[1]

Figure number in text to link discussion to visual

Citation: Placement separates writer's ideas from source information

Content note

To see the contrast between these mainstream and underground comics, compare the two covers in fig. 1. The *Amazing Fantasy* cover (left) includes the Comics Code Authority approval stamp in its upper right corner, while the *Snarf* cover (right) does not. The *Snarf* cover actually pokes fun at covers like the one at left; on the *Amazing Fantasy* cover, superhero Spider-Man dangles from a high

Topic sentence: Claim supported by visual, analysis

Figure number links visual to text discussion

Fig. 1. Mainstream versus Underground Comics. Spider-Man (left) extols (and exhibits) his prowess as superhero, while (right) a less conventional comic book "hero" struts his stuff. (Left: Cover from Jack Kirby and Steve Ditko, *Amazing Fantasy* #15. [New York: Marvel Comics, 1962]; right: Cover from Robert Crumb, *Snarf* #6 [Amherst: Kitchen Sink Enterprises, 1976])

Source information in caption

building by a thread, proclaiming his "awesome might" to the world, while on the *Snarf* cover, a geeky guy in an unwieldy homemade contraption wants to save the world by fighting "the big companies"—which include oil companies (the "Gas" industry this inventor is trying to boycott) and probably DC Comics, too.

Topic sentence: Claim supported by examples

Underground comics continue to be less well-known than superhero comics, but they are also better-respected among mature readers for their bold and inventive content. Graphic novels, such as Spiegelman's *Maus* and Harvey Pekar's *Our Cancer Year* (1994), have successfully addressed some of the most highly charged and sensitive subjects in modern society. Both of these show the subtlety of and the wide range of topics that underground comics explore. Other common themes of underground comics include sex and sexual identity, politics, and social issues (Daniels 165), as shown in Crumb's work, which is well known for its satirical approach to countercultural topics (Heller).

Illustrations referenced but not reproduced in paper

Refers to entire work: no page number

Topic sentence: Claim supported by example, visual, quotation

Mainstream superhero comics are set on an epic scale—depicting amazing feats, heroic battles between good and evil, and the like—while underground comics tend to focus on everyday life. Adrian Tomine, for example, has been called "a master of pseudorealistic stories" due to his ability to present an ordinary situation as profoundly interesting and complex (Weiner 58; see fig. 2). Comics like Tomine's also provide a subject or situation that readers can identify with more easily than, say, Superman's battles with Brainiac.[2]

Bibliographic note

The quirky perspectives of underground artists would be impossible in mainstream comics because the structure for producing and publishing mainstream comics limits the input of the artists working on them. The modern comic book industry is a huge business, selling not only comics, but also related merchandise such as T-shirts, toys, and video games, not to mention tickets to comic book–inspired movies. Story decisions involving major characters such as Batman or the Hulk have to be made with profits in mind. Because mainstream

Fig. 2. Comic whose characters face realistic challenges—the loss of a loved one, parental guilt—that readers can easily relate to. From Adrian Tomine, *Optic Nerve* #6, p. 22 (Montreal: Drawn and Quarterly, Feb. 1999).

comic publishers often change the creative teams working on their titles (Herndon) and because teams can include dozens of members (McCloud 180), individual artists can have only so much impact on a particular character or story. Most mainstream comics are the result of work done by many different people.

Online article: no page reference

Transition

In contrast, the individual artist in the underground realm has almost total control in creating his or her comic book. The creative teams working on underground titles are usually very small, and they rarely change (Herndon). Les Daniels, who has written several books about DC Comics' creations, notes that underground comic artists are not controlled by corporate interests that discourage "daring" material that might not sell (165, 180). This freedom allows for the uninhibited creativity that distinguishes underground comics from their more commercially oriented counterparts.

Signal phrase

Information from two passages, same source

Underground artists not only push the envelope in terms of content, but they also incorporate experimental visual devices, earning critical praise for breaking away from traditional comic layouts in favor of more artistic perspectives. Artists such as Daniel Clowes argue that comic art can be more evocative than film, especially in the use of nonlinear storytelling techniques (Hignite 18). *New York Times* columnist John Hodgman agrees: Discussing a moment of existential crisis in Kevin Huizenga's *Ganges* #1, he writes, "I have never seen any film or read any prose that gets at that frozen moment when we suddenly feel our mortality, when God is seen or denied, as effectively as a comic panel." Artist Chris Ware manipulates the borders and frames in his comics so extensively that even reading his works can feel like an art to be mastered (see fig. 3). The demands his comics place on the reader create an interaction between viewer and artist that is unheard of in the pages of superhero titles.

Claim supported by summary, quotation, visual example

Signal phrase with background; one-page article—no page number

While Ware and Clowes demonstrate how the page can be used to create innovative and complicated layouts, other underground artists excel at creating

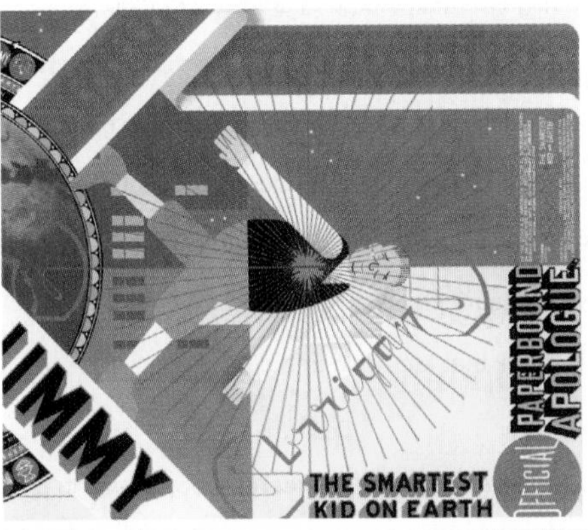

Title identifies illustration

Caption explains visual support of claim

Fig. 3. Cover from Chris Ware's *Jimmy Corrigan: The Smartest Kid on Earth* (New York: Pantheon, 2000). Critically acclaimed *Jimmy Corrigan* comics use visual storytelling techniques, pushing the limitations of comics and forcing the reader to work to achieve understanding.

simple, striking visuals. Unlike mainstream comics, which depict dynamic scenes through loud, flamboyant colors, underground comics often achieve their effects through simplicity. Frequently, they are printed in black and white or with limited colors, with characters rendered in clean, bold lines. The clarity and lack of clutter in such art allows for immediate, striking storytelling (see fig. 2).

Reference to earlier figure

Obviously, most underground comics are not intended for young children. Yet, because of the childish connotations of the term "comic," most adults overlook the fascinating work that underground comic artists do. The association of comics with superheroes and children has made reading comics a source of shame or embarrassment for many adults. As Clowes comments, "I think that the average reader is far more open to a well-designed book than a standard comic book. . . . Very few would feel comfortable reading a standard comic book pamphlet" (qtd. in Hignite 17). Artists such as Scott McCloud have changed this perception of comic books by offering a broader definition of what a comic is. According to McCloud, comics are "juxtaposed pictorial and other images in a deliberate sequence" (12). This definition includes not only what one might find in the latest Spider-Man comic, but also all the experimental work that McCloud and his underground colleagues are creating.

Signal phrase and paren-thetical page reference

Conclusion: Restatement of thesis—closure

McCloud and others have succeeded in bringing underground comics to a wider audience. Since the 1980s, comics have been finding their way into gallery and museum exhibitions, where the craftsmanship of the individual comic book artist can be better appreciated (Hignite 18). Major newspapers like the *New York Times* have begun featuring comics in their pages, including serialized graphic novels such as *George Sprott (1894–1975)* and *Watergate Sue*. The market for underground comics has also expanded through internet venues such as *eBay*, where interested readers can find not only new titles, but also classic comics otherwise available only in specialty shops. The internet has also become an outlet for direct distribution through artists' websites, making independent titles not only more accessible to consumers but also more affordable for individual artists to produce and market (Fenty, Houp, and Taylor, par. 1). While underground comics may never sell as well or be as large a part of popular culture as Superman and his ilk, their creators will likely continue to be heroes to anyone seeking courage, creativity, and artistic quality in their comics.

Article by more than one author, paragraph no. cited

Notes Heading (centered), new page

Content note: Pertinent information not central to project's claim

½″ 1. According to Schnakenberg, over 2 million copies of *Zap* comix were in print by 1999.

2. For an intriguing argument that the world of classic comic book superheroes is not so different from our own—including a discussion of how comics before World War II commented on then-current events—see Wright 1–28.

Bibliographic note

Works Cited

Heading (centered), new page; entries alphabetized by author

"The Comic Book Code." *Culture Shock.* PBS, n.d. Web. 17 Mar. 2009.

Web page: No author, no date

Daniels, Les. *Comix: A History of Comic Books in America.* New York: Outerbridge and Dienstfrey, 1971. Print.

½″

More than one author: Order of names reversed for first author

Fenty, Sean, Trena Houp, and Laurie Taylor. "Webcomics: The Influence and Continuation of the Comix Revolution." *ImageTexT* 1.2 (2004): 22 pars. Web. 18 Mar. 2009.

Journal article: Published only online, paragraph numbers

Online scholarly project: No authors—alphabetized by title

"'Good Shall Triumph over Evil': The Comic Book Code of 1954." *History Matters: The U.S. History Survey Course on the Web.* George Mason University, n.d. Web. 22 Mar. 2009.

Heller, Steven. "Zap Comics." *Print* May/June 2000: 100–05. *Academic Search Premier.* Web. 26 Mar. 2009.

Herndon, L. Kristen. "Mainstream Culture Is in Trouble, and Superman's Not Gonna Save It. But the Simpsons Might." *Art Papers* 21 (1997): 22–25. *Art Index.* Web. 10 Mar. 2009.

Journal article: Accessed through database

Hignite, M. Todd. "Avante-Garde and Comics: Serious Cartooning." *Art Papers* 26.1 (2002): 17–19. *Art Index.* Web. 10 Mar. 2009.

Hodgman, John. "Comics Chronicle." *New York Times* 4 June 2006, late ed., sec. 7: 18. *LexisNexis.* Web. 19 Mar. 2009.

Newspaper article: Accessed through database

McCloud, Scott. *Understanding Comics, the Invisible Art.* New York: Harper Perennial, 1994. Print.

Book (printed): Popular press

Specialized reference work: Accessed through database

Schnakenberg, Robert E. "Zap Comix." *St. James Encyclopedia of Popular Culture.* 2002. *Find Articles.* Web. 17 Mar. 2009.

Weiner, Stephen. "Beyond Superheroes: Comics Get Serious." *Library Journal* 7.2 (2002): 55–58. *Academic Search Premier.* Web. 10 Mar. 2009.

Wright, Bradford W. *Comic Book Nation: The Transformation of Youth Culture in America.* Baltimore: Johns Hopkins UP, 2001. Print.

Book (printed): Scholarly press

20 Documenting Sources: APA Style

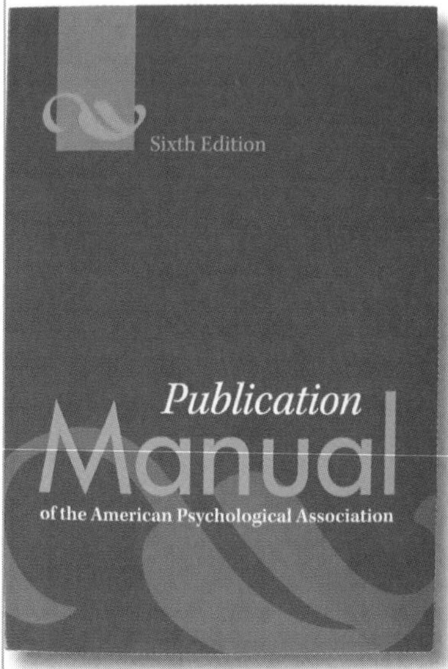

Sixth Edition
Publication
Manual
of the American Psychological Association

Developed by the American Psychological Association, APA style is used by researchers in psychology and many other social science disciplines, such as education, social work, and sociology. APA style requires that sources be cited in two ways:

- **Citation.** Provide an in-text citation in the body of your project for each source used.
- **Documentation.** Provide a reference list at the project's end.

More about ▶▶▶
Popular academic documentation styles, per discipline, 221–28
MLA style, 230–89
Chicago style, 333–60
CSE style, 361–85

Writing Responsibly **Citing and Documenting Sources**

When you cite and document sources, you acknowledge any material that you have borrowed from a source, and you join the conversation on your topic by adding your own interpretation. Simultaneously, you give interested readers (including your instructor) a way to join the conversation: Accurate entries in the text and your reference list allow your audience to find and read your sources so that they can evaluate your interpretation and learn more about the subject themselves. Accurate entries also demonstrate the care with which you have written your research project and reinforce your reputation as a sound scholar.

20a Creating APA-Style In-Text Citations

In-text citations appear in the body of your project. They mark each use you make of a source, regardless of whether you are quoting, paraphrasing, or drawing on an idea from the source. In-text citations include just enough information for readers to locate the source in your reference list, which appears at the end of the project (followed by endnotes, if any). They also alert readers to shifts between *your* ideas and those borrowed from a source.

1. Place in-text citations so readers know where borrowed material starts and stops.

When you incorporate a quotation, paraphrase, summary, or idea from a source into your own prose, carefully consider the placement of the in-text citation, keeping the following goals in mind:

- To make clear exactly which material is drawn from the source
- To avoid distracting your reader

More about ▸▸▸
What you *must* to cite, 109–11
What you do not *need to* cite, 111–13
Signal phrases, 181

You can cite a source in your text in two ways:

- **Signal phrase.** Include the author's name (first initial[s] and surname for the first mention and just the surname for each mention thereafter) and an appropriate verb in your sentence; place the date of publication, in parentheses, immediately following the author's name. For quotations or paraphrases of anything less than the entire argument, place a page reference, in parentheses, at the end of the borrowed passage.

  G. H. Edwards (1992) found that beliefs regarding men and women transcend gender. . . .

  A signal phrase often makes it easier for readers to determine where your ideas end and borrowed material begins. It also allows you to integrate the borrowed material into your sentence and to put the source in context by adding your own interpretation and the qualifications of the source author. For these reasons, most of your summaries, paraphrases, and quotations should be introduced by a signal phrase.

- **Parenthetical note.** In parentheses, provide the author's surname, followed by a comma and the year in which the source was published. Place the note immediately after the borrowed material.

  Subtypes or subcategories of beliefs emerge from within gender categories (Edwards, 1992).

  Parenthetical notes are most appropriate when citing more than one source, when establishing facts, or when the author is not especially important to the point you are making.

NOTE The reference list entry is the same, regardless of whether you use a signal phrase or a parenthetical note:

author — pub. date — title — publication info.

Edwards, G. H. (1992). The structure and content of the male gender role stereotype: An exploration of subtypes. *Sex Roles: A Journal of Research, 27,* 553–561.

Example 1, 293
Example 14, 299
Example 9, 297

Provide enough information in your in-text citation for readers to locate the source in the reference list. In most cases, the author's sur-

Quick Reference → Formatting APA In-Text Citations

name and the date of publication is sufficient. Occasionally, you may need to provide more information; when citing a specific part of a source or using a quotation, for example, you would also provide page numbers. Use paragraph number(s) or a section heading if no page numbers are available. When citing works by authors with the same surname, also include the authors' initials.

2. Adjust in-text citations to different types of sources.

The exact form of an in-text citation depends on the type of source you are citing. The examples that follow cover the most common types. For more unusual sources, study the general principles outlined here and adapt them to your special circumstances or consult the *Publication Manual of the American Psychological Association,* 6th ed. (available in any library).

APA In-Text Citations

1. One author
2. Two authors
3. Three to five authors

1. One author

a. Signal phrase

signal phrase

Plummer (2001) indicates that boys begin pressuring one another to conform in childhood, telling each other to toughen up or to stop acting like a baby.

b. Parenthetical note

This pressure to conform to recognized masculine norms typically begins at a very young age, and boys may tell each other to toughen up or to stop acting like a baby (Plummer, 2001).

c. Specific page or section cited If you are quoting directly from your source or paraphrasing or summarizing a specific section, include the author's name in a signal phrase, the year of publication immediately after the author's name, and a page reference at the end of the cited passage. This not only provides source information but also makes clear what part of your text comes from the source.

> Plummer (2001) argues that an overt pressure to conform to recognized norms of masculinity typically begins at a very young age, with boys discouraging one another from being "soft" or "artistic" (p. 18).

APA In-Text Citations

If you cannot use a signal phrase, include all three pieces of information at the end of the passage cited.

> This overt pressure to conform to recognized norms of masculinity typically begins at a very young age, with boys discouraging each other from being "soft" or "artistic" (Plummer, 2001, p. 18).

Example 2, 302

2. Two authors List two authors by surnames in the order listed by the source; be sure to use this same order in your reference list entry. In a signal phrase, spell out the word *and* between the two surnames; in a parenthetical citation, replace the word *and* with an ampersand (&).

> signal phrase (*and* spelled out)
> Carpenter and Readman (2006) define physical disability as "the restriction of activity caused by impairments, for example, the loss of a limb, involuntary movements, loss of speech or sight" (p. 131).

> Medical doctors define the word *disability* as "an individual problem of disease, incapacity, and impairment" (Carpenter & Readman, 2006, p. 131).
> parenthetical note (ampersand)

3. Three to five authors When a source has three, four, or five authors, list them all in your first in-text citation of the source.

> The research of Oller, Pearson, and Cobo-Lewis (2007) suggests that bilingual children may have a smaller vocabulary in each of their languages than monolingual children have in their sole language.

In subsequent citations, list only the first author, representing the others with the abbreviation *et al.,* which stands for the Latin phrase *et alii,* "and others." In APA style, this abbreviation should not be underlined or italicized.

> The bilingual children in the study were all Spanish-English speakers (Oller et al., 2007).

NOTE *al.* is an abbreviation, so it requires a period; *et* is a complete word, so it does not. There should be no punctuation between the author's name and *et al.*

---

4. Six or more authors If the source has six or more authors, use only the surname of the first author plus *et al.*

> The researchers note that "there is less direct experimental evidence for effect of grazing animal species on biodiversity" (Rook et al., 2003, p. 141).

5. Group or corporate author Provide the full name of the group in your parenthetical note or signal phrase. If you are going to cite this source subsequently, use the group's name in a signal phrase and insert its acronym (the first letters of each word in a name or phrase) in parentheses. In subsequent in-text references, use only the acronym.

> full name
> In 2003 the National Commission on Writing in America's Schools and Colleges (NCWASC) demanded that "the nation's leaders . . . place writing squarely in the center of the school agenda, and [that] policymakers at the state and local levels . . . provide the resources required to improve writing" (p. 3).
> acronym

Alternatively, include the full name in a parenthetical citation, and insert the acronym in square brackets following.

> If writing is to improve, our society "must place writing squarely in the center of the school agenda, and policymakers at the state and local levels must provide the resources required to improve writing" (National Commission on Writing in America's Schools and Colleges [NCWASC], 2003, p. 3).
> full name
> acronym

APA In-Text Citations

6. Unnamed author When no author is listed for a source, use the first few words of the title in your in-text citation instead.

> On average, smokers shave about twelve minutes off their life span for every cigarette smoked ("A Fistful of Risks," 1996, pp. 82–83).
> title

Set titles of articles or parts of books in quotation marks and titles of books, periodicals, and other longer works in italics.

Only if the source lists its author as anonymous should you use that word (without italics or quotation marks) in a parenthetical citation; avoid using *anonymous* in a signal phrase.

7. Two or more sources by the same author When citing two or more sources by the same author in a single citation, name the author once but include all publication years, separating them with commas.

> Wynn's work explores the ability of human infants to perform mathematical functions, such as addition and subtraction (1992, 2000).
>
> [pub. date 1] [pub. date 2]

> Human infants have shown surprising abilities to perform mathematical functions, such as addition and subtraction (Wynn, 1992, 2000).
>
> [pub. date 1] [pub. date 2]

8. Author with two or more works published in the same year When your reference list includes two or more publications by the same author in the same year, add a letter following the year (*2006a, 2006b*). Use these year-and-letter designations in your in-text citations.

> The brain not only controls the senses of sight and sound, but it also plays an important role in associating emotions such as fear with particular situations (Barinaga, 1992b).
>
> [source letter assigned]

9. Two or more authors with the same surname If your reference list includes works by different authors with the same surname, include the authors' initials to differentiate them.

Example 6, 304

Rehabilitation is a viable option for many juvenile offenders, whose immaturities and disabilities can, with institutional support and guidance, be overcome as the child matures (M. Beyer, 2006).

first initial + surname

If more than one author is listed, include initials for the first author only.

10. Reprinted or republished work Include both dates in your in-text citation, with the original date of publication first and a slash between dates.

Example 8, 305

Danon-Boileau (2005/2006) takes a cross-disciplinary approach to the study of language disorders in children.

orig. date / reprint date

APA In-Text Citations

11. Source cited more than once If you cite the same work more than once in a single paragraph, provide the parenthetical note only once. If you use information from a different page in the source within that paragraph, provide only the new page number.

In a 2007 study, 100 physicians were observed in role-playing activities to see if "physician perceived control" might make a doctor more empathetic to his or her patients (Silvester, Patterson, & Koczwara, p. 519). One interesting result was the difference between ratings by assessors (favoring doctors who listened to personal stories and let the patients lead) and ratings by patients (favoring physicians who focused on providing reassurance and information). While patients may judge a doctor's empathy partly by his or her willingness to listen, they also want "opportunities for informed decision making" (p. 525).

pub. year / 1st citation (complete) / 2nd citation (pg. no. only)

12. Two or more sources in one citation To cite more than one source in a single parenthetical note, list the sources in the same order in which they appear in the reference list, using a semicolon to separate them.

> When placed in well-structured rehabilitative programs, juvenile offenders—even those who commit serious crimes such as murder—can become more mature thinkers, more involved and loving members of their families, and more successful workers and learners (Beyer, 2006; Burns & Hoagwood, 2002).

13. Indirect source When referring to source material you have learned about through its mention in another source, mention the name of the original source in a signal phrase. In your parenthetical note, include *as cited in* followed by the name of the author of the source in which you found the information, and conclude with the year of that source's publication. Whenever possible, consult the original source instead.

> Choy, Fyer, and Lipsitz (as cited in King, 2008) make the distinction that people with phobias, unlike those with general anxiety, can identify specific causes for their feelings of nervousness and dread.

In the reference list, provide only the source you used: For the example above, include a reference list entry for King, not Choy, Fyer, and Lipsitz.

14. Website or other electronic source For a brief reference to an entire online source that readers can retrieve, provide the URL in a parenthetical note, but do not include the source in the reference list.

> The Olympics assume great importance to the local community, as demonstrated by the website for California State University–Sacramento in the period before Olympic trials were to be held on the campus. Three out of four news bulletins on the university's home page were connected to the Olympics (http://www.csus.edu/).
>
> URL

Examples 20–21, 312–13

When citing a specific passage or engaging in a substantial way with an online or electronic source, cite it as you would any other source and include it in your reference list.

APA In-Text Citations

> The website *Psychology Matters* reports that cell-phone use while driving can impair performance as badly as drinking alcohol does: "Cell-phone use is associated with a four-fold increase in the odds of getting into an accident—a risk comparable to that of driving with blood alcohol at the legal limit" ("Driven to Distraction," 2006).

Cite specific page numbers only when they are fixed, such as in a PDF file. When there are no fixed page numbers, you may use paragraph numbers if they are visible on the page (abbreviated as *para.*). If there are neither page numbers nor visible paragraph numbers, you can refer to section headings (enclosed in quotation marks and shortened if too long) and identify the number of the paragraph within that section ("Conclusions," para.2).

More about ▸▸▸ Interviews, 131–35

15. Personal communication, interview, or email For sources such as personal email messages and phone calls that your readers cannot retrieve and read, mention the communication in your text or provide a parenthetical note, but do not include an entry in the reference list.

> The scientist himself was much more modest about the development
>
> message author — source type — date
>
> (S. J. Gould, personal communication, November 13, 1986).

Quick Reference APA Reference List Entries

APA Reference List Entries

1. **One author**
2. **Two authors**
3. Three to seven authors
4. Eight or more authors

▶▶▶Annotated visual of where to find author, title, publication, and other information, on foldout following p. 385

20b Preparing an APA-Style Reference List

The reference list, which comes at the end of your research project, includes the sources you have cited in your text. The format of each entry in the reference list depends in part on the type of source you are citing, such as a printed book, an article in an electronic journal or accessed through a database, or an audio recording.

Books—Printed and Electronic

In a printed book, the information you need to create a reference list entry appears on the title and copyright pages. In an online book or e-book, print and electronic publication information appears at the top or bottom of the first page or is available through a link.

1. One author

a. Printed The basic entry for a printed book looks like this:

Author's surname, Initial(s). (Date of publication). *Title of work: Subtitle of work.* Place of publication: Publisher.

Here is an example of an actual citation:

For books, only first word of title and subtitle (plus names) are capitalized.

Morrison, J. R. (2007). *Diagnosis made easier: Principles and techniques for mental health clinicians.* New York, NY: Guilford Press.

b. E-book When citing an electronic book, the electronic retrieval information replaces the traditional publishing information. Use a digital object identifier (DOI) number if available or the URL of the home page for the website from which you retrieved the book at the end of the entry. If the electronic book is also available in print, note the electronic version in brackets (for example: *DX Reader, Adobe Digital Editions, Google Books*) after the title.

Spencer, H. (1890). *Principles of psychology* (Vol. 1, 3rd ed.) [Google Books version]. Retrieved from http://www.archive.org/index.php

URL

2. Two authors When there are two authors, list them in the order they appear on the title page of the source with a comma and ampersand (&) between them.

Tech

Citing Electronic Sources: Digital Object Identifiers (DOIs) and URLs

Because URLs change and links break, the APA now recommends using a digital object identifier (DOI) whenever available. The DOI is a unique alphanumeric string assigned to the text, and it can usually be found on the first page of the article or in the full citation page for the article if you located it with a database. Use a URL only when no DOI is available, citing the home page of the publisher or journal; you may need to do a web search to find this information if you located the text through a database. Provide the URL for the home page of a database instead of the publisher or journal only when the availability of the document is limited (such as discontinued journals or dissertations). When your citation ends with a DOI or URL, do *not* add a period after it. Break a DOI or URL (if necessary) only before a punctuation mark, and do not add a hyphen.

APA Reference List Entries

author 1 author 2

Tavris, C., & Aronson, E. (2007). *Mistakes were made (but not by me): Why we justify foolish beliefs, bad decisions, and hurtful acts.* New York, NY: Harcourt.

Use an ampersand (&) between names.

3. Three to seven authors If the book has three to seven authors, list all of their names.

Oltmanns, T. F., Neale, J. M., & Davison, G. C. (1992). *Case studies in abnormal psychology.* New York, NY: Guilford Press.

Use an ampersand (&) between the last two names.

4. Eight or more authors When the book has eight or more authors, list the first six authors' names with a comma after each name, then insert an ellipsis, and finish with the last author's name.

More about ▸▸▸ et al., 295

Brown, P. O., Cepko, C. L., Elledge, S. J., Hudspeth, A. J., Kim, P. S., Oren, M., . . . Zou, L. (2003). *The Harvey lectures: Series 97, 2001–2002.* New York, NY: Wiley-Liss.

5. Unnamed (anonymous) author Start the entry with the title followed by the publication data. Alphabetize the entry in the reference list using the first significant word in the title (not an article such as *a, an,* or *the*).

And still we conquer! The diary of a Nazi Unteroffizier in the German Africa Corps. (1968). University, AL: Confederate Publishing.

If the author is listed as "Anonymous," use that word in place of the author's name.

Anonymous. (1971). *Go ask Alice.* Englewood Cliffs, NJ: Prentice Hall.

6. Two or more books by the same author For multiple books by the same author (or authors), arrange the entries in order of publication (from least to most recent).

Tonkiss, F. (2005). *Space, the city and social theory: Social relations and urban forms.* Malden, MA: Polity.

Tonkiss, F. (2006). *Contemporary economic sociology: Globalization, production, inequality.* New York, NY: Routledge.

When books were written by the same author(s) in the same year, alphabetize the entries by title and add the letter *a* following the publication date of the first entry, *b* following the publication date of the second entry, and so on.

Cervone, D., & Shoda, Y. (1999a). *The coherence of personality: Social-cognitive bases of consistency, variability, and organization.* New York, NY: Guilford Press.

Cervone, D., & Shoda, Y. (1999b). Social-cognitive theories and the coherence of personality. In D. Cervone & Y. Shoda (Eds.), *The coherence of personality: Social-cognitive bases of consistency, variability, and organization.* New York, NY: Guilford Press.

Works written by a single author should be listed *before* sources written by that same author plus a coauthor, regardless of publication dates.

APA Reference List Entries

Morrison, J. R. (2007). *Diagnosis made easier: Principles and techniques for mental health clinicians.* New York, NY: Guilford Press.

Morrison, J. R., & Anders, T. F. (1999). *Interviewing children and adolescents: Skills and strategies for effective* DSM-IV *diagnosis.* New York, NY: Guilford Press.

When citing multiple sources by an author and various coauthors, alphabetize entries by surname of the second author.

Clarke-Stewart, A., & Allhusen, V. D. (2005). *What we know about childcare.* Cambridge, MA: Harvard University Press.

Clarke-Stewart, A., & Brentano, C. (2006). *Divorce: Causes and consequences.* New Haven, CT: Yale University Press.

7. Group or corporate author List the sponsoring organization as the author of a book (or other publication) by a corporation, institution, or government agency. Use the full name, and alphabetize it in the reference list according to the name's first significant word. If the same group or corporation is also listed as the publisher, replace the name of the publisher with the word *Author.*

Fabian Society, Commission on Life Chances and Child Poverty. (2006). *Narrowing the gap: The final report of the Fabian Commission on Life Chances and Child Poverty.* London, England: Author.

8. Author and editor or translator List the author first, followed by the publication date of the translation or edition. After the title, include in parentheses the editor's or translator's name, followed by the abbreviation *Trans.* for translator or *Ed.* for editor. If the original publication of the work was in an earlier year, provide that information, in parentheses, at the conclusion of the entry.

pub. date of trans.

Danon-Boileau, L. (2006). *Children without language: From dysphasia to autism* (J. Grieve, Trans.). New York, NY: Oxford University Press. (Original work published 2005)

APA Reference List Entries

5. Unnamed (anonymous) author
6. Two or more books by the same author
7. **Group or corporate author**
8. **Author and editor or translator**
9. Edited book or anthology as a whole
10. Selection from an edited book or anthology

9. Edited book or anthology as a whole Treat the editor as the author.

Ghosh, R. A. (Ed.). (2005). *CODE: Collaborative ownership and the digital economy.* Boston, MA: MIT Press.

For a book with multiple editors, change the abbreviation from *Ed.* to *Eds.*

10. Selection from an edited book or anthology Begin with the selection's author, followed by the publication date of the book and the selection's title (with no quotation marks or other formatting). Then insert the word *In,* the editors' names, and the title of the book or anthology (italicized). Next include page numbers for the entire selection (even if you used only part of it). Conclude the entry with the publication information for the book in which the selection appeared.

selection author — selection title — selection pg. nos.

Smither, N. (2000). Crime scene cleaner. In J. Bowe, M. Bowe, & S. Streeter (Eds.), *Gig: Americans talk about their jobs* (pp. 96–103). New York, NY: Crown.

APA Reference List Entries

Example 10, 306

11. Edition other than the first Insert the edition number (*2nd ed., 3rd ed.*) or edition name (*Rev. ed.* for "revised edition") after the book's title. (The edition number or name should appear on the title page.)

Johnson, J. B., & Reynolds, H. T. (2005). *Political science research methods* (5th ed.). Washington, DC: CQ Press.

12. Entry in a reference work Format an entry in a reference work as you would a selection from an edited book. For signed articles, include the author's name. (Articles in reference works often carry the author's initials only, so you may need to cross-reference the initials with a list of contributors in the front or back of the book.) If an article is unsigned, begin with its title.

a. Printed

Treffert, D. A. (2000). Savant syndrome. In A. E. Kazdin (Ed.), *Encyclopedia of psychology* (pp. 144–148). New York, NY: Oxford.

b. Online Add the complete URL for the entry if the work is open access or the URL for the homepage of the database if the work is available by subscription only.

French, M. D. (2006). Schizophrenia. In Y. Jackson (Ed.), *Encyclopedia of multicultural psychology.* [ebook version]. Retrieved from http://www.gale.cengage.com

access date

database name

Major depression. (2009). In *Medline Plus encyclopedia.* Retrieved from http://www.nlm.nih.gov/medlineplus/ency/article/000945.htm

URL

13. Dissertation The title of a published dissertation is italicized; the title of an unpublished dissertation is not. Note the type of document in parentheses after the title.

a. Abstracted in DAI, obtained from database

Kelley, E. (2008). *Parental depression and negative attribution bias in parent reports of child symptoms* (Doctoral dissertation). Retrieved from ProQuest Dissertations and Theses database. (UMI No. 3315753)

database

accession number

b. Abstracted in DAI, obtained from university

Song, L. Z. (2003). *Relations between optimism, stress and health in Chinese and American students* (Doctoral dissertation). *Dissertation Abstracts International: Section B. Sciences and Engineering, 64*(09), 4650.

c. Unpublished

Luster, L. (1992). Schooling, survival and struggle: Black women and the GED (Unpublished doctoral dissertation). Stanford University, CA.

title (unpublished)

APA Reference List Entries

Periodicals—Printed and Electronic

A periodical is a publication issued at regular intervals—newspapers are generally published every day, magazines every week or month, and scholarly journals four times a year. For periodicals, include not only the title of the article (no quotation marks or italics) but also the title of the periodical (in italics, all important words capitalized). The type of publication information you include depends on the type of periodical you are citing.

▶▶▶Annotated visual of where to find author, title, publication, and other information, on foldout following p. 385

14. Article in a scholarly journal The information needed to create a reference list entry for a printed journal article appears on the cover or table of contents of the journal and on the first and last page of the article. For articles downloaded from a database, the information appears either on the screen listing the articles that fit your search terms or on the first (and last) page of the downloaded file. For articles that appear in journals that are published solely online, the needed information may be on the website's home page, in the journal's table of contents, or on the first page of the article.

More about ▶▶▶ Searching databases, 52–58, 68–71

NOTE APA style requires writers to include the issue number after the volume number only when each issue of the journal starts with page 1.

APA Reference List Entries

a. Printed The basic citation for an article in a printed journal looks like this:

Author's surname, Initial(s). (date of publication). Article title. *Title of Journal, vol no.*(issue no.), pages.

Here is an example of a citation for a journal whose pagination does not start with page 1 in each issue:

author · date · article title · journal title · vol. · pgs.

Fancher, R. E. (2009). Scientific cousins: The relationship between Charles Darwin and Francis Galton. *American Psychologist, 64,* 84–92.

Here is an example for a journal that is paginated by issue:

More about ▶▶▶ Formatting author information: examples 1–10, 302–06

Rothman, S., & Lichter, S. R. (2001). Environmental cancer. *Society, 38*(4), 20–27.

b. Online or accessed through a database Most articles published recently are tagged with a digital object identifier, or DOI. The DOI is a permanent identifier that will not change from library to library or data-

More about ▶▶▶ DOIs, 302

base to database. The DOI makes URLs, database names, and access dates—in most cases—unnecessary. Whenever a DOI is provided, include it at the end of your citation. Include a URL only when no DOI has been assigned or the article is not widely available. Include an access date only when the article is likely to change.

The basic citation for an article in an online journal or accessed through an online database that has a DOI is the same as for a printed journal article except that the DOI appears at the end of the citation:

Rozin, P. (2007). Exploring the landscape of modern academic psychology: Finding and filling the holes. *American Psychologist, 62,* 754–766. doi: 10.1037/1091-7527.25.4.468

DOI

For an article in an online journal that does *not* include a DOI, replace the DOI with the phrase *Retrieved from* followed by the URL of the journal home page.

Mann, T. L. (1993). A failure of nonshared environmental factors in predicting sibling personality differences. *Journal of Psychology 127*(1), 79–86. Retrieved from http://web.heldref.org/pubs/jrl/about.html

URL (permalink)

APA Reference List Entries

15. Article in a magazine

a. Printed or accessed through a database Provide the full publication date of the issue (year, month, and day; or year and month).

Gladwell, M. (2007, November 12). Dangerous minds. *The New Yorker,* 36–45.

If the volume and issue number of the magazine are available, include that information as you would for a journal article.

Example 14, 308

Pelusi, N. (2009, January). Neanderthink: The appeal of the bad boy. *Psychology Today, 42*(1), 58–59.

b. Online Provide similar information for online magazines as you would for print magazines, including volume and issue numbers when available. Most online magazines do not include stable page numbers, however, so cite the home page for the magazine.

Chamberlin, J. (2009, July/August). Strong families, safe children. *Monitor on Psychology, 40*(7). Retrieved from http://www.apa.org/monitor

Some magazines that have both print and online versions do not include volume or issue numbers on the website. Include the publication date given in the article.

Pelusi, N. (2009, January 1). Neanderthink: The appeal of the bad boy. *Psychology Today.* Retrieved from http://www.psychologytoday.com/

APA Reference List Entries

No retrieval dates are needed unless the material may change over time, as in wikis. Similarly, because most online magazines can be searched through the online index, exact URLs for the articles are not necessary. They should be included only when the information would be difficult to locate otherwise (as with newsletter articles).

Goldberg, M. (2006, February 24). Saving the neighborhood. *Salon.* Retrieved from http://www.salon.com

16. Article in a newspaper The information you need to create a reference list entry for a printed newspaper article is on the masthead of the newspaper (at the top of the first page) and on the first and last page of the article. For newspaper articles downloaded from a database, the information you need appears on the screen listing the articles that fit your search terms or on the first page of the article itself. For articles that appear in online versions of the newspaper, the information you need is usually at the top of the first page of the article.

a. Printed or accessed through a database

author — pub. date — title

Friedman, R. A. (2009, January 20). Sex and depression: In the brain, if not the mind. *The New York Times,* p. D6.

newspaper — sec./pg. no.

If the title of a newspaper does not include its place of publication, supply the city and state, in square brackets, following the title.

Sabo, B. (2006, July 30). Honored parents emphasize values. *The Patriot-News* [Harrisburg, PA], p. B4.

sec./pg. no.

If the pages of the article are not continuous, provide all page numbers, with a comma after each.

Chen, G. (2007, May 10). Electronic baby sitter: 18% of American toddlers have a TV set in their room. *The Post-Standard* [Syracuse, NY], pp. A1, A8.

The citation for a newspaper article downloaded from a database follows the model for a printed newspaper article, but it generally omits page numbers, as they are usually not included online.

b. Online Follow the format for a printed newspaper article, but omit the page reference and include the words *Retrieved from* and the URL for the newspaper's home page.

Friedman, R. A. (2009, January 20). Sex and depression: In the brain, if not the mind. *The New York Times.* Retrieved from http://www .nytimes.com/

17. Review Follow the model for the type of periodical in which the review appeared, and add the label *Review of the book* followed by the title and author of the reviewed work, in brackets, after the review's title.

Examples 14–16, 308–10

review author — review title — reviewed work

Balk, D. E. (2007). Diamonds and mummies are forever [Review of the book *Remember me A lively tour of the new American way of death, by L. T. Cullen*]. *Death Studies, 31*(10), 941–947. doi: 10.1080/07481180701603436

If the review is untitled, substitute the words *Review of the book* and the book's title.

Schredl, M. (2008). [Review of the book *The dream experience: A systematic exploration*] by Milton Kramer. *Dreaming, 18*(4), 280–286.

APA Reference List Entries

APA Reference List Entries

18. Letter to the editor Follow the model for the type of periodical in which the letter appeared, and insert the label *Letter to the editor* in brackets following the letter's title.

Royce, B. S. (2007, April 27). Carbon emissions [Letter to the editor]. *Times Literary Supplement, 5430,* 17.

If there is no letter title, substitute the words *Letter to the editor.*

19. Abstract It is always better to read and cite an article itself. However, if you relied only on the abstract, or summary, cite only the abstract to avoid misrepresenting your source and your research.

Loverock, D. S. (2007). Object superiority as a function of object coherence and task difficulty [Abstract]. *American Journal of Psychology, 120,* 565–591.

Bruce, A. S., Ray, W., & Carlson, R. A. (2007). Understanding cognitive failures: What's dissociation got to do with it? *American Journal of Psychology, 120,* 553–563. Abstract retrieved from http://ajp.press.illinois.edu/index.html

Other Electronic Sources

▶▶▶Annotated visual of where to find author, title, publication, and other information, on foldout following p. 385

While it is generally easy to find the information you need to create a complete citation for a book or an article in a periodical, websites can be a bit trickier. Most of the information you need will appear on the site's home page, usually at the bottom or top of that page, or on the web page you are citing. Sometimes, however, you may need to look further. Click on links with titles such as "About us" or "More information." Frequently, websites will not provide complete information, so include as much information in your entry as you can.

20. Website When referring to an entire website rather than a specific document, cite the URL of the site within your text; you do not need to list the website in your references.

Tech

Checking URLs and DOIs

DOIs. If your selection includes a DOI number, you can check it by visiting <crossref.org> and inserting the DOI into the search box.

URLs. Just before submitting your paper, test all the URLs; sometimes web addresses change or content is taken down. If the URL you provided no longer works, search for the work online by title or keyword; you may find it "cached" on the Web even though the owner of the original site has taken the work down. Then use the URL for the cached version in your bibliographic entry.

APA Reference List Entries

The website *Psychology Matters* provides information that anyone can access on everything from money issues to trauma (http://psychologymatters.apa.org).

21. Web page Following the author and the date (or *n.d.* if no date is available), provide the title of the page (with no formatting) and the URL for the specific page you are citing.

web page title

American Psychological Association. (2008). Getting a good night's sleep with the help of psychology. In *Psychology matters.* Retrieved from

URL for web page

http://www.psychologymatters.org/insomnia.html

If the website is untitled, add a description.

The Writing Center, University of North Carolina. (2007). Handouts and links: Sociology. Retrieved from http://www.unc.edu/depts/wcweb/handouts/sociology.html

22. Discussion list posting Include an entry only if the forum maintains an online archive that readers can access. If messages are protected by a password or unavailable to the general public (as with an email or instant message), use only an in-text citation. Provide the author's name or username, the exact date of the posting, and the subject line followed by a description of the message in brackets (for example: *Online forum comment* or *Electronic mailing list message*). Include the URL where the message can be found and the name of the list to which it was posted when this information is not part of the URL.

Arendes, L. (2008, July 9). Objectivity [Discussion list post]. Retrieved from news://sci.psychology.research/archived at http://groups.google.com/group/sci.psychology/research/

APA Reference List Entries

23. Article on a wiki Because wikis are written and edited collaboratively, there is no author to cite; begin with the article's title. Always include a retrieval date and direct URL. If the date of the most recent update is not noted, include the abbreviation *n.d.* in place of the date. Wiki titles are not italicized or otherwise formatted.

International relations. (n.d.). Retrieved April 22, 2008, from Political Science Wiki: http://polisci.wikidot.com/international-relations

24. Blog posting, comment on a blog posting

a. Blog posting

post author — post date — post title

Dean, J. (2009, January 1). Gratitude enhanced by focusing on end of pleasurable experience [Web log post]. Retrieved from www.spring.org.uk/2009_01_01_blogarchive.php

URL (post)

More about ▶▶▶ Reliability, 82–84

b. Comment on a blog posting

comment author — date posted — thread title

HLVictoria. (2004, January 11). Re: Sociology of weblogs [Web log comment]. Retrieved from http://blog.niceperson.org/2003/02/11/sociology-of-weblogs/#comment-62

URL

Audio and Visual Sources

The information you need to create an entry for most audio and visual sources will appear on the cover, label, or program of the work or in the credits at the end of a film or television show. As with other citations, italicize the titles of longer works, such as albums and films, and do not format the titles of shorter works such as single songs or single episodes of television programs.

25. Motion picture

release

Howard, R. (Director), & Grazer, B. (Producer). (2001). *A beautiful mind* [Motion picture]. United States: Warner Bros.

26. Online video or video blog (vlog)

ATTC Network. (2007, July 12). Michael–Clinical psychologist [Video file]. Retrieved from http://www.youtube.com/watch?v=4OAYT5P6xaQ

27. Television or radio broadcast

a. Series

Garcia, R. (Executive producer). (2008–2009). *In treatment* [Television series]. New York, NY: HBO.

b. Episode

Barclay, P. (Director). (2008). Mia: Week three [Television series episode]. In R. Garcia (Executive producer), *In treatment.* New York, NY: HBO.

c. Podcast

Mitchell, N. (Producer). (2008, March 15). The psyche on death row. *All in the mind.* [Audio podcast]. Retrieved from http://www.abc.net.au/rn/allinthemind/default.htm

28. Musical or other audio recording

a. CD, LP, or audiobook

Gore, A. (Writer), & Patton, W. (Narrator). (2007). *The assault on reason* [CD]. New York, NY: Penguin Audio.

APA Reference List Entries

b. Selection or song on a CD, LP, or audiobook

© date

Dilly, D., & Wilkin, M. (1959). The long black veil. On *Pioneering women of bluegrass* [CD]. Washington, DC: Smithsonian/Folkways Records.

recording date

(1996)

29. Lecture, speech, or conference presentation

Robinson, G. E. (2008, May 6). *Preventing violence against women.* Paper presented at the annual meeting of the American Psychiatric Association, Washington, DC.

Miscellaneous Sources

30. Government publication

a. Printed

National Institutes of Mental Health. (2008). *Bipolar disorder* (NIH Publication No. 3679). Washington, DC: U.S. Government Printing Office.

Example 7, 305

U.S. Department of Health and Human Services. (2005). *Steps to a healthier US.* Washington, DC: Author.

b. Online

U.S. General Accounting Office. (1993, September 21). *North American Free Trade Agreement: A focus on the substantive issues* (Publication No. GAO/T-GGD-93-44). Retrieved from General Accounting Office Reports Online via GPO Access: http://www.gpoaccess.gov/gaoreports/search.html

Campbell, C. (1987). *Writing with others' words: Native and non-native university students' use of information from a background reading text in academic compositions.* Washington, DC: Office of Educational Research and Improvement. (ERIC Document Reproduction Service No. ED287315)

31. Report (nongovernmental)

American Psychological Association. (2008). *Report of the Task Force on Gender Identity and Gender Variance.* Washington, DC: Author.

APA Reference List Entries

Example 7, 305

20c Using APA Style for Notes

APA style cites sources in the body of the text rather than in footnotes or endnotes. However, it does allow for content notes and author notes. *Content notes* provide relevant information that is not central to the argument of the paper; *author notes* acknowledge any help the writer received or any possible conflicts of interest. Content and author notes should appear in a footnote at the bottom of the page or in a list of endnotes on a new page following the reference list.

▶▶▶Sample content note, 332

20d Formatting a Paper in APA Style

The appearance of your paper reflects the care you have taken in writing it. If you are writing in the social sciences (or if your instructor asks you to), format your project using APA style. The following section explains how to format a student paper, and Heather DeGroot's paper at the end of this chapter provides a model.

▶▶▶Student research project (APA style): "The Power of Wardrobe," Heather DeGroot, 321–32

1. Margins and spacing

- Set one-inch margins at the top, bottom, left-, and right-hand sides of your paper.
- Indent the first line of each paragraph half an inch.

- Indent quotations of forty or more words half an inch from the left margin, and set as a block.
- Double-space the main text of the paper.
- Use a hanging indent for each reference list entry: The first line should be flush with the left margin with subsequent lines indented half an inch.

▶▶▶Sample reference list, 330–31

2. Typeface

More about ▶▶▶
Applying the principles of design, 207–15

Use a standard typeface such as Times New Roman or Arial in a readable size (usually 12-point).

3. Header and page number

Include a running head and a page number on every page of your document. The header is a shortened form of your title, usually the first two or three words. It should be in all-capital letters and should not exceed 50 characters, including punctuation and spaces. Position the running head flush left half an inch from the upper edge of the page. The page number should appear flush right on the same line. Both should be at least one inch from the left and right edges of the paper. Use your word processor's header feature to insert the header and to number the pages automatically. On the title page only, the phrase "Running head:" should precede the running head itself.

4. Title page

More about ▶▶▶
Developing a title, 164–65
Reconsidering your title, 195–96

- Insert the title, typed in upper- and lowercase letters, centered on the top half of the page.
- Insert a blank line and then type your name.
- Include the course number, the name of the instructor to whom the project will be submitted, and the date of submission, centered on separate lines.

A sample title page appears on p. 321.

5. Abstract

The abstract generally includes a one-sentence summary of the most important points in each section:

- Introduction: Problem under investigation
- Methods: Number and characteristics of participants, research methods
- Results: Your outcomes
- Conclusions: Implications of your results

The abstract follows the title page and appears on its own page, headed with the word *Abstract* centered at the top of the page.

More about ▶▶▶
Organizing, 148–60
Introductions, 150–52
Methods, 42–43
Conclusions, 150–52
Social scientific research structure, 226–29

6. Tables and figures

- Refer to tables and figures in the text, using the word *Table* or *Figure* followed by the number of the table or figure in sequence. (The first figure is Figure 1, the second table is Table 2.) Discuss the significance of tables and figures in the text, but do not repeat the information that appears in the table or figure itself.
- Include a caption with each figure, using the word *Figure* with the number assigned in the text. The caption, which follows the figure, should describe the figure briefly but not repeat the information in your text. If you borrowed the figure or the data to create your figure, include the source information at the end of your caption.
- Include a table number (preceded by the word *Table*) and, on the next line, the table title. The table number and title should precede the table. If you borrowed the table or the data to create the table, include source information in a note below the table.
- Place tables and figures (photographs, drawings, cartoons, graphs, and charts) on a new page, immediately following the one on which you refer to the table or figure.

▶▶▶Sample figure caption, APA style, 327

Writing Responsibly **Of Deadlines and Paper Clips**

Instructors expect students to turn in thoughtful, carefully proofread, and neatly formatted papers on time—usually in class on the due date. Another assumption is that the writer will clip (or staple) the pages of the paper *before* the paper is submitted. Do justice to yourself by being fully prepared: Do not hand in a stack of loose sheets or expect your instructor to provide a paper clip.

7. Printing, paper, and binding

Print your paper using a high-quality printer (make sure it has plenty of ink), on opaque, 8½ × 11–inch white paper. Most instructors do not want you to enclose your paper in a binder, but if you are in doubt, ask. If you do not use a binder, paper-clip the pages together.

More about ▸▸▸
Writing in the social, physical, and natural sciences, 226–29

Student Research Project: APA Style

In the sample student research project that follows, Heather DeGroot examines the influence that gender stereotypes can have on behavior. Her paper follows the format of an APA-style research report.

Page number flush right

The Power of Wardrobe:

Male Stereotype Influences

Title, centered, upper half of page

Heather DeGroot

Author's name

James Madison University

Institutional affiliation

Psychology 220

Dr. Lawrence

May 2, 2008

Other identifying information for class purposes (double spaced)

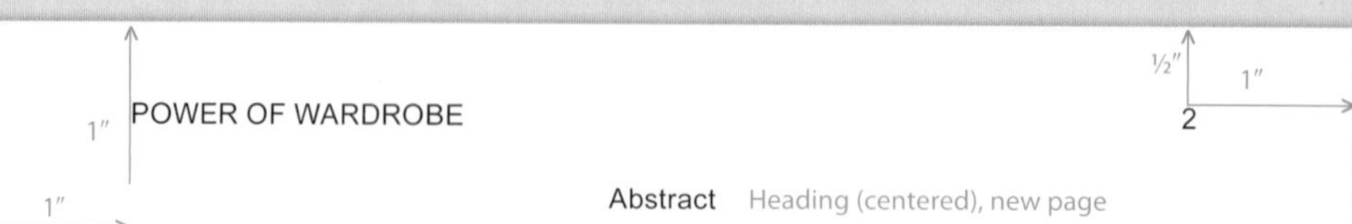

Abstract

Heading (centered), new page

This study explores the potential influence of stereotypical appearances on male subjects' stated opinions regarding entertainment perceived as "feminine." Results are based on responses from 26 undergraduate males. Data were analyzed using one-way variance tests and Tukey HSD post hoc tests. The findings show that participants were more likely to give a favorable rating to a "chick-flick" in the presence of a counterstereotypical male (M = 8.67, SD = 1.53) than in the presence of a stereotypical male (M = 5.31, SD = 1.97) or control proctor (M = 5.20, SD = 1.99). Results suggest that participants may have experienced gender role conflict.

Abstract: Summary of problem, methods, results, discussion

¶ indent: 5 spaces or ½"

The Power of Wardrobe: Male Stereotype Influences

Title: Centered

Stereotypes—expectations placed upon people because of their gender, race, or religion—may be discouraged in their most overt forms, but they continue to flourish in the media. In contemporary American culture, this sort of bias places an exaggerated emphasis on physical appearance. Such attitudes are not isolated features of media programming; rather, they influence many interactions in everyday life—especially among adolescents and young adults, for whom clothing, personal image, and identity tend to be inextricably bound (Sontag, Peteu, & Lee, 1999).

Text: Double spaced

Summary of whole source, so no page number

Impressions of other people can be classified into two categories: stereoypes and individuating information (Kunda & Thagard, 1996). Stereotypes focus on social categories, while individuating information is the focus of other factors, including personality, actions of the individual, and so forth. The stereotype effect, as defined by Monica Biernat (2003), is "a finding that individual members (comparable in all ways except their category membership) are judged in a direction consistent with group-level expectations or stereotypes" (p. 1019). Under such circumstances, people are judged more by the category in which one can group them than by their qualities or skills as individuals. However, according to Kunda and Thagard (1996), the division of these types of judgment is not always clear. This was the influence for their impression formation theory, in which stereotypes, traits, and behaviors are all constrained by positive and negative associations. In their research, they found that appearance was crucial in this process.

Introduction (funnel): Background, definitions, hypothesis

Signal phrase with parenthetical citation for date, page number

The influential power of stereotypes is particularly interesting when gender boundaries are crossed. In a 2003 study, researchers found that while membership

1"

1"

in a socioeconomic class or "power position" tended to give participants a biased or predetermined opinion about the beliefs and behaviors (such as work ethic) by which a person in another category lived, gender exerted at least as great an influence on the manner in which people were categorized (Vescio, Snyder, & Butz). Men in power positions were likely to be viewed differently than females in the same positions (Mansfield, 2006).

Date of publication in text, so omitted from parenthetical citation

Would these findings remain consistent if only one gender were used in the study? That is to say, can we identify intragender roles or stereotypes that similarly affect perception and beliefs about individuals? A study by G. H. Edwards (1992) found that beliefs regarding men and women transcend gender, for subtypes or categories emerge within each sex; for example, among American men one might be perceived as businessman, athlete, family man, or loser. Typically, such seeming variations represent varying degrees of a supposed normative "masculinity," rather than truly distinct expressions of a male gender role. Rudman and Fairchild (2004) write that "for men, a lifetime of experience observing one's peers being teased or ostracized for 'effeminate' behavior may evoke strong normative pressures toward highly masculine self-presentations" (p. 160). Plummer (2001) indicates that boys begin pressuring one another to conform in childhood, telling each other to toughen up or to stop acting like a baby.

Paraphrase of whole source, so no page number included

Direct quotation from PDF; page number included

The purpose of this study is to observe whether male participants are likely to be influenced by a stereotypically "male" opinion. Are college-aged males more swayed by the "jock" or "cool guy on campus" than by those with an "average Joe" or a "metrosexual" appearance? Hypothetically, male participants should more

Hypothesis

likely be swayed by the opinions of the stereotypical male than by those of the control group ("average Joe") or the experimental group (counterstereotypical).

Method

First-level heading (centered, bold)

Participants

Second-level heading (left, bold)

Twenty-six undergraduate males from a large Southeastern university, (mean age = 19) participated in this study in order to fill a course requirement in their general psychology classes.

Procedure

The participants were randomly assigned to one of three conditions in the study: the stereotypically "male" proctor group, the counterstereotypical proctor group, and the control group. The proctor was the same person in each condition, but his appearance was different in each. In the stereotypically male proctor condition, the proctor wore an outfit consisting of team sports apparel: a baseball cap, a basketball jersey, shorts, and sneakers (Figure 1a). In the counterstereotypical condition, he wore a long-sleeved, light pink button-down shirt (tucked in), creased khaki pants, and dress shoes (Figure 1b). In the control condition, the proctor wore a short-sleeved blue button-down shirt (not tucked in), khaki shorts, and sneakers (Figure 1c).

Methods: How study was conducted

The participants in each condition were told at the beginning of the experiment that they were participating in a memory-recall task. They were to identify what they could remember from a clip from the movie *Pretty Woman* (Marshall, 1990),[1] a stereotypical "chick-flick." During the ten-minute film clip, which was constant for each of the three conditions, the proctor read scripted lines such

Content note: Additional information, endnote

as "Oh! I love this part!" and "I'm seriously such a sap, but this film is just so good!" The script was a constant in each of the three conditions.

After the clip was viewed by all, the proctor then handed out a questionnaire to conduct the "memory-recall task." The questionnaire contained diversion questions such as "What color is the dress that Vivian (Julia Roberts's character) wears in the scene?" and "What game do Edward and Vivian play after the performance?" At the end of the questionnaire, the participants rated the movie on an opinion scale from 1 to 10, with 10 being the highest overall liking.

After the experiment was over, participants in each condition were debriefed as a group and were dismissed from the study.

Results

A one-way analysis of variance (ANOVA) was conducted on the data in order to determine whether males are more influenced by a stereotypically "male" proctor in comparison to the counterstereotypical and control-group proctors. The analysis demonstrated that at least one group was significantly different from the others, $F(2, 23) = 4.08$, $p < .05$. Tukey HSD post hoc tests were performed to measure the difference between the groups individually. The Tukey HSD revealed that the participants were more likely to give a favorable movie rating under the influence of the counterstereotypically masculine proctor ($M = 8.67$, $SD = 1.53$) than the stereotypically masculine proctor ($M = 5.31$, $SD = 1.97$) or the control proctor ($M = 5.20$, $SD = 1.99$) (see Figure 2).

Results: Summarizes data and research findings; includes figure

There were no significant differences in movie ratings between those in the stereotypically masculine proctor's group and those in the control proctor's. These

(a)

(b)

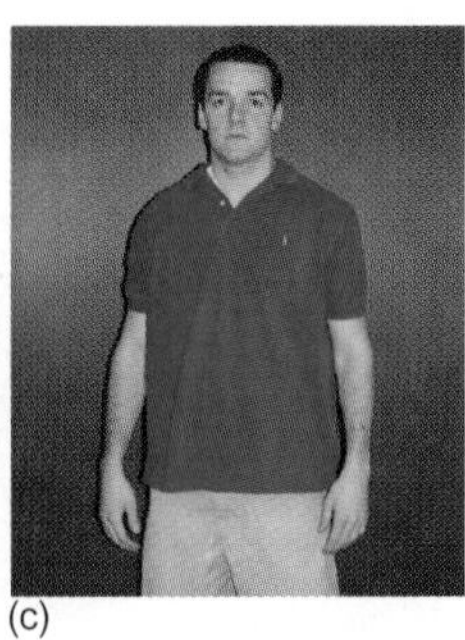
(c)

Figure 1. Male proctor in three conditions: (a) stereotypical, (b) counterstereotypical, and (c) control.

Figure caption: Label *(Figure)* and number in italics; caption below illustration

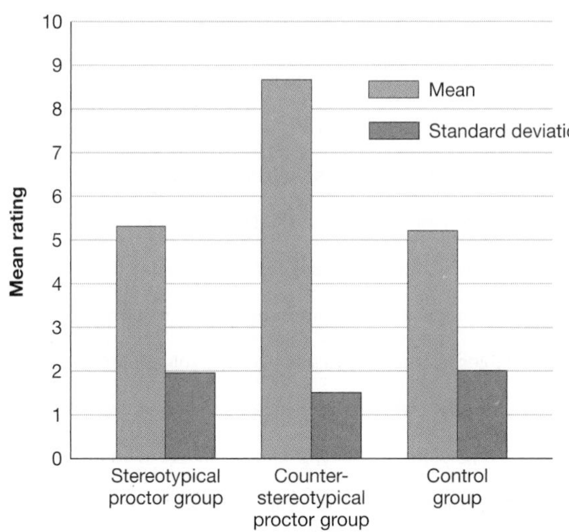

Figure 2. Tukey HSD post hoc test results for the three groups: Group with the stereotypical proctor, group with the counterstereotypical proctor, and control group.

results were contrary to the study's initial hypothesis, and they suggest that male participants are more likely to defy gender roles in the presence of a counter-stereotypical proctor than in the presence of a stereotypically masculine proctor.

Discussion

Discussion: Author's interpretation of data, conclusions, concerns, and questions for further study

The study elicited something beyond stereotypical responses from the participants. In fact, the participants may have experienced gender role conflict. Instead of scoring favorably when the masculine male proctor said he enjoyed the film, the participants instead scored the film lower than initially expected. The presence of a highly or moderately "masculine" male, though he made favorable comments in each condition, may have caused the participants to adhere more rigidly to socialized male gender roles and thus rate the movie lower than subjects in the atypically "masculine" proctor group, who did not feel the pressure to assert masculinity in their rating of *Pretty Woman* (McCreary et al., 1996).

Citations of six or more authors: First author plus *et al.*

Certain irregularities in the study provoked questions that might be investigated in future research. Due to factors beyond the researcher's control, each condition had a different number of participants. The counterstereotypical condition, which had significant findings, had the smallest number of participants; as a result, those scores are subject to greater statistical variation due to strong individual opinion. However, one might also question whether the number of males present influences a subject's tendency to admit to a counterstereotypical opinion or value judgment. If the study were to be replicated to find for stereotype differences alone, it would be crucial for the number of participants in each condition to be the same. On the other hand, a separate study might use multiple viewing groups of varying individual sizes to determine the effect of group size in gender-stereotype-determined valuations.

Another issue to consider is the effect of the fictional nature of the film to which the male viewers were asked to react. A recent study reported in *Business Week* suggested that men are more willing to show empathy when they know the stories eliciting their emotional response are fictional. Jennifer Argo, one of the authors of the study, is quoted as saying that fictional works provide "an excuse to relax gender stereotypes" (as cited in Coplan, 2008, p. 17). This factor was not considered in the study reported here.

References

Heading (centered), new page; references alphabetized by author single spaced with double space between entries

Biernat, M. (2003). Toward a broader view of social stereotyping. *American Psychologist, 58,* 1019–1027. doi: 10.1037/0003-066X.58.12.1019

5 spaces or ½″

Journal article: Accessed through data-base, DOI included

Magazine article: print version

Coplan, J. H. (2008, January 28). When it's all right for guys to cry. *Business Week, 4068,* 17.

Edwards, G. H. (1992). The structure and content of the male gender role stereotype: An exploration of subtypes. *Sex Roles: A Journal of Research, 27,* 533–551. doi: 10.1007/BF00290008

Kunda, Z., & Thagard, P. (1996). Forming impressions from stereotypes, traits, and behaviors: A parallel-constraint-satisfaction theory. *Psychological Review, 103,* 284–308. doi: 10.1037/0033-295X.103.2.284

Book: Scholarly press

Mansfield, H. C. (2006). *Manliness.* New Haven, CT: Yale University Press.

Film: Medium in brackets

Marshall, G. (Director). (1990). *Pretty woman* [DVD]. USA: Touchstone Pictures.

McCreary, D. R., Wong, F. Y., Wiener, W., Carpenter, K. M., Engle, A., & Nelson, P. (1996). The relationship between masculine gender role stress and psychological adjustment: A question of construct validity? *Sex Roles: A Journal of Research, 34,* 507–516. doi: 10.1007/BF01545029

Journal article: Online; PDF accessed—page numbers included

Plummer, D. C. (2001). The quest for modern manhood: Masculine stereotypes, peer culture and the social significance of homophobia. *Journal of Adolescence, 24,* 15–23. doi: 10.1006/jado.2000.0370

Rudman, L. A., & Fairchild, K. (2004). Reactions to counterstereotypic behavior: The role of backlash in cultural stereotype maintenance. *Journal of Personality and Social Psychology, 87,* 157–176. doi: 10.1037/0022-3514.87.2.157

Sontag, M. S., Peteu, M., & Lee, J. (1999). *Clothing in the self-system of adolescents: Relationships among values, proximity of clothing to self, clothing interest, anticipated outcomes and perceived quality of life.* Retrieved from Michigan State University Extension Web site: http://web1.msue.msu.edu/msue/imp/modrr/rr556098.html

Vescio, T. K., Snyder, M., & Butz, D. A. (2003). Power in stereotypically masculine domains: A social influence strategy X stereotype match model. *Journal of Personality and Social Psychology, 85,* 1062. doi: 10.1037/0022-3514.85.6.1062

Article on website: URL included

Notes Heading (centered), new page

1. This romantic comedy starring Julia Roberts and Richard Gere (dir. Garry Marshall) was extremely popular, grossing nearly $464 million worldwide, according to the site Box Office Mojo (www.boxofficemojo.com/movies/?id=prettywoman.htm). Nevertheless, participants had not seen the film before participating in this experiment.

Content note: Relevant information not central to argument

21 Documenting Sources: *Chicago* Style

IN THIS CHAPTER

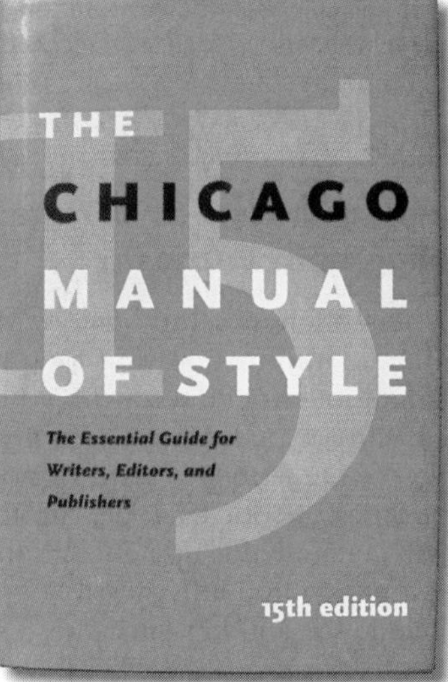

Written by editors at the University of Chicago Press, the *Chicago Manual of Style,* 15th ed., provides advice to help writers and editors produce clear and consistent copy for their readers. Many writers in the humanities and social sciences (in history, economics, and philosophy, for example) follow the guidelines provided by the *Chicago Manual* for citing and documenting sources. This chapter includes examples of the most common types of *Chicago*-style in-text citations and bibliography entries. For more information or for examples of less common types of sources, consult the *Chicago Manual* itself. You can also subscribe to the *Chicago Manual* online.

Editors at the University of Chicago Press recognize that readers from different disciplines may have different expectations about how in-text citations and bibliography entries should look, so the *Chicago Manual* provides an author-date system similar to that of the American Psychological Association (APA) and the Council of Science Editors (CSE) for writers in the sciences. It also provides a note and bibliography system for writers in the humanities and social sciences. If your readers (including your instructor) expect you to use the author-date system, consult the *Chicago Manual* itself or follow the style detailed in the APA and CSE chapters in this book.

More about ▸▸▸
Popular academic documentation styles per discipline, 222
MLA style, 230–89
APA style, 290–332
CSE style, 361–85

Writing Responsibly **Citing and Documenting Sources**

When you cite and document sources, you acknowledge any material from which you have quoted, paraphrased, summarized, or drawn information, and you join the conversation on your topic by adding your own interpretation. Simultaneously, you give interested readers (including your instructor) a way to join the conversation.

Accurate entries in the text and bibliography allow your audience to find and read your sources so that they can evaluate your interpretation and learn more about the subject themselves. Accurate entries also demonstrate the care with which you have written your research project and reinforce your reputation as a sound scholar.

More about ▸▸▸
Entering conversations and supporting your claims, 173–90

21a Creating *Chicago*-Style Notes and Bibliography Entries

The note system offered by the *Chicago Manual* allows you to include full bibliographic information in a footnote or endnote or to use an abbreviated footnote or endnote with a bibliography. Including abbreviated notes with a bibliography is recommended.

Examples of the *complete* form of notes and bibliography entries for different types of sources appear in the next section. An *abbreviated* note will generally include enough information for readers to recognize the work and find it in the bibliography. Generally, a shortened note will include the author's surname, a shortened version of the title that includes the title's key words in the same order as they appear on the title page, and the page number you are citing. Here is an example of an abbreviated note and a bibliography entry for the same book:

NOTE (ABBREVIATED) 1. Vancouver, *Voyage of Discovery*, 283.

BIBLIOGRAPHY Vancouver, George. *A Voyage of Discovery to the North Pacific Ocean and Round the World, 1791–1795*. Edited by W. Kaye Lamb. London: Hakluyt Society, 1984.

A complete bibliographic note or bibliography entry will include three parts: the author's name, the title of the work, and the publication information (print, electronic, or both). The information you include in each of these parts will differ depending on the type of source you are citing. There are many models, and every variation cannot be covered. You may have to adapt a model to your special circumstances.

Books—Printed and Electronic

In a printed book, the information you need to create a note and bibliography entry (with the exception of a page number) is on the title and copyright pages. In an online or e-book, print and electronic

▸▸▸Student research project (*Chicago* style): "Exploration and Empire," Abrams Conrad, 354–60

Quick **Reference** *Chicago*-Style Notes and Bibliography Entries

Chicago **Note & Bibliography Entries**

▶▶▶Annotated visual of where to find author, title, publication, and other information, on foldout following p. 385

publication information often appears at the top or bottom of the first screen or is available through a link.

1. One author

a. Printed The basic note for a printed book looks like this:

> Ref. No. Author's first name Surname, *Title: Subtitle* (Place of Publication: Publisher, Date of publication), Page(s).

Here is an example of an actual note:

> 1. Michael Novak, *The Universal Hunger for Liberty: Why the Clash of Civilizations Is Not Inevitable* (New York: Basic Books, 2004), 96–98.

The basic bibliography entry for a printed book looks like this:

> Author's surname, First name. *Title: Subtitle.* Place of publication: Publisher, date of publication.

Here is an example of an actual bibliography entry:

> Novak, Michael. *The Universal Hunger for Liberty: Why the Clash of Civilizations Is Not Inevitable.* New York: Basic Books, 2004.

The *Chicago Manual* allows for either full publishers' names (as above) or abbreviated versions (*Basic,* for example). Be consistent within a paper. This chapter uses full names.

b. Database

> 2. W. E. B. Du Bois, *The Souls of Black Folk* (Chicago: A. C. McClurg & Co., 1903; Bartleby.com, 1999), http://www.bartleby. com/114/.

> Du Bois, W. E. B. *The Souls of Black Folk.* Chicago: A. C. McClurg & Co., 1903. Bartleby.com, 1999. http://www.bartleby.com/114/.

If the online book is *not* available in print or is not yet in final form and might change by the time your readers seek it out, provide your access date in parentheses following the URL.

c. E-book

3. Charles C. Mann, *1491: New Revelations of the Americas before Columbus* (New York: Knopf Publishing Group, 2006), Adobe Reader e-book.

Mann, Charles C. *1491: New Revelations of the Americas before Columbus.* New York: Knopf Publishing Group, 2006. Adobe Reader e-book.

Tech

Guidelines for Formatting URLs

As you format notes and bibliography entries for online sources, you will find that not all URLs fit on one line. The *Chicago Manual* recommends breaking a URL (if necessary) after a slash (/) or double slash (//) or before a dot or other punctuation.

2. Two or three authors

4. Peter Bernstein and Annalyn Swan, *All the Money in the World* (New York: Random House, 2008), 122.

5. Cynthia Kuhn, Scott Swartzwelder, and Wilkie Wilson, *Buzzed: The Straight Facts about the Most Used and Abused Drugs from Alcohol to Ecstasy,* 3rd ed. (New York: W. W. Norton & Co., 2008), 225.

Bernstein, Peter, and Annalyn Swan. *All the Money in the World.* New York: Random House, 2008.

Kuhn, Cynthia, Scott Swartzwelder, and Wilkie Wilson. *Buzzed: The Straight Facts about the Most Used and Abused Drugs from Alcohol to Ecstasy.* 3rd ed. New York: W. W. Norton & Co., 2008.

Chicago Note & Bibliography Entries

1. One author
2. **Two or three authors**
3. **More than three authors**
4. Unnamed (anonymous) author
5. Editor (no author)

3. More than three authors

6. Peter M. Senge and others, *The Necessary Revolution: How Individuals and Organizations Are Working Together to Create a Sustainable World* (New York: Random House, 2008), 83.

Senge, Peter M., Bryan Smith, Nina Kruschwitz, Joe Laur, and Sarah Schley. *The Necessary Revolution: How Individuals and Organizations Are Working Together to Create a Sustainable World.* New York: Random House, 2008.

4. Unnamed (anonymous) author If no author is listed, begin with the title.

7. *Terrorist Hunter: The Extraordinary Story of a Woman Who Went Undercover to Infiltrate the Radical Islamic Groups Operating in America* (New York: Ecco-HarperCollins, 2003), 82.

Terrorist Hunter: The Extraordinary Story of a Woman Who Went Undercover to Infiltrate the Radical Islamic Groups Operating in America. New York: Ecco-HarperCollins, 2003.

5. Editor (no author)

8. Susan E. Cook, ed., *Genocide in Cambodia and Rwanda: New Perspectives* (New Haven, CT: Yale Center for International and Area Studies, 2004), 79.

Cook, Susan E., ed. *Genocide in Cambodia and Rwanda: New Perspectives.* New Haven, CT: Yale Center for International and Area Studies, 2004.

For a book with multiple editors, change the abbreviation *ed.* to *eds.*

6. Author and editor or translator

9. John Locke, *The Second Treatise of Government*, ed. Thomas P. Peardon (Indianapolis: Oxford University Press, 1990), 124.

10. Stefan Chwin, *Death in Danzig*, trans. Philip Boehm (New York: Harcourt, 2004), 24.

Locke, John. *The Second Treatise of Government*. Edited by Thomas P. Peardon. Indianapolis: Oxford University Press, 1990.

Chwin, Stefan. *Death in Danzig*. Translated by Philip Boehm. New York: Harcourt, 2004.

7. Selection from an edited book or anthology

selection author — selection title — title of book in which selection appears

11. Rebecca Arnold, "Fashion," in *Feminist Visual Culture*, ed. Fiona Carson and Claire Pajaczkowska (New York: Routledge, 2001), 212.

Arnold, Rebecca. "Fashion." In *Feminist Visual Culture*, edited by Fiona Carson and Claire Pajaczkowska, 207–22. New York: Routledge, 2001.

selection pgs.

8. Edition other than the first

12. James A. Herrick, *The History and Theory of Rhetoric: An Introduction*, 3rd ed. (Boston: Allyn & Bacon, 2005), 50.

Herrick, James A. *The History and Theory of Rhetoric: An Introduction*. 3rd ed. Boston: Allyn & Bacon, 2005.

9. Introduction, preface, foreword, or afterword by a different writer

13. Mario Andretti, foreword to *Race to Win: How to Become a Complete Champion*, by Derek Daly (Minneapolis: Quayside-Motorbooks, 2008), 7.

pg. cited

***Chicago* Note & Bibliography Entries**

Andretti, Mario. Foreword to *Race to Win: How to Become a Complete Champion*, by Derek Daly, 7–8. Minneapolis: Quayside-Motorbooks, 2008.

intro. pgs.

10. Entry in a reference work For a well-known reference work such as the *American Heritage Dictionary* or the *Encyclopedia Britannica,* a bibliography entry is optional.

a. Printed

s.v. Abbreviation of the Latin phrase *sub verbo,* "under the word"

14. *The American Heritage Dictionary*, 2nd college ed., s.v. "plagiarism."

b. Online

15. *Dictionary.com*, s.v. "plagiarism," http://dictionary.reference.com/browse/plagiarism.

11. Multivolume work

a. All volumes If you use information from all volumes in a multivolume work, follow the model for a bibliography entry below.

Tarbell, Ida. *The Life of Abraham Lincoln.* 2 vols. New York: Lincoln Memorial Association, 1900.

Provide a note only when you cite a specific passage in one of the volumes; follow the model in part b below.

b. One volume

16. Ida Tarbell, *The Life of Abraham Lincoln* (New York: Lincoln Memorial Association, 1900), 1:173.

vol. pgs.

Tarbell, Ida. *The Life of Abraham Lincoln.* Vol. 1. New York: Lincoln Memorial Association, 1900.

Chicago **Note & Bibliography Entries**

Chicago Note & Bibliography Entries

12. Book in a series

book title

17. Oleg V. Khlevnyuk, ed. *The History of the Gulag: From Collectivization to the Great Terror.* Annals of Communism (New Haven, CT: Yale University Press, 2004), 186–87.

series title

Khlevnyuk, Oleg V., ed. *The History of the Gulag: From Collectivization to the Great Terror.* Annals of Communism. New Haven, CT: Yale University Press, 2004.

13. Sacred text

book lines version

18. 1 Kings 3:23–26 (King James Version).

verse

19. Qur'an 17:1–2.

Sacred texts are usually omitted from the bibliography.

14. Dissertation For an unpublished dissertation, include the type of document (*PhD dissertation,* which can be abbreviated *PhD diss.*), the university where it was submitted, and the date of submission.

20. Jessica Davis Powers, "Patrons, Houses and Viewers in Pompeii: Reconsidering the House of the Gilded Cupids" (PhD diss., University of Michigan, 2006), 43–57.

Powers, Jessica Davis. "Patrons, Houses and Viewers in Pompeii: Reconsidering the House of the Gilded Cupids." PhD diss., University of Michigan, 2006.

For a published dissertation, format the note and bibliography entry as you would for a book.

Example 1, 336

▸▸▸Annotated visual of where to find author, title, publication, and other information, on foldout following p. 385

Periodicals—Printed and Electronic

A periodical is a publication issued at regular intervals—newspapers are generally published every day, magazines every week or month, and scholarly journals four times a year. For periodicals, include not only the title of the article (in quotation marks) but also the title of the periodical (in italics). The type of publication information you include depends on the type of periodical you are citing.

15. Article in a scholarly journal The information you need to create a note and bibliography entry for a printed journal article appears on the cover or title page of the journal and on the first and last page of the article. For articles downloaded from a database, the information appears on the screen listing the articles that fit your search terms or on the first (and last) page of the file you download. For articles that appear in journals published solely online, you will find the publication information on the website's home page, in the journal's table of contents, or on the first page of the article.

a. Printed The basic note for an article in a printed journal looks like this:

Ref. No. Author's first name Surname, "Title of Article," *Title of Journal* Vol. No., no. Issue number (Date of publication): Pages.

Chicago style recommends that you always include both the volume number and issue number in your citation of a journal. When a journal is paginated by volume and each issue starts with p. 1, you must add the issue number after the volume number. However, you may choose to omit the issue number when a journal is paginated by volume—for example, if issue 1 ends on p. 175 and issue 2 begins on p. 176. Regardless of which style you choose or which your instructor asks you to follow, be sure to remain consistent through the essay.

Paginated by Issue or Volume (required for journals paginated by issue)

21. Bill McCarron, "Basilisk Puns in *Harry Potter and the Chamber of Secrets*," *Notes on Contemporary Literature* 36, no. 1 (Winter 2006): 2.

vol. no. / issue no.

McCarron, Bill. "Basilisk Puns in *Harry Potter and the Chamber of Secrets*." *Notes on Contemporary Literature* 36, no. 1 (Winter 2006): 2.

Note: Although recommended, including the month is optional when you include the issue number.

Optional Style for Journals Paginated by Volume

22. Jason Phillips, "The Grape Vine Telegraph: Rumors and Confederate Persistence," *Journal of Southern History* 72 (November 2006): 770.

vol. no.

Phillips, Jason. "The Grape Vine Telegraph: Rumors and Confederate Persistence." *Journal of Southern History* 72 (November 2006): 753–88.

b. Accessed through a database Most researchers locate journal articles through subscription databases available through their college library. Frequently, articles indexed in such databases are also available in HTML (hypertext markup language, the coding system used to create websites and web pages) or PDF (portable document format, a method created by Adobe for sharing documents across platforms without losing formatting) format through the database. If the article you are citing is available in PDF format, include the page numbers you are citing in your note and the page range in your bibliography entry. If the article is available only in HTML format, add a subhead or paragraph number to your note if this will help readers locate the passage you are citing. To cite an article accessed through a subscription database, add the URL of the database's home page at the end of your entry. If the article is accessible through an open-access database, include the URL for the article itself. More and more academic journals are also adding digital object identifiers (DOIs); if the article you are citing includes a DOI, add it in place of the article's page numbers.

23. Michael J. Furlong and Sandra L. Christenson, "Engaging Students at School and with Learning: A Relevant Construct for *All* Students," *Psychology in the Schools* 45, no. 5 (May 2008), doi: 10.1002/pits.20302, http://www.ebscohost.com.

DOI

database home page

Chicago Note & Bibliography Entries

More about ▸▸▸ DOIs, 303

Furlong, Michael J., and Sandra L. Christenson. "Engaging Students at School and with Learning: A Relevant Construct for *All* Students." *Psychology in the Schools* 45, no. 5 (May 2008). doi: 10.1002/pits.20302, http://www.ebscohost.com.

c. Online Online journals usually do not provide page numbers. Provide the issue number (if available), and include the DOI (if there is one) and the URL for the article.

24. Jeremy Adelman, "An Age of Imperial Revolutions," *American Historical Review* 113, no. 2 (April 2008), doi: 10.1086/ahr.113.2.319, http://www.journals.uchicago.edu/doi/full/10.1086/ahr.113.2.319.

Adelman, Jeremy. "An Age of Imperial Revolutions." *American Historical Review* 113, no. 2 (April 2008). doi: 10.1086/ahr.113.2.319, http://www.journals.uchicago.edu/doi/full/10.1086/ahr.113.2.319.

***Chicago* Note & Bibliography Entries**

16. Article in a magazine Omit volume and issue numbers, and replace the parentheses around the publication date (month and year; or month, day, and year) with commas.

a. Printed

25. Marian Smith Holmes, "The Freedom Riders," *Smithsonian,* February 2009, 72.

Holmes, Marian Smith. "The Freedom Riders." *Smithsonian,* February 2009, 70–75.

b. Accessed through a database

26. Jesse Ellison, "The Refugees Who Saved Lewiston," *Newsweek,* January 17, 2009, 69, http://www.lexisnexis.com/.

Ellison, Jesse. "The Refugees Who Saved Lewiston." *Newsweek,* January 17, 2009, 69. http://www.lexisnexis.com/.

c. Online

27. Mike Madden, "What's Love Got to Do with It?" *Salon,* January 28, 2009, http://www.salon.com/news/feature/2009/01/28/stimulus/.

Madden, Mike. "What's Love Got to Do with It?" *Salon*, January 28, 2009. http://www.salon.com/news/feature/2009/01/28/stimulus/.

17. Article in a newspaper (signed) Because page numbers may differ from edition to edition, omit them and use section letters or numbers (if available) instead.

a. Printed

28. John M. Broder, "Geography Is Dividing Democrats over Energy," *New York Times*, January 26, 2009, national edition, sec. 1.

Broder, John M. "Geography Is Dividing Democrats over Energy." *New York Times,* January 26, 2009, national edition, sec. 1.

If the city in which the newspaper is published is not identified on the newspaper's masthead, add it in italics; if it might be unfamiliar to readers, add the state, also.

29. Jim Kenneally, "When Brockton Was Home to a Marathon," *Brockton (MA) Enterprise,* April 20, 2006, sec. 1.

Kenneally, Jim. "When Brockton Was Home to a Marathon." *Brockton (MA) Enterprise,* April 20, 2006, sec. 1.

For well-known national newspapers (such as the *Christian Science Monitor, USA Today,* and the *Wall Street Journal*), no city or state is needed. If you are unsure whether the newspaper is well known, consult your instructor or a reference librarian.

Chicago **Note & Bibliography Entries**

15. Article in a scholarly journal
16. Article in a magazine
17. Article in a newspaper (signed)
18. Article or editorial in a newspaper (unsigned)
19. Review

b. Accessed through a database

30. John M. Broder, "Geography Is Dividing Democrats over Energy," *New York Times,* January 26, 2009, late edition, sec. A, http://lexisnexis.com.

Broder, John M. "Geography Is Dividing Democrats over Energy." *New York Times,* January 26, 2009, late edition, sec. A. http://lexisnexis. com.

c. Online

Chicago **Note & Bibliography Entries**

31. Steve Chapman, "Moderating the Terror War," *Chicago Tribune,* January 25, 2009, http://www.chicagotribune.com/news/columnists/chi-oped0125chapmanjan25,0,1998584.column.

Chapman, Steve. "Moderating the Terror War." *Chicago Tribune,* January 25, 2009. http://www.chicagotribune.com/news/columnists/chi-oped0125chapmanjan25,0,1998584.column.

18. Article or editorial in a newspaper (unsigned) When no author is named, begin notes and bibliography entries with the name of the newspaper, not the title of the article.

32. *Los Angeles Times,* "Health before Ideology," January 27, 2009, sec. A.

Los Angeles Times, "Health before Ideology," January 27, 2009, sec. A.

19. Review

33. Ben Brantley, "Rash and Unadvis'd in Verona Seeks Same," review of *Romeo and Juliet,* directed by Michael Greif, *New York Times,* June 25, 2007, sec. E.

Brantley, Ben. "Rash and Unadvis'd in Verona Seeks Same." Review of *Romeo and Juliet,* directed by Michael Greif. *New York Times,* June 25, 2007, sec. E.

Other Electronic Sources

Although it is usually easy to find citation information for books and articles in periodicals, websites can be a bit trickier. Most of the information you need will appear at the bottom or top of the web page or on the site's home page. Sometimes, however, you may need to look further. Click on links such as "About us" or "More information." Frequently, websites will not provide complete information; provide as much information as you can. If no author is listed, place the site's sponsor in the "author" position. If key information is missing, include a phrase describing the site, in case the URL changes.

20. Website or wiki The basic note for a website looks like this:

Ref. No. Author, Website Title, Sponsoring Organization (if not clear from title), URL of site's home page.

Here is an example of an actual note:

34. Christine Roth, Victorian England: An Introduction, University of Wisconsin–Oshkosh, Department of English, http://www.english.uwosh .edu/VictorianEngland.htm.

The bibliography entry for this note looks like this:

Roth, Christine. Victorian England: An Introduction. University of Wisconsin–Oshkosh, Department of English. http://www.english .uwosh.edu/VictorianEngland.htm.

The *Chicago Manual* indicates that access dates should be omitted except where significant updates are likely or when changes in the field can have a significant effect (as in medicine).

21. Web page or wiki article When referring to a specific page or article on a website or wiki, place that page's title in quotation marks.

Chicago **Note & Bibliography Entries**

35. Montana Historical Society, "Lewis and Clark County History Project," Montana History Wiki, Montana Historical Society, http://montanahistorywiki.pbwiki.com/Lewis+and+Clark+County+History+Project.

Montana Historical Society. "Lewis and Clark County History Project." Montana History Wiki, Montana Historical Society. http://montanahistorywiki.pbwiki.com/Lewis+and+Clark+County+History+Project.

Chicago **Note & Bibliography Entries**

22. Discussion list or blog posting Omit bibliography entries for electronic communications unless your instructor requires one; a mention in the text or an in-text citation (parenthetical note, footnote, or endnote) is sufficient. For a blog entry, include the title; for a comment on a blog posting, include the phrase "comment on" before the title of the blog and "comment posted" before the date.

post author — post title — blog title

36. Francis Heaney, "The Tie Project, days 164–173," *Heaneyland!,* July 28, 2007, http://www.yarnivore.com/francis/archives/001900.html#more.

23. CD-ROM Unless the CD-ROM is also published as a printed book, place the format information after the publication information, not after the title; city and date of publication are needed only if there is more than one version or edition of the source or if it is published periodically.

37. *History through Art: The 20th Century,* Fogware Publishing, CD-ROM.

History through Art: The 20th Century. Fogware Publishing. CD-ROM.

Audio and Visual Sources

The information you need for creating notes and bibliography entries for most audio and visual sources will appear on the cover, label, or program, or in the credits at the end of a film or a television show. Begin with the author, director, conductor, or performer, or begin your citation with the name of the work, depending on what your project emphasizes.

24. Motion picture (film, video, DVD)

38. Jason Reitman, dir., *Juno,* DVD, written by Diablo Cody (2007; Los Angeles: Fox Searchlight Home Entertainment, 2008).

Reitman, Jason, dir. *Juno.* DVD. Written by Diablo Cody, 2007. Los Angeles: Fox Searchlight Home Entertainment, 2008.

25. Music or other audio recording

39. Johannes Brahms, *Piano Concerto no. 1 in D minor, op. 15,* Berliner Philharmoniker, dir. Claudio Abbado, 1986, Philips Classics Productions, BMG D153907. Compact disc.

Brahms, Johannes. *Piano Concerto no. 1 in D minor, op. 15.* Berliner Philharmoniker. Dir. Claudio Abbado. 1986. Philips Classics Productions. BMG D153907. Compact disc.

26. Performance

40. Lauren Ambrose, *Romeo and Juliet,* dir. Michael Greif, Delacorte Theatre, New York, July 1, 2007.

Ambrose, Lauren. *Romeo and Juliet.* Directed by Michael Greif. Delacorte Theatre, New York, July 1, 2007.

27. Work of art If a reproduction of the work appears in your project, identify the work in a figure caption. If you discuss the work but do not show it, cite it in your notes but do not provide an entry in your bibliography.

41. Alexander Calder, *Two Acrobats,* 1929, wire sculpture, Menil Collection, Houston.

Chicago **Note & Bibliography Entries**

More about ▶▶▶
Figure captions (*Chicago* style), 351–52, 355

Miscellaneous Sources

28. Government publication For documents published by the U.S. Government Printing Office (or GPO), including the publisher is optional.

42. U.S. Department of Education, Office of Innovation and Improvement, *Charter High Schools: Closing the Achievement Gap* (Washington, DC: U.S. Government Printing Office, 2006).

Or (Washington, DC, 2006).

U.S. Department of Education, Office of Innovation and Improvement. *Charter High Schools: Closing the Achievement Gap.* Washington, DC: U.S. Government Printing Office, 2006.

Or Washington, DC, 2006.

Chicago **Note & Bibliography Entries**

29. Interview

a. Printed or broadcast

43. Barack Obama, interview by Maria Bartiromo, *Closing Bell,* CNBC, March 27, 2008.

Obama, Barack. Interview by Maria Bartiromo. *Closing Bell.* CNBC, March 27, 2008.

b. Online

44. Barack Obama, interview by Maria Bartiromo, *Closing Bell,* CNBC, March 27, 2008; transcript posted March 27, 2008, http://www.cnbc.com/id/23832520.

Obama, Barack. Interview by Maria Bartiromo. *Closing Bell.* CNBC, March 27, 2008. Transcript posted March 27, 2008, http://www.cnbc.com/id/23832520.

c. Unpublished Typically, unpublished interviews appear as in-text citations or notes. When they appear in bibliographies, the entries should include the interviewee's name, the date, the name of the interviewer, information regarding the availability of a tape or transcript, and the place of the interview.

Gunderson, Sarah. 2008. Interview by Samantha Cade. Tape recording.

May 9. Hope Community Center, St. Paul, MN.

30. Personal communication Unless your instructor requires it, no bibliography entry is required.

a. Letter

45. Evan Marks, letter to the author, August 13, 2005.

b. Email

46. Amy E. Robillard, email message to the author, March 14, 2007.

31. Indirect source

47. Theophrastus, *The Characters of Theophrastus,* ed. and trans.

J. M. Edmonds (New York: G. P. Putnam, 1929), 48, quoted in Henry

Gleitman, *Psychology* (New York: W. W. Norton & Co., 2000), 553.

Theophrastus. *The Characters of Theophrastus.* Translated and edited by

J. M. Edmonds. New York: G. P. Putnam, 1929, 48. Quoted in Henry

Gleitman, *Psychology* (New York: W. W. Norton & Co., 2000), 553.

***Chicago* Note & Bibliography Entries**

21b Using *Chicago* Style for Tables and Figures

The *Chicago Manual* recommends that you number tables and figures in a separate sequence (*Table 1, Table 2, Figure 1, Figure 2*) both in the text and in the table title or figure caption. Tables and figures should be placed as close as possible after the first text reference. If you use abbreviations in such illustrations, make sure they will be clear to readers. Discuss visuals in the text, but do not repeat the information contained in the table or figure itself, or in an accompanying caption. For tables, provide a brief identifying title and place it above the table. For figures, provide a caption that includes any information about the figure that readers will need to identify it, such as the title of a work of art, the artist's name, the work's location, and a brief description. If the figure, table, or information used to create these illustrations comes from

Tech

Creating Footnotes and Endnotes

Most word processing programs, including Microsoft *Word* and Google *Docs,* allow you to insert footnotes and endnotes easily. This automated system for inserting footnotes will automatically renumber all the notes in your project if you add or delete one. However, the software for managing notes may not provide many formatting options, so check with your instructor in advance to make sure the software's default format is acceptable.

another source, provide a source note. Source notes for tables generally appear below the table, while source information for figures appears at the end of the figure caption.

21c Using *Chicago* Style for Content Notes

Content notes offer ideas and information that clarify or justify a point in your text. They can also be used to acknowledge the contributions of others (such as tutors and classmates) in the preparation of your research project. If a paper includes both content notes and bibliographic notes, *Chicago* recommends that writers use footnotes (labeled with symbols) for content notes and endnotes (numbered sequentially) for bibliographic notes.

More about ▸▸▸
Taking content notes, 97–99
Designing an academic research essay, 215–17

21d Formatting a Paper in *Chicago* Style

The *Chicago Manual* provides detailed instructions about manuscript preparation for authors submitting their work for publication, but it does not offer formatting instructions for college projects. Follow the formatting instructions provided in chapter 17 or chapter 19 (MLA style), or consult your instructor.

The *Chicago Manual* recommends numbering bibliographic notes consecutively throughout the paper, using superscript (above-the-line) numbers in the body of the paper:

> While acknowledging that not all scholars agree, Mann observes, "If Monte Verde is correct, as most believe, people were thriving from Alaska to Chile while much of northern Europe was still empty of mankind and its works."[8]

Writing Responsibly **Of Deadlines and Paper Clips**

Instructors expect students to turn in thoughtful, carefully proofread, and neatly formatted papers on time—usually in class on the due date. They also expect writers to clip (or staple) the pages of the paper *before* the paper is submitted. Do justice to yourself by being fully prepared: Do not hand in a stack of loose sheets or expect your instructor to supply a paper clip.

If endnotes are used, type the heading "Notes" at the top of a new page following the end of the text, and type the notes below. (You may need to insert a page break and type the word "Notes" if your word processor has automatically created endnotes on the last page of your paper.)

To begin your list of works cited, type the heading "Bibliography" or "Works Cited" at the top of a new page. (Ask your instructor which heading is preferred.) Entries should be set with a hanging indent: The first line of each entry is set flush with the left margin, and subsequent lines are indented. Entries should also be alphabetized by the author's surname. If you used more than one source by the same author (or authors), replace the author's name with three hyphens in entries after the first:

Obama, Barack. *The Audacity of Hope: Thoughts on Reclaiming the American Dream.* New York: Crown, 2006.

---. *Dreams from My Father: A Story of Race and Inheritance.* New York: Crown, 1995.

Student Research Project: *Chicago* Style

The following excerpts are taken from a research project written by Abrams Conrad for a history course at American University. His formatting has been modified to show both abbreviated notes with a list of works cited and full notes without one.

More about ▶▶▶
Using abbreviated notes, 334, 358

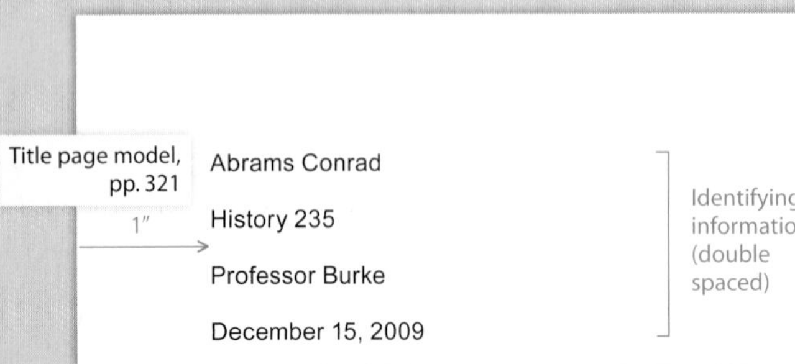

Conrad 1

Title page model, pp. 321

Abrams Conrad

History 235

Professor Burke

December 15, 2009

Identifying information (double spaced)

Title (centered)

Exploration and Empire: James Cook and the Pacific Northwest

Descriptive title

Exploration of the Pacific Northwest begins and ends with Captain James Cook, the first British explorer to reach the area, map it, and study its peoples. The men who explored and studied the area in his wake had sailed and trained under his command. While others sailed to the Pacific Northwest, their motivation was largely for trade; Cook's voyage and those of his successors were motivated as much by a desire to understand the region and its peoples as by the desire for financial gain.

Thesis at end of first paragraph to guide reader

In the late 1770s, the Pacific Northwest was the globe's last temperate coast to be explored and mapped, primarily due to its remoteness. Cook's third voyage, begun in 1778, was undertaken to discover a Northwest Passage, an inland waterway connecting the Pacific Ocean with the Atlantic that would shorten the sailing time from Europe to Asia. The Admiralty had instructed him "to search for, and to explore, such Rivers or Inlets as may appear to be of a considerable extent and pointing towards Hudsons or Baffins Bay."[1] While his findings were negative—he all but eliminated the possibility of an inland passage—he was the first Briton to make contact with the area and truly to study the geography and culture of the region.*

Quotation integrated into text; source in endnote

*The Captain Cook Society's website <http://captaincooksociety.com/ccsu52.htm> offers a number of engravings of Pacific Northwestern peoples and their habitat based on paintings and illustrations created during Cook's voyage to the Pacific Northwest.

Symbol, not number, in content note footnote

Cook made anchor in Nootka Sound for most of April 1778 and then ventured north along the Canadian coast, searching for a waterway northeast, until he put in at Prince William Sound.[2] He made a detailed survey of the coast, a portion of which is shown in Figure 1.

Summary in text with bibliographic endnote

Figure callout in text

Cook's third voyage was also strategic: to thwart Spanish and Russian claims to the Pacific Northwest.[3] With the Spanish in the south and moving north, and the Russians in the north and moving south, the northwest coast, or "New Albion," was a place where the British could establish a claim and perhaps eventually a colony.[4] Another reason for Cook's exploration of the Northwest was the man

Transition

Figure 1. A chart of the northwest coast of America and the northeast coast of Asia, explored in the years 1778 and 1779. Prepared by Lieut. Henry Roberts, under the immediate inspection of Capt. Cook, 1794, David Rumsey Map Collection, davidrumsey.com.

Figure identified in caption

himself. Cook was the quintessential explorer; he "never missed an opportunity to chart a reef or an island," wrote Ernest Dodge of the Peabody Museum in Salem, Massachusetts.[5] Cook stood out because he was so methodical. He was exact in his measurements and never missed an opportunity to learn or write about indigenous peoples.

Signal phrase with background information

Cook's explorations of the Pacific Northwest ended with his death in the Hawaiian Islands in early 1779, but his explorations of the Pacific Northwest had direct consequences for traders. James King, who took over command of the expedition after Cook's death, received 800 Spanish dollars in return for twenty sea otter pelts he brought back from the Pacific Northwest—and those were the ragged ones; King received 120 dollars each for pelts in pristine condition, an immense amount of money at that time.[6] It is doubtful the price ever went that high again,[7] but this sum put the region on the map for traders and spawned a new series of voyages.

Claim in topic sentence; supporting facts in balance of paragraph

Footnote callouts placed at natural pause

What made Cook so important to the Pacific Northwest were the explorations of the area by those who had sailed with him. In this regard, it is interesting to compare the results of those who sailed under Cook with those who did not. Some of the first voyages to the area after Cook's death were the trading voyages of James Hanna and James Strange. Hanna sailed from Macao to Nootka Sound (in what is now British Columbia) in 1784–86.[8] His voyage produced few results except those of trade, collecting more than 500 skins.[9] Strange sailed from India; his mission was to proceed to the Northwest, trade at Nootka Sound and Alaska, make discoveries, and sail through the Bering Strait and Arctic Ocean, as far

Claim in topic sentence; synthesis of information for support in paragraph north as the North Pole.[10] While his instructions stated discovery as the primary goal, his investors looked upon trade as the focus of the expedition, and Strange ended up doing neither very well. He brought back barely 600 skins, not enough to offset the costs of the voyage, and though he tried to put together another trip, he was unsuccessful.[11] His voyage also proved a burden to Hanna, who returned to the Northwest for a second voyage immediately after Strange and found few furs because of Strange's expedition.[12] What the Strange voyage was notable for, other than reflecting some of the more distasteful bureaucratic aspects of the East India Company, was the growing interest in the Northwest.[13]

John Meares led a voyage in 1785 to the Gulf of Alaska, where he anticipated better trading and finer pelts. He proved ignorant both of Russian control over the area and of the harsh Alaskan climate.[14] Meares reached Cook Inlet in September and found the Russians controlling the trade in the area, so he moved east to Prince William Sound.[15] He thought wintering in the waters off what is now Alaska would be less risky than wintering in the Hawaiian Islands (then called the Sandwich Islands), where Cook had been killed six years before, yet he managed to lose twenty-three men from disease.[16] He also got his ship stuck in the ice and was released only with warm weather and the help of George Dixon and Nathanial Portlock (both had sailed with Cook), who provided aid if he promised to leave at once.[17]

Notes

Heading (centered), new page

If notes and list of works cited used, notes abbreviated

"Ibid." (abbreviation of *ibidem,* Latin for "in the same place") used when source cited in note immediately above; page number added when different

1. Cook, *The Journals,* 220–24.

2. Ibid., 230.

3. Rose, "Captain Cook," 102–9.

4. Schwantes, *The Pacific Northwest,* 41.

5. Dodge, *Beyond the Capes,* 15.

6. Schwantes, *The Pacific Northwest,* 43.

7. Ibid.

8. Blumenthal, *The Early Exploration,* 3.

9. Dodge, *Beyond the Capes,* 43–44.

Journal article

10. Gough, "India-Based Expeditions," 219.

11. Ibid., 217–19.

12. Blumenthal, *The Early Exploration,* 4.

13. Gough, "India-Based Expeditions," 219.

14. Ibid., 220.

15. Ibid.

16. Ibid.

Reference work; Use "s.v," *sub verbo,* "under the word" (Latin)

Two citations in same footnote separated with a semicolon

17. Blumenthal, *The Early Exploration,* 4; *Oxford Dictionary of National Biography,* s.v. "John Meares," http://www.oxforddnb.com/.

Works Cited

Book: Editor, no author

Blumenthal, Richard W., ed. *The Early Exploration of Inland Washington Waters: Journals and Logs from Six Expeditions, 1786–1792*. Jefferson, NC: McFarland, 2004.

Book: Editor and author; one volume from multivolume work

Cook, James. *The Journals of Captain James Cook on His Voyages of Discovery*. Vol. 3. Edited by J. C. Beaglehole. Cambridge: Cambridge University Press, 1967.

Dodge, Ernest S. *Beyond the Capes: Pacific Exploration from Captain Cook to the* Challenger, *1776–1877*. Boston: Little, Brown, 1971.

Book (printed): Popular press

Journal article: Accessed through a database, URL of database home page provided

Gough, Barry M. "India-Based Expeditions of Trade and Discovery in the North Pacific in the Late Eighteenth Century." *Geographical Journal* 155, no. 2 (July 1989): 215–23, http://www.jstor.org/.

Rose, J. Holland. "Captain Cook and the Founding of British Power in the Pacific." *Geographical Journal* 73, no. 2 (February 1929): 102–22, http://www.jstor.org/.

Schwantes, Carlos A. *The Pacific Northwest: An Interpretive History*. Lincoln: University of Nebraska Press, 1989.

Book (printed): Scholarly press

Notes Heading (centered), new page

If no list of works cited included, complete note used first time and abbreviated note thereafter

Book: Editor and author, one volume from multivolume work

1. James Cook, *The Journals of Captain James Cook on His Voyages of Discovery,* vol. 3, edited by J. C. Beaglehole (Cambridge: Cambridge University Press, 1967), 220–24.

2. Ibid., 230.

Journal article: Accessed through a database, URL of database home page provided

3. J. Holland Rose, "Captain Cook and the Founding of British Power in the Pacific," *Geographical Journal* 73, no. 2 (February 1929): 102–9, http://www.jstor.org/.

Book (printed): Scholarly press

4. Carlos A. Schwantes, *The Pacific Northwest: An Interpretive History* (Lincoln: University of Nebraska Press, 1989), 41.

Book (printed): Popular press

5. Ernest S. Dodge, *Beyond the Capes: Pacific Exploration from Captain Cook to the* Challenger, *1776–1877* (Boston: Little, Brown, 1971), 15.

6. Schwantes, *The Pacific Northwest,* 43.

Same work, same page as note above, so only "ibid." needed

7. Ibid.

Book (printed): Editor but no author

8. Richard W. Blumenthal, ed., *The Early Exploration of Inland Washington Waters: Journals and Logs from Six Expeditions, 1786–1792* (Jefferson, NC: McFarland, 2004), 3.

9. Dodge, *Beyond the Capes,* 43–44.

10. Barry M. Gough, "India-Based Expeditions of Trade and Discovery in the North Pacific in the Late Eighteenth Century," *Geographical Journal* 155, no. 2 (July 1989): 219, http://www.jstor.org/.

Same work as above but different pages, so "ibid." plus page number needed

11. Ibid., 217–19.

12. Blumenthal, *The Early Exploration,* 4.

13. Gough, "India-Based Expeditions," 219.

22 Documenting Sources: CSE Style

IN THIS CHAPTER

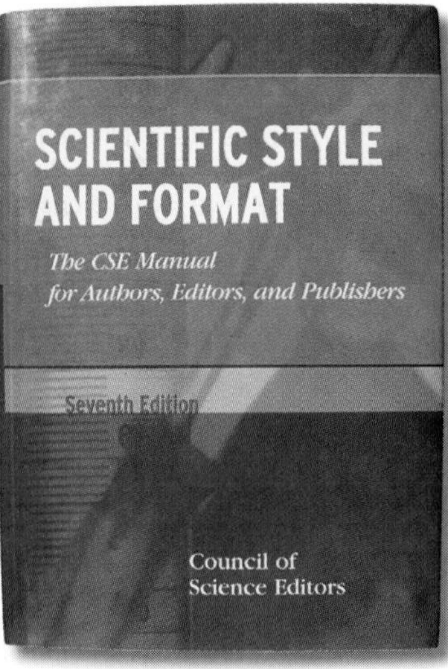

Writers in the sciences customarily use formatting and documentation guidelines from *Scientific Style and Format: The CSE Manual for Authors, Editors, and Publishers,* 7th ed., published by the Council of Science Editors (CSE). CSE style requires that sources be cited briefly in the text and documented in a reference list at the end of the project. The goal of providing in-text citations and a list of references is to allow readers to locate the sources and to distinguish the writer's ideas from those borrowed from other sources.

22a Creating CSE-Style In-Text Citations

More about ▸▸▸
Popular academic documentation styles per discipline, 222
MLA style, 230–89
APA style, 290–32
Chicago style, 333–60

In-text citations, which appear in the body of your paper, identify any material borrowed from a source, whether it is a quotation, paraphrase, summary, or idea. The CSE offers three formats for citing sources in the body of the project:

- name-year
- citation-sequence
- citation-name sequence

The *name-year system* requires you to include the last name of the author and the year of publication in parentheses whenever the source is cited:

> Advances have clarified the role of betalains and carotenoids in
> author date
> determining the color of flowers (Groteworld 2006).

More about ▶▶▶
Signal phrases, 109–11, 181–86
Signal verbs, 183

If you use the author's name in a *signal phrase,* include just the year of publication in parentheses:

> author date
> Christoffel (2007) argues that public health officers adopted the strategies
> signal phrase
> they did because they were facing a crisis.

The name-year system tells readers immediately how current your source is—this is particularly crucial in the sciences—and who wrote it. This system requires many rules for creating in-text citations (for example, how to create in-text citations for several authors, organizations as authors, and so on), which can make it difficult to apply the rules consistently. (For the details of creating in-text citations using the name-year system, consult the CSE style manual, *Scientific Style and Format,* 7th ed.)

The *citation-sequence* and *citation-name systems* use a superscript number (a single number for each source) to refer the reader to a list of references at the end of the report.

Place reference numbers after punctuation marks. When drawing information from multiple sources, include multiple citations, separated by commas.

> Some testing of the River Invertebrate Prediction and Classification System (RIVPACS) had already been conducted.[1] Biologists in Great Britain then used environmental data to establish community type,[2] and two studies developed predictive models for testing the effects of habitat-specific sampling.[3, 4] These did not, however, account for the earlier RIVPACS research.[1]

When using the *citation-sequence system,* arrange the sources in your reference list in order of first mention in your research report and then number them. (The first work cited is number 1, the second work cited is number 2, and so on.) When using the *citation-name system,* alphabetize sources and then number them. (The first work alphabetically is number 1, the second work alphabetically is number 2, and so on.)

The citation-sequence and citation-name systems need no rules about how to form text citations, but they do require you to renumber citations if sources are added or deleted. Since the word processor's

Creating Superscript Numbers

The footnoting function in your word processing program will not work for inserting reference numbers for the citation-sequence or citation-name systems because it will only insert the reference marks in sequence (*1, 2, 3, . . .*), whereas the CSE system requires that you use the same superscript number for a source each time you cite it. Instead, insert superscript numbers manually, without using your word processing program's footnote function, and type your list of references separately. (Use the Help function to learn about inserting superscript numbers.)

footnoting system cannot be used, this renumbering must be done manually, which requires you to work carefully to avoid errors. Also, readers must turn to the reference list to see the name of the author and the source's date of publication.

Check with your instructor about which system to use, and use it consistently. If your instructor does not have a preference, consider the advantages and drawbacks of each system before making your choice.

22b Preparing a CSE-Style Reference List

A research report or project in CSE style ends with a list of cited references. How you format those references depends on which system you use.

▶▶▶Annotated visual of where to find author, title, publication, and other information, on foldout following p. 385

Books—Printed and Electronic

In a printed book, you can find most or all of the information you need to create a reference list entry on the copyright and title pages. In an online or e-book, print and electronic publication information often appears at the top or bottom of the first page or is available through a link.

1. One author

a. Printed The basic format for a printed book looks like this:

Name-year system

Author's surname First and Middle Initials. Date of publication. Title: subtitle. Place of publication: Publisher. Number of pages.

Quick Reference **CSE Reference List Entries**

Citation-sequence and citation-name systems

No punctuation between surname and initials and no period or space between initials

Ref. No. Author's surname First and Middle Initials. Title: subtitle. Place of publication: Publisher; date of publication. Number of pages.

NOTE Book titles are neither italicized nor underlined in CSE style.

Lines after the first align with the author's name, not the reference number.

Here are examples of actual citations:

CSE Reference List Entries

1. One author
2. Two or more authors
3. Group or corporate author

Name-year system

Field RI. 2007. Health care regulation in America: complexity, confrontation, and compromise. New York: Oxford University Press. 336 p.

Citation-sequence and citation-name systems

1. Field RI. Health care regulation in America: complexity, confrontation, and compromise. New York: Oxford University Press; 2007. 336 p.

b. Online

Name-year system

Stroup A. 1990. A company of scientists: botany, patronage, and community at the seventeenth-century Parisian Royal Academy of Sciences [Internet]. Berkeley (CA): University of California Press [cited 2007 Mar 10]. Available from: http://ark.cdlib.org/ark:/13030/ft587006gh/

print publication information

access date

URL (permalink)

Citation-sequence and citation-name systems

2. Stroup A. A company of scientists: botany, patronage, and community at the seventeenth-century Parisian Royal Academy of Sciences [Internet]. Berkeley (CA): University of California Press; 1990 [cited 2007 Mar 10]. Available from: http://ark.cdlib.org/ark:/13030/ft587006gh/

CSE Reference List Entries

2. Two or more authors

Name-year system

Jamieson BGM, Dallai R, Afzelius BA. 1999. Insects: their spermatozoa and phylogeny. Enfield (NH): Science Publishers. 555 p.

Follow the order of authors on the title page. No *and* before last author.

Citation-sequence and citation-name systems

3. Jamieson BGM, Dallai R, Afzelius BA. Insects: their spermatozoa and phylogeny. Enfield (NH): Science Publishers; 1999. 555 p.

If the source has more than ten authors, list the first ten; after the tenth author, insert the words *and others*.

3. Group or corporate author

Name-year system

Institute of Medicine Committee on the Use of Complementary and Alternative Medicine by the American Public. 2005. Complementary and alternative medicine in the United States. Washington, DC: National Academies Press, 337 p.

Citation-sequence and citation-name systems

4. Institute of Medicine Committee on the Use of Complementary and Alternative Medicine by the American Public. Complementary and alternative medicine in the United States. Washington, DC: National Academies Press; 2005. 337 p.

4. Edited book

Name-year system

Whelan CT, Mason NJ, editors. 2005. Electron scattering: from atoms, molecules, nuclei, and bulk matter. New York: Kluwer Academic/Plenum. 340 p.

Citation-sequence and citation-name systems

5. Whelan CT, Mason NJ, editors. Electron scattering: from atoms, molecules, nuclei, and bulk matter. New York: Kluwer Academic/Plenum; 2005. 340 p.

5. Selection from an edited book or conference proceedings

Name-year system

selection author | selection title | book title | selection pages

Berkenkotter C. 2000. Scientific writing and scientific thinking: writing the scientific habit of mind. In: Goggin MD, editor. Inventing a discipline: rhetoric scholarship in honor of Richard E. Young. Urbana (IL): National Council of Teachers of English. p. 270–284.

Citation-sequence and citation-name systems

6. Berkenkotter C. Scientific writing and scientific thinking: writing the scientific habit of mind. In: Goggin MD, editor. Inventing a discipline: rhetoric scholarship in honor of Richard E. Young. Urbana (IL): National Council of Teachers of English; 2000. p. 270–284.

CSE Reference List Entries

To cite a paper published in the proceedings of a conference, add the number and name of the conference, the date of the conference, and the location of the conference (separated by semicolons and ending with a period) after the title of the book and before the publication information:

48th Annual American Society for Cell Biology Conference; 2008 Dec 13–17; San Francisco, CA.

6. Translation

Name-year system

Aristotle. 1939. On the heavens. Guthrie WKC, translator. Cambridge (MA): Harvard University Press. 378 p.

Citation-sequence and citation-name systems

7. Aristotle. On the heavens. Guthrie WKC, translator. Cambridge (MA): Harvard University Press; 1939. 378 p.

7. Multivolume work

Name-year system

Taketani M. 2001. The formation and logic of quantum mechanics. Nagasaki M, translator. River Edge (NJ): World Scientific. 3 vol.

Citation-sequence and citation-name systems

8. Taketani M. The formation and logic of quantum mechanics. Nagasaki M, translator. River Edge (NJ): World Scientific; 2001. 3 vol.

8. Dissertation For dissertations published by University Microfilms International (UMI), include the access number.

Name-year system

Song LZ. 2003. Relations between optimism, stress and health in Chinese and American students [dissertation]. Tucson (AZ): University of Arizona.

access information location access no.

107 p. Available from: UMI, Ann Arbor, MI; AAI3107041.

CSE Reference List Entries

CSE Reference List Entries

▶▶▶Annotated visual of where to find author, title, publication, and other information, on foldout following p. 385

No punctuation between surname and initials and no period or space between initials

Journal titles: Omit punctuation, articles (*an, the*), and prepositions (*of, on, in*), and abbreviate most words longer than 5 letters (except 1-word titles like *Science* and *Nature*).

Citation-sequence and citation-name systems

9. Song LZ. Relations between optimism, stress and health in Chinese and American students [dissertation]. Tucson (AZ): University of Arizona; 2003. 107 p. Available from: UMI, Ann Arbor, MI; AAI3107041.

If the location of the school is not listed on the title page of the dissertation, place square brackets around this information: [Tucson (AZ)].

Periodicals—Printed and Electronic

The information needed to document a printed journal article is on the cover or table of contents of the journal and the first and last page of the article. For articles downloaded from a database, the information you need appears on the screen listing the articles that fit your search terms or on the first (and last) page of the file you download. For journal articles published online, the information you need appears on the website's home page, on that issue's web page, or on the first screen of the article.

9. Article in a scholarly journal

a. Printed The basic citation for an article in a scholarly journal looks like this:

Name-year system

Author's surname First and Middle Initials. Year of publication. Title: subtitle. Abbreviated Journal Title. Vol. number(Issue number):page numbers.

Citation-sequence and citation-name systems

Ref. No. Author's surname First and Middle Initials. Title: subtitle. Abbreviated Journal Title. Year of publication;Vol. number(Issue number):page numbers.

Here is an actual citation of each type:

Name-year system

Cox L. 2007. The community health center perspective. Behav Healthc. 27(3):20–21.

Citation-sequence and citation-name systems

10. Cox L. The community health center perspective. Behav Healthc. 2007;27(3):20–21.

b. Accessed through a database Most researchers locate journal articles through subscription databases available through their college library. Frequently, articles indexed in such databases are available in HTML or PDF format through a link from the database. As yet, the CSE does not provide a model, but since most library databases are by subscription, readers will probably find the URL of the database's home page more useful than a direct link to the article itself. If a digital object identifier (DOI) is available, include it.

More about ▸▸▸ DOIs, 20 Tech

Name-year system

Borrok D, Fein JB, Tischler M, O'Loughlin E, Meyer H, Liss M, Kemner KM. 2004. The effect of acidic solutions and growth conditions on the adsorptive properties of bacterial surfaces. Chem Geol. 209(1–2):107–119. In Science Direct [Internet] [cited 2004 Aug 7]. Available from: http://www.sciencedirect.com doi: 10.1016/j.chemgeo.2004.04.025

(Labels: database; medium; access date; URL (database home page); DOI)

No period after URL or DOI

Citation-sequence and citation-name systems

11. Borrok D, Fein JB, Tischler M, O'Loughlin E, Meyer H, Liss M, Kemner KM. The effect of acidic solutions and growth conditions on the adsorptive properties of bacterial surfaces. Chem Geol. 2004;209(1–2):107–119. In Science Direct [Internet] [cited 2004 Aug 7]. Available from: http://www.sciencedirect.com doi:10.1016/j.chemgeo.2004.04.025

c. Online Omit page numbers for online articles. When a subscription is not required to access the article, provide a direct permalink URL to the article; otherwise, provide the URL of the home page. If a DOI is provided, include it.

CSE Reference List Entries

7. Multivolume work
8. Dissertation
9. Article in a scholarly journal
10. Article in a magazine
11. Article in a newspaper

Name-year system

Patten SB, Williams HVA, Lavorato DH, Eliasziw M. 2009. Allergies and major depression: a longitudinal community study. Biopsychosoc Med [Internet] [cited 2009 Feb 5];3(3). Available from: http://www.bpsmedicine.com/content/3/1/3 doi: 10.1186/1751-0759-3-3

URL (permalink)

DOI

No period after URL or DOI

Citation-sequence and citation-name systems

12. Patten SB, Williams HVA, Lavorato DH, Eliasziw M. Allergies and major depression: a longitudinal community study. Biopsychosoc Med [Internet]. 2009 [cited 2009 Feb 5];3(3). Available from: http://www.bpsmedicine.com/content/3/1/3 doi:10.1186/1751-0759-3-3

CSE Reference List Entries

10. Article in a magazine

a. Printed

Name-year system

Gladwell M. 2006 Oct 16. The formula. New Yorker:138–149.

Citation-sequence and citation-name systems

13. Gladwell M. The formula. New Yorker 2006 Oct 16:138–149.

b. Accessed through a database

Name-year system

Gladwell M. 2006 Oct 16. The formula. New Yorker:138–149. In EbscoHost [Internet] [cited 2008 Apr 23]. Available from: http:www.ebscohost.com/

Citation-sequence and citation-name systems

14. Gladwell M. The formula. New Yorker 2006 Oct 16:138–149. In EbscoHost [Internet] [cited 2008 Apr 23]. Available from: http://www.ebscohost.com/

c. Online

Name-year system

Coghlan A. 2007 May 16. Bipolar children—is the US overdiagnosing? NewScientist.com [Internet] [cited 2007 May 19]. Available from: URL (permalink) http://www.newscientist.com/channel/health/mg19426043.900-bipolar-children--is-the-us-overdiagnosing.html/

Citation-sequence and citation-name systems

15. Coghlan A. Bipolar children—is the US overdiagnosing? NewScientist .com [Internet]. 2007 May 16 [cited 2007 May 19]. Available from: http://www.newscientist.com/channel/health/mg19426043.900-bipolar-children--is-the-us-overdiagnosing.html/

11. Article in a newspaper

a. Printed

Name-year system

LaFraniere S. 2009 Feb 6. Scientists point to possible link between dam and China quake. New York Times (Late Ed.). Sect. A:1 (col. 3).

edition section col. no. 1st pg.

Citation-sequence and citation-name systems

16. LaFraniere S. Scientists point to possible link between dam and China quake. New York Times (Late Ed.). 2009 Feb 6;Sect. A:1 (col. 3).

b. Accessed through a database

Name-year system

LaFraniere S. 2009 Feb 6. Scientists point to possible link between dam and China quake. New York Times. Sect. A:1. In LexisNexis [Internet] [cited 2009 Feb 28]. Available from: http://www.lexisnexis.com/

Citation-sequence and citation-name systems

17. LaFraniere S. Scientists point to possible link between dam and China quake. New York Times. 2009 Feb 6;Sect. A:1. In LexisNexis [Internet] [cited 2009 Feb 28]. Available from: http://www.lexisnexis.com/

c. Online

Name-year system

Include permalink URL if available; if not, use URL of home page.

LaFee S. 2006 May 17. Light can hold fatal attraction for many nocturnal animals. San Diego Union-Tribune [Internet] [cited 2006 May 20] [about 11 paragraphs]. Available from: http://www.signonsandiego.com/news/science/

length

Citation-sequence and citation-name systems

18. LaFee S. Light can hold fatal attraction for many nocturnal animals. San Diego Union-Tribune [Internet]. 2006 May 17 [cited 2006 May 20] [about 11 paragraphs]. Available from: http://www.signonsandiego.com/news/science/

CSE Reference List Entries

Other Electronic and Miscellaneous Sources

The information needed to document a website or web page usually appears at the top or bottom of the home page or web page. You may also need to look for a link to a page labeled "About us" or "Contact us." Frequently, information needed for a complete reference list entry is missing, but you should provide as much information as you can.

12. Website

Name-year system

In the name-year system, a sample reference entry for a website looks like this:

Author. Title of website [Medium (internet)]. Publication date [Access date]. Available from: URL (home page)

Here is an example of an actual entry:

MIT news [Internet]. 2009 Feb 9 [cited 2009 Mar 10]. Available from: http://web.mit.edu/newsoffice/index.html/

The site has no author, so the reference list entry begins with the name of the site's sponsor.

Citation-sequence and citation-name systems

When referencing an entire website, the only difference in the citation-sequence and citation-name systems is the addition of the reference number at the beginning of the entry.

13. Web page When documenting a web page or document on a website, provide the URL for the web page, not the site's home page.

Name-year system

article author / article title / website / URL (web page)

Schorow, S. 2009 Feb 5. Aliens at sea: anthropologist Helmreich studies researchers studying ocean microbes. MIT News [Internet] [cited 2009 Mar 10]. Available from: http://web.mit.edu/newsoffice/2009/alien-ocean-0205.html

Citation-sequence and citation-name systems

19\. Schorow, S. Aliens at sea: anthropologist Helmreich studies researchers studying ocean microbes. MIT News [Internet]. 2009 Feb 5 [cited 2009 Mar 10]. Available from: http://web.mit.edu/newsoffice/2009/alien-ocean-0205.html

CSE Reference List Entries

14. Discussion list or blog posting

Name-year system

time posted / disc. list / medium

Hall A. 2004 Aug 5, 11:33 am. Biology of deep Gulf of Mexico shipwrecks. In: FISH-SCI [Internet discussion list]. [Lulea (Sweden):

National Higher Research and Education Network]; [cited 2005 Jan 30] [about 4 paragraphs]. Available from: http://segate.sunet.se/archives/fish-sci.html

Citation-sequence and citation-name systems

20. Hall A. Biology of deep Gulf of Mexico shipwrecks. In: FISH-SCI [Internet discussion list]. [Lulea (Sweden): National Higher Research and Education Network]; 2004 Aug 5, 11:33 am [cited 2005 Jan 30] [about 4 paragraphs]. Available from: http://segate.sunet.se/archives/fish-sci.html

CSE Reference List Entries

15. Email message

Name-year system

email author / time sent / subject line / email recipient / length

Martin SP. 2005 Nov 18, 3:31 pm. Revised results [Email]. Message to: Lydia Jimenez [cited 2005 Nov 20] [about 2 screens].

Citation-sequence and citation-name systems

21. Martin SP. Revised results [Email]. Message to: Lydia Jimenez. 2005 Nov 18, 3:31 pm [cited 2005 Nov 20]. [about 2 screens].

16. Government document If no author is listed, use the name of the governing nation and the government agency that produced the document, and include any identifying number.

Name-year system

Department of Health and Human Services (US). 1985 May. Women's health. Report of the Public Health Service Task Force on Women's Health Issues. PHS:85-50206.

Citation-sequence and citation-name systems

22. Department of Health and Human Services (US). Women's health. Report of the Public Health Service Task Force on Women's Health Issues; 1985 May. PHS:85-50206.

22c Formatting a Paper and Reference List in CSE Style

▶▶▶Example student report, CSE style, 377

The CSE does not specify a format for the body of a college report, but most scientific reports include the following sections:

- Abstract
- Introduction
- Methods
- Results
- Discussion
- References

Ask your instructor for formatting guidelines, refer to the general formatting guidelines provided in chapter 17, or follow the formatting guidelines for APA style.

Start a new page for your reference list, and title it "References." CSE style does not indicate whether you should indent the lines after the first. (The manual itself shows entries both ways: aligned at left with an extra space between entries, as in the journals *Cell* and *Science,* and with the second and subsequent lines indented.) Ask your instructor which format to use.

More about ▶▶▶
Writing an abstract, 225–28
Writing a scientific report, 225–28
Designing an academic research essay, 215–17
Formatting a paper in APA style, 317–20

Name-Year System List entries in alphabetical order by author's last name or first keyword of the title (first word, omitting articles such as *the, a,* or *an*) if no author or editor is listed. Do not number the entries.

Citation-Sequence System Number your entries in order of their appearance in your paper. Each work should appear in your reference list only once, even if it is cited more than once in your report. Double-check to make sure that the numbers in your reference list match the numbers in your text.

Writing Responsibly **Of Deadlines and Paper Clips**

Instructors expect students to turn in thoughtful, carefully proofread, and neatly formatted papers on time—usually in class on the due date. They also expect writers to clip (or staple) the pages of the paper *before* the paper is submitted. Do justice to yourself by being fully prepared: Do not hand in a stack of loose sheets or expect your instructor to supply a paper clip.

Citation-Name System Alphabetize the entries in your reference list first, and then number them. Each work should appear in your reference list only once, even if it is cited more than once in your paper. Double-check to make sure that the numbers in your reference list match the numbers in your text.

Student Research Project: CSE Style

In the sample laboratory report, "The Effects of Hardy-Weinberg, Natural Selection, and Allelic Frequency on *Drosophila melanogaster*," Alicia Keene of the University of Maryland explains the findings of her experiment with fruit flies. The in-text citations and the entries in the reference list are formatted in the name-year style.

Running head ½″ from top on all pages; 1″ from right margin

Title page follows APA guidelines. Because the CSE does not specify a format for papers, use a standard format like APA or ask your instructor for guidelines.

The Effects of Hardy-Weinberg, Natural Selection, and

Allelic Frequency on *Drosophila melanogaster*

Alicia Keene

Professor Raupp

Biology 103

2 May 2008

Information on title page is double-spaced and centered on the page. The title and author information appear in the top third of the page following APA style.

Abstract (less than 120 words) summarizes the experiment, its goals, methods, results, and discussion.

Abstract

Goals

The objective of this experiment is to demonstrate the selection process within a *Drosophila melanogaster* population. *Drosophila* are the ideal animals for genetic study because of their short life cycle, the ease with which males and females can be differentiated, their four pairs of large chromosomes, and their numerous offspring per mating. This experiment will show the effects of Hardy-Weinberg, natural selection, and allelic assortment on *Drosophila.* Using processes of immobilization and surveillance, the fruit flies will be directly observed through processes of immobilization, surveillance, and mating. The preliminary results reveal that Hardy-Weinberg, natural selection, and allelic assortment do in fact have effects on fruit flies.

Discussion

Methods

Results

The Effects of Hardy-Weinberg, Natural Selection,

and Allelic Frequency on *Drosophila melanogaster*

The study of *Drosophila* has been very important to the understanding of human genetics. During the early days of genetic study, before the discovery of DNA and the advent of sophisticated equipment and processes such as electron microscopes and gene splicing, many genetic concepts such as crossing over, gene linkage, and mutation events were discovered using *Drosophila* (Ives 1921). These fruit flies are especially useful for demonstrating the processes of natural selection because they have short life spans, a small number of genes, and pronounced sexual characteristics. They also have the advantages of being cheap to raise and easy to maintain (Geiger 2002).

Reference to the general ideas of a source

Paper structure includes introduction, methods, results, and discussion.

Charles Darwin's theory of evolution proposes that species adapt over generations in response to the pressures of natural selection because the offspring of individuals with advantageous traits have greater reproductive success (that is, more of their offspring reproduce) (Mader 2007, p. 118).

Wingedness is one characteristic that varies in *Drosophila melanogaster.* If the number of fruit flies with wings increases over successive generations, it can be assumed that, at least in the past, wingedness was advantageous (Hoikkala, Aspi 1993; Marcillac, Bousquet, Alabouvette, Savarit, Ferveur 2005). If, however, fruit fly populations return to Hardy-Weinberg equilibrium, that is, if their allelic frequencies do not change over successive generations, then wingedness is unlikely to have been an advantageous trait (Mader 2007, p. 154).

Reference to multiple sources

Citation of a specific passage from a source

A final area of interest is allelic assortment, whether certain alleles are inherited together. The characteristics of wingedness and eye color are being observed here to determine whether these two traits are inherited together.

The first portion of this study will focus on wingedness. The hypothesis is that wingedness is advantageous (wingless fruit flies would become prey more frequently than their winged cousins) and, therefore, the number of individuals with wings will increase over three generations. The second portion of this study examines whether the fruit fly population returns to Hardy-Weinberg equilibrium. The hypothesis for this portion of the study is that the population will in fact return to Hardy-Weinberg equilibrium.

Introduction lays out the ideas and hypotheses of the experiment

Methods

Step 1: Obtain a vial of wild *Drosophila melanogaster.*

Step 2: Immobilize the flies. Invert the vial with food inside, so that the flies will not fall into the food. (The food is sticky and will kill the flies because they will not be able to get out of it once they wake up.)

Step 3: Pump carbon dioxide into the tube; the flies will become anesthetized in a few seconds.

Step 4: Transfer the immobilized flies onto a carbon dioxide plate, which will continue to pump carbon dioxide onto the flies in order to keep them immobilized.

Step 5: Separate the flies into two groups—winged and wingless.

Step 6: Count and record the number of each type of fly present.

Step 7: Select 50 specimens of each type and place the selected flies into a fresh vial. This is the P_1 generation of flies.

Step 8: Place any remaining flies on the carbon dioxide plate into the “fly morgue.” This is necessary to avoid confusion between generations.

After a week, repeat steps 1–8 with generation P_1. Label the vial with this new generation of flies F_1.

After another week, repeat steps 1–6 with the F_1 generation flies. Label the vial containing their offspring F_2. Then separate the flies into three piles: winged, wingless, and winged with red eyes. The new phenotype of winged flies with red eyes is representative of the heterozygous winged trait; the other two phenotypes are homozygous dominant or recessive. After recording the numbers for each of the phenotypes, remove the remaining flies to the “fly morgue.”

There are three possible outcomes for the F_2 generation. The first is if a winged mated with a winged; since winged is dominant, the offspring would have wings. For a dominant trait to be shown, it needs only one allele because the dominant allele will mask the recessive.

WW	WW
WW	WW

The second is if a wingless mated with a wingless; since wingless is recessive, the offspring would have no wings. For a recessive trait to be shown, it needs to have two recessive alleles.

ww	ww
ww	ww

The third is if a wingless mated with a winged. If the winged parent were homozygous, all the offspring would have wings, since winged is dominant.

Ww	Ww
Ww	Ww

If, however, the winged parent were heterozygous, a quarter of the offspring would be wingless.

Ww	Ww
Ww	ww

Heterozygous flies are distinguishable from their homozygous siblings because they have red eyes, while homozygous dominant have wings and sepia-colored eyes.

Results

Results provide clear illustration of data.

Table 1. The numerical value of each type of fly during the three generations studied.

Genotype	P_1 generation before selection	P_1 generation after selection	F_2 generation
Winged	50	32	230
Wingless	45	17	183
Winged with Red Eyes	0	0	95

Table 2. Frequency of wingedness in the F_2 generation (expected vs. actual). The expected numbers are calculated by using the Hardy-Weinberg equation. The actual numbers are the numbers recorded from the experiment. χ^2 is generated by using the Chi Square formula.

Table captions label and explain data included.

Genotype	Expected Frequency	Actual Frequency	χ^2	At H-W Equilibrium?
Winged	0.42	0.45	0.005	Yes
Wingless	0.46	0.36	0.077	Yes
Winged with Red Eyes	0.12	0.19	0.34	Yes

Table 3. Natural selection probabilities. Number of winged flies lost to predation vs. number of wingless flies lost to predation. Predictions come from the null hypothesis that was 1:1; the actual numbers come from the P_1 generation after natural selection (Table 1).

	Winged	Wingless
Predicted	25/50 = 0.50	25/50 = 0.50
Actual	32/49 = 0.65	17/49 = 0.35

Discussion

Discussion summarizes findings of report.

The purpose of this lab was threefold:

- to look at the effect natural selection had on fruit flies
- to determine whether allelic assortment occurred
- to determine whether fruit fly populations returned to Hardy-Weinberg equilibrium

The results indicate that natural selection does occur. The hypothesis was that wingless flies would be killed by predators in greater numbers than winged flies. As it turns out, the wingless were targeted more frequently than the winged (Table 3). This indicates that fruit flies do undergo natural selection and that having wings is beneficial to survival.

In-text reference to specific table of data.

The results also indicate that the fruit flies returned to Hardy-Weinberg equilibrium (Table 2). That is, they returned to equilibrium after they underwent selection.

When winged flies are crossed with wingless, they produce heterozygous flies with a phenotype similar to that of a homozygous dominant. There is only one phenotypic difference between the two types of flies and that is that heterozygous flies have red eyes and homozygous dominants have sepia-colored eyes. The fact that heterozygous flies have red eyes and wings indicates that the allele for eye color and the allele for wings are inherited together because red eyes are a recessive trait.

Heading (centered), new page, references alphabetized by author

References

Geiger P. 2002. Introduction to *Drosophila melanogaster.* [Internet] Tucson (AZ): University of Arizona, General Biology Program for Teachers, Biology Department [cited 2008 Apr 30]. Available from: http://biology.arizona.edu/sciconn/lessons2/geiger/intro.htm

Web page: Date cited and URL of web page provided

Hoikkala A, Aspi J. 1993. Criteria of female mate choice in *Drosophila littoralis, D. montana,* and *D. ezoana.* Evolution 47(3):768–778. In Academic Search Premier [Internet] [cited 2008 Apr 28]. Available from: http://web.ebscohost.com

Journal article: Accessed through a database, no DOI; URL of database home page provided; no period after URL

Ives JD. 1921. Cross-over values in the fruit fly, *Drosophila ampelophila,* when the linked factors enter in different ways. Am Naturalist 6:571–573.

Print journal article: title of journal abbreviated

Mader, S. 2007. Lab manual. 9th ed. New York: McGraw-Hill. 528 p.

Marcillac F, Bousquet F, Alabouvette J, Savarit F, Ferveur, JF. 2005. A mutation with major effects on *Drosophila melanogaster* sex pheromones. Genetics 171(4):1617–1628. In Academic Search Premier [Internet] [cited 2008 Apr 28]. Available from: http://web.ebscohost.com doi: 10.1534/genetics.104.033159

Journal article: Accessed through a database, with DOI

Documentation Matters

MLA Documenting a Source:

Book (Printed)

author | title | publication information | medium

Morrison, Toni. *A Mercy*. New York: Knopf, 2008. Print.

place of publication | publisher | publication date

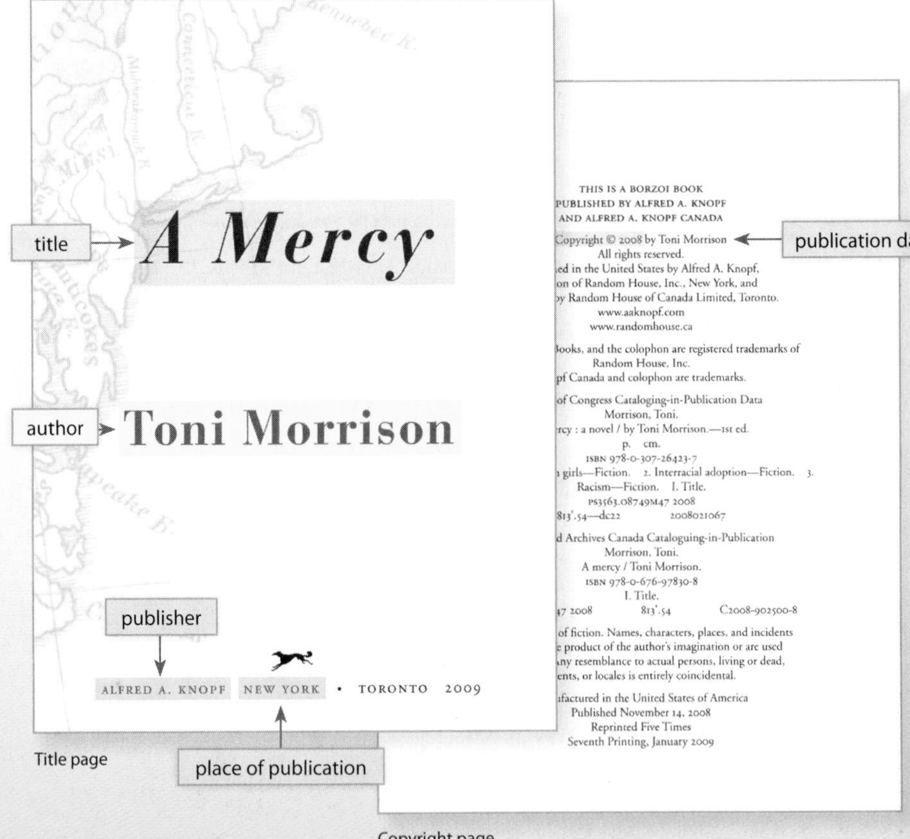

title
A Mercy
author
Toni Morrison
publisher
ALFRED A. KNOPF NEW YORK • TORONTO 2009
place of publication
THIS IS A BORZOI BOOK
PUBLISHED BY ALFRED A. KNOPF
AND ALFRED A. KNOPF CANADA
Copyright © 2008 by Toni Morrison
publication da
All rights reserved.
Published November 14, 2008
Reprinted Five Times
Seventh Printing, January 2009

Title page

Copyright page

Look for the information you need to document a printed book on the book's title page and copyright page. If more than one location for the publisher is listed on the title page, use the first. (For more about documenting a book, see pp. 230–55.)

Short Work on a Website

author · web page title · website title · sponsor/publisher

Kukkonen, Karin. "The Rhetoric of Comics." *Project Narrative Weblog.* Ohio State University,

medium · access date

College of the Humanities, 4 Nov. 2008. Web. 2 Dec. 2008.

©date/last update

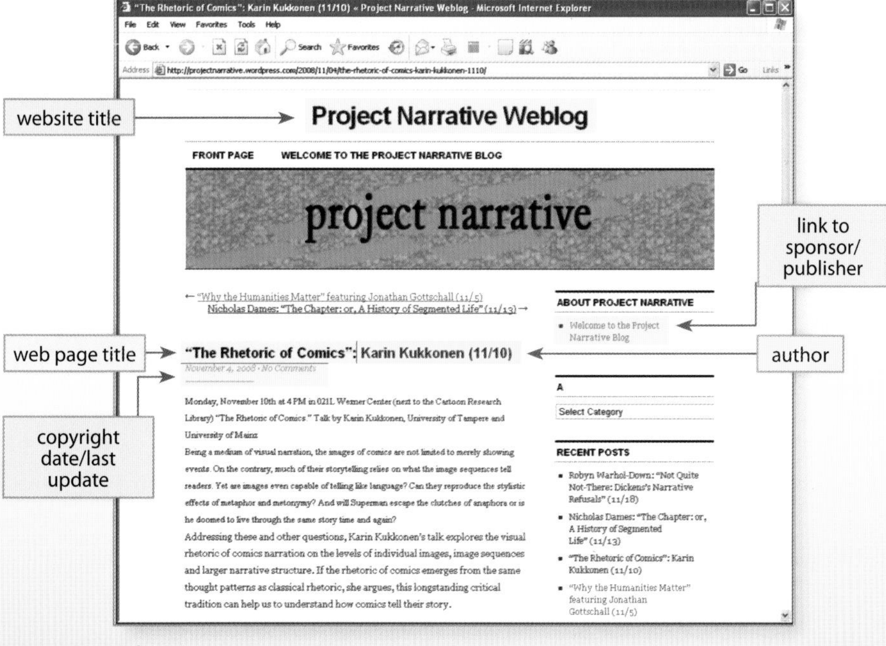

Web page

Frequently, the information you need to create a complete entry in the list of works cited is missing or difficult to find on web pages. Look at the top or bottom of the web page or home page or for a link to an "About" or "Contact Us" page. If no sponsor or publisher is listed, use *n.p.*; if no publication date is available, use *n.d.* (For more about documenting online sources, see pp. 260-63.)

APA Documenting a Source:

Book (Printed)

authors publication date title and subtitle

Tavris, C., & Aronson, E. (2007). *Mistakes were made (but not by me): Why we justify foolish beliefs, bad decisions, and hurtful acts.* Orlando, FL: Harcourt.

publication information: place of publication, publisher

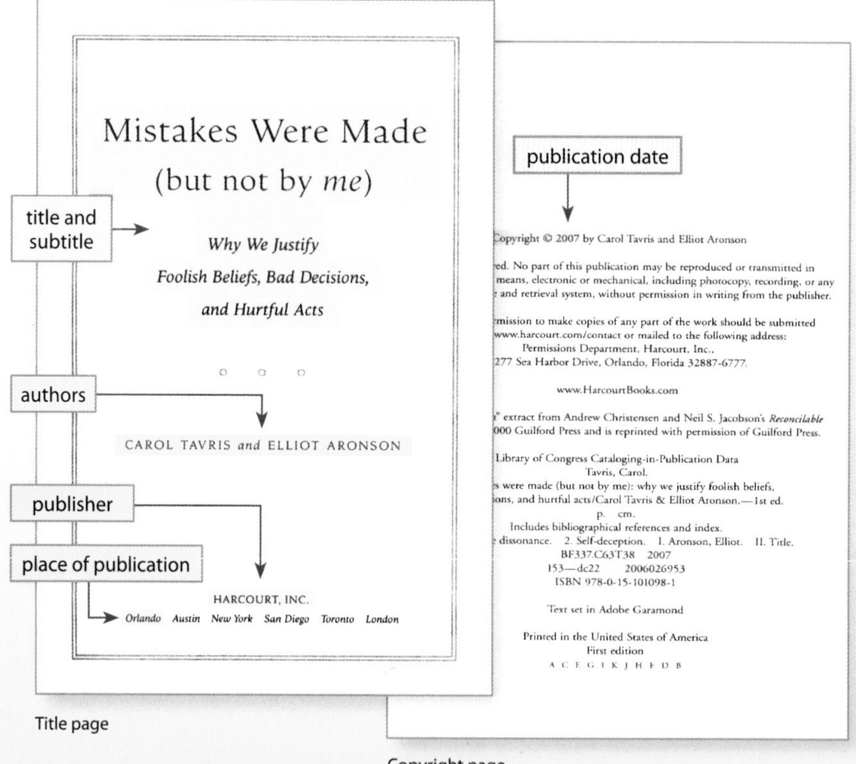

Mistakes Were Made
(but not by *me*)

Why We Justify Foolish Beliefs, Bad Decisions, and Hurtful Acts

CAROL TAVRIS *and* ELLIOT ARONSON

HARCOURT, INC.
Orlando Austin New York San Diego Toronto London

Copyright © 2007 by Carol Tavris and Elliot Aronson

ed. No part of this publication may be reproduced or transmitted in means, electronic or mechanical, including photocopy, recording, or any and retrieval system, without permission in writing from the publisher.

mission to make copies of any part of the work should be submitted www.harcourt.com/contact or mailed to the following address:
Permissions Department, Harcourt, Inc.,
277 Sea Harbor Drive, Orlando, Florida 32887-6777.

www.HarcourtBooks.com

" extract from Andrew Christensen and Neil S. Jacobson's *Reconcilable* 000 Guilford Press and is reprinted with permission of Guilford Press.

Library of Congress Cataloging-in-Publication Data
Tavris, Carol.
s were made (but not by me): why we justify foolish beliefs, ions, and hurtful acts/Carol Tavris & Elliot Aronson.—1st ed.
p. cm.
Includes bibliographical references and index.
dissonance. 2. Self-deception. I. Aronson, Elliot. II. Title.
BF337.C63T38 2007
153—dc22 2006026953
ISBN 978-0-15-101098-1

Text set in Adobe Garamond

Printed in the United States of America
First edition
A C E G I K J H F D B

Title page

Copyright page

Look for the information you need to document a printed book on the book's title page and copyright page. If more than one location for the publisher is listed on the title page, use the first or the publisher's home office location (if indicated). (For more about documenting a book, see pp. 290–99.)

Journal Article from an Online Database

author | year | article title and subtitle

Fancher, R. E. (2009). Scientific cousins: The relationship between Charles Darwin and Francis Galton.

publication information | digital object identifier

American Psychologist 64, 84–92. doi:10.1037/a0013339

journal title | volume | pages

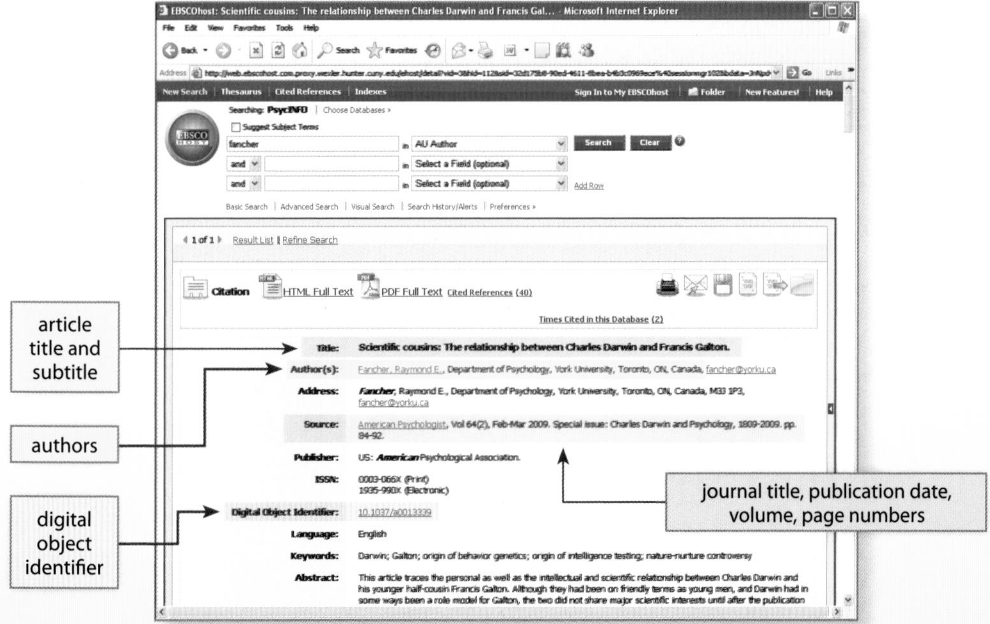

Database screen

Look for the information you need to document an article you accessed through an online database on the search results screen, the full record of the article, or the first and last pages of the article itself. Include a digital object identifier (DOI) if one is provided. No access date is needed. (For more about documenting an article accessed through an online database, see pp. 308–11.)

Journal Article (Printed)

authors · article title and subtitle

Cantor, Nancy, and Steve Schomberg. "What We Want Students to Learn: Cultivating Playfulness and Responsibility in a Liberal Education." *Change* 34.6 (2002): 47-49. Print.

journal title · issue · pages · volume · year · medium

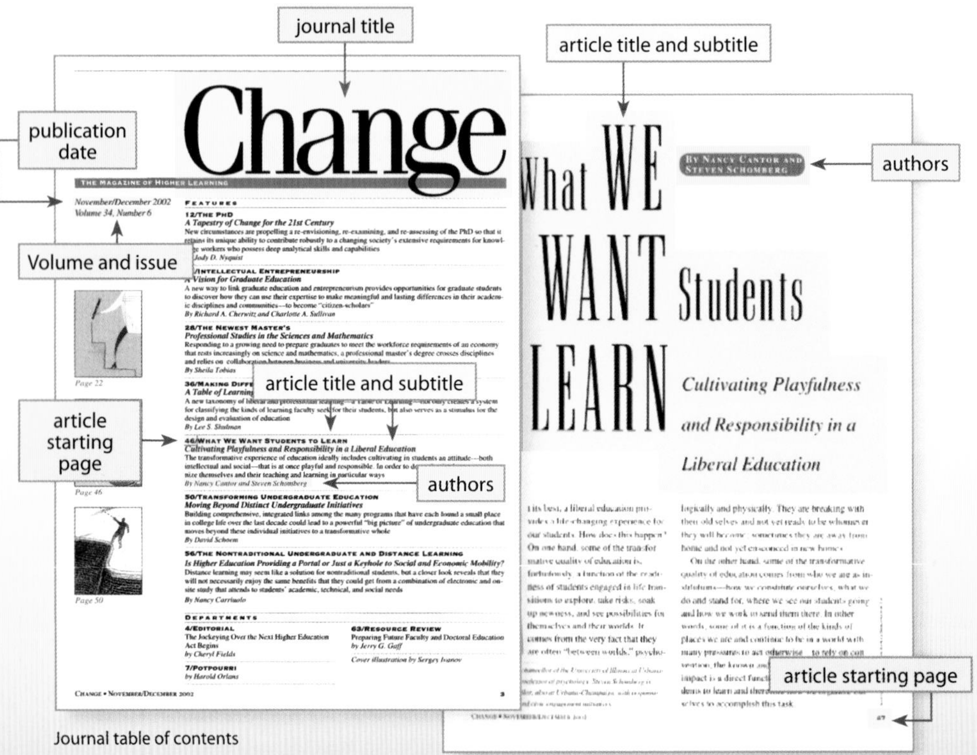

Change

THE MAGAZINE OF HIGHER LEARNING

November/December 2002
Volume 34, Number 6

FEATURES

12/THE PHD
A Tapestry of Change for the 21st Century
New circumstances are propelling a re-envisioning, re-examining, and re-assessing of the PhD so that it retains its unique ability to contribute robustly to a changing society's extensive requirements for knowl-ge workers who possess deep analytical skills and capabilities
Jody D. Nyquist

/INTELLECTUAL ENTREPRENEURSHIP
A Vision for Graduate Education
A new way to link graduate education and entrepreneurism provides opportunities for graduate students to discover how they can use their expertise to make meaningful and lasting differences in their academic disciplines and communities—to become "citizen-scholars"
By Richard A. Cherwitz and Charlotte A. Sullivan

Page 22

28/THE NEWEST MASTER'S
Professional Studies in the Sciences and Mathematics
Responding to a growing need to prepare graduates to meet the workforce requirements of an economy that rests increasingly on science and mathematics, a professional master's degree crosses disciplines and relies on collaboration between business and university leaders
By Sheila Tobias

36/MAKING DIFF
A Table of Learning
A new taxonomy of liberal and professional learning—a Table of Learning—not only creates a system for classifying the kinds of learning faculty seek for their students, but also serves as a stimulus for the design and evaluation of education
By Lee S. Shulman

46/WHAT WE WANT STUDENTS TO LEARN
Cultivating Playfulness and Responsibility in a Liberal Education
The transformative experience of education ideally includes cultivating in students an attitude—both intellectual and social—that is at once playful and responsible. In order to d nize themselves and their teaching and learning in particular ways
By Nancy Cantor and Steven Schomberg

Page 46

50/TRANSFORMING UNDERGRADUATE EDUCATION
Moving Beyond Distinct Undergraduate Initiatives
Building comprehensive, integrated links among the many programs that have each found a small place in college life over the last decade could lead to a powerful "big picture" of undergraduate education that moves beyond these individual initiatives to a transformative whole
By David Schoem

Page 50

56/THE NONTRADITIONAL UNDERGRADUATE AND DISTANCE LEARNING
Is Higher Education Providing a Portal or Just a Keyhole to Social and Economic Mobility?
Distance learning may seem like a solution for nontraditional students, but a closer look reveals that they will not necessarily enjoy the same benefits that they could get from a combination of electronic and on-site study that attends to students' academic, technical, and social needs
By Nancy Carriuolo

DEPARTMENTS

4/EDITORIAL
The Jockeying Over the Next Higher Education Act Begins
by Cheryl Fields

7/POTPOURRI
by Harold Orlans

63/RESOURCE REVIEW
Preparing Future Faculty and Doctoral Education
by Jerry G. Gaff

Cover illustration by Sergey Ivanov

CHANGE • NOVEMBER/DECEMBER 2002 3

Journal table of contents

What WE WANT Students LEARN

BY NANCY CANTOR AND STEVEN SCHOMBERG

Cultivating Playfulness and Responsibility in a Liberal Education

47

First page of article

Look for the information you need to document a journal article on the cover or table of contents of the journal and on the first and last pages of the article. (Turn to the last page of the article for the last page number.) (For more about documenting an article from a printed or online periodical, see pp. 255–59.)

Journal Article from an Online Database

authors | article title and subtitle

Cantor, Nancy, and Steve Schomberg. "What We Want Students to Learn: Cultivating Playfulness

journal title | issue | pages | database

and Responsibility in a Liberal Education." *Change* 34.6 (2002): 47-49. *Academic Search*

medium | access date | volume | year

Premier. Web. 2 Dec. 2008.

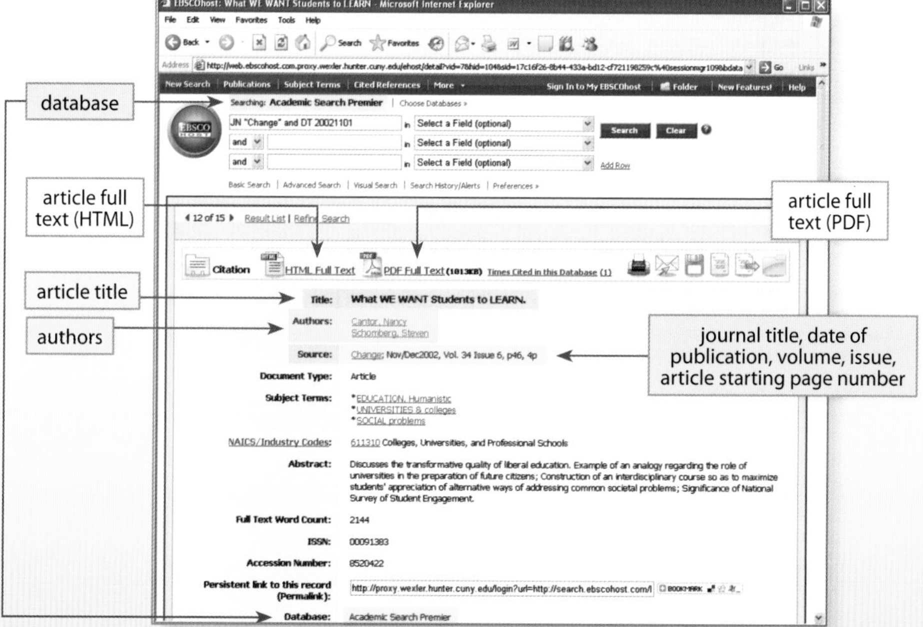

Database screen: full record for article

Look for the information you need to document an article you accessed through an online database on the search results screen, the full record of the article, or the first and last pages of the article itself. The access date is the date you last consulted the source; record this date in your notes. (For more about documenting an article accessed through an online database, see pp. 256–57.)

Journal Article (Printed)

author — year — article title and subtitle

Fancher, R. E. 2009. Scientific cousins: The relationship between Charles Darwin and Francis Galton.

publication information

American Psychologist 64, 84–92.

journal title — volume — pages

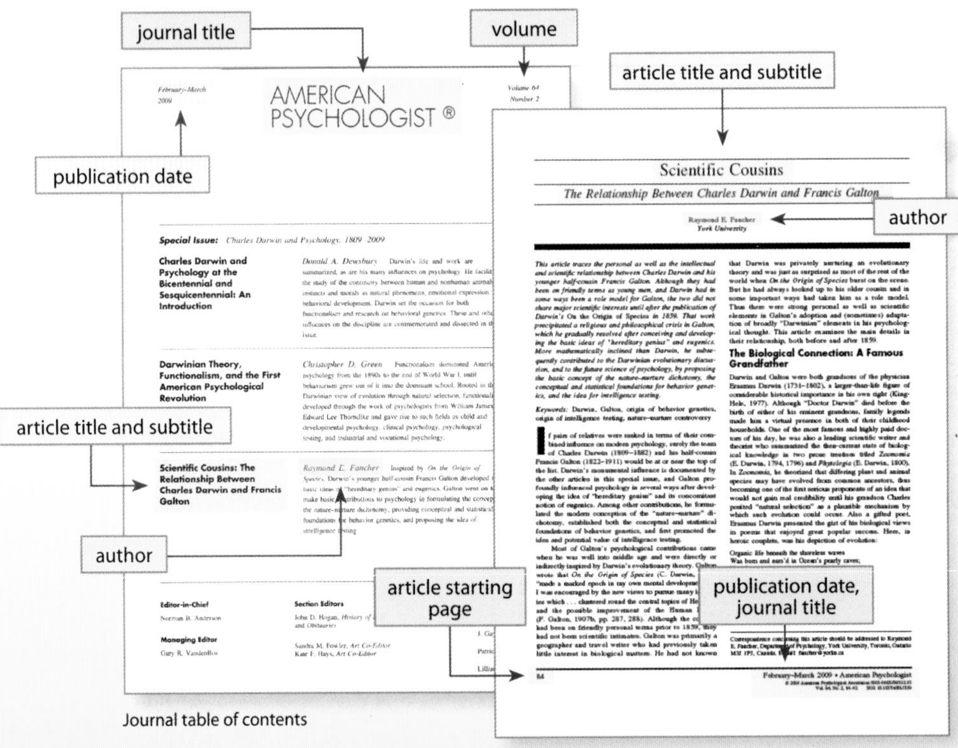

Journal table of contents

First page of article

Look for the information you need to document a journal article on the cover or table of contents of the journal and on the first and last pages of the article. (Turn to the last page of the article for the last page number.) If each issue of the journal begins with page 1, include the issue number, in parentheses, after the volume number. (For more about documenting an article from a printed or online periodical, see pp. 307–11.)

Short Work on a Website

corporate author/publisher — ©date/last update — web page title and subtitle — retrieval statement — URL for web page — retrieval date

American Psychological Association. (2005). The fast and the furious: Psychologists figure out who gets road rage and find ways to calm them down. Retrieved March 31, 2009, from http://www.psychologymatters.org/roadrage.html

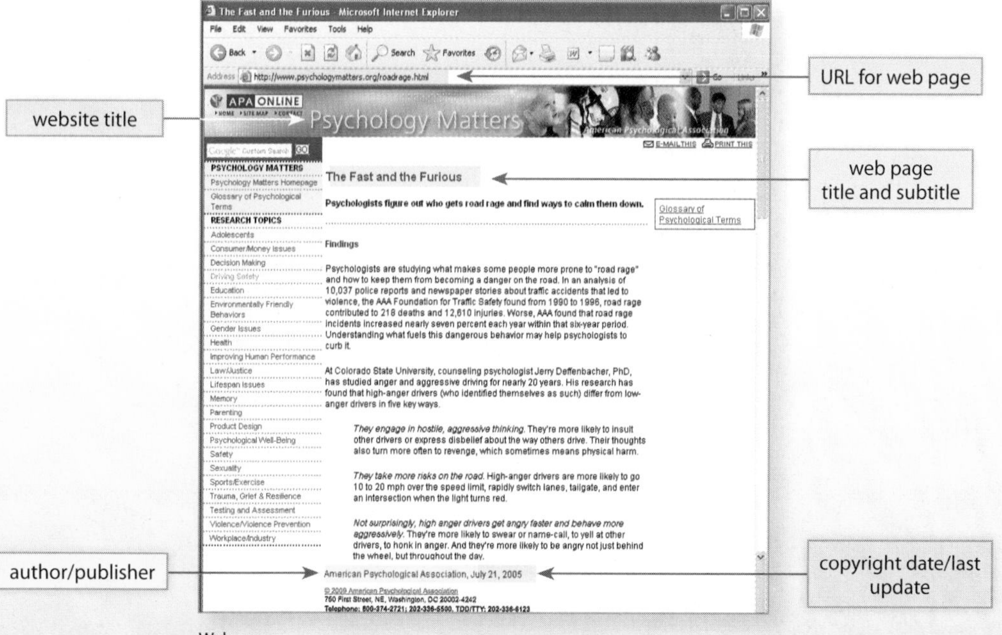

Web page

Frequently, the information you need to create a complete entry in the reference list is missing or difficult to find on web pages. Look at the top or bottom of the web page or home page or for a link to an "About" or "Contact Us" page. If no author is cited, move the title to the author position. If the web page is untitled, add a description (in brackets) in place of the title. If the page was created and published by the same group, omit the publisher name from the retrieval statement (as here); if not, add the publisher's name before the URL (*Retrieved from APA website:*). (For more about documenting online sources, see pp. 312–14.)

Appendix

Resources in the Disciplines

This appendix contains an annotated list of research resources in a variety of academic disciplines. The resources are grouped into four broad categories—Humanities, Social Sciences, Natural Sciences and Mathematics, and Professional Disciplines—that cover most of the academic disciplines. Each broad category is then subcategorized for user convenience. A list of associations and organizations concludes each category.

General Databases

Many libraries subscribe to these databases, which are excellent starting points for research.

EBSCOhost <search.ebscohost.com/> Subscription-based service including multiple subject-specific databases from which searchers can select.

JSTOR <www.jstor.org/> Full-text database of more than 1,000 journals in the humanities, social sciences, and sciences.

OCLC FirstSearch <firstsearch.oclc.org/> WorldCat. Subscription-based service including multiple subject-specific databases from which searchers can select.

Humanities

General

Wilson Humanities Index: 1974–date. Wilson. Available through Ovid. Check your library for a subscription. Bibliographic database that cites articles from the most popular English-language scholarly journals and periodicals and many other specialized magazines.

Library of Congress Humanities and Social Sciences Division: Databases and E-resources <openlibrary.org/a/OL419954A/Library_of_Congress._Humanities_and_Social_Sciences_Division> Information about the 70,000-volume general reference collection, online catalogs, subscription databases, CD-ROMs, bibliographies and guides, and internet resources.

Project Muse <muse.jhu.edu/> Johns Hopkins UP. Check your library for a subscription. Full-text articles in the humanities and social sciences.

Voice of the Shuttle <vos.ucsb.edu/> Online database of resources in the humanities and some social sciences.

Art

Artcyclopedia <www.artcyclopedia.com/> Searchable online encyclopedia organized by artist, artwork, museum, medium, subject, nationality, movement, and gender.

Art Index Retrospective: 1929–1984. Wilson. Check your library for a subscription. An extensive multi-language index of art history texts.

Grove Art Dictionary Online <www.oxfordartonline.com/public/> Oxford UP. Contains 45,000 articles on every aspect of the visual arts from prehistory to the present day. Compiled over 15 years, it represents the work of more than 6,800 international scholars.

Heilbrunn Timeline of Art History <www.metmuseum.org/toah/> Overview of the history of art as illustrated and represented in the Metropolitan Museum of Art's collection.

Film

The Film Encyclopedia: The Complete Guide to Film and the Film Industry. Ephraim Katz (New York: Collins, 2008). A single-volume reference with entries on such categories as major figures in film, film organizations, terminology, theories, and industry advances.

The Library of Congress: Motion Picture and Television Reading Room <www.loc.gov/rr/mopic/> Access to and information about the field provided by the Motion Picture, Broadcasting, and Recorded Sound Division of the Library of Congress.

Motion Picture Association of America <www.mpaa.org> General guide to the American motion picture, home video, and television industries.

The New Biographical Dictionary of Film. David Thomson (New York: Knopf, 2002). Contains 1,300 entries from film critic Thomson. Not comprehensive; rather, it draws on Thomson's opinions and critiques about artists.

History

Dictionary of American History, 2nd ed. rev., vol. 1. Ed. James Truslow Adams and R. V. Coleman (New York: Scribner's, 1940). Contains more than 6,000 articles covering a wide range of military, political, social, and economic subjects.

Encyclopedia of African-American Culture and History: The Black Experience in the Americas. 6 vols. Ed. Colin A. Palmer (New York: Cengage, 2005). Also available as e-book. Covers the African-American experience from 1619 to 2005.

Princeton's Guide to History Web Sites <www.princeton.edu/~pressman/hiswebs.htm> Comprehensive guide to general web resources in history.

Languages

Cambridge Encyclopedia of Language, 2nd ed. David Crystal (New York: Cambridge UP, 1997). General study of language covering words, speech, writing, and thought.

MLA Bibliography (New York: Modern Language Association). Available through EBSCO, ProQuest, Cengage/Gale, OCLC. The core resource for languages and literatures; virtually all libraries subscribe to this database.

Literature

Academy of American Poets <www.poets.org/audio> Includes more than 150 sound files of recited poetry.

Bibliographic Guide to the Study of the Literature of the USA, 5th ed. Clarence Louis Frank Gohdes (Durham, NC: Duke UP, 1984). Extensive list of books and articles on the literature of the United States.

Cambridge Bibliography of English Literature, 3rd ed. Ed. Joanne Shattock (New York: Cambridge UP, 2000). Extensive list of books and articles in English literature.

The Internet Public Library's Guide to Literature <www.ipl.org/div/subject/browse/hum60.00.00/> Critical and biographical websites about authors and their works that can be browsed by author, title, or nationality and literary period.

MLA Bibliography (New York: Modern Language Association). Available through EBSCO, ProQuest, Cengage/Gale, OCLC. The core resource for languages and literatures; virtually all libraries subscribe to this database.

Music

American Song Database <amso.alexanderstreet.com/> Check your library for a subscription. Database of American music, with an emphasis on history. More than 58,000 tracks compiled.

The Garland Encyclopedia of World Music Online <glnd.alexanderstreet.com/> Comprehensive online resource devoted to music research on all the world's peoples; includes 9,000 pages of information, essays, and images.

Grove Dictionary of Music and Musicians, 2nd ed. Charles Newell Boyd (New York: Oxford UP, 2001). Largest single reference work on Western music. Included in Oxford Music Online (see next entry).

Oxford Music Online <www.oxfordmusiconline.com/> Includes the *Oxford Dictionary of Music, Grove Music Online* (biographies), and the *Oxford Companion to Music.*

Philosophy

Cambridge Dictionary of Philosophy, 2nd ed. Ed. Robert Audi (New York: Cambridge UP, 1999). Short reference work on philosophy, including coverage of specific philosophers and concepts.

Oxford Companion to Philosophy, new ed. Ed. Ted Honderich (New York: Oxford UP, 2005). Encyclopedia of philosophers, branches of philosophy, and concepts; also includes timeline and visual representations, or "maps," of the field.

Routledge Encyclopedia of Philosophy Online <www.rep.routledge.com> Online resource for philosophy and its related disciplines.

Stanford Encyclopedia of Philosophy <plato.stanford.edu/> Regularly updated and maintained by field experts.

Religion

Encyclopedia of Religion. 15 vols. Ed. Lindsay Jones (Detroit: Macmillan Reference, 2005). Comprehensive reference on religion worldwide across its recorded history.

Encyclopedia of Religion and Society. William H. Swatos Jr. and Peter Kivisto (Walnut Creek, CA: AltaMira Press/Sage, 1998). Broad reference tool in the study of religion and society. Also available online at <hirr.hartsem.edu/ency/acss.htm>.

Theater

The Cambridge Guide to Theater. Martin Banham (New York: Cambridge UP, 1995). Comprehensive guide to the history and current practice of theater throughout the world.

Literary Resources—Theater and Drama <andromeda.rutgers.edu/~jlynch/Lit/theatre.html> Lists several theater, drama, and performance arts resource sites.

Associations and Organizations in the Humanities

Academy of Motion Picture Arts and Sciences <www.oscars.org/>
American Comparative Literature Association <www.acla.org/>
American Philosophical Practitioners Association <www.appa.edu/>
American Psychological Association <www.apa.org/>
American Society for the History of Rhetoric <www.ashr.org/Resources.html>

American Society of Composers, Authors, and Publishers <www.ascap.com/index.aspx>
Association of Art Historians <www.aah.org.uk/>
Modern Language Association <www.mla.org/>
Theater Development Fund <www.tdf.org/>
The World History Association <www.thewha.org/>
Yahoo! Listing of Religious Organizations <dir.yahoo.com/society_and_culture/religion_and_spirituality/organizations/>

Social Sciences

General

International Bibliography of the Social Sciences <www.lse.ac.uk/collections/IBSS/> Online bibliography for social science and interdisciplinary research produced by the Library at the London School of Economics and Political Science.

Project Muse <muse.jhu.edu/> Johns Hopkins UP. Full-text articles in the humanities and social sciences.

Voice of the Shuttle <vos.ucsb.edu/> Online database of resources on the humanities and some social sciences.

Anthropology

Anthrosource <www.aaanet.org/publications/anthrosource/> American Anthropological Association. Check your library for a subscription. Online database of full-text anthropology resources.

Encyclopedia of Anthropology. Ed. H. James Birx (Walnut Creek, CA: Sage, 2005). Covers physical and biological anthropology, archaeology, cultural and social anthropology, linguistics, and applied anthropology.

Communications

Communication and Mass Media Complete. Accessible through EBSCO (see "General Databases"). Check your library for a subscription. Database that indexes articles from more than 690 journals (including full text for 380), all in the fields of communications and mass media.

Communication Studies: A SAGE Full-Text Database <www.sagefulltext.com/loginform.htm> Check your library for a subscription. Includes full-text articles from SAGE journals in communication.

Criminal Justice

Abstracts Database: National Criminal Justice Resource Service (NCJRS) <www.ncjrs.gov/App/AbstractDB/AbstractDBSearch.aspx> Federally sponsored database that provides information regarding criminal justice in the United States.

Criminal Justice Abstracts: 1968–present (Thousand Oaks, CA: Sage Publications). Available through ProQuest. Check your library for a subscription. Criminology database covering scholarly and professional works on topics such as "crime trends, crime prevention and deterrence, juvenile delinquency, . . . police, courts, punishment and sentencing."

Economics

The American Economic Association Online <www.aeaweb.org/index.php> Collection of information for research in economics. Includes URLs for associations and publications along with contents, abstracts, data files, and full-text links to many economics periodicals and journals.

The Concise Encyclopedia of Economics <www.econlib.org/library/CEECategory.html> Ed. David R. Henderson (Liberty Fund, 2008). A wealth of economic analysis by 150 leading economists.

Education

Bibliographic Guide to Education (Boston: G. K. Hall, 2001). Recent education publications cataloged by Teachers College and Columbia University, supplemented with publications in the field of education cataloged by the Research Libraries of the New York Public Library.

Education Full Text. Wilson. Check your library for a subscription. Bibliographic database that indexes more than 770 education-related English-language periodicals and yearbooks published in the United States and elsewhere, over 400 of which are peer reviewed.

ERIC: Education Resources Information Center: 1966–present <www.eric.ed.gov/> Check your library for a subscription. Searchable database of full-text and bibliographic resources focused on education.

Geography

A Dictionary of Geography. Susan Mayhew (New York: Oxford UP, 1997). More than 6,000 concise entries for words and terms encountered in both human and physical geography.

The Library of Congress Geography and Map Reading Room <www.loc.gov/rr/geogmap/> Cartographic and geographic information for all parts of the world.

Political Science

Encyclopedia of Government and Politics. Ed. Mary Hawkesworth and Maurice Kogan (New York: Routledge, 2003). Provides a systematic account of politics and political studies, assesses both traditional and contemporary approaches, and projects the paths of future research.

FactCheck.org, A Project of the Annenberg Public Policy Center <www.factcheck.org/> Monitors the factual accuracy of statements by major U.S. political players in TV ads, debates, speeches, interviews, and news releases.

Information Sources in Political Science, 5th ed. Ed. Stephen Green and Douglas Ernest (Santa Barbara, CA: ABC-CLIO, 2005). Comprehensive bibliography of American and international politics covering print and electronic materials published in English, primarily in the United States and the United Kingdom.

U.S. Government Made Easy <www.usa.gov/> Topics and links related to American government.

Psychology

Bibliographic Guide to Psychology (Detroit: G. K. Hall, 2003). Psychology publications cataloged by the Library of Congress and the Research Libraries of the New York Public Library.

PsycARTICLES. American Psychological Association Databases, 1894–present. <www.apa.org/psycarticles/> Check your library for a subscription. Database containing full-text articles from 71 psychology journals published by the American Psychological Association and several other psychology associations.

Sociology

Sociology: A Guide to Reference and Information Sources, 3rd ed. Stephen H. Aby, James Nalen, and Lori Fielding (Santa Barbara, CA: Greenwood, 2005). Descriptions of approximately 610 major reference sources in sociology, its subdisciplines, and the related social sciences.

The Socio Web, an Independent Guide to Sociological Resources on the Internet <www.socioweb.com/> Independent guide to sociological resources available on the internet.

Women's Studies

American Library Association's College and Research Libraries—Women's Studies Section <www.libr.org/wss/wsslinks/> Provides access to a wide range of resources in support of women's studies.

Women's Studies Encyclopedia. Ed. Helen Tierney (Santa Barbara, CA: Greenwood, 1999). Information about women from all fields and disciplines of study in such areas as violence against women, women in public life, and women in specific countries and regions.

Associations and Organizations in the Social Sciences

American Anthropological Association <www.aaanet.org/>
American Educational Research Association <www.aera.net/>
American Political Science Association <www.apsanet.org/>
American Sociological Association <www.asanet.org/>
Association of American Geographers <www.aag.org/>
International Association of Business Communicators <www.iabc.com/>
International Political Science Associations <www.ipsa.org/site/>
League of Women Voters <www.lwv.org//AM/Template.cfm?Section=Home>
National Association for Business Economics <www.nabe.com/>
National Communication Association <www.natcom.org/>
National Education Association <www.nea.org/>
National Women's Studies Association <www.nwsa.org/>

Natural Sciences and Mathematics

General

Science Reference Center. Found in *EBSCOhost* (see "General Databases"). Indexes full-text reference works and periodicals in the sciences.

Web of Science. ISI Web of Knowledge. 1970–present. <www.isiwebofknowledge.com/> Check your library for a subscription. Includes the *Science Citation Index Expanded* and covers 150 disciplines.

Astronomy and Astrophysics

Encyclopedia of Astronomy and Astrophysics <eaa.crcpress.com/> Ed. Paul Murdin. Taylor & Francis Group. Contains more than 3,000 articles covering a broad range of topics in astronomy and astrophysics.

University of Buffalo's Astronomy and Astrophysics: Internet Resources <library.buffalo.edu/asl/guides/astronomy.html> Contains selected astronomy resources freely available on the internet.

Biology

Oxford Dictionary of Biology, 6th ed. Ed. Robert Hine (New York: Oxford UP, 2008). Comprehensive coverage of biology, biophysics, and biochemistry, including biographical entries on key scientists.

The University of Wisconsin/Madison Library's Biology Resources Guide <www.library.wisc.edu/guides/biology/> Comprehensive listing of useful links for biology research.

Chemistry

American Chemical Society Publications <pubs.acs.org/> Comprehensive collection of the most-cited peer-reviewed journals in the chemical and related sciences.

TOXNET <toxnet.nlm.nih.gov/> Databases on toxicology and environmental health created and supported by the Division of Specialized Information Services, National Library of Medicine.

Ecology and Environmental Science

The Dictionary of Ecology and Environmental Science. Ed. Henry W. Art (New York: Holt, 1993). More than 8,000 entries, with definitions, for terms and concepts from environmental biology, chemistry, geology, and physics.

TOXNET. See entry under "Chemistry."

The University of Connecticut's Guide to Resources for Environmental Science <www.lib.uconn.edu/research/bysubject/environm.htm> Comprehensive list of useful links for research in ecology and environmental science.

Geology

Encyclopedia of Geology. Richard C. Selley and Ian R. Plimmer (Philadelphia: Elsevier, 2004). Covers all aspects of geology and new investigative techniques pertaining to earth history, earth materials, surface processes, regional geology, economic geology, engineering geology, petroleum geology, geochemical and mineral exploration, and the history of geology.

Geology.com <geology.com/> Current information about geology in an accessible format.

Health and Medicine

The Gale Encyclopedia of Nursing and Allied Health, 2nd ed. Ed. Jacqueline L. Longe (Farmington Hills, MI: Gale Cengage, 2006). Covers a wide range of subjects related to nursing and the allied health professions including diseases and disorders, tests and procedures, equipment and tools, human biology and body systems, nursing and allied health professions, and current health issues.

Lippincott's Nursing Center <www.nursingcenter.com/home/index.asp> Information from more than 50 nursing journals.

Miller-Keane Encyclopedia and Dictionary of Medicine, Nursing, and Allied Health, rev. reprint 7th ed. Ed. Benjamin Miller, Clare Brackman Keane, and Marie O'Toole (Philadelphia: Saunders, 2005). Provides medical definitions and covers topics across the health care spectrum.

University of Delaware Library's Resources for Health and Exercise Sciences <www2.lib.udel.edu/subj/hesc/internet.htm> Comprehensive, annotated list of links, databases, and print and electronic journals relating to sports medicine and management, athletics and fitness, and recreation and leisure.

Mathematics

CRC Concise Encyclopedia of Mathematics, 2nd ed. Ed. Eric W. Weisstein (Boca Raton, FL: Chapman & Hall/CRC, 2002). Contains mathematical definitions, formulas, figures, tabulations, and references.

Wolfram MathWorld <mathworld.wolfram.com/> Collaboratively created clearinghouse for researcher-contributed new mathematical discoveries. An educational resource.

Physics

McGraw-Hill Dictionary of Physics, 3rd ed. (New York: McGraw-Hill, 2003). Defines words and phrases encountered in physics.

Physics and Astronomy Online <www.physlink.com/> Comprehensive physics and astronomy research and reference website.

Associations and Organizations in the Natural Sciences and Mathematics

American Association of Physicists in Medicine <www.aapm.org/>
American Astronomical Society <aas.org/>
American College of Sports Medicine <www.acsm.org//AM/Template.cfm?Section=Home_Page>
American Mathematical Society <www.ams.org/>
American Medical Association <www.ama-assn.org/>
American Physical Society <www.aps.org/>
Association for Environmental Health and Sciences <www.aehs.com/>
Biology News Net <www.biologynews.net/>
Center for International Environmental Law <www.ciel.org/>
Geological Organizations and Agencies <geology.com/groups.htm>
International Council of Nurses <www.icn.ch/>
International Organization for Chemical Sciences in Development <www.iocd.org/index.shtml>
World Health Organization <www.who.int/en/>

Professional Disciplines

Business

Encyclopedia of Business, 2nd ed. Ed. Jane A. Malonis and Gale Group (Farmington Hills, MI: Gale, 1999). Essays by business school professors, members of the business community, and business writers covering 700 business topics including internal business functions such as finance, human resources, and marketing and external elements that affect businesses, such as technology, environmental concerns, and federal laws.

Rutgers Business Research Guide <www.libraries.rutgers.edu/rul/rr_gateway/research_guides/busi/business.shtml> Descriptions of databases and hundreds of reference books on a variety of business and management topics.

Law

American Legal Systems: A Resource and Reference Guide. Tony M. Fine (New York: Yeshiva University, Benjamin N. Cardozo School of Law, 1997). Overview of the American legal system and the interrelationships between and among its institutions and legal authorities.

Lexis/Nexis Academic <www.lexisnexis.com/us/lnacademic/> Sometimes accessible through college libraries. Indexes approximately 6,000 news, business, and legal resources. Includes case citations from 1789 to present.

Library of Congress Guide to Law Online <www.loc.gov/law/help/guide.php> Annotated guide to sources of information on government and law prepared by the Public Services Division of the Law Library of Congress.

Associations and Organizations in the Professional Disciplines

Academy of International Business <aib.msu.edu/resources/Professionalorgs.asp>
American Association for Justice <www.justice.org/cps/rde/xchg/justice/hs.xsl/default.htm>
American Bar Association <www.abanet.org/>
American Civil Liberties Union <www.aclu.org/>
American Society of International Law <www.asil.org/>
Business and Professional Women's Foundation <www.bpwfoundation.org/i4a/pages/index.cfm?pageid=1>
Business Professionals of America <www.bpa.org/>
International Academy of Business and Economics <www.iabe.com/domains/iabex/Default.aspx>

Credits

Text Credits

Chapter 1: 7 Tag cloud from del.icio.us. Reproduced with permission of Yahoo! Inc. ©2009 Yahoo! Inc. DELICIOUS and the DELICIOUS logo are registered trademarks of Yahoo! Inc. and by permission of Amy Rupiper Taggart.

Chapter 2: 16–17 Brent Staples, "How Hip-Hop Lost Its Way and Betrayed Its Fans," *New York Times,* 5/12/05, p. A26. © 2005 The New York Times. All rights reserved. Used by permission and protected by the Copyright Laws of the United States. The printing, copying, redistribution, or retransmission of the Material without express written permission is prohibited.

Chapter 3: 30 Fig. 3.2, Adam Ostrow, "Facebook Quitters: Find Out When Someone De-Friends You," August 31, 2009. Mashable, the Social Media Guide. Reproduced by permission from http://mashable.com/2009/08/31/facebook-friends-checker/. **34 Fig. 3.4,** Librarians' Internet Index: Online Subject Directory under "Business" at <<http://lii.org/pub/topic/busfinjobs>. Copyright © 2008, Librarians' Internet Index, LII. All rights reserved. **Fig. 3.5,** screenshot from Librarians' Internet Index: online subject directory under "Business: Corruption & Fraud" at Lib.org <<http://lii.org/pub/topic/corruptfraud>. Copyright © 2008, Librarians' Internet Index, LII. All rights reserved.

Chapter 4: 36 Chapter Opener, Courtesy of Villa Lagoon, Gulf Shores, Alabama. Designed by Theodore Dial of DAC-ART Building System. Copyright 2006-2008. All Rights reserved. Used by permission.

Chapter 5: 53 Fig. 5.1, Home Page and Database Access Page, Penrose Library, University of Denver <http://penrose.du.edu> and <http://penrose.du.edu/findit/EResources/index.cfm>. Reproduced by permission of Penrose Library, University of Denver. **56: Fig. 5.2,** ProQuest search results for "underground comics" AND "genre." Image published with permission of ProQuest LLC. © 2009, ProQuest LLC; all rights reserved. Further reproduction is prohibited without permission. **57: Fig. 5.3,** Link to Interlibrary Loan and Electronic Journals List, Home Page of Pollak Library, California State University, Fullerton <http://www.library.fullerton.edu/default.aspx>. Reproduced by permission of Pollak Library, California State University, Fullerton. **61: Fig. 5.5,** Search Screen for Maine InfoNet (Statewide Library Catalog) <http://mainecat.maine.edu>. © Maine Info Net 2009. **64: Fig. 5.6,** A Library Search by Subject, "The Bridge" (Carleton & St. Olaf College Libraries) for "english diaries—history and criticism" at <http://bridge.carleton.edu/search/a?a>. © The Bridge: Carleton & St. Olaf Libraries.

Chapter 6: 69 Fig. 6.1, A Simple Keyword Search on Google. © 2009 Google. **72 Fig. 6.2,** Advanced Google Search. © 2009 Google. **77 Fig. 6.3,** Using Research Guides, from Colorado State University Libraries website http://lib.colostate.edu/research/>. Used by permission of Colorado State University Libraries.

Chapter 7: 80 Chapter Opener from FactCheck.org <www.factcheck.org/elections-2010/campaign_2010_begins.html>. "Campaign 2010 Begins" by Brooks Jackson and Justin Bank, February 5, 2009. Copyright © 2003–2009, Annenberg Public Policy Center of the University of Pennsylvania. <http://www.factcheck.org/elections-2010/campaign_2010_begins.html>. Used by permission. **84 Fig 7.2,** Determining Reliability by Assessing Citations. EBSCO Host Academic Search Premier navigation toolbar. Reproduced by permission from EBSCO Host Copyright Agent. **89 Fig. 7.4,** Weighing Source Reliability. Google search page for "link owl english purdue edu." © 2009 Google. **90 Fig. 7.1,** Exercise: Evaluating Web Pages. Left: "Turnitin" resources at: <http://www.plagiarism.org.research_cite-05-23-07>. Reproduced from <<http://www.plagiarism.org.research_cite-05-23-07>. Right: html version of pamphlet on plagiarism for students, accessed 5/23/07 at <http://www.indiana.edu/~wts/pamphlets/plagiarism.shtml>. Courtesy of The Trustees of Indiana University.

Chapter 8: 96 Fig. 8.1, Sample Research Entry from Blog "Gettin' Lit'rit" showing tag for "Case selection" in a research project about a Supreme Court case <https://www.blogger.com/start>. Blogger © 2009 Google. pp. 101-102: Yugi Noguchi, "On Capitol Hill, Playing WikiPolitics." *Washington Post* 4 Feb 2006:A1. © 2006 The Washington Post. All rights reserved. Used by permission and protected by the Copyright Laws of the United States. The printing, copying, redistribution, or retransmission of the Material without express written permission is prohibited. **104** Claudia Milne, "On the Grounds of the Fresh Water Pond: The Free-Black Community at Five Points, 1810-1834," *International Journal of Historical Archaeology* (June

2002). With kind permission from Springer Science+Business Media. Copyright © 2002.

Chapter 10: 120 Chapter opener. Left: Joshua Shaw, "Annotated Bibliography of Writings in Feminism and Aesthetics," *Hypatia,* Vol. 18, No. 4, Fall/ Winter 2003, pp. 258-272. Copyright 2003; Reprinted with permission of John Wiley & Sons, Inc. Right: Linda Cockey & Kathryn Kalmanson, "Annotated Bibliography on Musician Wellness." *American Music Teacher,* June 1, 2002. Copyright 2002 Music Teachers National Association, Inc. Used by permission. All rights reserved.

Chapter 17: 205 Fig. 17.1, A Web Page from the John Adams Library at the Boston Public Library <http://www.Johnadamslibrary.org>. Courtesy of the John Adams Library at the Boston Public Library. **209 Fig. 17.4,** Use of Color and White Space in Web pages. Left: screenshot from Museum of Contemporary Art, Los Angeles <http://www.moca.org/museum/exhibitiondetail.php?id=352>. Reproduced by permission of the Museum of Contemporary Art. Jean-Michel Basquiat, *Philistines,* 1982. Acrylic and oil paintstick on canvas, 72 x 123 inches. Collection of Mr. and Mrs. Thomas E. Worrell Jr. © 2010 The Estate of Jean-Michel Basquiat / ADAGP, Paris / ARS, New York. Right: screenshot from <http://www.c-span.org>. Reproduced by permission of C-SPAN Networks. **212 Fig. 17.6,** Use of Lines (Rules) and Borders. A web page of CNN.com. Reproduced by permission of Copyright Agent, Cable News Network (CNN). **216 Fig 17.7,** "Courting the Youth Vote: The Obama Effect" by Lindsey C. Bohl, *Vanderbilt Undergraduate Research Journal, Volume 5,* 2009. Sponsored by the Office of the Provost, the Jean and Alexander Heard Library System, and the Office of Innovation through Technology. This journal provides open access to all of it content on the principle that making research freely available to the public supports a greater global exchange of knowledge. Copyright 2009. Reproduced by permission.

Chapter 18: 221 Classification under the Linnaean System. Illustration by Peter Halasz.

Chapter 19: 241 Audre Lorde, "Hanging Fire." Copyright © 1978 by Audre Lorde, from THE COLLECTED POEMS OF AUDRE LORDE by Audre Lorde. Used by permission of W.W. Norton & Company, Inc. David Mason, *Ludlow* (2007). Reprinted with permission of Red Hen Press. Copyright © 2007 by David Mason. **245 Fig 19.1,** Table in MLA Style from John Feather, *A History of British Publishing* (London: Croom Helm Ltd., 1988), quoted in Kelly J. Mays, "The Publishing World," *A Companion to the Victorian Novel,* ed. Richard Cronin, Patrick Branlinger, and William B. Thesing (New York: Wiley-Blackwell, 2002). © 1988 John Feather. Reprinted by permission of Routledge, an imprint of the Taylor & Francis Group. **283: Fig. 2** in student paper, "Holy Underground Comics, Batman!" by Lydia Nichols. Adrian Tomine, 8-panel cartoon "Optic Nerve #6," p. 22, from *Drawn and Quarterly,* February 1999. © 1999 by Adrian Tomine. Reproduced by permission.

Photo Credits

Chapter 1: 1 Bildarchiv Preussischer Kulturbesitz/Art Resource, NY; **Chapter 2: 11** PM Images/Getty Images; **12** ©Michael Newman/PhotoEdit; **Chapter 3: 24** ©Mascarucci/Corbis; **Chapter 5: 50** © Antatoly Maltsev/epa/Corbis; **Chapter 7: 67** Bildarchiv Preussischer Kulturbesitz/Art Resource, NY; **Chapter 7: 83 L** Courtesy of Rodale Publishing; **83 R** Courtesy of University of California Press, © 2011 Estate of Pablo Picasso/Artists Rights Society (ARS), New York; **91** Franklin D. Roosevelt Presidential Library and Museum; **Chapter 8: 93** Bildarchiv Preussischer Kulturbesitz/Art Resource, NY; **Chapter 9: 106 T** Courtesy of Louis Bloomfield; **106 C** Courtesy of Harold Garner; **106 B** Adrian Dennis/AFP/Getty Images; **Chapter 11: 128** Erich Lessing/Art Resource, NY; **129** Library of Congress; **Chapter 12: 141** Getty Images; **Chapter 13: 148 L** Radious/Superstock; **149 R** Lenora Gim/Getty Images; **Chapter 14: 161** © Car Culture/Corbis; **Chapter 15: 173** ©GraphicallyMinded/Alamy; **181** "Jacket Cover" from JIMMY CORRIGAN: THE SMARTEST KID ON EARTH by Chris Ware, © 2000, 2003 by Mr. Chris Ware. Used by permission of Pantheon Books, a division of Random House, Inc.; **Chapter 16: 191** Werner Forman/Art Resource, NY; **Chapter 17: 204** WPA Poster Collection, Library of Congress, Prints & Photographs Division; **Chapter 18: 223** ©Corbis; **Chapter 19: 281 L** SPIDERMAN: TM & © 2011 Marvel Characters, Inc. Used with permission. **281 R** Copyright © Robert Crumb, 2009. Used by permission, Agence Littéraire Lora Fountain & Associates, Paris, France; **285** "Jacket Cover" from JIMMY CORRIGAN: THE SMARTEST KID ON EARTH by Chris Ware, © 2000, 20003 by Mr. Chris Ware. Used by permission of Pantheon Books, a division of Random House, Inc.; **Chapter 21: 355** The David Rumsey Map Collection, www.davidrumsey.com <http://www.davidrumsey.com/>

Index

N

Q

R

S

X

Y